*A Reader's Guide to
African Literature*

A Reader's Guide
to African Literature

Compiled and edited by
HANS M. ZELL and HELENE SILVER

With contributions by
BARBARA ABRASH AND GIDEON-CYRUS M. MUTISO

AFRICANA PUBLISHING CORPORATION
NEW YORK

741452

Published
in the United States of America 1971
by Africana Publishing Corporation
101 Fifth Avenue
New York, N.Y. 10003

Library of Congress catalog card no. 76-83165
ISBN 8419-0018-3

Für Ursi

Photoset in Lumitype Latine and Optima
by St Paul's Press Ltd, Malta, and
printed in Great Britain

Contents

INTRODUCTION · vii '
REFERENCES · xviii
ACKNOWLEDGEMENTS · xx
PICTURE CREDITS · xxi

BIBLIOGRAPHY · 1
Bibliographies · 2
Critical Works · 4
Anthologies · 11

WRITINGS
IN ENGLISH · 20

WEST AFRICA · 20
Cameroon · 21
The Gambia · 22
Ghana · 22
Guinea · 27
Liberia · 27
Nigeria · 27
Sierra Leone · 43

CENTRAL AFRICA · 45
Sudan · 45

EAST AFRICA · 45
Ethiopia · 46
Kenya · 47
Tanzania · 50
Uganda · 50

SOUTHERN AFRICA · 52
Lesotho · 52
Malawi · 53
Rhodesia · 54
South Africa · 54
Zambia · 59

WRITINGS IN FRENCH
AND IN ENGLISH
TRANSLATION · 60

WEST AFRICA · 60
Cameroon · 60
Dahomey · 64
Guinea · 65
Ivory Coast · 66
Mali · 68
Nigeria · 69
Senegal · 69
Tchad · 74

CENTRAL AFRICA · 75
Congo-Brazzaville · 75
Congo-Kinshasa · 75

EAST AFRICA
Malagasy Republic · 76
Rwanda · 77
Somaliland · 77

POLITICALLY COMMITTED LITERATURE IN
ENGLISH: A SELECTION · 78

CHILDREN'S BOOKS · 86

STOP PRESS ADDENDUM · 94

SOME ARTICLES ON AFRICAN LITERATURE · 96

PERIODICALS AND MAGAZINES · 102

BIOGRAPHIES · 113

Peter Abrahams · 115
Chinua Achebe · 114
Ama Aidoo · 120
Timothy Aluko · 121
Elechi Amadi · 122
Ayi Kwei Armah · 123
Kofi Awoonor · 124
Francis Bebey · 126
Mongo Beti · 128
Dennis Brutus · 130
John Pepper Clark · 132
William Conton · 134
Bernard Dadié · 135
Birago Diop · 137
David Diop · 139
Mbella Sonne Dipoko · 140
R. Sarif Easmon · 142
Cyprian Ekwensi · 142
Alfred Hutchinson · 144
Legson Kayira · 145
Asare Konadu · 147
Alex La Guma · 148
Camara Laye · 150
Taban lo Liyong · 152
Ezekiel Mphahlele · 154
James Ngugi ·154

Abioseh Nicol · 159
Lewis Nkosi · 160
Flora Nwapa · 163
Onuora Nzekwu · 163
Grace Ogot · 164
Gabriel Okara · 165
Christopher Okigbo · 166
Yambo Ouologuem · 168
Sembène Ousmane · 170
Ferdinand Oyono · 172
Guillaume Oyono-Mbia · 174
Peter K. Palangyo · 175
Okot p'Bitek · 176
Lenrie Peters · 177
Jean-Joseph
  Rabéarivelo · 178
Richard Rive · 180
David Rubadiri · 181
Sahle Sellassie · 182
Francis Selormey · 183
Léopold Senghor · 184
Robert Serumaga · 187
Wole Soyinka · 189
Efua Sutherland · 193
Amos Tutuola · 195
Tchicaya U Tam'si · 197

ESSENTIAL ADDRESSES · 200

PUBLISHERS · 200
BOOKSELLERS AND DEALERS · 205

INDEX · 207

Introduction

The study of Africa and of African literature is generating an unprecedented interest today: African studies is one of the fastest-growing academic disciplines, and the general public are equally excited by their recent discovery of the African arts — visual, theatrical, and literary. In the United States, African literature is now being introduced — often for the first time — as a significant part of the syllabus in schools, colleges, and universities.

What is African literature and what makes an African writer? The search for a definition has brought much debate: is it the literature written *in* Africa, or *about* Africa? Is it solely the literature produced by people living in or originating from Africa; or can the writings of a non-African who utilizes an African setting be accepted as African literature? Does Joseph Conrad's *Heart of Darkness* qualify? What about Joyce Cary, Graham Greene, Robert Ruark, Ernest Hemingway? Does African literature embrace only the indigenous languages, or should it include English, French, Portuguese, Afrikaans? Then there is the question of boundaries: North African writing belongs to such a radically different tradition from that of the literature south of the Sahara. Yet the recent Pan-African Cultural Festival was held in Algeria and perhaps points towards more unity of thought among writers of the entire continent. Lastly, what is the position of native white South African writers? At a seminar on African literature and the universities held at Fourah Bay College in Freetown, Sierra Leone, in 1963, a motion was put forward which defined African literature as 'any work in which an African setting is authentically handled, or to which experiences which originate in Africa are integral'. Chinua Achebe, however, feels that one cannot cram African literature into a small, neat definition, and goes on to say, 'I do not see African literature as one unit but as a group of associated units — in fact the sum total of all the *national* and *ethnic* literatures of Africa.' He believes that 'any attempt to define African literature in terms that overlook the complexities of the African scene at present is doomed to failure'.[1] The German scholar Janheinz Jahn, too, has his own concept of 'neo-African literature'. In the introduction to his monumental bibliography he argues that it is the style that characterizes Neo-African literature and not the author's language, birthplace, or colour of skin.[2]

Whatever the definitions, African literature in English is still in its infancy. With a few exceptions, for example the early novels of Peter Abrahams, *major* creative activity did not start until the nineteen-fifties.[3] The publication date of Amos Tutuola's *The Palm-wine Drinkard*, in 1952, is generally taken as a starting point of contemporary African-English literature. Published with little style editing, its unconventional use of English provoked a great deal of controversy, especially among Tutuola's fellow writers in Nigeria; but the novel surged to sudden prominence and instant success largely owing to a rave review by Dylan Thomas writing in the London *Observer*.

The journal *Black Orpheus* was founded by Ulli Beier and Janheinz Jahn in September 1957. Its maiden issue included the first English translations of some of Léopold Senghor's verse, poetry by Gabriel Okara, an essay on Tutuola by Gerald Moore, and contributions by the two joint editors. Later, in 1961, Ulli Beier was also influential in establishing the Mbari Club in Ibadan, set up with the aim of getting artists and writers together to talk, to publish books, and stage exhibitions. Like *Black Orpheus*, it served as an important platform for creative African writing, and such major writers as Wole Soyinka, Christopher Okigbo, John Pepper Clark, and Dennis Brutus made an early appearance in the publications of the Mbari Club. Cyprian Ekwensi's *People of the City* was issued by a small London publisher in 1954. It was not, however, until 1958 that Chinua Achebe's important first novel, *Things Fall Apart*, was published by Heinemann's. Faber and Faber, already the publishers of Tutuola and Peter Abrahams, brought out the autobiographical *Down Second Avenue* by Ezekiel Mphahlele in 1959. Later it was reissued in paperback by Seven Seas Books, an East German publisher.

The pioneering paperback *African Writers Series* was begun by Heinemann Educational Books as a considerable gamble in 1962. It originally catered largely for an educational market in Africa, but today is enjoying deserved success and popularity well beyond that continent. The first title in the series by Chinua Achebe (who also acted as general editor to the series), the paperback reissue of *Things Fall Apart*, has now sold more than 300,000 copies. An increasing number of books are added every year, and in 1971 the AWS will reach a hundred titles.

There was an almost complete lack of interest in the series by any American publisher until as recently as two years ago, but today there is strong competition for marketing rights for the titles. American publishers appear to have badly neglected African literature — short of the odd exception, such as Doubleday's edition of Sembène Ousmane's *God's Bits of Wood*, published in 1962, or *The African* by William Conton, issued by Little, Brown two years earlier. The situation is now changing drastically. For example, 1969, saw a marked increase of paperback reissues of the writings of Achebe, Ekwensi, Ngugi, Abrahams, and others, produced by major U.S. publishing houses. It was an American publisher too, Houghton Mifflin of Boston, who first published Ayi Kwei Armah's highly successful *The Beautyful Ones Are Not Yet Born*, which was hailed by the *New York Times* as 'a rarity, not only in the first rank of African novels, but perhaps in the first rank of recent novels anywhere'. Another prominent U.S. publisher, Random House, recently issued Wilfred Cartey's important critical study of African literature; and in 1971 Doubleday's will launch an impressive program of creative writing from Africa. With the establishment of the Africana Publishing Corporation in New York, there is now even a publisher with a list exclusively devoted to the publication and dissemination of books on African studies, arts, and literature.

The output of African literature by major publishers has increased enormously during the past three years or so. During 1968 and 1969 over 180 new titles, or paperback reissues, were published. Whereas Barbara Abrash was able to list some 200 English-language titles in her bibliography issued in 1967, this number has now increased to over 400 in this volume. Yet during the past two years there has been relatively little *original* writing (in book form) from West Africa, one exception being

Armah's first novel already mentioned. In Nigeria, major writers such as Achebe or Okara were too preoccupied with the implications of the civil war to devote much time to writing. Christopher Okigbo, perhaps the most promising of contemporary African poets, was killed in action in September 1967. Soyinka was imprisoned for almost two years, and all we had from him were *Two Poems from Prison*, which managed to reach a London publisher. In East Africa, on the other hand, a whole new crop of writers is suddenly emerging, largely due to the activities and enter-prise of the East African Publishing House in Nairobi. After the success of Kenya's James Ngugi, we now also have the first modern novels from Ethiopia, Uganda, and Tanzania.

The francophone scene got under way considerably earlier when works by the Malagasy poets Jean-Joseph Rabéarivelo and Jacques Rabémananjara were published in the nineteen-thirties and 'forties. The first significant, or at least well-known novel came from the pen of the Senegalese Bakary Diallo, entitled *Force bonté*, and published in Paris in 1926.[4] Two further novels followed several years later: from Dahomey, Paul Hazoumé's *Doguicimi* (1935), and from Senegal, Ousmane Socé's *Karim* (1948). Then we had the first verse collections by Léopold Senghor and the Malian poet Fily Dabo Sissoko.

It was not, however, until the nineteen-fifties that any substantial number of novels by Africans began to appear. Notable among these novelists were Ferdinand Oyono, Bernard Dadié, Sembène Ousmane, Mongo Beti, and Camara Laye. Laye's *L'enfant noir*, published in 1953, caused a considerable stir in Parisian literary circles and has now established itself as one of the most important novels to have come from Africa. Camara Laye and Mongo Beti were probably the first African novelists writing in French to become known in English-speaking countries. *L'enfant noir* was translated and published in both the U.S. and Britain in 1954/5, and Beti's *Mission terminée* came out in an English translation in 1958. More recently we have had translations of works by Ferdinand Oyono and Birago Diop. The journal *Présence Africaine* of the Society of African Culture, founded in 1947 under the leadership of Alioune Diop, a Senegalese resident in Paris, has been an important instrument for cultural expression of African and Negro thought. *Présence Africaine* is not only a journal, but also a bookshop and a publishing house, and it remains the chief outlet for French-African authors, for creative as well as political, sociological, and historical writings. Several major French publishing houses, however, now have new works by Laye and Dadié, but Beti, Oyono, and Ousmane have recently remained silent, Ousmane being more active in the field of the cinema. There are two recent novels that have aroused particular attention: Francis Bebey's *Le fils d'Agatha Moudio*, a novel by a Cameroonian, also published by Éditions C.L.E. in Yaoundé, Cameroon, and awarded the Grand Prix Littéraire de l'Afrique Noire. The novel by a young writer from Mali, Yambo Ouologuem, entitled *Le devoir du violence*, received the Prix Renaudot 1968, making Ouologuem the first African writer to receive a major French literary award. The book created a small literary sensation and an English translation is to be published shortly.

Much-needed critical interpretations and studies are now beginning to appear; urgently needed, too, are basic source-materials and annotated guides to the literature and criticism available. This bibliography aims to meet this need. A number of bibliographies have, of course, already been published on the subject. The present volume aims to *supplement* – and update – and *not* replace existing bibliographies. It does, however, differ from them not only in scope, but also in so far as it provides annotations on the literature, together with extracts from book reviews. Lastly, but by no means least important, very considerable emphasis is laid upon *availability*.

A really exhaustive and definitive bibliography of African literature has yet to be produced, but Janheinz Jahn's *Bibliography of Neo-African Literature* published in 1965, is certainly the most useful, scholarly and comprehensive reference work published to date.[5] There have been quarrels about Jahn's criteria of inclusion and his somewhat questionable definition of 'neo-African literature'. The bibliography fails to make any distinction between significant and less significant writings. Nevertheless, despite its shortcomings it remains within its framework the most reliable and accurate source so far available. Jahn has promised supplements to his bibliography, but these have not been forthcoming at the time of going to press. However, being aware of the bibliography's inevitable gaps he has invited others to fill in the omissions and to correct the errors. Two scholars in particular have taken Jahn up on the invitation: Paul Páriscy, of the Hungarian Academy of Sciences, published a supplement to the Jahn bibliography in *The Journal of the New African Literature and the Arts*,[6] and in 1969 followed this up by a supplementary and most valuable bibliography in book form.[7] In the United States Bernth Lindfors (now at the University of Texas) has done the most bibliographic research in African literature. The September 1968 issue of the *African Studies Bulletin* featured his *Additions and Corrections to Janheinz Jahn's Bibliography of Neo-African Literature*.[8] He has also published a survey of American university and other library collections of African literature.[9]

One of the earliest efforts to compile in a single source references to all published African creative writing was Janheinz Jahn's *Approaches to African Literature* (with John Ramsaran), which listed some 250 items covering African, Caribbean, and black American writing, as well as works by European authors handling African themes.[10] Ramsaran's updated and revised edition followed in 1965 as *New Approaches to African Literature*, which now also included some Portuguese writings and African vernacular literature.[11] In 1962 the Deutsche Afrika-Gesellschaft in Bonn published its *Schöne Schriften aus Afrika*.[12] Based on an exhibition, it is a catalogue of contemporary African writing and includes works from the Caribbean, North and South Africa, and Arabic writings, accompanied by brief biographical details about each author. Although this was a laudable early effort, the list is not entirely reliable and much of the bibliographic data is rather incomplete.

In 1962 also appeared Dorothy Porter's *Fiction by African Authors*.[13] This was a preliminary checklist, which she supplemented by a bibliographic essay entitled *African and Caribbean creative writing. A bibliographic survey*, which appeared in *African Forum* in the spring of 1966.[14] Both were valuable at the time. During 1962 and 1963 two further bibliographies appeared: Gerald Moser's *African Literature in the Portuguese Language*[15] and *Bibliographie africaine et malgache* by Roger Mercier.[16] The latter is perhaps a bit over-ambitious in its title, since its listings are confined to literature in French, though within this scope it is a reliable source. In 1964 came the publication of a useful list of Malagasy authors compiled by Clive Wake and John Reed, *Modern Malagasy Literature in French*,[17] and Vincent Bol and Jean Allary's *Littérateurs et poètes noirs*[18], the second part of the latter being a bibliographic essay covering creative writing in English and French from Africa, the Caribbean, and the Americas.

Inspired and prompted by the publication of *Schöne Schriften aus Afrika*, Margaret Amosu produced her bibliography *Creative African Writing in the European Languages*, also in 1964.[19] This covers a great deal of ground and is especially valuable for its inclusion of North African literature. Mrs Amosu subtitles her list *a preliminary bibliography*, and though inevitably out-of-date now, it is (as an early attempt) a most useful compilation.

Another extremely valuable though by no means exhaustive bibliography of francophone African writing was published in 1965: Thérèse Baratte's *Bibliographie auteurs africains et malgaches de langue française.*[20] Political, sociological, economic, and historical literature by African authors is included, in addition to creative writing. It is notable in so far that prices are given and items no longer available are indicated accordingly. A second revised and updated edition of this bibliography appeared in 1968.[21] On a more limited scale, I produced a small bibliography, *Writings by West Africans*, which was based on an exhibition held in Freetown, Sierra Leone in 1967. It covered creative as well as political and historical literature of an original nature by West African authors of both English- and French-speaking nations. This list, too, unfortunately became dated soon after publication. The National Book League in London has produced several useful, if limited, reading lists. Claude Wauthier's exhaustive survey *L'Afrique des Africains — inventaire de la négritude*,[23] published in English as *The Literature and Thought of Modern Africa*, lists the works of some 150 black African writers, with an emphasis on the modern trend of African nationalist thought.[24] It is an impressive study and the bibliography which it includes is a particular asset. However, the year 1963 is the termination point for the main substance of the book and therefore much of the new creative writing is not taken into account.

Black African Literature in English since 1952: Works and Criticism, compiled by Barbara Abrash and published in 1967, was warmly welcomed and to date has probably been the most functional and practical guide for the student of African literature.[25] It lists both books and articles as well as reviews of each work cited where such have been published. Mrs Abrash was also the first to attempt the listing of works of writers anthologized but not published separately, and those writers whose stories, plays or poetry have appeared dispersed in various anthologies. We have adopted this idea for the present volume.

The latest (11th) edition of *The Reader's Adviser* edited by Winifred F. Courtney and published in 1968 now gives much improved and expanded coverage to African literature, and special attention is devoted to Abrahams, Senghor, Achebe, Mphahlele, Tutuola, and Soyinka.[26] However, the guide is of course limited to listings of material published or distributed in the U.S.A.

The most recent bibliography, *A New Bibliography of African Literature*, already mentioned, comes from the Hungarian scholar Paul Páricsy.[27] This volume is largely supplementary to the Jahn bibliography, giving details of material not covered by Jahn, as well as listing new literature that has appeared since 1965.

Current bibliographies of new African writing are featured in each issue of the biannual (yearly as from 1971) *African Literature Today*, covering both books and periodical articles from all parts of the world.[28] Annual compilations have been included in the September or December issues of *The Journal of Commonwealth Literature*.[29] The annual *MLA International Bibliography* has coverage of African literature since the number appearing in June 1968; earlier material was listed under the 'Commonwealth Literature English' section.[30] However, the MLA bibliography lists only *scholarship* on African literature, and creative works such as novels, plays, poetry, etc., are not included unless they are published with a critical introduction of some significance. In the volume appearing in June 1968 (for 1967) the section on African writing comprised 241 entries out of a total of 21,633 entries; in the June 1969 issue (for 1968) it comprised 401 out of 24,126. The recently launched *Africana Library Journal* provides extensive bibliographic coverage (books only) of new creative writing from Africa.[31] More selectively, there are also listings in the monthly *Current Bibliography of African Affairs*.[32]

The various national bibliographies of Great Britain, France, and the United States are the obvious primary sources for new material. In Africa, the development of national bibliographic services is making constant progress. National bibliographies, or at least some official listings of material deposited at national libraries, now exist for several African nations. Legal deposit of any printed material is required in most countries but is not always strictly enforced or carefully supervised, and small publishers and printers tend to ignore the publications ordinance or are not aware of it. As a result, hardly any of the national bibliographies are truly exhaustive.

The University of Ibadan was one of the forerunners in national bibliographic activities, and since 1950 has issued *Nigerian Publications*.[33] Published quarterly and cumulated annually, it lists material in English and in the vernacular languages as well as 'Nigeriana' published outside Nigeria, and it provides a directory of publishers and printers. Arranged similarly, and again including vernacular literature, is the *Ghana National Bibliography*, which commenced publication in 1968; annual cumulations covering the years 1965 and 1966 are now available.[34] From Sierra Leone we have *Sierra Leone Publications*, annual lists issued since 1962, which cite only English publications; vernacular literature is covered by the Sierra Leone Literacy Bureau in Bo.[35]

Unfortunately, national bibliographies are so far unavailable for many East African countries, though current material is recorded in the bibliographies that appear in certain periodicals such as *Tanzania Notes and Records*[36] and *Uganda Journal*,[37] both published twice yearly. The Institute of African Studies at Haile Selassie I University publishes its

annual *Ethiopian Publications*.[38] The national archives of Malawi and
Rhodesia both publish a *List of Publications Deposited in the Library of the
National Archives* annually.[39,40]

Similarly, most of the francophone African nations still lack adequate
bibliographic services. However, an impressive annual bibliography
comes from the Malagasy Republic, the *Bibliographie annuelle de Madagascar*.[41] To date three cumulations have appeared for 1964, 1965, and
1966. Its listings include books and articles that have appeared in periodicals. For South Africa several good sources are available: *The South
African National Bibliography*, published quarterly (and also available as
a weekly card-catalogue service), is cumulated into annual volumes and
compiled by the State Library in Pretoria.[42] It records all publications
received under the terms of the Copyright Act published in the Republic
of South Africa and South West Africa. For research into African literature, however, more important is *Africana Nova*, which includes all
the vernacular writings not covered by the *South African National Bibliography*.[43] It was published between 1959 and 1969 by the South African
Library in Cape Town and most back numbers are still available. Works
by and about African authors writing in Portuguese — not covered by this
bibliography — may be traced in the *Boletin Internacional de Bibliografia
Luso-brazileira*.[44]

A useful inventory of bibliographic resources for African literature
is Albert Gérard's *Bibliographical Problems in Creative African Literature*.[45]
Current developments and national bibliographic activities in Africa are
discussed and outlined in depth in *The Bibliography of Africa*, the proceedings and papers of the International Conference on African Bibliography
held at Nairobi in December 1967.[46] A summary of the report on the conference was also published separately in *Africa*, the journal of the International African Institute.[47]

Thus the problems of definition, of scope, and of up-to-dateness can
be seen as central to the bibliographic coverage of African literature. In
this guide we are attempting to provide a *current* and comprehensive
framework for African literature today, to create the bibliographic foundation which is so obvious and imperative a need for this expanding, new,
and exciting literature.

Scope and Arrangement of this Guide

A Reader's Guide to African Literature lists 820 works by *black* African
authors south of the Sahara writing in English and in French. Reference
material, critical works, and anthologies (many by non-Africans) are also
included. While this bibliography aims to be a comprehensive reference
tool within the above categories, for many librarians and students of
African literature it will necessarily be supplementary to reference
works and bibliographies already published.

The bibliography — reference and critical works and anthologies apart —
is grouped under two major sections: Part I, 'Writings in English', and
Part II, 'Writings in French'. Within these divisions the arrangement

is by country, and alphabetically by author. In the section covering writings in English we list 317 works, and though we have tried to be as comprehensive as possible, the listing is by no means complete. The French-language section gives details of 197 titles, and includes English translations. This second section is strictly selective, and briefer annotations are given to the titles. Here we give emphasis to literature still available, but we include a number of books now out-of-print that are judged to be significant.

All entries are numbered consecutively throughout the book, and the author index refers to these numbers. Writers who have not published separately but whose work appears in any of the anthologies are also indexed comprehensively. Index numbers in these cases are prefixed with the letter 'A', followed by the entry number of the relevant anthology.

OMISSIONS AND EXCEPTIONS

It has not been easy to keep the bibliography to manageable proportions, and we have had to *exclude* writings in Portuguese and in Arabic as well as literature by North African and white South African writers. The mass of Onitsha market novels, popular pamphlet literature, and chap-books from Nigeria and from Ghana are excluded. The important exceptions to this are the early Achebe and Ekwensi short stories, which are now collector's items. Regrettably, the vast output of vernacular literature has had to be omitted — for example, the works by the great Swahili poet Shabaan Robert and other Swahili literature,[50] and the late Chief D. O. Fagunwa's writings in Yoruba.[51] With reluctance, we have also decided to exclude the entire impressive range of writing from the Caribbean, much of which is so closely linked to African literature and the 'Négritude' movement. Familiar names such as Aimé Césaire, Léon Damas, and Frantz Fanon are therefore entirely missing from the bibliography.

Though this is a bibliography of *contemporary* African literature, some of the classic early works such as Olaudah Equiano's *Narrative*, recently reissued, and Thomas Mofolo's *Chaka*, first published in translation in 1931, are included.

A number of papers presented to the (American) African Studies Association annual meetings (and still available in xerox form) are included, but theses and dissertations are omitted.

Lastly, a word about folkloristic literature, i.e. collections of legends, myths, tales, ballads, etc. Such material has been covered only selectively; we have concentrated mainly on recently published literature and reprints. For comprehensive coverage on African folklore and oral literature readers should consult the annual MLA bibliographies.[52]

We hope that these carefully considered omissions will mean in fact that coverage under the terms we have defined will make this a more complete and functional reference tool than would otherwise have been possible.

FEATURES

Children's books by African authors are featured in a separate section, with indications of approximate age-groups.

Politically committed literature has been and remains closely tied to the development of African literature, and exerts a considerable influence on creative writing. For this reason we have included a list of such works in a separate section, compiled by Gideon-Cyrus M. Mutiso.

We have also felt it desirable to provide an annotated select list of articles on creative African literature that have appeared in magazines and periodicals. Barbara Abrash contributed this section.

A novel feature, we believe, is our inclusion of a series of fairly extensive biographies on some of the major authors represented in the bibliography. To obtain accurate and up-to-date biographic details on certain of the authors has been a formidable task; this explains the disparity in length and treatment in some cases. We have put stress on 'letting the writers speak for themselves', and have therefore included a large number of quotes from writers voicing their views on their own and other authors' works.

REVIEWS AND ANNOTATIONS

This guide differs from previously published bibliographies in that it has two new features: (a) annotations on almost all titles listed, and (b) extracts from reviews on a great many of the entries. We wish to emphasize that — with the exception of the section on bibliographies — the annotations are entirely *descriptive* and *not critical*; they are intended to place, not judge, the books. They have been prepared, as far as possible, from actual reading or examination of each book. In some cases we have been unable to obtain or examine a copy of a book and have had to rely on publishers' blurbs alone. The annotations vary in length, but this is not meant in any way to reflect on the quality of any book.

The reviews originate largely from major literary magazines on African literature such as *Black Orpheus, Présence Africaine, Transition,* and *African Literature Today,* and as well as from important scholarly periodicals such as *West Africa, African Affairs, Africa Today,* and *Africa Report,* which frequently carry book reviews of new African writers and critics reviewing their own literature. In many cases relevant reviews were not available, or we were unable to obtain them. Therefore a considerable number of significant books do not feature any reviews; again, we want to stress emphatically that omission of a review *or* the inclusion of one or two extracts does *not* necessarily reflect on the importance or quality of any title. It could be argued, therefore, that the inclusion of review extracts is altogether questionable, particularly since we have only listed reviews that were generally favourable (or quoted favourable extracts) —provided we were in a position to examine at least two such positive reviews. Needless to say, in a great many cases equally unfavourable reviews have appeared of the same books. Take for example Lenrie Peters' novel *The Second Round*: Gerald Moore, the noted English critic, writing in *East Africa Journal,* considers it 'a distinguished and memorable work of imagination',[53] and his statement is supported by that of another reviewer, Charles Larson, in *Africa Report,* who says it is 'the most impressive title Heinemann has added to its African Writers Series in a long time'.[54] However, the South African Lewis Nkosi doesn't agree at all. Writing in the same *Africa Report* one month later, he dismisses the novel as 'one of the real disasters of African fiction'.[55] Another example of how sharply divided critics can be on any one book is the case of *Wind versus polygamy* by Obi Egbuna: it 'entertains immensely', it is 'a remarkable novel', says Mbella Sonne Dipoko, reviewing the novel in *Présence Africaine*.[56] Yet Ronald Dathorne in *Black Orpheus* bluntly calls it 'the worst African novel I have ever read'.[57] In spite of these differences of opinion, we did feel reviews ought to be featured to make for somewhat livelier and more stimulating reading. In many cases they provide a mirror reflecting the views of African novelists, playwrights, and poets on their own literature.

AVAILABILITY AND PRICES

Previously published bibliographies (except Baratte) have unfortunately neglected the important factor of *availability*. Many teachers and instructors are repeatedly placing on their reading lists or syllabuses books that are in fact unobtainable and long out-of-print. We have therefore considered stress on availability to be highly desirable. In addition to complete bibliographic data, we have provided the names of publishers of *both* English and American editions, together with details of *prices* (again, listing both English *and* American retail prices where applicable). Out-of-print items are clearly indicated as such. Inevitably, a few of the books listed as being available may become out-of-print by the time this bibliography comes off the press.

Prices, which of course are subject to change, are listed in the currency of the country of publication, or at the official dollar prices established by American exclusive distributors. Dollar prices quoted by American distributors or dealers are, in most cases, not the simple dollar equivalent of sterling, French franc, or other currencies. It is the price at which the publication can be sold from the United States taking into account transatlantic freight and other costs of maintaining an American sales depot. English prices are given throughout in the new decimal currency, regardless of publication date: it is emphasized that these prices are approximate only, since at the time of going to press many titles were still listed in the old currency. Our rule-of-thumb conversions to the new currency may not always correspond with the actual new prices quoted by publishers. For the African Writers Series (Heinemann Educational Books) U.K. prices are quoted: overseas prices are normally at least 5p cheaper.

ADDRESSES

Essential addresses are provided in an appendix. There is a list of major book dealers specializing in African literature and/or holding substantial stocks in this area. An international list of publishers whose programmes include creative African writing is also included.

A BASIC LIBRARY OF AFRICAN LITERATURE

We have asterisked * a number of works —limited to *books still in print* —

which in our opinion form a basic and representative collection of African creative writing — fiction, drama, and poetry — as well as some outstanding anthologies, critical and reference works. Tabulating the costs for the nucleus of such an 'instant' library (in hardcover editions where available), the total outlay comes to about \$410 (£170.80) or, without material in French, to \$270 (£112.50). The same collection in paperback form, where available, could cost substantially less. Other tabulations[58] provide the following figures: *all* material in English, including bibliographies, critical works, anthologies, and (where published) English translations of francophone writing, \$1.025 (£427.10), covering everything *still in print*. Politically committed literature is \$135 (£56.25), children's books about \$68 (£28.30). All literature in French, including bibliographies, critical works, anthologies, etc. would come to \$275 (£114.60).

Considering that libraries today have the unique opportunity to assemble the literature of almost an entire continent (and the material represented in this volume covers the most substantial portion of black African writing today), the total cost involved seems a remarkably inexpensive and wise investment.

New York City. September 1970.   H. M. Z.

References

1 Chinua Achebe: 'English and the African writer', *Transition*, vol. 4, no. 18, 1965.
2 New York, Frederick Praeger; London, Deutsch, 1965.
3 For an interesting account of the development of creative writing in West Africa see E. N. Obiechina's 'The growth of written literature in English-speaking West Africa', *The Conch*, vol. 1, no. 2, September, 1969 (see p. 104).
4 The *first* African novel in French has been attributed to Massyla Diop (1885–1933), whose *Le reprouvé, roman d'une Sénégalaise* appeared in instalment form in the mid-1920's in the *Revue Africaine Artistique et littéraire* (published in Dakar), all issues of which are now extremely scarce.
5 New York, Frederick Praeger; London, Deutsch, 1965 (see entry 9).
6 *The Journal of the New African Literature and the Arts*, no. 4, Fall, 1967 (see p. 105).
7 *A new bibliography of African literature*, Budapest, Center for Afro-American Research, Hungarian Academy of Sciences, 1969 (see entry 16).
8 *African Studies Bulletin* vol. 11, no. 2, September, 1968 (see p. 108).
9 *African Studies Bulletin* vol. 11, no. 3, December, 1968 (see p. 108).
10 Ibadan, Ibadan University Press, 1959 (see entry 19).
11 Ibadan, Ibadan University Press, 1965, 2nd edn. 1970.
12 Bonn, Deutsche Afrika-Gesellschaft, 1962.
13 *African Studies Bulletin*, vol. 5, no. 2, September, 1962.
14 *African Forum*, vol. 1, no. 4, Spring 1966.
15 *Journal of General Education*, vol. 13, 1962.
16 *Revue de Littérature comparée*, no. 37, 1963.
17 *Books Abroad*, no. 38, 1964.
18 Léopoldville (Kinshasha), Congo, Bibliothèque de l'Étoile. ('Cahiers Documents pour l'Action, 3'), 1964 (see entry 4).
19 Ibadan, Institute of African Studies, University of Ibadan, 1964 (see entry 2).
20 Paris, Office de Coopération Radiophonique, O.C.O.R.A., 1965.
21 *ibid.*, new edition, 1968 (see entry 3).
22 Freetown, Sierra Leone University Press, 1967 (see entry 130).
23 Paris, Ed. du Seuil, 1964 (see entry 63).
24 London, Pall Mall Press; New York, Frederick Praeger, 1967 (see entry 64).
25 New York, Johnson Reprint Corp., 1967 (see entry 1).
26 New York, R. R. Bowker Co., 1968.
27 Budapest, Center for Afro-American Research, Hungarian Academy of Sciences, 1969 (see entry 16).
28 London, Heinemann Educational Books, 1968 – (see p. 102).
29 London, Heinemann Educational Books, 1965–1969 (Nos. 1–8; now available from Swets & Zeitlinger, Amsterdam); London, Oxford University Press, 1970 – (No. 9) (see p. 105).
30 New York, Modern Language Association. (The bibliographies are *not* available separately. The complete annual volumes can be obtained from Kraus Reprint Co., New York.)
31 New York, Africana Publishing Corp., 1970 – (see p. 108).
32 Washington, D.C., African Bibliographic Center, 1965 – (now distributed by Greenwood Periodicals, Westport, Conn.) (see p. 109).
33 Ibadan, Ibadan University Press, 1950 – .
34 Accra, Ghana Library Board (P.O.B. 663), 1968 – .
35 Freetown, Sierra Leone Library Board (P.O.B. 326), 1962 – .
36 Dar es Salaam, Tanzania Society (P.O.B. 511), 1936 – (formerly published as *Tanganyika Notes and Records*).
37 Kampala, Uganda Society (P.O.B. 4980), 1963 – .
38 Addis Ababa, Institute of Ethiopian Studies, Haile Selassie I University, 1965 – .
39 Zomba, National Archives of Malawi (P.O.B. 62), 1965 – (as *Malawi National Bibliography*, 1968 –).
40 Salisbury, National Archives of Rhodesia (P.O.B. 8043), 1961 – (as *Rhodesia National Bibliography*, 1969 –).
41 Tananarive, Bibliothèque Universitaire et Bibliothèque Nationale (B.P. 908), 1967 – .
42 Pretoria, The State Library, 1959 – (formerly published as *Publications received by the State Library*, 1933 –1958).
43 Cape Town, The South African Library (Queen Victoria Street), 1959–1969. (Ceased with the December 1969 issue. Back numbers still available are: No. 3, 1959; no. 1, 1960; no. 1, 1961; nos. 2 and 4, 1963; and nos. 1–4, 1964–1969 complete).
44 Lisbon, Fundación Calouste Gulbenkian, 1960 – .
45 *The Journal of General Education*, vol. 14, no. 1, April, 1967.
46 London, Frank Cass; New York, Africana Publishing Corp., 1970.
47 *Africa* vol. 28, no. 3, July 1969.
48 Vernacular literature is well covered by both the Jahn and Páricsy bibliographies already cited. For early vernacular titles the missionary journal *Books for Africa* (London, 1931 –) is an important source. It was the bulletin of the International Committee on Christian Literature for

Africa. This organization ceased to exist in July 1958, and its work was taken over by the Christian Literature Council.

49 Shabaan Robert's complete works have recently been reissued in twelve paperback volumes published by Thomas Nelson and Sons, London.

50 For comprehensive coverage of Swahili literature and folklore, see also Marcel van Spaandonck, *Practical and systematical Swahili bibliography: Linguistics 1850–1963.* Leiden, Netherlands, E. J. Brill, 1965 (pp. 29–49).

51 Some of Fagunwa's writings are now available in translation (see entry 257).

52 See footnote 30.

53 *East Africa Journal,* November 1965.

54 *Africa Report,* vol. 11, no. 8, November 1966.

55 *Africa Report,* vol. 11, no. 9, December 1966.

56 *Présence Africaine,* no. 53, 1965.

57 *Black Orpheus,* no. 17, 1965.

58 All these estimates are approximate only. British prices will tend to be lower throughout. *Not* considered in the estimates are the G. K. Hall catalogue-card reprints, nor any reprints priced above $25.00.

Acknowledgements

For supplying review extracts and photographs of authors we are grateful to the following publishers: Heinemann Educational Books Ltd, London; Longman Group Ltd, London; Oxford University Press, London and New York; Hutchinson Publishing Group, London; Faber and Faber Ltd, London; William Collins and Sons, London and New York; East African Publishing House, Nairobi; Editions C.L.E., Yaoundé; The Transcription Centre, London; and a special note of thanks must go to Geoffrey Jones of Présence Africaine in Paris.

Our thanks to International University Bookseller's *Africana Center* in New York, which enabled us to examine many African literature titles held in stock there.

Several people have supplied valuable and helpful comments and suggestions while reading the manuscript. Above all, we are most grateful to Bernth Lindfors of the University of Texas (Editor of *Research in African Literatures*); Eldred Jones of the University of Sierra Leone (Editor of *African Literature Today*), John Povey of the African Studies Center at the University of California at Los Angeles, and last but not least to Katy Brooks and Heather Karolyi. We also wish to acknowledge the help of Gisela Bickford in the compilation of the extensive index.

For permission to quote extracts from the copyright material listed below we are grateful to the following publishers:

Africana Publishing Corporation and Heinemann Educational Books Ltd for J. P. Clark, *America, their America*, Cosmo Pieterse and Donald Munro, *Protest and Conflict in African Literature*, and Gabriel Okara, *The Voice* (from the introduction by Arthur Ravenscroft); Africana Publishing Corporation and the Scandinavian Institute of African Studies for Per Wästberg, *The Writer in Modern Africa*; Cambridge University Press for Camara Laye, *L'enfant noir* (edited by Joyce Hutchinson), Abioseh Nicol, *Two African Tales*, and Birago Diop, *Contes choisies* (edited by Joyce Hutchinson); Grove Press Inc. for Janheinz Jahn, *Neo-African Literature: a history of black writing*, and Amos Tutuola, *The Palm-wine Drinkard*; Longman Group Ltd and Humanities Press Inc. for Davidson Nicol, *Africa: a subjective view*; Longman Group Ltd and Deborah Rogers Ltd for Lewis Nkosi, *Home and Exile*; National Educational Television, New York, for *African Writers of Today* series of interviews nos. 3 and 6; Northwestern University Press for Lalage Bown and Michael Crowder, *The Proceedings of the First International Congress of Africanists*, and Ulli Beier, *Introduction to African Literature*; Oxford University Press for A. C. Brench, *The novelists' Inheritance in French Africa*, Gerald Moore, *Seven African Writers*, Clive Wake, *An anthology of African and Malagasy poetry in French*, John Reed and Clive Wake, *Léopold Senghor: Prose and Poetry*, Birago Diop, *Tales of Amadou Koumba* (edited and translated by Dorothy Blair), and Davidson Nicol, *The truly married women*; Pall Mall Press Ltd for Claude Wauthier, *The Literature and Thought of Modern Africa*; Alfred A. Knopf Inc. for Peter Abrahams, *Tell Freedom*.

For permission to quote extracts from various journals and magazines, we are indebted to the editors and publishers of the following publications: *African Arts/Arts d'Afrique*, *African Literature Today*, *Black Orpheus*, *Cultural Events in Africa*, *The Journal of Commonwealth Literature*, *The Journal of the New African Literature and the Arts*, *Présence Africaine*, and *Transition*.

Picture Credits

Peter Abrahams, courtesy of Heinemann Educational Books Ltd., London

Chinua Achebe, photograph by Lotte Meitner-Graf, courtesy of Heinemann Educational Books Ltd., London

Ama Ata Aidoo, photograph by John Goldblatt, courtesy of The Transcription Centre, London

Timothy Aluko, courtesy of Heinemann Educational Books Ltd., London

Ayi Kwei Armah, photograph by Douglas Harris, courtesy of Houghton Mifflin Co., Boston

Kofi Awoonor, photograph by Sandra Gatten, courtesy of Heinemann Educational Books Ltd., London

Francis Bebey, photograph by Irmelin Lebeer, courtesy of the author Mongo Beti, courtesy of Heinemann Educational Books Ltd., London

Okot p'Bitek, courtesy of The Transcription Centre Ltd., London

Dennis Brutus, courtesy of Heinemann Educational Books Ltd., London

John Pepper Clark, courtesy of Heinemann Educational Books Ltd., London

Bernard Dadié, courtesy of Editions Seghers, Paris

Mbella Sonne Dipoko, photograph by Lütfi Ozkök, courtesy of Heinemann Educational Books Ltd., London

Cyprian Ekwensi, courtesy of Hutchinson Publishing Group Ltd., London

Alex la Guma, courtesy of The Transcription Centre, London

Camara Laye, courtesy of William Collins & Sons, London

Taban lo Liyong, courtesy of Heinemann Educational Books Ltd., London

Ezekiel Mphahlele, courtesy of the author

James Ngugi, courtesy of Heinemann Educational Books Ltd., London

Davidson Nicol, courtesy of the author.

Lewis Nkosi, photograph by Bill Orchard, courtesy of The Transcription Centre, London

Gabriel Okara, photograph by Isaac Uzuegbu, courtesy of Andre Deutsch and Heinemann Educational Books Ltd., London

Christopher Okigbo, courtesy of Heinemann Educational Books Ltd., London

Yambo Ouologuem, courtesy of Editions du Seuil, Paris

Sembene Ousmane, courtesy of Presses de la Cite, Paris

Ferdinand Oyono, courtesy of Heinemann Educational Books Ltd., London

Guillaume Oyono-Mbia, photograph by Valerie Wilmer, courtesy of The Transcription Centre, London

Lenrie Peters, courtesy of Heinemann Educational Books Ltd., London

David Rubadiri, courtesy of East African Publishing House

Richard Rive, courtesy of Heinemann Educational Books Ltd., London

Sahle Sellassie, courtesy of Heinemann Educational Books Ltd., London

Francis Selormey, courtesy of Heinemann Educational Books Ltd., London

Leopold Sédar Senghor, courtesy of Heinemann Educational Books Ltd., London

Robert Serumaga, photograph by Valerie Wilmer, courtesy of Heinemann Educational Books Ltd., London

Wole Soyinka, courtesy of The Transcription Centre, London

Amos Tutuola, courtesy of Faber & Faber Ltd., London

Tchicaya U Tam'si, photograph by Jalabert, courtesy of Heinemann Educational Books Ltd., London

Bibliography

BIBLIOGRAPHIES

*1 **Abrash, Barbara** comp. and ed.
Black African Literature in English, since 1952: Works and criticism
New York, Johnson Reprint Corp., 1967. 92 pp. $3.95
A bibliography of creative works of literature by black African writers, along with selected relevant criticism. Amos Tutuola's *Palm-wine Drinkard* is taken as a starting point. Gives 463 entries, covering both books and periodical articles, together with a list of literary magazines. Includes listings of authors whose work has appeared in anthologies. There is an introductory essay by John Povey.
'. . . an invaluable list.'
Ezekiel Mphahlele — *Africa Today*[1]

*2 **Amosu, Margaret** comp. and ed.
Creative African Writing in the European Languages: a preliminary bibliography
(Special supplement to *African Notes* Bulletin of the Institute of African Studies)
Ibadan, Institute of African Studies, Univ. of Ibadan, 1964. 35 pp. 5s.0d. [Nigeria]
Lists works by 251 authors including South African writers 'irrespective of colour, whose work is clearly inspired (for better or for worse) by their relation to the African social and political situation of that country.' Now somewhat out-of-date, but as a preliminary bibliography still valuable. Notable for its inclusion of writings by North African authors.

*3 **Baratte, Thérèse** comp. and ed.
Bibliographie auteurs africains et malgaches de langue française
(2nd revised and enlarged edition)
Paris, Office de Coopération Radiophonique, 1968. 78 pp. F3.00
Covers not only creative writing, but also historical and political literature. Perhaps the most comprehensive source to date: includes prices and details of availability. Country-by-country arrangement, with author index.
'. . . an accurate, convenient and up-to-date list including practically every title by African and Malagasy authors writing in French . . . it is gratifying [therefore] to see such detailed information delivered in such a legible attractive form.'
Gary Spackey — *African Literature Today*[2]

4 **Bol, V. P.**, and **Allary, J.**
Littérateurs et poètes noirs
Léopoldville, Bibliothèque de l'Étoile (BP 3375), 1964. 79 pp., out-of-print
This volume is divided into two sections: the first provides a basic introduction to French African writing; the second is a bibliographic essay which systematically lists creative writing by francophone African authors as well as that from English-speaking West and South Africa, the Caribbean and the Americas.

*5 **East, N. B.** comp. and ed.
African Theatre: a checklist of critical materials
New York, Africana Publishing Corp., 1970. 48 pp. $3.75
This bibliography draws together wide-ranging references to secondary materials related to African drama. It is divided into seven areas: Bibliographies; General; North; South; East; West; and Films. Appearing in part in the Spring, 1969 issue of *Afro-Asian Theatre Bulletin*, it has now been expanded and brought up-to-date.

6 **Harvard University Library, Cambridge, Mass. Widener Library Shelflist**
No. 2, Africa. Classification schedule
Classified list by call number. Alphabetical list by author or title. Chronological listing
Cambridge, Mass., Harvard Univ. Press (for Harvard Univ. Library) 1965. 196 pp. $25.00
Classification '10,000' covers African Literature titles (classified listing pp. 267—301), added to the Widener library since 1960. Some authors are wrongly classified: Tutuola and Ekwensi, for example, appear under South African authors.

7 **Howard University Library**
Dictionary Catalog of the Jesse E. Moorland Collection of Negro Life and History
(Photographic reprint of catalogue card-index)
Nine volumes, 150,000 cards
Boston, G. K. Hall, 1970. $665.000

8 **Howard University Library**
Dictionary Catalog of the Arthur B. Spingarn Collection of Negro Authors
(Photographic reprint of catalogue card-index)
Two volumes, 31,400 cards
Boston, G. K. Hall, 1970. $150.00
This collection of Negro authors is the result of fifty years of effort by Arthur B. Spingarn, a New York attorney and authority on Negro life and history, to assemble all significant writings by persons of African descent throughout the world. The bulk of the collection consists of more than 8,000 volumes. Among them there is a great deal of early Afro-American writing; slave narratives and biographies; works by Caribbean authors, Afro-Cuban and Afro-Brazilian poets, novelists and essayists, as well African literature in the vernacular languages and in English and French.

[1]vol. 15, no. 6, Dec./Jan. 1969
[2]no. 3, 1969

2

*9 Jahn, Janheinz comp. and ed.
A Bibliography of Neo-African Literature: from Africa, America and the Caribbean
London, Deutsch, 1965. 336 pp. £4.20
New York, Praeger, 1965. 359 pp. out-of-print
The most comprehensive and authoritative bibliographic source to date. Jahn's volume lists 1,184 works by African authors, noting both translations and country of origin for each writer. Jahn's criteria for the inclusion of a writer — based on his definition of 'neo-African literature' outlined in his book *Muntu* (see 38) — has been much debated by a number of African scholars, but his bibliography, nevertheless, remains an extremely valuable reference tool. Individual supplements to Jahn's bibliography have appeared in the Sptember 1968 issue of *African Studies Bulletin*, and *Journal of the New African Literature and the Arts*, no. 4, 1968. Jahn's new *Bibliography of Creative African Writing* is expected to be published during the course of 1971.

10 Memmi, Albert comp.
Bibliographie de la littérature Nord-Africaine d'expression française, 1945–1962
Paris and The Hague, Mouton, 1965 (Ouvrages sur la culture Nord-Africaine, 3). 48 pp.
New York, Humanities Press, distr. $2.75
A useful bibliographic inventory of French-language North-African literature (*not* covered by this bibliography) by authors from Algeria, Morocco and Tunisia. It cites over 500 entries, covering both books and periodical articles.

11 Naaman, A. Y. and **Achiriga, J. J.**
Ébauche d'une bibliographie de la littérature nègre d'expression française
Legon, Univ. of Ghana, Dept. of Modern Languages, 1966. 23 pp. out-of-print [?]

12 National Book League, London
Bibliography prepared for the World Festival of Negro Arts
London, National Book League, 1966. 7½p out-of-print [?]
A selected bibliography specially designed for the First World Festival of Negro Arts, held in Dakar, Senegal, 1966, representing the Negro's contribution to literature.

13 National Book League, London
Fiction, Drama and Poetry from the Commonwealth
London, National Book League, 1966. 43 pp. 20p
An annotated reading list prepared for the 'Commonwealth in Books' exhibition held in London, October 1966, containing 301 entries, of which 75 are on African literature.

14 National Book League, London, and **The African Centre, London**
Contemporary African writing, 1967
London, National Book League, 1967. 48 pp. 10p
This annotated catalogue of an exhibition held at the National Book League premises in September 1967 lists 170 books, including African contributions in History, Politics, Law and Economics. A small separate section surveys francophone African writing.

15 Northwestern University Libraries. Evanston, Ill.
Catalog of the African Collection of the Northwestern University Library
(Photographic reprint of catalogue card-index)
2 volumes, 28,300 cards
Boston, G. K. Hall, 1963. 1,350 pp. $120.00
This catalogue provides a partial guide to the collection, which includes a great deal of African literature.

*16 Páricsy, Pál comp.
A New Bibliography of African Literature
Budapest, Center for Afro-Asian Research of the Hungarian Academy of Sciences, 1969 (Studies on Developing Countries, no. 24). 108 pp. $1.80
Consists of two parts: Part I 'An additional bibliography to J. Jahn's *A Bibliography of Neo-African Literature from Africa, America and the Caribbean*'; Part II 'A preliminary bibliography of African writing (from 1965 to the present)'. Part I lists 361 entries additional to the Jahn coverage of African writing. Part II lists 377 titles. Follows the Jahn style for bibliographic description. There are a great many listings of non-trade and 'out-of-the-way' materials, especially those published in South Africa, Nigeria and East Africa. Part of this bibliography was previously published in *Journal of the New African Literature and the Arts*, no. 4, 1968.

17 Porter, Dorothy comp.
A Catalogue of the African Collection in the Moorland Foundation, Howard University Library
Compiled by students in the program of African Studies
Washington, D.C., Howard University Press, 1958. 398 pp. $8.00
Includes details of 289 African literature items in the collection. (See also 18)

18 Porter, Dorothy ed.
Supplement to the Catalogue of the African Collection in the Moorland Foundation of the Howard University Library
Comp. by H. P. Alexander
Washington, D.C., Catholic University, 1963. 106 pp.

19 Ramsaran, John
New Approaches to African Literature: A guide to Negro-African writing and related studies
Ibadan, Ibadan University Press, 1965. 192 pp. (out-of-print)
Ibadan, Ibadan University Press, 1970 (2nd edn.). 182 pp. £2.5.0. ⌈Nigeria⌉
New York, Africana Publishing Corp. distr. $4.95
A useful bibliographic inventory, recently re-issued in a new edition. It introduces various aspects of African, Caribbean and Black American writing, followed by extensive and up-to-date book lists, details of critical articles, and book reviews.
'... produced with great clarity and simplicity ... an essential tool for the study of African literature ... Mr Ramsaran has approached the task of bibliography with loving care.'
                    Eldred Jones — *Bull of the Assoc.*
                    for African Literature in English[1]

20 Schomburg Collection of Negro Literature and History (New York Public Library Catalog)
(Photographic reprint of catalogue card-index)
9 volumes, 177,000 cards
Boston, G. K. Hall, 1962. 8,474 pp. $605.00
First supplement, 2 volumes, 37,100 cards
Boston, G. K. Hall, 1964. 1,769 pp. $95.00
The Schomburg Collection is considered one of the most important sources in the world for the study of Negro life and cultures. Material in the collection is classified by the Dewey Decimal System and may be located through the catalogue, which arranges author, title and subject entries in a single alphabetical list.

21 Shears, Gillian comp.
African Literature
London, Dillon's University Bookshop (Malet Place, W.C.1) 1966. 8 pp. gratis
A list presented to the meeting of the African Studies Association at Indiana University, October, 1966.

22 University of London: School of Oriental and African Studies
Library Catalogue of the School of Oriental and African Studies
(Photographic reprint of catalogue card-index)
15,400 entries
Boston, G. K. Hall, 1963. 618 pp. $50.00
First supplement: 11,300 cards
Boston, G. K. Hall, 1965. 540 pp. $45.00

23 von Meijer, Gillian comp.
African Arts
London, Dillon's University Bookshop (Malet Place, W.C.1) 1970. 21 pp. gratis
The third part of this catalogue — perhaps one of the most comprehensive of its nature ever

issued by a bookseller — covers literature. It gives author, title, bibliographic data, and prices, but *not* names of relevant publishers.

CRITICISM

24 Actes du Colloque sur la littérature africaine d'expression française, Dakar, 26–29 mars 1963
(Université de Dakar, Publ. de la Faculté des Lettres et Sciences Humaines, langues et littératures, no. 14)
Dakar, Université de Dakar, Faculté des Lettres et Sciences Humaines, 1965. 276 pp. F51.50.
Contains the proceedings of a conference on francophone African writing, held in Dakar, Senegal, in 1963. Includes papers on the novel, on poetry, and on negritude. There are studies on three individual writers: Cheikh Hamidou Kane, Ferdinand Oyono, and Tchicaya U'Tam'si. Among the contributors are Camara Laye, Armand Guibert, Thomas Melone, Roger Mercier, Janheinz Jahn, Gerald Moore, and Anthony Brench.

25 American Society of African Culture, New York
Some Modern African Writers: sketches and works
New York, American Soc. of African Culture, 1964. 19 pp. out-of-print

26 Balogun, S. I.
Notes and Exercises on Modern Poetry from Africa
Ibadan, Onibonoje Press, 1967, 55 pp. 3s 6d.
Background notes based on the West African Examinations Council's selections.

*27 Beier, Ulli ed.
Introduction to African Literature: an anthology of critical writings from 'Black Orpheus'
London, Longmans, 1967. 272 pp. £1.50
Evanston, Ill., Northwestern University Press, 1967. 272 pp. $7.50
An anthology of critical writing on African and Afro-American literature and oral tradition, with contributions by Ezekiel Mphahlele, Gerald Moore, Janheinz Jahn, Abiola Irele, John Ramsaran, Robert July, Lewis Nkosi, Jan Knappert, O. R. Dathorne, Ulli Beier himself, and many more.
'... I strongly recommend this book to anyone interested in African literature. As a collection of major critical essays on major African writers, as a balanced survey of modes of African literary expression, as an "introduction" of sufficient strength to stimulate both the beginner and the initiate, and as a record of the intellectual life that has pulsed

[1]no. 4, Mar. 1966

through the pages of Black Orpheus, *it is not likely to be surpassed for many years to come.'*

Bernth Lindfors — *Africa Report*[1]

'All in all this is a valuable and attractive volume which ought to form part of the library of every school or college where literature is taught.

Robert Green — *Mawazo*[2]

28 **Belinga, Enos M. S.**

Littérature et musique populaire en Afrique noire
Paris, Ed. Cujas, 1965. 259 pp. F10.00
Examines African music and literatures in the context of their ancient traditions.

29 **Bown, Lalage,** and **Crowder, Michael** eds.

The Proceedings of the First International Congress of Africanists, Accra, 11th—18th December 1962
London, Longmans, 1964 369 pp. out-of-print
Evanston, Ill., Northwestern University Press, 1964. 369 pp. $5.95
Contents include: 'Folklore and Literature' by Bernard B. Dadié (pp. 199—219), and 'African Literature' by Ezekiel Mphahlele, (pp. 220—232).

*30 **Brench, A. C.**

The Novelists' Inheritance in French Africa: writers from Senegal to Cameroon
London and New York, Oxford University Press, 1967 (Three Crowns Book). 152 pp. 52½p/$1.85
The writings of Birago Diop, Camara Laye, Ferdinand Oyono, Mongo Beti, Jean Malongo, Bernard Dadié, Ake Loba, Cheikh Hamidou Kane, and Sembène Ousmane are examined both as works of literature and as writing that came into being as a result of historical events. Bibliographical and biographical notes accompany the text (see also 31).

*31 **Brench, A. C.**

Writing in French from Senegal to Cameroon
London and New York, Oxford University Press, 1967 (Three Crowns Book). 160 pp. 52½p/$1.85
Untranslated extracts from the work of the novelists considered in the preceeding entry, intended to be representative of each writer's work. The selection complements the essays in *The novelists' inheritance in French Africa,* but it may be used separately. Bibliographical, biographical, and introductory notes are provided for each passage.

'With these two books A. C. Brench . . . makes an important contribution to a still somewhat neglected field.

Frederic Michelman — *Africa Report*[3]

*32 **Cartey, Wilfred**

Whispers from a Continent: the literature of contemporary black Africa

New York, Random House, 1969. 397 pp. $8.95
New York, Vintage Books, 1969. 397 pp. $2.45
London, Heinemann Educ. Books, 1971. 397 pp. £2.25 (£1.50 pap.)
This is an in-depth survey of African writing during the last thirty years. Cartey groups his study under two major themes. In the section 'The Movement Away', he covers Auto-biography; Disillusionment and Breakup; The Colonial World; The Falling away; Alienation and Flight; Apartheid; The Lost Generation; Urban Political Reality; and The Search. Under the second theme, 'The Movement Back', he includes Homecoming and Reentry; Exile and Return; Négritude. Belief and Man's Faith; and Rebirth.

'. . . his interpretation might be a very special one since his vision as a West Indian combines a degree of external detachment denied the African yet his sense of identifying blackness grants him a more intimate perception than the totally external European critic . . . this book is the boldest attempt yet to survey the field of African literature and it is an impressive and able work that will become a significant reference.'

John Povey — *Africa Today*[4]

33 **Chadwick, H. M.** and **Chadwick, Nora, K.**

The Growth of Literature
Vol. III: The Tatars, Polynesia, Some African Peoples, General Survey.
(Reprint of ed. London, 1940)
London and New York, Cambridge University Press, 1969. 928 pp. £6.50/$22.50

34 **Colin, Ronald**

Littérature africaine d'hier et de demain
Paris, Association pour le développement Educatif et Culturel, 1965. 192 pp. out-of-print.

35 **Colin, Roland**

Les contes noirs de l'Ouest Africain, témoins majeurs d'un humanisme
Paris, Présence Africaine, 1957. 206 pp. out-of-print
Study of traditional African literature, with a preface by Léopold Senghor.

36 **Cook, Mercer,** and **Henderson, Stephen E.**

The Militant Black Writer in Africa and the United States
Madison, Univ. of Wisconsin Press, 1969. 136 pp. $4.50 ($1.95 pap.)

[1]vol. 12, no. 9, Dec. 1967
[2]vol. 1, no. 3, June 1968
[3]vol. 12, no. 9, Dec. 1967
[4]vol. 17, no. 2, Mar.—Apr. 1970

The two essays that make up this volume were originally delivered in shorter form as papers at the first meeting of a two-day symposium, 'Anger, and Beyond — The Black Writer and a World in Revolution', held in Madison, Wisconsin, in August 1968. In his paper 'African Voices of Protest', Professor Cook traces the development of black African literature through the works of representative African writers from the nineteenth century to the present. He explores basic themes: independence, identity, African personality, and African socialism, and draws a parallel between the concepts of African 'Négritude' and the black American 'Soul'. The second essay, by Stephen Henderson, is entitled 'Survival Motion'; this is a study of the black writer and the black revolution in America.

'Mercer Cook's "African Voices of Protest" is certainly an excellent introduction for anyone wishing to read a basic introductory essay on the revolutionary aspects of contemporary black African writing.'

Charles Larson — Research in African Literatures[1]

37 **Deuxième Congrès des Écrivains et Artistes Noirs, Rome, 26 Mars — 1 Avril, 1959** [Proceedings] 2 vols.
Vol. 1: L'Unité des cultures négro-africaines 435 pp. F13.00
Vol. 2: Responsabilité des hommes de culture 368 pp. F12.00
Paris, Présence Africaine, 1959.
Two special issues of Présence Africaine, nos. 24/25, and nos. 27/28, covering the proceedings of the second congress of Negro writers held in Rome, April 1959.

38 **Dudley, D. R.**, and **Lang, D. M.** eds.
The Penguin Companion to Literature
Vol. 4: Classical and Byzantine, Oriental and African
Harmondsworth, Penguin Books, 1969 (Penguin Reference Books, R 37) 360 pp. 52½p
Baltimore, Penguin Books, 1969, 360 pp. $2.25
Section four of this volume (pp. 333 — 60) covers African literature, and consists of 114 short bio-bibliographies of the major African writers, together with a list of recommended reading.

37 **Eliet, Édouard**
Panorama de la littérature négro-africaine (1921—1962)
Paris, Présence Africaine, 1965. 268 pp. F20.40
A critical anthology of French-African writing, with extracts from the works of Rabéarivelo, Senghor, Césaire, Fodeba, Rabemananjara, Diop, Oyono, Dadié, Laye, Fanon, and others, and an interpretation of the meaning of negritude.

'... deserves high praise ... enables the reader, made weary and sceptical by too many subtle arguments on négritude, to return to the poems and novels of African writers and discover in them virtue that transcends the historical moment.'

Emile Snyder — African Forum[2]

38 **Jahn, Janheinz**
Muntu: an outline of Neo-African culture
(Trans. from the German by Marjorie Greene)
London, Faber, 1961. 272 pp. £1.50
New York, Grove Press, 1961 (Evergreen E. 332). 267 pp. $2.45
A wide-ranging survey of the African cultural situation and its clash with Western traditions. The study embraces art, religion, history, dance, philosophy and literature. The latter, a chapter entitled 'Hantu. History of Literature' traces the beginnings of 'neo-African' literature and then goes on to discuss contemporary African literature. South African writing and the works of Camara Laye and Amos Tutuola are singled out for special attention.

'Jahn has created a very detailed, schematic outline of what he calls "neo-African culture," a culture which he sees arising out of the older more traditional African ways ... so read Muntu; no one in Africa can afford not to, for in spite of its sometimes illogically reached conclusions it does represent a comprehensive viewing of the belief and prejudices upon which the African leaders of today will most likely be acting.'

Gary Gappert — Transition[3]

*39 **Jahn, Janheinz**
A History of neo-African literature: writing in two continents
(Trans. from the German by Oliver Coburn and Ursula Lehrburger)
London, Faber, 1968. 301 pp. £3.50
New York, Grove Press (publ. as Neo-African literature. A History of Black Writing), 1969. 301 pp. $7.50 ($2.45 pap.)
The book is divided into four main sections. The first deals with the cultural and historical background of African literature and contains accounts of early and little-known writers of African descent. Part two, 'The African Scene', discusses oral literature, Afro-Arabic literature, and 'apprentice' and 'protest' work in the European and African Languages. The third part, 'The American Scene' examines verse and prose in Latin America, the Caribbean and the U.S.A., and lastly, 'The New Problems' discusses the achievements of African literature, recent developments and the négritude school. Each

[1]vol. 1, no. 1, 1970
[2]vol. 2, no. 4, Spring 1967
[3]vol. 1, no. 2, Dec. 1961

chapter is followed by a bibliography which lists the primary and most important secondary sources.
'... presented with an admirable scholarly approach ... Mr. Jahn has a lot to say on African oral traditions, especially prompted by what he feels to be a betrayal of African culture by the approach of the social anthropologist ... the book is a piece of historical documentation aimed at serving as a pointer to further reading and research.'
G. R. Gacheche — Busara[1]

'... Jahn's conception of neo-African literature now receives a certain clarification which gives point and a measure of significance to his formidable (and even forbidding) bibliography ... appears to me invaluable, not only because of the information which it gives, but also because of its demonstration of the continuity of the African imagination, taking new forms in its contact with the European genius, to give inspiration and life to an original mode of literary expression.'
Abiola Irele — The Journal of Modern African Studies[2]

40 July, Robert W.
The Origins of Modern African Thought: its development in West Africa during the nineteenth and twentieth centuries.
New York, Praeger, 1967. 512 pp. illus. $10.00
London, Faber, 1968. 512 pp. £3.50
This book provides a detailed analysis of West African reactions to Westernization and European and American penetration in the nineteenth and early twentieth centuries. The author examines the lives, careers and ideologies of some forty West Africans who were the leaders of their time in such fields as theology, law, business, politics, journalism, literature and education. Edward W. Blyden, Bishop Samuel Ajayi Crowther, Henry Carr, Africanus Horton, Joseph E. Casely Hayford, Herbert Macaulay and Blaise Diagne are among those studied. Contemporary African thought is briefly surveyed in an epilogue entitled 'The emergence of the modern West African', and the volume concludes with an extensive bibliography.

*41 Kesteloot, Lilyan
Les écrivains noirs de langue française: naissance d'une litterature (3rd rev. edn)
Brussels, Universite Libre de Bruxelles, Institut de Sociologie, 1965. 340 pp. FB 240
A history and analysis in great depth of black African writing in French. The book grew out of a doctoral thesis submitted to the University of Brussels in 1961, and is now already in its third edition. The history of the negritude movement is analysed in detail and there is heavy emphasis on the writings of Aimé Césaire (from Martinique), Léon Damas (from Guyana), Frantz

Fanon (also from Martinique), Birago Diop, Léopold Senghor, David Diop and Jacques Rabemananjara. A comprehensive bibliography is appended. (An English translation of this volume will be published by Temple University Press in 1971.)

'... Mlle. Kesteloot's book is very readable and a valuable sociological and literary document.'
S. K. Dagbo — African Affairs[3]

*42 Lo Liyong, Taban
The Last Word. Cultural Synthesism
Nairobi, East African Publ. House, 1969. 210 pp. EAshs. 8.00
Evanston, Northwestern Univ. Press; distr. $2.00
The first critical commentary on African literature to be published in East Africa, this is a collection of essays some of which have previously appeared in Transition, Busara, Africa Report and elsewhere. Contents include Taban Lo Liyong's thoughts on Tutuola and the subject of negritude. There is a commentary on Okot p'Bitek's Song of Lawino; reviews of Ngugi's Weep not Child and David Cook's anthology Origin East Africa. Among other chapter titles are 'Tibble, Tutuola, Taban and Thugs', 'Negroes are not Africans', and 'African Students in Washington, D.C.'.

'Taban's books, especially The Last Word rank among the most seriously discussed East African books, only months after their appearance ... one of the most outspoken commentaries on black people published in Africa up to the present'.
A. S. Bukenya — Mawazo[4]

'With this slim book of essays he introduces himself as a powerful voice, a spectacular and audacious intelligence ... His work is contentious, irreverent, and exciting ... He writes on what interests him — and that, often, is what angers him: American arrogance, African self-indulgence, intellectual slackness, pettiness ... His book is a Magna Carta for African greatness.'
Basil Busacca — Africa Report[5]

43 Makward, Edris
Is there an African Approach to African Literature?
Los Angeles, University of California, African Studies Center, 1969. 50c.
A paper read at the African Studies Association annual meeting, Los Angeles, October 16—19, 1968.

[1]vol. 2, no. 1, 1969
[2]vol. 7, no. 3, 1969
[3]vol. 67, Oct. 1968
[4]vol. 2, no. 3, June 1970
[5]vol. 15, no. 8, Nov. 1970

44 **Melone, Thomas**
De la négritude dans la littérature négro-africaine
Paris, Présence Africaine, 1962. 141 pp. F5.00
Examines the philosophy of negritude through an analysis of the major writings by French-African novelists and poets.

*45 **Moore, Gerald** ed
African Literature and the Universities
Ibadan, Ibadan University Press (for Congress for Cultural Freedom), 1965. 152 pp. 15s.0d.
[Nigeria]
New York, Africana Publishing Corp., distr.
$3.00
The record of two seminars held at the University of Dakar and at Fourah Bay College, the University of Sierra Leone, in March and April 1963. The conferences grew out of a conviction that university initiative throughout Africa was needed to ensure the introduction of African literature to first-degree arts courses. There are papers on the African novel, poetry and négritude, with a record of lively and at times heated discussions among the participants. These included Ezekiel Mphahlele, Janheinz Jahn, Camara Laye, Sembène Ousmane, Eldred Jones, Davidson Nicol, and many others.
'. . . one of Gerald Moore's best contributions to African literary studies . . . the meetings, and the resulting book shed new light on the communications gap and the differences in approach between the two leading intellectual and literary traditions in contemporary Africa.'
Ellen Conroy Kennedy — *Africa Report*[1]

*46 **Moore, Gerald**
Seven African Writers
London and New York, Oxford University Press, 1962 (Three Crowns Book) (reprinted with corrections and extended bibliography 1966). 108 pp. 32½p/$1.15
Short critical studies of the works and style of Senghor, Mphahlele, David Diop, Laye, Tutuola, Achebe and Beti, each accompanied by a detailed bibliography, which has been brought up to date for the corrected reprint issued in 1966. In his introduction, Gerald Moore traces and interprets the concept of negritude, which he considers fundamental to an understanding of French African writing.
'. . . absolutely indispensable to anybody who wishes to make a serious study of new African writing . . . Gerald Moore not only gives us a great deal of factual background information about the seven writers, but also an extremely sober and balanced judgement of the literary merits of the seven authors.'
O. A. — *Black Orpheus*[2]

'Mr Moore's analysis of literary attitudes, his handling of the morphology of myths (especially of Camara Laye and Amos Tutuola) and the rich

elegance of his prose equally remove his work from the dry, pedantic and detached world of pure literary criticism . . . He comes to his task with quiet enthusiasm, reflection and warmth.'
Mbella Sonne Dipoko — *Présence Africaine*[4]

*47 **Moore, Gerald**
The Chosen Tongue: English writing in the tropical world
London, Longmans, 1969. 222 pp. illus. £2.25
(90p pap., for *African* market only)
New York, Harper and Row, 1970. 222 pp. illus.
$6.00
A critical examination of English writing of tropical Africa and the Caribbean. In Moore's words, 'quite apart from their common use of English, these areas have direct historical, cultural and ethnic links with one another.' The study is grouped around four central themes: 'The Islands', 'The Continent', 'The City', and 'Guinea'. Its literary achievements are evaluated in the light of the historical, geographical, social and cultural backgrounds that have helped to shape its development.
'. . . a work which from start to finish impresses with its structural and thematic unity . . . should be read, I warmly recommend, for its scholarly excellence and perceptive critical insights into the literature it surveys, however disturbing its undercurrent of linguistic nationalism.'
Sunday O. Anozie — *The Conch*[4]

'. . . Taking Moore's new book together with "Seven African Writers", his work is the most rigorous and sensitive criticism yet written on African and Caribbean authors. Moore's commentary is informative and sensible in content, and eminently readable in expression.'
R. W. Noble — *West Africa*[5]

48 **National Educational Television, New York**
African Writers of Today (6 programs)
New York, N.E.T. 1964 (10 Columbus Circle, N.Y. 10019)
6 Films of 30 minutes each, $4.90 rental fee per program, scripts available separately at $3.00 each.
(Available from Indiana University Extension Program)
A series of six films (about 30 minutes each) produced by N.E.T., consisting of interviews with thirteen African writers and literary figures. *Program 1*: Walter Allen (former literary

[1]vol. 13, no. 1, Jan. 1968
[2]no. 13, Nov. 1963
[3]vol. 17, no. 45, 1963
[4]vol. 2, no. 1, Mar. 1970.
[5]no. 2769, 4 July 1970

editor of the *New Statesman*), Amos Tutuola, and Ulli Beier interviewed by the series host Lewis Nkosi. *Program 2*: A discussion of francophone African writers — David Rubadiri, Léopold Senghor, Bernard Fonlon and Wole Soyinka interviewed by Nkosi. *Program 3*: Ezekiel Mphahlele is interviewed by two fellow South Africans, Richard Rive and Lewis Nkosi. *Program 4*: Wole Soyinka and Lewis Nkosi interview Chinua Achebe and discuss his novels. *Program 5*: Professor William Abraham (author of *The Mind of Africa*, see 639) is interviewed by Soyinka and Nkosi. *Program 6*: David Rubadiri interviewed by Joseph Kariuki and Lewis Nkosi.

Each script is between 8 and 10 pages, on foolscap mimeographed sheets. All were recorded in 1964, and filmed in Paris, London, Ibadan, and Blantyre, Malawi. Slightly abridged transcripts of this series have also been reprinted in *Africa Report*, vol. 9, no. 7, July 1964 (pp. 7—21).

49 Nouvelle somme de poésie du monde noir

Paris, Présence Africaine, 1966. 575 pp. F8.00
Another special issue (no. 57) of *Présence Africaine* devoted to the 'new sum of poetry from the negro world'. A brief introduction is provided by Léon Damas and a preface by Aimé Césaire.

50 Pagéard, Robert

Littérature négro-africaine: le mouvement littéraire contemporaine dans l'Afrique noire d'expression française (2nd edn.)
Paris, Le Livre Africain, 1966. 140 pp. F7.20
A history and analysis of contemporary African writing in French. The author considers creative writing as well as political and historical literature from the early colonial days to the present time. Bio-bibliographical notes are included in an appendix.

51 Páricsy, Paul J.

Researches in African Oral Literature in the European Socialist Countries
Waltham, Mass., African Studies Assoc., Brandeis Univ., 1970. $2.50
A paper presented to the 1969 annual meeting of the African Studies Association, and available in xerox form.

*52 Pieterse, Cosmo, and Munro, Donald eds.

Protest and Conflict in African Literature
London, Heinemann Educ. Books, 1969. 192 pp.
£1.25 (50p pap.)
New York, Africana Publishing Corp. 192 pp.
$4.50 ($2.45 pap.)
An attempt to define and analyse some of the impulses and features that characterize African literature as a *genre* inspired the series of talks and discussions which were held in 1968 at the Africa Centre in London, the main substance of which form the contents of this volume. The series 'sought to popularize the growing body of what is generally called African literature while at the same time trying to avoid discussions consisting mainly of meaningless generalities.' The essays range widely from the politics of negritude to protest against apartheid, and from cultural conflict to satire of the élite. Contributors include: Gerald Moore, Clive Wake, James Ngugi, Dennis Brutus, Jeannette Macaulay, and many others.

'. . . *a welcome addition to the accumulating criticism of African literature . . . these studies indicate new directions in the study of the themes of African literature.*'

Pio Zirimu — *Mawazo*[1]

53 Premier congrès international des écrivains et artistes noirs

Compte rendu complet 2 vols.
Paris, Présence Africaine, 1956/57. 408 pp.,
363 pp. F12.00 each
The complete proceedings and individual papers submitted to the first international conference of Negro writers, held in Paris, September 19—22, 1966, issued here as two special numbers of the journal *Présence Africaine*, nos. 8/9/10 and 14/15.

54 Press, John ed.

Commonwealth Literature; unity and diversity in a common culture
London, Heinemann Educ. Books, 1965. 223 pp.
out-of-print
Extracts from the proceedings of a conference held in Leeds, September 1964. Papers include: 'The Use of English in Nigeria,' by J. O. Ekponyong, 'Nationalism and the Writer,' by Eldred Jones, and, 'The Novelist as Teacher,' by Chinua Achebe.

55 Ramsaran, John, and Jahn, Janheinz

Approaches to African Literature
Non-English writings by Janheinz Jahn, and English writing in West Africa by John Ramsaran
Ibadan, Ibadan University Press, 1959. 31 pp.
out-of-print
Pioneering bibliographic essays, now out-of-print, and superseded by Ramsaran's *New approaches to African literature* (see 19).

*56 Sartre, Jean-Paul

Black Orpheus
(Trans. from the French by S. W. Allen)

[1]vol. 2, no. 2, Dec. 1969

Paris, Présence Africaine, 1963. 65 pp. F5.00
An English translation — here published separately — of Sartre's introductory essay to the Senghor anthology published in 1948. This is a manifesto of negritude and the black soul. (see 113).

57 Société Africaine de Culture
Colloque sur l'art nègre
1er Festival mondial des arts nègres, Dakar, 1–24 Avril, 1966.
Colloque, function et signification de l'art nègre dans la vie du peuple et pour le peuple (30 Mars—9 Avril)
Paris—Présence Africaine, 1967. 645 pp. F36.00
The complete proceedings of the First Festival of Negro Arts held in Dakar, Senegal, April 1966.

58 Society of African Culture
Colloquium on Negro Art
1st World Festival of Negro Arts.
Function and significance of the African Negro art in the life of the people and for the people.
Paris, Présence Africaine, 1968. 599 pp. F44.50
The English translation of the Colloquium. Articles on literature include: 'Oral literature' by G. Calame-Griaule; 'African oral literature' by John Mbiti; 'Negro-African oral literature' by Basile-Juléat Fouda; 'Meaning and function of the traditional Negro-African Theatre' by Bakary Traoré; 'Modern Negro-African theatre' by Wole Soyinka; 'Black writers in a troubled world" by Langston Hughes; and 'Modern African poetry' by Lamine Diakhaté.

59 Traoré, Bakary
Le théâtre négro-africain et ses fonctions sociales
Paris, Présence Africaine, 1958. 160 pp. F8.50
An analysis of the origin and development of black African theatre viewed in a social setting. The study is confined to writings 'd'expression française.'

60 Tucker, Martin
Africa in Modern Literature: a survey of contemporary writing in English
New York, Ungar, 1967. 316 pp. $7.50
A study that 'differs in scope from other works of literary criticism on African writing in that it is an attempt to survey literature about Africa written in English in the twentieth century, and thus treats American and English writers, as well as Africans, as an integral part of "African literature" as a whole. In effect, the book — arranged in terms of regional settings: West, East, Central and South Africa respectively — includes detailed analyses of the works by Joyce Cary, Joseph Conrad, Graham Greene, Elspeth Huxley, and several other European and American writers. African literature by West Africans is comprehensively surveyed in a

separate chapter. There is a detailed reading list.

' . . . this is a book on which literary historians and literary critics alike will come to depend . . . will become a standard for those who wish to know where African literature has been and where it may well be going.'
Robert Cobb — *Africa Report*[1]

61 von Grunebaum, G. E.
French African Literature: some cultural implications
(Publ. of the Institute of Social Studies, series minor, vol. 5)
The Hague, Mouton, 1964. 41 pp. Dfl. 5.-
New York, Humanities Press, distr. $1.25
An appreciation of the African writer 'd'expression française', with an emphasis on the works of Aimé Césaire and Léopold Senghor as well as some Maghrebi authors.

*62 Wästberg, Per ed.
The Writer in Modern Africa
Stockholm, Almqvist and Wiksell (for Scandinavian Inst. of African Studies), 1968. 123 pp. Sw. Kr. 15.-
New York, Africana Publ. Corp., 1969, 123 pp. $2.95
The proceedings of the African-Scandinavian Writers' Conference sponsored by the Scandinavian Institute of African Studies, held at Häselby Castle near Stockholm, Febuary 6 —9, 1967. In his foreword, Per Wästberg describes this volume as 'a collage of voices from Africa . . . a confrontation of temperaments, the outcome of which is not measured in tangible results. Views, not facts." Among the contributions in this collection are Wole Soyinka's paper 'The writer in a modern Africa state", and there are childhood memories by Dan Jacobson, Dennis Brutus, James Ngugi, and George Awoonor-Williams. Other contributors include Lewis Nkosi, Mbella Sonne Dipoko, Eldred Jones and Kateb Yacine, the Algerian poet and novelist. Each paper is followed by a general discussion.

' . . . is one of the most valuable documents available for those of us who are concerned with African literature.'
John Povey — *African Studies Review*[2]

' . . . remarkable for two or three contributions of exceptional sanity and directness.'
Gerald Moore — *Research in African Literatures*[3]

[1]vol. 13, no. 3, Mar. 1968
[2]vol. 13, no. 1, Apr. 1970
[3]vol. 1, no. 1, 1970

63 Wauthier, Claude
L'Afrique des africains: inventaire de la négritude
Paris, Seuil, 1964 (Coll. L'Histoire immédiate).
320 pp. F18.00
For English *translation*, see 64.

64 Wauthier, Claude
The Literature and Thought of Modern Africa: a survey
(Trans. from the French by Shirley Kay)
London, Pall Mall, 1967. 323 pp. 87½p (pap.)
New York, Praeger, 1967. 323 pp. $8.00
A revised and enlarged version of the original French edition (see 63). It is a wide-ranging study covering the period from the beginning of the Second World War to 1963, and it cites the works of some 150 black African writers, including copious quotations from them. The volume embraces creative writing from the entire African continent as well as politically committed literature. Emphasis is on the modern trend of African nationalist thought and there are, for example, extracts from Sekou Touré's study on African Marxism, the speeches of Kwame Nkrumah and Jomo Kenyatta's social survey of the Kikuyu. Notes and references and an extensive bibliography are appended.
'... cool and self-effacing in approach, Mr Wauthier ... examines, through the works of more than 150 writers, the correspondence between the demand for national independence and a cultural revival that includes, along with the purely literary aspects of négritude, anthropology, history, law, theology and folklore.'
Nadine Gordimer — *The Nation*[1]

'... the political emphasis in Wauthier's analysis makes this book one of the most informative guides for understanding contemporary African literature yet written — a book and an approach to African literature that were long overdue ... The slave narratives, W. E. B. DuBois and Marcus Garvey, Négritude in the West Indies and West Africa, the American Civil Rights movement of the 1960's, are all related. Wauthier skillfully weaves these threads together in a book likely to be regarded as a landmark of African literary scholarship for years to come."
Charles R. Larson — *Africa Report*[2]

ANTHOLOGIES

*65 **Angoff, Charles,** and **Povey, John** eds.
African Writing Today
New York, Manyland Books, 1969. 304 pp. illus.
$6.95
The major portion of this volume comprises the special African number of *The Literary Review*. It introduces a largely new generation of African writers, though Sarif Easmon, Eldred Jones, Ama Ata Aidoo, Taban lo Liyong, George Awooner-Williams and Joe de Graft are among more familiar names included. John Povey provides an introductory essay, 'The quality of African writing today', which is followed by short stories, verse and a novella 'Under the Iroko Tree' by Joseph Okpaku, editor of *The Journal of the New African Literature and the Arts*. Biographical notes supplement the text.

66 Beier, Ulli ed.
Black Orpheus; an anthology of new African and Afro-American stories
London, Longmans, 1964. 160 pp. 61p (35p pap.)
New York, McGraw-Hill, 1965. 156 pp. out-of-print
Sixteen stories representing the three main streams of African and Afro-American fiction, grouped under three main sections entitled 'New Realities', 'Tradition', and 'Experiments'.
'... interesting, illuminating, and at times touching and troubling.'
Thomas Parkinson — *Jnl. of the New African Literature and the Arts*[1]

*67 **Beier, Ulli** comp. and ed.
African Poetry: an anthology of traditional African poems
London and New York, Cambridge University Press, 1966. 80 pp. illus. 62½p (35p pap.)/$2.75 ($1.95 pap.)
The poems in this book (which is intended as a school reader), are from widely different tribes and cultures, including those of the Yoruba and Ewe of West Africa, the Zulu and Bushmen of South Africa, the Galla and Swahili of East Africa, and the ancient Egyptians, and are arranged by themes such as Death, Sorrow, War, Love, People and Animals. There are notes on the poems and sources are cited.

68 Beier, Ulli ed.
The Origin of Life and Death: a collection of creation myths from Africa
London, Heinemann Educ. Books, 1966 (African Writers Series, no. 23). 96 pp. 25p
New York, Humanities Press, distr. $1.00

[1]vol. 204, June 26, 1967
[2]vol. 12, no. 9, Dec. 1967

[1]vol. 3, Spring 1967

The creation myths in this collection originate from all over Africa and from many different languages. They provide a cross-section of the amount, variety and vitality of the form of the traditional story.
'... a perfect little gem ... will serve as an invaluable reference book for the student of African culture.'
Charles Larson — Africa Report[1]

*69 Beier, Ulli ed.
Political Spider: an anthology of stories from 'Black Orpheus'
London, Heinemann Educ. Books, 1969 (African Writers Series, 58). 118 pp. 30p
New York, Africana Publishing Corp., 1969. 118 pp. $1.50
Many of the best-known names in African writing made an early appearance in the pioneering magazine *Black Orpheus*. This selection gathers together some of their stories and extracts from novels. Most were written in English but there are also translations from the Yoruba, French and Portuguese.

70 Berry, John P.
Africa Speaks: a prose anthology with comprehension and summary passages
London, Evans, 1970. 128 pp. 45p
An introduction to modern African literature with prose selections chosen for their subject interest, literary merit and suitability for language study. The passages are followed by questions and exercises, with particular emphasis on comprehension and summary work.

Brench, A. C.
Writing in French from Senegal to Cameroun
See 31

71 Brownlee, P. and **Rose, B. W.** eds.
Commonwealth Short Stories
London, Nelson, 1966, 212 pp. 42½p
Contributions from Ghana and Sierra Leone are included in this volume of Commonwealth short stories.

Cartey, Wilfred
Palaver. Modern African Writings
See 695

72 Caverhill, Nicholas, ed.
Recueil des textes Africains: an anthology of modern African writing in French
London, Hutchinson, 1967. 178 pp. 62½p
A collection of self-contained extracts from modern African authors writing in French. The first half of the anthology is made up primarily of traditional African folk-tales and some character sketches, while the second half

contains passages describing African childhood and education. There are biographical details on the authors, and a vocabulary.

*73 Clark, Leon E. ed.
Coming of Age in Africa: Continuity and Change
('Through African Eyes', unit I)
New York, Praeger, 1969. 106 pp. $1.48
The first book in a six-volume series established to develop curriculum materials for the study of other cultures. Its aim is to let Africans speak for themselves and to let students think for themselves. This first volume contains contributions by Luis Bernado Honwana and Anna Apoko, extracts from Okot p'Bitek's *Song of Lawino*; Laye's *African Child*, and poetry by Kwesi Brew, Ismael Hurreh (from Somalia) and Léopold Senghor.

74 Dathorne, O. R. ed.
African Poetry for Schools and Colleges
London, Macmillan, 1969. 166 pp. 42½p
The poetry selections contained herein were 'chosen to show their varied approaches to writing verse'. They cover oral poetry, 'made up of all that is sung, chanted, or declaimed', poetry in the vernacular languages (in translation) early poetry in English and French, and contemporary verse. The second portion of the book is reserved for extensive notes on the poems themselves, accompanied by biographical details on the authors, and indexes of first lines, translators and authors.

*75 Dathorne, Oscar Ronald, and **Feuser, Willfried** eds.
Africa in Prose
Harmondsworth, Middx., Penguin Books, 1969 (Penguin African Library, AP 24). 384 pp. 40p
Baltimore, Penguin Books, 1969. 384 pp. $1.75
A collection of forty-four extracts: writing from the entire African continent, providing a view of African prose from the early twentieth century to the present day. The editors' aim is 'to show that there is a recognizable prose tradition that goes back to the beginning of this century', and therefore they include several pieces not available elsewhere. There is an introduction by the editors, who also give biographical notes, and a brief commentary accompanying each extract.

76 Denny, Neville comp.
Pan African Short Stories
London, Nelson, 1966. 240 pp. 42½p
New York, Humanities Press, distr. $1.50
A broad and varied sampling of modern African writing south of the Sahara by authors 'preoccupied with the experience of individual

[1]vol. 12, no. 9, Dec. 1967

Africans adjusting themselves to life in a continent where the pace of change is faster than that which any other people have ever known.' There are stories by Efua Sutherland, Grace Ogot, Cyprian Ekwensi, Chinua Achebe, Gabriel Okara, James Ngugi, Alex la Guma, William Conton, and several others, with exercises and notes on each story.
' . . . the exercises form by far the most important part of the book. The intelligently framed questions and suggestions, even if some are twice removed from the immediate contexts of the stories, will stimulate critical reading and appreciation, and encourage practice.'

Theo Vincent — Black Orpheus[1]

77 Diboti, Ekoa M., and Dogbeh, Richard eds.
Voix d'Afrique: echos du monde — livre de lecture (Cours moyen et 1er cycle du second degré)
Paris, Inst. Pédagogique Africain et Malgache, 1965. 256 pp. illus. F9.00
A reader for primary schools in Africa. Extracts from African (and some French) novels and poetry are used to illustrate scenes from everyday life in Africa — school, family, playtime, sports, hunting etc. — and also provide descriptions of the country, its traditions, its legends and its heritage.

78 Dick, John B. ed.
The Cambridge Book of Verse for African schools
London and New York, Cambridge University Press, 1966. 120 pp. 32½p
An anthology of English poetry that includes a section of poems by modern African poets.

79 Dick, John, B.
African Forum
London and New York, Cambridge Univ. Press, 1968. 101 pp. 37½p $1.40
Comprehension and composition exercises aimed primarily at senior classes in African secondary schools 'to help each pupil to think and talk and write more fluently about his own experience, his own society, his own ideas and the ideas of others.' Extracts from the writings of a variety of African writers from Thomas Mofolo and Samuel Johnson to Camara Laye and Wole Soyinka are included.

80 Doob, Leonard ed.
Ants Will not Eat your Fingers: a selection of traditional African poems
New York, Walker, 1966. 127 pp. $3.95
This collection of traditional African poems in translation utilizes a wide variety of sources. They are presented in alphabetical arrangement by tribe or society. The book, the editor says, 'makes no trivial claim that the verses are typical of the society from which, out of context,

they have been ripped; that the societies are representative of sub-saharan Africa; or that the translations are faithful or scholarly.' A complete list of sources is appended.

Doob, Leonard
see also 702

81 Drachler, Jacob ed.
African Heritage: an anthology of Black African personality and culture
New York, Crowell, 1962. 256 pp. out-of-print
New York, Collier, 1964. 286 pp. $1.25
London, Collier-Macmillan, 1964. 286 pp. 37½p
Divided into three main themes, 'African Voices', 'Afro-American Responses', and 'Through the Eyes of Others', this volume presents a great deal of material, ranging from four tales from Togoland and songs from Dahomey, to articles by Melville and Frances Herskovits' 'Creative Impulses in Dahomean Poetry' and Thomas L. Hodgkin's 'The African Renaissance'.
' . . . one of the most significant anthologies.'
Dorothy Porter — African Forum[2]

*82 Edwards, Paul comp.
Modern African Narrative: an anthology
London, Nelson, 1966. 204 pp. 47½p
New York, Humanities Press, distr. $1.75
An anthology 'with a difference' in that it includes works by white South Africans such as Nadine Gordimer and Dan Jacobson, Doris Lessing from Rhodesia, and a contribution by the Egyptian novelist Waguin Ghali. There is an extract from Kariuki's Mau Mau Detainee. Other authors represented in this collection are Peter Abrahams, Chinua Achebe, Cyprian Ekwensi, Ezekiel Mphahlele, James Ngugi, and Abioseh Nicol, among others. Each passage is preceded by an introduction.
' . . . very useful . . . Mr Edwards is rendering a valuable service in that his anthologies have covered a far wider field than that normally embraced by the general reader's idea of "African Literature".'
Peter Young — Bull. of the Assoc. for African Lit. in English[3]

'This collection is to be recommended for whetting the appetite for modern African literature.'
J. D. — West Africa[4]

83 Edwards, Paul comp.
Through African Eyes 2 vols.

[1]no. 21, Apr. 1967
[2]vol. 1, no. 4, Spring 1966
[3]no. 4, Mar. 1966
[4]no. 2587, Dec. 31, 1968

London, Cambridge University Press, 1966. 122
pp. 126 pp. 27½p each.
A sampling of African writing in the form of
prose extracts. This collection includes less
familiar early authors of the eighteenth and
nineteenth centuries, in addition to well-known
contemporary writers, such as Peter Abrahams,
Chinua Achebe, Amos Tutuola, Camara Laye,
Abioseh Nicol, Cyprian Ekwensi, Mongo Beti,
Ezekiel Mphahlele, and a great many more.

84 Forrest, R.
An African Reader
London, Longmans, 1965. 180 pp. 30p

85 Hamann, Walter ed.
Auteurs neo-Africains d'expression française
(Diesterwegs neusprachliche Bibliothek, 4181)
Frankfurt, Diesterweg, 1968. 73 pp. illus. DM
2.80
Short extracts of francophone African poetry
and prose writings, accompanied by extensive
notes and biographical data, the latter in
German.

86 Hughes, Langston, and Reynault, Christiane eds.
Anthologie africaine et malgache
Paris, Seghers, 1962. 307 pp. F18.50
Short stories, essays and poetry. The majority
of contributions by English-speaking authors
(in French translation) are drawn from Langston
Hughes's *An African Treasury* (see 88). These
are supplemented by original French writings
by Camara Laye, Ferdinand Oyono, Ousmane
Socé, Bernard Dadié, Birago Diop, David Diop,
Sekou Touré, and several others.

*87 Hughes, Langston ed.
Poems from Black Africa
Bloomington, Ind., Indiana University Press,
1966. 158 pp. illus. $1.75/72½p
Poetry from all parts of Africa. Its emphasis lies
on English-speaking poets, but it also includes
contributions from the Congo, Madagascar and
Senegal (in translation) and three poems by
Valente Malangatana from Mozambique. A
section on oral tradition appears too. Mr Hughes
contributes a foreword and biographical notes
on the authors.
*'Mr Hughes's anthology is another in an impressive
series of personal contributions to the cause of literature by black men. It is also a guide to the discovery
of the intimate heart of Africa through its more
remarkable forms of literary expression.'*
Abiola Irele — *Présence Africaine*[1]

*88 Hughes, Langston ed.
*An African Treasury: articles, essays, stories, poems
by black Africans*
New York, Crown, 1960. 207 pp. out-of-print

London, Gollancz, 1961, 207 pp. out-of-print
New York, Pyramid Books, 1961. 192 pp. 50c
An extensive selection of African writing
from articles by Tom Mboya, Ezekiel Mphahlele
and Peter Abrahams to stories and poetry by
Efua Sutherland, Richard Rive, Abioseh Nicol,
Wole Soyinka and many others; also included
are speeches of Kwame Nkrumah, Efik folk tales,
and letters in the Lonely Hearts column of
Johannesburg's *Drum magazine,* all reflecting the
voice of the new Africa.
*'Mr Hughes has done the cause of African literature
a great service.'*
Bernard Fonlon — *Présence Africaine*[2]

89 Ikiddeh, Ime comp.
Drum Beats: an anthology of African writing
Leeds, E. J. Arnold, 1968. 155 pp. 42½p
A collection of African narrative prose, intended
for school level and aimed primarily at young
people outside the African continent. All
extracts — many of which relate to childhood
experiences — are from the major works of
the most popular African authors, but the com-
piler has also included some writings by lesser
known writers such as Waguih Ghali from
Egypt and Nkem Nwanko and Chukwuemeka
Ike, both from Nigeria. In making his selection
Ime Ikiddeh places high value on variety — of
setting, theme and style. Introductory and biographical notes accompany each contribution.

*90 Irele, Abiola ed.
*Lectures Africaines: a prose anthology of African
writing in French*
London, Heinemann Educ. Books, 1969. 118
pp. 52½p
New York, Humanities Press, distr. $1.75
Introduces francophone African writing
through a selection of extracts from novels and
stories by Birago Diop, Bernard Dadié, Camara
Laye, Sembène Ousmane, Ferdinand Oyono,
Mongo Beti and Cheikh Hamidou Kane. Each
extract is preceded by a critical commentary
and a brief biography of the author.

91 Justin, André
*Anthologie africaine des écrivains noirs d'expression
française*
Paris, Institute Pédagogique Africaine, 1962. 190
pp. F2.90
Passages from prose works of the major French
African writers of West Africa, the Congo and
Madagascar.

*92 Kesteloot, Lilyan
Anthologie négro-africaine: panorama critique de.

[1]vol. 21, no. 49, 1964
[2]vol. 6/7, no. 34/35

prosateurs, poètes et dramatourges noirs du XXème siècle
Verviers, Belgium, Gérard, 1967 (Collection marabout université, no. 129). 432 pp. illus. F7.50

A comprehensive survey of writings by Negro authors from Africa, the Americas and the Caribbean. It features fiction, drama and poetry as well as extracts from periodical articles. The selections are preceded by an introduction by Madame Kesteloot, and there are brief biographical notes on each author.

93 Koelle, Sigismund Wilhelm
African Native Literature: or, Proverbs, Tales, Fables and Historical Fragments in the Kanuri or Bornu language
Graz, Austria, Akademische Druck-und Verlagsanstalt, 1968 (Reprint of edn, London, 1854). 434 pp. $10.50

A reprint — with a new introduction by David Dalby — of a study aimed to present the reader with both unaltered specimens of oral Kanuri literature and the structure of one of West Africa's most important languages. Sigismund Koelle, who was at Fourah Bay College in Freetown for five years, is also the author of the monumental *Polyglotta Africana*, a collection of some two hundred African vocabularies.

*94 Komey, Ellis Ayitey and Mphahlele, Ezekiel eds.
Modern African Stories
London, Faber, 1964. 227 pp. 90p
London, Faber, 1966. 227 pp. 42½p
An anthology of twenty-five stories, contributed by such authors as Ghana's Christina Aidoo and South Africa's Can Themba. Other contributions come from Nigeria, Sierra Leone and Kenya.
' . . . in *imaginative literature in English, West Africa has produced a cultural protest, East Africa a political protest and South Africa a racial protest. Any collection should, in some measure, reflect these genres. This the present one does, more successfully than any of its predecessors.'*
O. R. Dathorne — *Black Orpheus*[1]

*95 Larson, Charles ed.
African Short Stories. A collection of contemporary African writing.
New York, Macmillan, 1970. 210 pp. $1.50
Preceded by a fairly lengthy introduction, this collection brings together twelve short stories from seven different African countries. It includes contributions by Sembène Ousmane, Abioseh Nicol, Amos Tutuola, Birago Diop, Barbara Kimenye, Alex La Guma, James Ngugi, Cameron Duodo, Ezekiel Mphahlele, and others.

96 Litto, Frederic M. ed.
Plays from Black Africa
New York, Hill and Wang, 1968. 316 pp. $5.95 ($1.95 pap.)

A collection of six plays, each preceded by an introduction and notes on the authors, 'formed with the double intention of introducing the playreading public to the best (by Western standards) dramatic writing in Africa today and providing theatre companies with a selection of highly stageable plays from Africa.' The plays are Lewis Nkosi's *Rhythm of violence*, John Pepper Clark's *Song of a goat*, Alfred Hutchinson's *The rain-killers*, Efua Sutherland's *Edufa* — all these also published separately elsewhere — together with *The jewels of the shrine* by James Ene Henshaw, and Ghanaian Henri Ofori's *The literary society.*

97 Lomax, Alan and Abdul, Raoul eds.
3000 Years of Black Poetry
New York, Dodd, Mead, 1970. 261 pp. $6.95
A wide-ranging anthology of black voices, from Akhenaton in the Egypt of the fourteenth century B.C. to Langston Hughes, Gwendolyn Brooks and Leroi Jones. African poetry is represented by the early traditional songs and verse of the Hottentots, Susus, Ewes, Yorubas and Zulus, to contemporary poetry from the pens of Senghor, David Diop, Bernard Dadié, Paulin Joachim, Gabriel Okara, Christopher Okigbo, Wole Soyinka, Lenrie Peters, and a host of other writers.

*98 Moore, Gerald and Beier, Ulli eds.
Modern Poetry from Africa (New, enlarged and revised edn)
Harmondsworth, Middx. and Baltimore, Penguin Books, 1963 (Penguin African Library, AP 7). (rev. edn) 1968 192 pp. 17½p/$1.25
A revised and considerably expanded version of a popular anthology that draws on sixteen countries to present the work of African poets writing in English, French and Portuguese (the latter two in translation). Substantial coverage is given to the poetry of John Pepper Clark, George Awoonor-Williams, Christopher Okigbo and Wole Soyinka. The poetry of negritude too, gets a fair share, notably the works of Léopold Senghor, David Diop, Birago Diop, and the Congolese poets Tchicaya U Tam'si and Antoine-Roger Bolamba. There is an introduction, notes on the authors, and an index of first lines.
'The editors' introduction . . . is among the most informative pieces written on the modern literature of Africa south of the Sahara.'
R. W. Noble — *West Africa*[2]

[1] no. 18, Oct. 1965
[2] no. 2693, Jan. 11, 1969

*99 Mphahlele, Ezekiel ed.
African Writing Today
Harmondsworth, Middx. and Baltimore,
Penguin Books, 1967. 347 pp. 37½p/$1.75
An anthology 'intended to give the intelligent
reader a map of themes and styles of African
writing in the metropolitan languages —English,
French and Portuguese'. It provides a wide
cross-section of recent African literature by
authors from fifteen different countries, and
is especially strong on writings from Nigeria,
Senegal, South Africa and Mozambique. There is
a brief introduction and biographical notes on
each author.
'... the most comprehensive book of its kind to come
out of Africa so far ... the book is very rich and
contains much that has literary value.'
        Mbella Sonne Dipoko — *Présence Africaine*[1]

'European and African readers alike should delight in
Ezekiel Mphahlele's anthology of African prose and
poetry, releasing us as it does from the agonized
neuroticism of much European writing to which we
have become addicted ... should be read by all who
are in danger of despairing over the future of African
literature.'
        Lenrie Peters — *African Affairs*[2]

100 Mushiete, Paul
*La littérature française africaine ; petite anthologie des
écrivains noirs d'expression française*
Leverville (Congo-Kinshasa), Bibliothèque de
l'étoile, 1957. 40 pp. out-of-print

101 Nolen, Barbara ed.
*Africa is People: firsthand accounts from contempo-
rary Africa*
New York, Dutton, 1967. 270 pp. illus. $6.96
Thirty-four selections culled from books,
journals, interviews, and eyewitness accounts.
The editor places emphasis on autobiographical
narratives by African writers, and she includes
extracts from R. W. Cole's *Kossoh Town Boy*,
Mbonu Ojike's *My Africa*, Camara Laye's *The
Dark Child*, Noni Jabavu's *Drawn in Colour*, and
Legson Kayira's *I Will Try*. Additional contribu-
tions are by Chinua Achebe, Peter Abrahams,
Ulli Beier, Léopold Senghor, as well as other
African, American and European scholars and
journalists. Each selection is prefaced by a brief
lead-in, which introduces the author and places
the excerpt within its context.

102 Okpaku, Joseph O. ed.
New African Literature and the Arts, vols. 1 & II
New York, Crowell (with Third Press), 1970.
(Apollo Editions). 358 pp., 282 pp. illus. $8.95
ea. ($3.95 ea. pap.)
The editor of *The Journal of the New African
Literature and the Arts* here brings together in
two volumes the contributions that appeared

in the first six numbers (1966 –68) of this magazine. The books include essays, poetry, short
stories, drama, as well as articles on music,
dance, art and the cinema. In volume I the
editor provides three introductory essays. (see
also p. 105).
'... an impressive collection of essays, poetry,
criticism, drama and graphics ... strikes me as an
excellent and varied introduction to African contemporary art.'
        Nancy Donovan — *Africa Report*[3]

103 Packman, Brenda ed.
*Etoiles africaines: morceaux choisis de la littérature
de l'Afrique noire*
London, Evans, 1968. 72 pp. 30p
Introducing some of the major works of African
writing in French, using extracts from several
novels, this collection is aimed at students who
have outgrown juvenile readers but who are
not yet ready to embark upon full-length novels.

104 Perham, Margery ed.
Ten Africans
London, Faber, 1936 (New edn, 1963). 356 pp.
illus. £2.00
Evanston, Ill., Northwestern Univ. Press, 1963.
356 pp. illus. $4.95
These are intimate life stories of ten Africans,
who range from an old chief in the bush to an
Oxford girl undergraduate. Each informant is
from a different tribe —Bemba, Xhosa, Kikuyu,
Yoruba, Zulu and so on. The stories 'show how
Africans of various tribes, types and ages saw
themselves and their lives before the second
world war, and especially how they had taken
the impress of British power and influence.'

105 Pieterse, Cosmo ed.
Ten One-Act plays
London, Heinemann Educ. Books, 1968 (African
Writers Series, 34). 304 pp. 37½p
New York, Humanities Press, distr. $1.25
Ten plays —four from West Africa, by Pat Maddy,
Femi Euba, Ime Ikiddeh and Kwesi Kay; three
from East Africa, by Ganesh Bagchi (born in
India) and Kuldip Sondhi (contributing two
plays), and another three from South Africa,
by Athol Fugard, Alfred Hutchinson and Arthur
Maimane. There is an introduction by the editor,
notes on the plays, and directions for producing
them.

106 Pieterse, Cosmo ed.
Eleven Short African Plays
London, Heinemann Educ. Books, 1971

[1] no. 63, 1967
[2] vol. 66, no. 265, Oct. 1967
[3] vol. 15, no. 8, Nov. 1970 (ter. of vol. I)

(African Writers Series, 78), ca. 120 pp. 60p (in preparation).

This collection includes 'Ancestral Power' and 'Lament,' by Kofi Awoonor, 'God's Deputy,' by Sanya Dosunmu, 'The Scar,' by Rebecca Njau, 'Resurrection,' by Richard Rive. 'Overseas,' by Mbella Sonne Dipoko, 'The Magic Pool,' by Kuldip Sondhi, 'This Time Tomorrow,' by James Ngugi, and David Lytton's, 'Epidsodes of an Easter Rising.' Cosmo Pieterse contributes his own play, 'Ballad of the Cells,' and provides an introduction and biographical notes on the authors.

107 **Radford, W. L.**
African Poetry for Schools
Nairobi, East African Publ. House, 1970. EAsh. 4.95.
An anthology aimed primarily at pupils in the upper classes of primary school and in the first and second years of secondary school in Africa. The author provides an introduction, along with detailed notes and teaching suggestions.

108 **Reed, John,** and **Wake, Clive** comp. and eds.
A Book of African Verse
London, Heinemann Educ. Books, 1964 (African Writers Series, 8). 119 pp. 30p
New York, Humanities Press, distr. $1.00
A wide-ranging selection of verse by thirty African poets from eleven countries. It includes some translations by the editors of poems originally written in French. The book features a critical introduction, biographical notes on each poet, twenty pages of notes on the poems, and an index of first lines.
'... this verse anthology appeared soon after the Beier/Moore one and is a useful companion as only six poems are duplicated. Reed and Wake are not so much concerned with modern verse. There is some poetry in the traditional manner.'
O. R. Dathorne — *Bull. of the Assoc. for African Lit. in English*[1]

109 **Ridout, Ronald,** and **Jones, Eldred** eds.
Adjustments: an anthology of African and Western writing
London, Edward Arnold, 1966. 164 pp. 30p
An attempt to put the work of African writers side by side with works from other traditions, such as those of Jack London and Richard Parker. Contains extracts from works by two Sierra Leonean writers, Sarif Easmon and William Conton; and from Achebe's *No longer at ease*; and Ngugi's *Weep not, Child.*

110 **Rive, Richard** ed.
Modern African Prose
London, Heinemann Educ. Books, 1964 (African

Writers Series, 9). 230 pp. 40p
New York, Humanities Press; distr. $1.25
An anthology of contemporary writing by Africans in English — covering both established as well as lesser-known authors — and intended primarily for use in schools and by students. One of the early endeavours of its kind, it includes extracts from novels and complete short stories by eighteen writers; eight from South Africa, eight from West Africa and three from East Africa. There are notes and an introduction by the editor.

111 **Rutherford, Peggy,** ed.
Darkness and Light: an anthology of African writing
Johannesburg, Drum Publications, 1958. 208 pp.
London, Faith Press, 1958. 208 pp. 45p
New York, Grosset (published as *African Voices*), 1959 (Universal Library, 105). 208 pp. $1.45
New York, Grosset; 1970. $2.25
This is one of the very first anthologies of African writing published; it has recently been reissued. It features folk tales, short stories, extracts from novels, and poetry, including a variety of contributions by lesser-known authors. The editor provides an introduction and biographical notes on each writer.

*112 **Sainville, Léonard** ed.
Anthologie de la littérature négro-africaine: romanciers et conteurs négro-africains, 2 vols.
Paris, Présence Africaine, 1963 and 1968. 456 pp. 644 pp., F25.00, F.46.25
A comprehensive anthology of neo-African writing, with extracts from works by African, Caribbean and North American authors. Although there are brief extracts from writings by Nigerian and other English-speaking writers, this anthology puts heavy emphasis on francophone African literature.

*113 **Senghor, Léopold Sédar** ed.
Anthologie de la nouvelle poésie nègre et malgache
Paris, Presses Universitaires de France, 1948. 228 pp. out-of-print
Paris, Presses Universitaires de France, 1969. 228 pp. F25.00
A pioneering anthology of modern African and Malagasy poetry in French — recently reissued — with its now famous introductory essay by Jean-Paul Sartre, 'Orphée noir' (Black Orpheus), in which he defines the concept of negritude (see also 58).
'*Quand cette anthologie, établie par Senghor, préfacée par Sartre, parut pour la première fois en 1948, ce fut comme si un immense éclair déchirait la grande nuit coloniale où se trouvait ensevelie l'Afrique ... L'anthologie de Senghor rassemblait,*

[1]no. 2, 1967

en un bouquet admirable, les blus belles fleurs de poésie nées sous les tropiques, fleurs de colère ou de révolte, couleur de sang ou couleur de nuit, mêlant l'odeur de la haine au parfum de l'amour, fleurs écloses en Haiti, à la Guadeloupe, à la Martinique, en Guyane, en Afrique noire, à Madagascar, fleurs vénéneuses ou chargées de sucs miraculeux.'
Jeune Afrique[1]

114 **Sergeant, Howard** ed.
Commonwealth Poems of Today
London, John Murray, 1967. 288 pp. £1.25 (52½p pap.)
An anthology of some 250 poems from Commonwealth countries, including recent verse from the Gambia, Ghana, Kenya, Malawi, Nigeria, Rhodesia, Sierra Leone, South Africa, Tanzania, Uganda and Zambia.

115 **Sergeant, Howard** ed.
New Voices from the Commonwealth
London, Evans, 1968. 208 pp. £1.25 (52½p pap.)
Reflecting the cultural diversity of the Commonwealth, this volume includes a substantial portion of poetry from African countries, by established as well as little-known African poets.

116 **Sergeant, Howard** ed.
Poetry from Africa
Oxford and New York, Pergamon Press, 1968 (Commonwealth and Int. Library: Pergamon poets, 2). 108 pp. 37½p/$1.75.
A selection from the work of Gabriel Okara, Gaston Bart-Williams, Kwesi Brew and David Rubadiri, accompanied by biographical notes.

117 **Shapiro, Norman R.** ed. and trans.
Négritude: Black poetry from Africa and the Caribbean
New York, October House, 1970. $7.50
Presents all the major exponents of negritude in the original French, with parallel English translations. Includes verse by Aimé Césaire, Léon Damas, Léopold Senghor, Tchicaya U Tam'si, Bernard Dadié, Joseph Bognini, and many others.

*118 **Shelton, Austin, J., jr.** ed.
The African Assertion: a critical anthology of African literature
New York, Odyssey Press, 1968. 273 pp. $2.45 pap.
This critical anthology of sub-Saharan African writing contains extracts from both poetry and prose drawn from a wide variety of African literature. There is an introduction by the editor and the book concludes with a section 'Readings, Topics and Questions for further Study', followed by a suggested reading list.
' . . . an excellent anthology . . . will serve well at

the core of survey courses in African literature.'
Robert McDowell — Africa Today[2]

119 **Tibble, Anne** ed.
African-English Literature: a survey and anthology
London, Peter Owen, 1965. 304 pp. £1.62½
New York, October House, 1965. (1969 pap. ed.) 304 pp. $2.95
Preceded by a brief historical outline, the first part of this anthology offers a short survey of the most important written prose and poetry of Africa south of the Sahara. The second part of the book provides a selection of African-English prose and poetry, accompanied by a bibliography. Covering the output of thirty-seven African writers, from both English- and French-speaking African nations, the anthology's intention reflected in the choice of selections, is 'not only to present African writers, but to make the best — that is, the already significantly individual — African writers more widely known.'

*120 **Wake, Clive** ed.
An Anthology of African and Malagasy Poetry in French
London and New York, Oxford University Press, 1965. 181 pp. 47½p/$1.55
Following a detailed introduction, this anthology presents, among others, the works of Rabearivelo, Senghor, Rabemananjara, Diop, Dadié, U'Tam'si, Bognini, Bebey and Ranaivo. Notes on each poet and an index of first lines supplement the text.

*121 **Whiteley, W. H.** comp.
A Selection of African Prose, 2 vols.
Vol. 1: *Traditional oral texts*
Vol. 2: *Written prose*
London and New York, Oxford University Press, 1964 (Oxford Library of African Literature) 216 pp., 194 pp., £1.25 ea./$4.50 ea.
An anthology of African prose initiated by UNESCO as the first in a series of anthologies. The first volume, *Traditional oral texts*, presents a representative selection from the oral tradition, representative both from a geographical point of view and from that of genre. Volume two provides a sampling of material written up to 1963 by African authors from different parts of the continent.
'Nowadays new anthologies are always coming out of Africa, but this present work is remarkable both for the great variety of material it has assembled together and for the manner in which Dr Whiteley has approached his task. It is only too easy to compile an anthology which may do credit to the editor's scholarship, or his industry, or his sense of

[1]no. 466, Nov. 26, 1969
[2]vol. 15, no. 6, Dec./Jan. 1969

mission but which remains lifeless and unreadable. Dr Whiteley has produced a lively and very readable book.'

Chinua Achebe — from the *Foreword*

122 **Young, T. Cullen** ed.
African New Writing; short stories by African writers
London, Lutterworth Press, 1947. 125 pp. out-of-print
Comprises fourteen stort stories, ten of them by Nigerian authors.

PART I: WRITINGS IN ENGLISH

WEST AFRICA

ANTHOLOGIES, CRITICAL WORKS, AND
BIBLIOGRAPHIES

123 Bassir, Olumbe ed.
An anthology of West African verse
Ibadan, Ibadan Univ. Press, 1957. 80 pp. out-of-print.

124 Edwards, Paul comp.
West African Narrative: an anthology for schools
London, Nelson, 1966. 256 pp. 45p. illus. map.
New York, Humanities Press, distr, $1.75
This selection of prose writings by West Africans is designed especially for school use. The earliest piece of writing comes from Equiano's autobiography, published in 1789, and the most recent from the pen of Francis Selormey, a short story entitled 'The witch'. All the writing is narrative, ranging through fiction, history and biography. Although most of the passages were originally written in English, translations from Hausa, Tiv and French literature also appear. There is a general account of writing in West Africa, and each writer's work is introduced by critical and explanatory notes.

*125 Gleason, Judith
This Africa: novels by West Africans in English and French
Evanston, Ill., Northwestern University Press, 1965. 186 pp. $6.50
A detailed analysis of twenty-five African novels, seventeen of them originally in French and eight in English. Styles and traditions are discussed in relation to their settings. Mrs Gleason groups her study under the following chapter headings: (1) The styles of the conquerors; (2) The heroic legacy in Africa, (3) Village life, (4) City life, and (5) The inner life. A bibliography of books and articles is appended.
'This is a splendid book. Not only does it reveal the volume and vitality of West African fiction, but it is also a first-rate piece of literary criticism.'
Robert Cobb — *Africa Report*[1]

126 Moore, Jane Ann
The Middle Society: five orientations towards husband-wife roles in West African novels
Waltham, Mass., African Studies Assoc, Brandeis Univ., 1968. $1.00
A paper presented to the 1967 annual meeting of the African Studies Association, and available in xerox form.

*127 Nwoga, Donatus I. ed.
West African Verse: an annotated anthology

London, Longmans, 1967. 239 pp. 42½p
A comprehensive introduction to West African poetry, from the pioneers to the present day, including translations from the French. Early poets include Gladys May Casely-Hayford, Raphael Armattoe, Dennis Osadebay, and Michael Dei-Anang. Modern poetry is represented by the writings of Abioseh Nicol, Gabriel Okara, Christopher Okigbo, John Pepper Clark, Wole Soyinka, Léopold Senghor, Bernard Dadié, and several others. Notes following each poem are designed to help in the analysis of the poems and in the appreciation of each poet. The first, line-by-line explanations define difficult words or words used in a sense special to the poem. These are followed by interpretations of meaning and comments on the technique of poetic expression; further line-by-line explanations clarify images and figures of speech that might present problems to the reader. Finally, questions are asked that aid individual study. Biographical notes on each writer are also included.

128 St John-Parsons, Donald ed.
Our Poets Speak: an anthology of West African verse
London, Univ. of London Press, 1966. 64 pp. 27½p
An anthology primarily aimed at young readers in secondary schools in Africa. The poems were deliberately selected to vary widely in theme and style, and in the measure of their success. Among the poets represented are well-known names such as Abioseh Nicol and Frank Parkes, in addition to those whose works appear for the first time: Jacob Stanley Davies and Simon Pederek, from Sierra Leone and Ghana respectively, are among the latter. The editor's approach is 'let the poets speak for themselves', and the text aims to promote enjoyment, appreciation and constructive criticism. There are notes on the poems, brief biographies of the authors and an index of first lines, and the selection is preceded by an introduction by O. R. Dathorne and a foreword by Eldred Jones.

*129 Taiwo, Oladele
An Introduction to West African Literature
London, Nelson, 1967. 192 pp. 47½p
The first part of this book describes aspects of

[1]vol. 10, no. 10, Nov. 1965

African life and culture that feature prominently in West African writing; oral traditions are then discussed and an attempt is made to relate them to the way of life of West African people. The author tries to determine to what extent they influenced contemporary literature in West Africa. In the second part characteristics of the major literary forms — the novel, poetry and drama — are discussed, and negritude is considered in some detail. Part three, lastly, consists of a detailed analysis of four well-known works by West African authors: Camara Laye's The African Child, Cyprian Ekwensi's People of the City, Chinua Achebe's No longer at ease, and Wole Soyinka's The Lion and the Jewel.
' . . . the author has succeeded admirably in producing what he intended: a simple book of critical exposition for a first course in African literature.'
John Povey — Africa Report[1]

130 **Zell, Hans Martin** comp. and ed.
Writings by West Africans — in print at December 1967
(2nd revised and enlarged edn)
Freetown, Sierra Leone University Press, 1968.
31 pp. Le 1.00/$1.00
Provides a listing of 365 'in-print' books by West African authors from both English- and French-speaking nations. Originally published as a guide to an exhibition held in Freetown in April, 1967, it covers creative as well as political and historical literature of an original nature.

Cameroon

WORKS
*131 **Dipoko, Mbella Sonne**†
A few Nights and Days
London, Longmans, 1966. 184 pp. £1.05
The few nights and days in this novel cover the life of an African student living and working in Paris. He seduces a French girl, later on falls in love with her, and they decide to get married. The girl's parents reluctantly give their consent, provided that they stay in France, while the boy's parents, on the contrary, insist that he should return home. In collusion with his prospective father-in-law, the boy secretly leaves France without telling the girl and thereby unwittingly occasions the ultimate tragedy. The girl commits suicide when she discovers the plot.
' . . . Dipoko is equally at home in English and French . . . He is one of the few African writers who has comfortably bridged the gap between two very

different cultural milieus . . . a fine piece of writing.'
Lewis Nkosi — Africa Report[2]
' . . . a different type of African novel, smaller in scope, egocentric, non-tribal, and almost (dare we say it?) non-African. Mr Dipoko appears to be moving away from the type of novel that critics have come to expect of African writers . . . the characters in the book are not grown up and they are cruel and spiteful. But, what the hell, it's a novel not a religious parable and it really doesn't matter if he is showing us more than he thinks he is. That is one virtue, one bonus, of the well-made novel and probably a reason for the success of most novels.'
Paul Theroux — Transition[3]

132 **Dipoko, Mbella Sonne**†
Because of Women
London, Heinemann Educ. Books, 1969 (African Writers Series, 57). 178 pp. £1.05 (45p pap.)
The author describes this novel as 'a study in pleasure and change. The story of a woman who dreams of founding a large family. The novel tries to show the deep joy there is in women.' It is a study of sex and society in contemporary Cameroon.

133 **Maimo, Sankie**
I am Vindicated
Ikenne, Nigeria, Author, 1959. 50 pp. out-of-print
(Reprinted in Early West African poetry and drama. Nendeln, Liechtenstein, Kraus Reprint, 1970. $15.00)

134 **Maimo, Sankie**
Sov-Mbang the Soothsayer
Yaoundé, Éd. C.L.E., 1969 (Collection Abbia).
58 pp. CFA 100
New York, Africana Publ. Corp., distr. $1.25
Elements of satire, folk tale and biblical legend are interwoven in this play, which presents the clash of the traditional with the modern in Cameroon society.

Oyono-Mbia, Guillaume
see 476—478.

[1]vol. 14, nos. 5 and 6, May—June 1969
[2]vol. 11, no. 9, Dec. 1966
[3]vol. 4, no. 27, 1966

†Dipoko, though Cameroonian, writes in English, and his works are not available in French.

The Gambia

Ghana

WORKS

135 Kinteh, Ramatoulie
Rebellion
New York, Philosophical Library, 1968. 79 pp.
$4.00
A three-act play by a hitherto little-known
Gambian woman writer. The plot is centered
around Nysata, a girl from a typical African
home in a patriarchical society, and her father,
chief Lamin Kuyateh, who is converted from
his conservative views to a more progressive
way of thinking.

136 Peters, Lenrie
Poems
Ibadan, Mbari, 1964. 44 pp. 30p

*137 Peters, Lenrie
The Second Round
London, Heinemann Educ. Books, 1965 (African
Writers Series, 22). 192 pp. 90p (40p pap.)
New York, Humanities Press, distr. $3.00 ($1.25
pap.)
In his first novel, Lenrie Peters relates the story —
through the person of Dr Kawa, a young doctor
returning home after several years at medical
school in England — of emotional and mental
disintegration, and of family hate and disloyalty
in Freetown society.
'. . . a distinguished and memorable work of imagination.'
                    Gerald Moore — *East Africa Journal*[1]

'. . . the most impressive title Heinemann has added
to its African writers series in a long time . . . has
outreached a whole generation of young African
novelists.'
                    Charles Larson — *Africa Report*[2]

*138 Peters, Lenrie
Satellites
London, Heinemann Educ. Books, 1967 (African
Writers Series, 37). 112 pp. 90p (42½p pap.)
Contains twenty-one poems from the Mbari
collection (see 136) and an additional thirty-four
previously unpublished poems.
'*Lenrie Peters has an uncommonly sophisticated
talent . . . his imagination roams over a limitless
area of the earth.*'
                                    West Africa[3]

ANTHOLOGIES AND CRITICAL WORKS

139 Awoonor, Kofi, and **Adali-Mortty, G.**
Messages: Poems from Ghana
London, Heinemann Educ. Books, 1970 (African
Writers Series, 42) 190 pp. 70p
A new verse collection from Ghana. Some of the
names which appeared in the pioneering *Voices
of Ghana* (see 142) contribute fresh verse here,
other names are new. Includes poetry by Joe de
Graft, A. Kayper Mensah, Ayi-Kwei Armah,
Amu Djoleto, Ellis Ayiteh Komey, Cameron
Duodo, Kojo Gyinaye Kyei, Kofi Sey, Frank
Kobina Parkes, Efua Sutherland, E. A. Winful,
and by Kofi Awoonor himself. There are bio-
graphical notes on the authors

140 Kotei, S. I. A. ed.
Ghanaian Writers and their Works
Accra, George Padmore Research Library on
African Affairs, 1961. out-of-print

141 O'Sullivan, Rev. John ed.
*The New Generation: prose and verse from the
secondary schools and training colleges of Ghana*
Accra, State Publishing Corp. 1968. 31 pp. 25p
This is the third collection of stories and poems
published under the patronage of the Ghana
Association of Teachers of English from the
winning entries in their annual creative writing
competition for the secondary schools and training colleges of Ghana.

142 Swanzy, Henry ed.
Voices of Ghana
Accra, Ministry of Information and Broadcast-
ing, 1958. 266 pp. out-of-print
A collection of literary contributions to the
Ghana Broadcasting system during 1955 to
1957.

143 Watts, Margaret E. ed.
*The New Generation: prose and verse from the
secondary schools and training colleges of Ghana*
Accra, State Publishing Corp., 1967. 58 pp. 40p
A collection of prize-winning entries from the
second creative writing competition organized
by the Ghana Association of Teachers of English.
George Awoonor-Williams, who contributes a
small preface, says of them: 'some of the stories
in this book bear a certain mark of genius, some
may be derivative; but they all have the simple
stamp of innocence'.

WORKS

144 Abbs, Akosua (pseud. for **E. Nockolds**)
Ashanti Boy
London, Collins, 1959. 256 pp. 62½p
The story of Kofi Boetang's struggles to obtain

---

[1] Nov. 1965
[2] vol. 11, no. 8, Nov. 1966
[3] Nov. 9, 1968

a formal education despite his illiterate father's opposition and indifference. Revealing the character and attitude of European teachers in the Ghana schools system, the story ends on the eve of Ghana's independence in 1957, with Kofi's resolution to become a doctor.

145 Abruquah, Joseph W.
The Catechist
London, Allen and Unwin, 1965. 202 pp. out-of-print
A biographical novel describing the life of the writer's father, a dedicated and loving man desirous to see his daughters well married and determined that his sons enjoy a better education than he had.

146 Abruquah, Joseph W.
The Torrent
London, Longmans, 1968. 280 pp. £1.25 (50p pap.)
New York, Humanities Press, distr. $1.50 pap.
Portrays a boy, Josiah Afful, growing up in Ghana, from his life in Nzima village to secondary school at Cape Coast: from the shelter of a family background to the problems common to adolescence, in school, sex and personal relationships.

'Mr Abruquah's critical insights into educational policies and practices transferred to the first African secondary schools from English public schools are lively and entertaining.'
R. W. N. — *West Africa*[1]

*147 Aidoo, Ama Ata
The Dilemma of a Ghost
London, Longmans, 1965. 50 pp. 25p
The plot of this play centres on the difficulties encountered by a black American girl who marries into a Ghanaian family, and the tensions and conflicts that ensue between the girl and her husband's family.

'. . . the directness and poetic qualities of Miss Aidoo's art make the play a very interesting, and, quite often, moving experiment indeed.'
Mbella Sonne Dipoko — *Présence Africaine*[2]

148 Aidoo, Ama Ata
Anowa
London, Longmans, 1969. 72 pp. 50p
A symbolic play based on an old Ghanaian legend: The beautiful Anowa refuses the suitors chosen by her parents and decides to marry the man of her own choice. The action is set in Ghana towards the end of the nineteenth century.

149 Aidoo, Ama Ata
No Sweetness Here. A collection of short stories.
London, Longman, 1970. 134 pp. 50p

New York, Doubleday, 1971 (with an introduction by Ezekiel Mphahlele).
Contemporary Ghana sets the background for this collection of eleven short stories. They explore the tensions and conflicts between the rural and urban societies in modern Ghana.

150 Ako, O. Dazi
The Seductive Coast: poems, lyrical and descriptive, from West Africa.
London. Ouseley, 1906. 164 pp. out-of-print

*151 Armah, Ayi Kwei
The Beautyful Ones Are Not Yet Born
Boston, Houghton Mifflin, 1968. 215 pp. $4.95
London, Heinemann Educ. Books, 1969 (African Writers Series, 43) 200 pp. (50p pap.)
New York, Macmillan, 1969. 180 pp. $1.50
The misspelled title of this novel derives from an inscription on an Accra bus. It tells the story of a railway freight clerk — a story of greed and corruption, of squalor and decay — and, foremost, it is a study of politics and politicians in a newly independent African nation. The Macmillan paper edition has an introduction by Ama Ata Aidoo.
'. . . Armah has taken the predicament of Africa in general, Ghana in particular, and distilled its dispair and its hopelessness in a very powerful, harsh, deliberately unbeautiful *novel.'*
Eldred Jones — *African Literature Today*[3]

'. . . what is impressive about The Beautyful Ones *is the way in which it expresses the disillusion and cynicism engendered in Ghana in the last years of Nkrumah, which his fall only seemed to compound.'*
West Africa[4]

*152 Armah, Ayi Kwei
Fragments
Boston, Houghton Mifflin, 1970. 287 pp. $5.95
The main theme of Armah's second novel is the shattered spiritual vision of a young African returning home after five years in America. He finds his homeland's society materialistic and eager to adopt Western ways and values, and soon sees himself surrounded by career-minded and corrupt people.

*153 Armattoe, Raphael Ernest Grail
Between the Forest and the Sea: collected poems
Londonderry, Lomeshie Research Centre, 1950 (New edn. 1952) 78 pp. (180 pp.) out-of-print

[1] July 5, 1960
[2] vol. 30, no. 58
[3] no. 3, 1969
[4] no. 2691, 28, Dec. 1968

154 **Asare, Bediako**
Rebel
London, Heinemann Educ. Books, 1969 (African Writers Series, 59). 160 pp. £1.25 (40p pap.)
New York, Humanities Press; distr. $3.75
The story of a man and his wife reacting against their tribe and a conservative fetish priest, over leaving the traditional tribal village of Pachanga.
'... tells the story of a sad and dying village and its survivors. It relates the movements of Ngurumo, a young man with a vision, who leads his people through a maze of local fetish priests, rites and terrors across a dangerous forest and into a land that is green, bright and open ... The struggle of young Ngurumo against deeply maintained tribal customs is sincere, if at times it seems contrived ... The story is simple and the language unpretentious, and the impact of change and hope gives strength and quality to the novel.'
Sheila Wilson — *Africa Report*[1]

155 **Awooner-Renner, Kweku Bankole**
This Africa
London, Central Books, 1943. 72 pp. out-of-print
A poetry collection.

Awoonor, Kofi see **Awoonor-Williams, George**

156 **Awoonor-Williams, George**
Rediscovery and other poems
Ibadan, Mbari, 1964. 36 pp. 25p
'... the work of this young Ghanaian poet is coolly rational.'
O. A. — *Black Orpheus*[2]

157 **Bediako, Asare Kwabena**
Don't Leave Me Mercy
Accra, Anowuo Educational Publ., 1966. 119 pp. 3s. 6d. [Ghana]
'Echoes from Owusu's marriage life. Richly entertaining and educative,' reads the sub-title of this novel.

158 **Bediako, Asare Kwabena**
A Husband for Esi Ellua
Accra, Anowuo Educational Publ., 1968. 179 pp. 5s. 6d. [Ghana]
A novel.

*159 **Brew, Kwesi**
The Shadows of Laughter
London, Longmans, 1969. 76 pp. 50p
A verse collection of forty-six poems, many of them hitherto unpublished. This is Kwesi Brew's only published volume, although his verse has been very widely anthologised.

160 **Casely-Hayford, Joseph E.**
Ethiopia Unbound: studies in race emancipation
London, C. M. Philipps, 1911. 211 pp. out-of-print

London, Frank Cass, 1969 (Reprint: Africana Modern Library) 215 pp. £3.00
New York, Humanities Press, distr. $9.00
This is one of the earliest literary works from Africa and the first West African 'novel'. Its hero and protagonist is a man from the Gold Coast who goes to London to prepare himself for a legal career and who finally returns to his native country, but now finds himself a stranger there. He is saddened and angered by what he discovers in his homeland. The result is this book which, containing a great deal of historical, literary and philosophical references, is principally an early declaration of negritude and an attempt to rally all black people to the defence of their culture, their achievements and racial pride. It is also an appeal for unity and national regeneration to the people of West Africa, based on the concept of *Ethiopianism*, i. e. the crystallization of religious and political notions with Ethiopia, which at that time was (with Liberia) the only independent nation in colonial Africa.

161 **Danquah, Joseph Boakye**
The Third Woman: a play in five acts
London, United Society for Christian Literature, 1943. 151 pp. out-of-print

162 **Danquah, Joseph Boakye**
Liberty; a page from the life of J. B. Danquah
Accra, H. K. Akyempong, 1960. 34 pp. out-of-print

163 **De Graft, J. C.**
Sons and Daughters
London and New York, Oxford Univ. Press, 1964 (Three Crowns Books). 53 pp. 27½p 90c
The major characters of the play, the children of Aaron Ofosu, try to fulfil their ambitions against their father's wish; it is a drama of the tensions that result from the clash of two generations.

164 **De Graft, J. C.**
Through a Film Darkly
London, Oxford Univ. Press, 1970 (Three Crowns Book). 70 pp. 50p
First performed at the Ghana Drama Studio, Accra, this new play explores the racial tension underlying the lives of two married couples, and the cause of the hero's hatred of Europeans.

165 **De Graft-Hanson, J. O.**
The Secret of Opokuwa
Accra, Anowuo Educational Publ., 1967. 72 pp. illus. 17½p
When Opokuwa, Agyeman and Boafo, three children in a Ghanaian village, learn that the

[1] vol. 14, no. 7, Nov. 1969
[2] no. 17, June 1965

British Governor in Cape Coast plans to seize the State Stool during the yam festival, they set out to work to defeat the plan. 'Written for the entertainment of both children and adults,' says the sub-title.

166 **Dei-Anang, Michael Francis**
Wayward Lines from Africa
London, United Society for Christian Literature, 1946. 47 pp. out-of-print
(Reprinted in *Early West African poetry and drama.* Nendeln, Liechtenstein, Kraus Reprint, 1970. $15.00)
A volume of verse.

167 **Dei-Anang, Michael Francis**
Africa Speaks; a collection of original verse, with an introduction on 'Poetry in Africa.'
Accra, Guinea Press, 1959. 99 pp. out-of-print

168 **Dei-Anang, Michael Francis**
Okomfo's Anokyo's golden stool: a play in three acts
Ilfracombe, Devon, Stockwell, 1960. 54 pp. out-of-print
This play is based on the traditional story of the Ashanti Golden Stool.

169 **Dei-Anang, Michael Francis**
Ghana Semi-tones
Accra, Presbyterian Book Depot, 1962. 28 pp. out-of-print
A collection of eighteen new poems.

170 **Dei-Anang, Michael Francis**
Two Faces of Africa
Accra, Waterville Publ. Co., 1965. 124 pp. out-of-print
Another poetry collection.

171 **Dei-Anang, Michael Francis** and **Warren, Jaw**
Ghana Glory: poems on Ghana and Ghanaian life
London, Nelson, 1965. 69 pp. photog. 62½p
In this joint collection two poets, a Ghanaian and an Englishman, combine their talents to present great moments of Ghana's history in narrative verse. Kwame Nkrumah has provided a foreword.

172 **Djoleto, Amu**
The Strange Man
London, Heinemann Educ. Books, 1967 (African Writers Series, 41). 279 pp. £1.25 (55p pap.)
New York, Humanities Press; distr. $4.00 ($1.25 pap.)
The funeral of his brother is the point of departure for the story of old Mensah, a respected member of his village community. In this account of his life, his boyhood in the village is retraced through school under a tyrannical headmaster to a minor position in the civil service, his

problems with his own family and his success as a businessman in the last days of the Gold Coast and the early days of Ghana.

173 **Duodo, Cameron**
The Gab Boys
London, Deutsch, 1967. 208 pp. £1.25
London, Collins (Fontana Books) 1969. 201 pp. 30p
The gab boys — so called because of their gaberdine trousers — are the sharply dressed youngsters that idle and lurk about a Ghanaian village, mistrusted and considered delinquent by their elders. This is the story of one of them, a boy who runs away from village life, and after a series of adventures and setbacks finds a new life in Accra.

174 **Hihetah, Robert Kofi**
Painful Road to Kadjebi
Accra, Anawuo Educational Publ., 1966. 194 pp. 3s. 6d. [Ghana]
Presenting a picture of Ghanaian rural society, this novel recounts the story of Ewe, a man imprisoned in a manner everyone believes to be a miscarriage of justice.

175 **Konadu, Samuel Asare**
The Player who Bungled his Life
Accra, Waterville Publishing House, 1965. 81 pp. out-of-print

176 **Konadu, Asare**
Come Back Dora
Accra, Anowuo Educational Publ., 1966. 218 pp. 3s. 6d. [Ghana]
'A husband's confession and ritual,' reads the subtitle of this fictitious account of funeral practices among the Akan Society in central Ghana (see also 180).

177 **Konadu, Asare**
Shadow of Wealth
Accra, Anowuo Educational Publ., 1966. 160 pp. 3s. 6d. [Ghana]
A business executive's search for a mistress, ultimately upsetting the entire administration of his company.

178 **Konadu, Asare**
Night Watchers of Korlebu
Accra, Anowuo Educational Publ., 1967. 99 pp. 3s. 6d. [Ghana]
A novel of the African world of spirits, of the juju man, his powers, and his hold on the village community.

*179 **Konadu, Asare**
A Woman in her Prime
London, Heinemann Educ. Books, 1967 (African Writers Series, 40). 116 pp. 90p (40p pap.)

New York, Humanities Press; distr. $3.00 ($1.25 pap.)

Set in a Ghanaian society that considers it a grave misfortune for a woman to have reached middle age without having borne children, this novel describes the plight of such a woman, who remains childless despite three marriages.

180 **Konadu, Asare**
Ordained by the Oracle
London, Heinemann Educ. Books, 1969 (African Writers Series, 55). 160 pp. £1.25 (50p pap.)
A reissue, under a new title, of *Come Back Dora* (see 176), a novel that portrays a man's agony at the sudden death of his wife, and the long days and nights of ritual that follow.

181 **Obeng, R. E.**
Eighteenpence
Ilfracombe, Devon, Stockwell, 1943. 180 pp. out-of-print
Birkenhead, Willmer Bros., 1950. 167 pp. out-of-print
Among the very first West African novels to appear in English, *Eighteenpence* chronicles the life of Obeng-Akrofi; it also documents the judiciary and legal systems of the Gold Coast (now Ghana) during the colonial days.

182 **Okai, John**
Flowerfall
London, Writers Forum, 1969 (Writers Forum Poets, no. 25). 25 pp. 12½p
A sampling of five poems by a young Ghanaian writer.

183 **Parkes, Frank Kobina**
Songs from the Wilderness
London, Univ. of London Press, 1965. 64 pp. 27½p
A selection of poems by Frank Parkes, the former President of the Ghana Society of Writers. In this volume he writes primarily of the destiny of the new Africa.
'. . . Mr Parkes is one of the fine poets writing today about Africa and the world.'
Mbella Sonne Dipoko — *Présence Africaine*[1]

'. . . a landmark not only in Ghanaian poetry but in African poetry as a whole.'
M. Bulane — *The New African*[2]

184 **Selormey, Francis**
The Narrow Path
London, Heinemann Educ. Books, 1967 (African Writers Series, 27). 184 pp. 90p (35p pap.)
New York, Praeger, 1968. 190 pp. $4.95
In this semi-autobiographical novel of Selormey's childhood he recounts Kofi's upbringing in a village on the coast of Ghana during the nineteen-twenties. Kofi's father, headmaster

of a Catholic mission school, is a strict disciplinarian who brutally punishes the boy to keep him on 'the narrow path' of right behaviour.
'. . . Selormey writes with great freshness and simplicity; his tale moves swiftly and involves the reader completely in the hero's painful pilgrimage. His honesty is also frequently disarming . . . altogether this is a distinguished addition to African autobiography.'
Gerald Moore — *The Journal of Commonwealth Literature*[3]

'. . . The Narrow Path is a simple story . . . but it is told with great sympathy, and has the humour and the pathos of an African Huckleberry Finn.'
Abbia[4]

*185 **Sutherland, Efua Theodora**
Edufa
London, Longmans, 1969. 72 pp. 37½p
A play based upon the conflict between traditional belief and modern circumstances. The hero faces a personal crisis caused by the conflict between an education into an alien culture on the one hand, and his African cultural instincts on the other.

186 **Sutherland, Efua**
Foriwa
Accra, State Publishing Corp., 1967, 67 pp. 60p
The action of this three-act play, first performed in Akan at the Ghana Drama Studio in 1962, takes place in a dilapidated street in Kyerefaso, a small Ghanaian town.

*187 **Sutherland, Efua**
Vulture! Vulture!
Accra, State Publishing Corp., 1968. 32 pp. illus. music etc. 45 Np
Two rhythm plays.
'An attractively presented and illustrated paperback of two plays by one of Ghana's best known artistic personalities. These two rhythm plays — Vulture! Vulture! and Tahinta — are good examples of Mrs Sutherland's distinctive and highly animated work. The chorus, the hand-clapping and the simple action seem to make them ideal for use in schools.'
O. C. S. — *West Africa*[5]

Sutherland, Efua
See also 765.

[1] vol. 30, no. 58
[2] no. 52, 1969
[3] no. 6, Jan. 1969
[4] no. 17—18, Sept. 1967
[5] no. 2732, 11 Oct. 1969

Guinea

WORKS

188 Modupe, Prince
I was a Savage
London, Museum Press, 1958. 168 pp. out-of-print.
New York, Praeger (reissued as *A Royal African*), 1969. 188 pp. $4.95
Living in the U.S. for the greater part of his life, married to an American girl, Modupe, who was born in French-speaking Guinea, wrote this autobiographical novel in English. He narrates his childhood life as a Sousou boy on the slopes of the Fouta Djalon mountains; his many adventures from the birth ceremonies and the initiation rites to his eventual escape from bush life for good. Elspeth Huxley has contributed a foreword.

Liberia

ANTHOLOGIES

189 Banks-Henries, A. D. comp.
Poems of Liberia (1836–1961)
London, Macmillan, 1966, 133 pp. out-of-print
A cross-section of the works of Liberian poets writing during the nineteenth and twentieth centuries.

WORKS

190 Dempster, Ronald Tombekai
The Mystic Reformation of Gondolia
London, Dragon Press, 1953. 71 pp. illus. out-of-print
Subtitled as 'being a satirical treatise on moral philosophy'.

191 Dempster, Ronald Tombekai
To Monrovia Old and New
London, Dragon Press, 1958. 13 pp. out-of-print.
A booklet of patriotic verse in praise of Monrovia, the capital of Liberia.

192 Dempster, Ronald Tombekai
A Song out of Midnight
London, Dragon Press, 1959. 42 pp. out-of-print
A volume of verse produced as a souvenir for the Tubman-Tolbert inauguration on 4 January 1960.

193 Moore, Bai T.
Ebony Dust
Monrovia, Author, no date [1965?] 111 pp. illus. $1.00
A verse collection. Its main theme is Africa, but the author's impressions of America — where he was educated — Europe, and Asia are reflected in several other poems.

194 Moore, Bai T.
Murder in the Cassava Patch
Monrovia, Author, 1968 (privately printed; N. V. Drukkerij Bosch, Holland). 64 pp.
The mutilated body of Tene, the daughter of a well-known Liberian family from Bendabli, is discovered in a cassava patch, to the horror of the entire community. A kind of 'detective' story from Liberia.

Nigeria

ANTHOLOGIES AND CRITICAL WORKS

*195 Ademola, Frances ed.
Reflections
Lagos, African Universities Press, 1962 (New edn 1965). 123pp. (119 pp.) 5s. 6d.
This anthology of prose, drama, poetry and essays from Nigeria features all of the major contemporary Nigerian writers. In addition there are also contributions by some less prominent and less well established authors such as John Ekwere, David Owoyele, Ralph Opara and Mabel Segun. The foreword is by Dr Nnamdi Azikiwe.

196 Babalola, S. A.
The Content and Form of Yoruba Ijala
London and New York, Oxford Univ. Press, 1966 (Oxford Library of African Literature). 410 pp. £3.50/$11.20
Examines a type of oral poetry in the culture of the Yoruba-speaking people of Western Nigeria. The first part of this study is a critical introduction to Ijala, while the main body of the book is an annotated, classified anthology of Ijala poems, with the complete original texts facing the translations.

197 Banham, Martin ed.
Nigerian Student Verse, 1959
Ibadan, Ibadan Univ. Press, 1960, 36 pp. 3s.0d. [Nigeria]
New York, Africana Publishing Corp., distr. $1.00
This small anthology represents the best verse written by undergraduates of the University College of Ibadan, originally published in the student magazine *The Horn*. It is 'presented to the reader not as a great achievement, but as a useful experiment to give young writers the benefit of a wider audience.'

198 Beier, Ulli ed. and trans.
Three Nigerian Plays
London, Longmans, 1967. 89 pp. 32½p
New York, Humanities Press, distr. $1.25
Three plays from Nigeria in which each author

interprets an aspect of his traditional background. Two of the plays — *Moremi* by Duro Ladipo and *Born with the Fire on his Head* by Obotunde Ijimere — are based on Johnson's *History of the Yorubas*, whilst *The Scheme* by Wale Ogunyemi is based upon an incident that happened during the author's childhood. All three authors endeavour to express themselves in a language that owes much to classical Yoruba poetry. Ulli Beier provides an introduction and notes.

'. . . all three plays have a strong structure that lends inevitability to the events they record. One is surprised to learn that only Ladipo's "Moremi" has been performed, for the others appear to have a strong poetic and dramatic authority that acting would ignite into bold theatre.'

John Povey — *Africa Report*[1]

*199 Beier, Ulli ed. and trans.
Yoruba Poetry: an anthology of traditional poems
London and New York, Cambridge Univ. Press, 1970. 126 illus. £1.75/$5.50
A collection of traditional African verse brought together by Ulli Beier. There are notes on the poems and an introductory essay entitled 'On translating Yoruba poetry.'

200 Clark, John Pepper
The Example of Shakespeare
London, Longman, 1970. ca. 112 pp. ca. £1.25 (ca. 60p pap.)
Evanston, Northwestern University Press, 1970. ca. 112 pp. ca. $4.95
A series of essays on African (largely Nigerian) poetry, which Clark had previously published in *Transition, Présence Africaine, Black Orpheus* and elsewhere. Most of the essays appear in their original form or with few changes, and under the following chapter headings: 'The legacy of Caliban: an introduction to the language spoken by Africans and other "natives" in English literature from Shakespeare to Achebe', 'Themes of African poetry of English expression', 'The communication line between poet and public', 'Aspects of Nigerian drama', and 'Othello's useless scene'.

201 Collins, Harold
The New English of the Onitsha Chapbooks
Athens, Ohio, Ohio University Center for International Studies, 1968 (Papers in International Studies, Africa series, no. 1). 17 pp. $1.00
This is a short survey of and bibliographic essay on the popular Onitsha market literature, which ranges from such colourful titles as *Why boys don't trust their girl friends; Money hard to get but easy to spend; Beware of harlots and many friends; Beautiful Maria in the act of true love; How to avoid enemies and bad company;* and *Trust no-body in time because Human being is trickish and difficult.*

202 Collins, Harold R.
Amos Tutuola
New York, Twayne Publishers, 1969 (Twayne's World Authors Series, 62). 146 pp. $4.50
A critical study and analysis of Tutuola's work. Mr. Collins traces his early life, the beginnings of his writing career, the reception of his work in Nigeria, and concludes with an appreciation of Tutuola's literary powers. Notes, references and a select bibliography are included.

203 Fuja, Abayomi ed.
Fourteen Hundred Cowries
London and New York, Oxford Univ. Press, 1962. 172 pp. illus. 80p/$2.60
Thirty-one traditional stories from Yorubaland, mostly concerned with ancient beliefs. Originally written in verse-form and recited by Yoruba story-tellers, they are here retold by the editor.

204 Gbadamosi, Bakare, and **Beier, Ulli** comps.
Yoruba Poetry: traditional Yoruba poems
Ibadan, Ministry of Education, Gen. Publ. Section, 1959. 96 pp. out-of-print

205 Gbadamosi, Bakare, and **Beier, Ulli** eds.
Not Even God is Ripe Enough
London, Heinemann Educ. Books, 1968 (African Writers Series, 48). 64 pp. 30p
New York, Humanities Press, distr. $1.25
'Not even God is ripe enough to catch a woman in love' is the theme of one of twenty Yoruba stories translated into English in this volume. Among others are: 'Every trickster will be fooled once'; 'A young man can have fine cloth like an elder, but he can never have rags like an elder'; 'When life is good for us, we become bad'; and 'He who shits on the road will meet flies on his return'.

'. . . the stories are built around old Nigerian proverbs but the language and vigorous style of the narrator of these tales, Bakare Gbadamosi, is very present, immediate, modern.'

Bessie Head — *The New African*[2]

206 Johnston, H. A. S. comp. and trans.
A Selection of Hausa Stories
London and New York, Oxford Univ. Press, 1966 (Oxford Library of African Literature). 292 pp. £1.75/$5.60
A collection of fairy tales, proverbs, animal stories, supplemented by historical legends and a number of 'true' stories collected from the rich oral tradition of the Hausas. Mr Johnston provides a lengthy introduction and an appendix of the original Hausa versions of the stories.

[1]Vol. 14, nos. 5 and 6, May—June 1969
[2]no. 56, 1969

207 Killam, G. D.
The Novels of Chinua Achebe
London, Heinemann Educ. Books, 1969. 112 pp.
£1.25 (50p pap.)
New York, Africana Publishing Corp., 1969. 112
pp. $3.95 ($1.75 pap.)
This first full-length critical commentary devoted to the writings of Chinua Achebe discusses his four novels and the short stories, utilizing copious extracts from Achebe's work. The author aims to interpret the sociological and anthropological significance of Achebe's works, in addition to their literary merit.

208 Laurence, Margaret
Long Drums and Cannons: Nigerian dramatists and novelists
London, Macmillan, 1968. 208 pp. £1.50
New York, Praeger, 1969. 208 pp. $5.95
Long Drums and Cannons — a title adapted from Christopher Okigbo's poem 'Heavensgate' — is a critical interpretation of the works of modern Nigerian dramatists and novelists; it is 'an attempt to show that Nigerian prose writing in English has now reached a point where it must be recognized as a significant part of the world literature). The first five chapters are devoted to an analysis and appreciation of works by Soyinka, Clark, Achebe, Tutuola, and Ekwensi. Chapter six, 'Other Voices', deals with Aluko, Amadi, Nwankwo, Nwapa, Nzekwu and Okara. An epilogue and bibliography by the author completes the volume.
'. . . the value of the volume lies in its commendable unity and the assistance it might give to the student who wishes to arrive at the center of Nigerian works without too much pain. The plots are there, fully described for him, and the judgments are never too risky or adventurous to be off center.'
Lewis Nkosi — *Africa Report*[1]

209 Lindfors, Bernth
Nigerian Chapbook Heroines
Waltham, Mass., African Studies Assoc., Brandeis Univ., 1968. $1.00
A paper on Onitsha market literature, presented to the 1967 annual meeting of the African Studies Association and available in xerox form.

*210 Lindfors, Bernth
Anos Tutuola and his Critics
Los Angeles, African Studies Center, U.C.L.A., 1969. 50c.
A thorough examination of the international reception that greeted Tutuola's works. The contradictory, sometimes superficial and unsubstantiated nature of the comments are noted, and Mr Lindfors' final plea is for more scholarly research on Tutuola and his work. This essay also appeared in *Abbia*, no. 22, 1969; it was originally a paper given at the African Studies

Association annual meeting at Los Angeles, 16–19, October 1968.

211 Lindfors, Bernth
The Folktale as Paradigm in Chinua Achebe's Arrow of God
Waltham, Mass., African Studies Assoc., Brandeis Univ.,1970. $2.50
A paper given at the African Studies Association annual meeting, Montreal, 1969, and available in xerox form.

*212 Ravenscroft, Arthur
Chinua Achebe
London, Longmans (for British Council), 1969 (Writers and their Work Series, no. 209). 40 pp. 17½p
A brief appreciation and critical commentary of Achebe's four novels, with introductory biographical notes and a select bibliography.
'. . . a fine, balanced study, pervaded with insight and common sense. It treats Achebe and his novels with the respect and solid critical standards of judgment that such an important artist and his works deserve . . . what impresses above all is Ravenscroft's perceptive and repeated insistence that Achebe refuses in any of his novels to simplify what are in reality complex questions of history, politics, religion and morality.'
Donald J. Weinstock — *Research in African Literatures*[2]

213 Ricard, Alain
Wole Soyinka and Leroi James: an attempt at a comparative study of their concept of nationalism in drama
Waltham, Mass., African Studies Assoc., Brandeis Univ., 1970. $2.50
A paper contributed to the African Studies Association annual meeting, Montreal, 1969, and available in xerox form.

214 Robinson, C. H.
Specimens of Hausa Literature
Farnborough, England, Gregg International Publ., 1969 (Reprint of edition, Cambridge, 1896). 134 pp. 53 pl. £10.00/$24.00

215 Skinner, Neil ed. and trans.
Hausa Readings: selections from Edgar's 'Tatsuniyoyi'
Madison, Univ. of Wisconsin Press, 1968. 279 pp. $5.00
A selection of thirty-two pieces taken from Major Edgar's *Lifafi na Tatsuniyoyi na Hausa*, with English annotations provided by the editor and translator. They are etiological tales, tall tales

---

[1]vol. 14, nos. 5 and 6, May–June 1969
[2]vol. 1, no. 2

and proverbs, riddles and folk history. For Frank Edgar's complete collection see 216.

216 **Skinner, Neil** ed. and trans.
Hausa Tales and Traditions 3 vols.
London, Cass, 1969. vol. 1 440 pp. £6.30
New York, Africana Publishing Corp., 1969. vol. 1 440 pp. $15.00 [Volumes 2 and 3 in preparation.]
A *magnum opus* of Hausa folk literature, *Lifafi na Tatsuniyoyi na Hausa* was originally collected, compiled and translated in three volumes by Major Frank Edgar, a British Administrative Officer in Northern Nigeria from 1905 until 1927. The collection embraces fables, history, riddles, songs, poems, proverbs, letters and religious and legal items.
'As one of the few extensive collections of African tradition that have been made to date, the contribution of Edgar and Skinner cannot be overestimated. It offers a diverse sample of Hausa tradition with broad possibilities for comparative purposes, a fact which is particularly important in view of the wide range of Hausa influence among neighboring peoples.'
Philip A. Noss — *Africa Report*[1]

217 **Syracuse University: Maxwell Graduate School of Citizenship and Public Affairs. Program of Eastern African Studies**
Onitsha Publications
(Program of Eastern African Studies, Occasional paper, no. 32) by Andre Nitecki
Syracuse, N.Y., Maxwell Graduate School of Citizenship and Public Affairs, 1967. 24 pp. $2.50
A listing — though by no means exhaustive — of a unique type of African literature, Onitsha market publications. Provides details of 77 titles and a list of publishers.

218 **Walsh, William**
A Manifold Voice: studies in Commonwealth literature
London, Chatto and Windus, 1969. 235 pp. £1.75
New York Barnes and Noble, 1970. 235 pp. $5.50
A critical study of Chinua Achebe's novels *Things Fall Apart, No longer at ease,* and *Arrow of God* is included in this volume of essays on a number of writers from all parts of the Commonwealth.

WORKS

219 **Achebe, Chinua**
The Sacrificial Egg, and other stories
Onitsha, Etudo Ltd, 1962. 32 pp. illus. out-of-print
The five short stories collected in this volume were written between 1952 and 1960. They are introduced by M. T. C. Echeruo.

*220 **Achebe, Chinua**
Things Fall Apart
London, Heinemann, 1958. 185 pp. £1.05
London, Heinemann Educ. Books, 1962 (African Writers Series, 1). 187 pp. 40p; (Students' edn, intro. by A. Higo) 212 pp. 30p
New York, Astor Honor, 1959. 215 pp. $1.95
Greenwich, Conn., Fawcett, 1969 (Premier Book, T 450). 192 pp. $0.75
The first of Achebe's four novels derives its title from W. B. Yeats' 'The Second Coming'. It is set in the eastern part of Nigeria and revolves around a double tragedy: that of its hero Okonkwo and that of his village, Umuofia. Though his entire life was dominated by fear, the fear of failure and weakness, Okonkwo was 'one of the greatest men of his time'. Through hard work and determination, Okonkwo becomes a prosperous and respected member of the Umuofia community, as well as being considered a great warrior. Though deep down Okonkwo is not a cruel man, he nevertheless acts thus with his son and wives. Afraid of being thought weak, it is his own machete that delivers the final blow to Ikemefuna, a child hostage he had reared for many years until the Oracle had decided he must die as tradition demanded. This is followed by his accidentally killing a clansman of Umuofia. As a result Okonkwo and his family are banished for seven years, and he finds refuge in the village of his wife's mother, Mbanta. During his exile, awaiting the return to his clan, Okonkwo sees the arrival of the first Christian missionaries. When he finally returns to Umuofia, Okonkwo finds that, here too, the Christans have built churches and entrenched themselves in his society. Okonkwo's opposition to them and the colonial administrators brings him to murder the white man's court messenger who tries to stop a meeting of the clan. But he finds himself alone in this warlike action; the villagers are too divided to follow his example, and, completely alienated from his people, he decides to take his own life.
'Not since Mister Johnson *has a novel about West Africa written in English shown such love and warmth for its subject as this first novel by a young Nigerian author.'*
Diana Speed — *Black Orpheus*[2]

'... breaks new ground in Nigerian fiction ... many books and anthropological treatises have told about the power of religious superstition, but here is one which forcefully but impartially gives us the reasons ...'
Mercedes Mackay — *African Affairs*[3]

[1] vol. 15, no. 9, Dec. 1970
[2] no. 5, May 1959
[3] vol. 57, no. 228, July 1958

Nigeria

*221 Achebe, Chinua
No Longer at Ease
London, Heinemann, 1960. 170 pp. £1.05
London, Heinemann Educ. Books, 1963 (African
Writers Series, 3) 176 pp. 35p
New York, Astor Honor, 1960. 170 pp. $1.95
Greenwich, Conn., Fawcett, 1969 (Premier Book,
T 449). 159 pp. $0.75
Generally regarded as a sequel to Achebe's first
novel, *Things fall apart*, the central character of
No longer at ease is the grandson of Okonkwo.
Obi, having been granted an education in England by the Umuofia Progressive Union, returns
to Lagos, where he obtains the prestigious position of Secretary to the government's Scholarship Board. In this new position he sets out with
high principles and idealism, but shortly ac-
cumulates a series of debts: his loan from the
Umuofia Union must be repaid, money is required at home to pay taxes and bills, and he
is altogether living too extravagantly to manage
prompt payments. Further complicating his life
is Obi's love for Clara, a nurse whom he met on
his homeward journey to Nigeria. However,
Clara is an 'osu', considered an outcast because
of her descent from slaves within the Ibo community. The Union and his father alike dis-
approve of his relationship and his mother
threatens to kill herself should her son go ahead
and marry this 'osu'. As pressures mount, Obi's
moral and intellectual opposition to bribery
gives way and he succumbs to corruption. The
results, ultimately, bring a sad and humiliating
end to a promising career.
'... the writer has a fine gift for narrative and he
never forces an issue or evades a conclusion. He has
a flat unemotional style which brings its own reality.
His characters are alive, but secondary to the settings
which produce them, and these settings explain their
actions. I have not yet read a book which brings
the Lagos scene so vividly to life, revealing the
circumstances which almost automatically lead to
corruption.'
Mercedes Mackay — *African Affairs*[1]

'Obi Okonkwo, the hero of this novel, is not an unusual
type. We all know dozens like him. He is not as unforgettable a character as his grandfather the warrior
Okonkwo, the hero of Things Fall Apart. But then
this new novel is about the new Nigerian middle
class, and like most bourgeoisies in the world the
Nigerian one does not produce particularly colourful
and memorable characters. The strength of the novel
does not lie in its characterization but in its brilliant
description and analysis of situations and conflicts ...
Mr Achebe has gained a new confidence. He presents
Nigerian life as it is — no need to justify or explain it.'
Omidiji Aragbabalu [pseud. for Ulli Beier] —
Black Orpheus[2]

*222 Achebe, Chinua
Arrow of God

London, Heinemann, 1964. 304 pp. £1.25
London, Heinemann Educ. Books, 1965 (African
Writers Series, 16). 296 pp. 45p
New York, John Day, 1967. 287 pp. $5.50
New York, Doubleday, 1969 (Anchor Book A
698: with an introduction by Kenneth Post) 266
pp. $1.45
Achebe's third novel is set in the Ibo villages
of Umuaro in Eastern Nigeria in the nineteen-
twenties, a time when colonialism was firmly
entrenched. At the centre of the novel is Ezeulu,
old and dignified chief priest of Ulu, the traditional God of his Umuaro people. Ezeulu, strug-
gling for power, finds that his authority as
spiritual leader is considerably strengthened
when a war he has been trying to prevent between his people and a neighbouring community
is brought to a halt by a British District Officer,
Captain Winterbottom. Though the latter is
totally ignorant of tribal customs and beliefs,
Ezeulu is greatly impressed by the knowledge
and power of the white man. As a result he
decides to send his son Oduche to the white
man's mission school, to learn the secrets of
such strength and 'to be my eyes and ears among
the whites'. Ultimately, however, this gives
cause for conflict, as the son, now converted to
Christianity and overzealous in his freshly acquired new religion, attempts to kill the python
of Idemili, the secret animal of traditional
religion. After this, Ezeulu turns to oppose the
colonial administration of the white man, but
his obstinacy and pride bring tragedy in the end.
'... more substantial than either of Achebe's two
earlier works — more complex than Things Fall
Apart and hence lacking the endearing simplicity of
that novel. Its great contribution is its shift of
emphasis from the clash of Africa with the outside
world to the internal tensions of Africa itself, a clash
which seems to be absent in much African writing ...
his novel is a human novel. His success in bringing
out the general humanity above the Africanness of
his themes is what gives him a high place among
African writers.'
Eldred Jones — *The Journal
of Commonwealth Literature*[3]

'... Achebe has done more than depict an African
society, to determinate a moment of its history ...
this novel is very important. Not only is it the most
serious African novel in English up to now; it can also
be added to the author's two preceding masterpieces
in order to reveal, in striking unity, the personal
vision of a lucid artist.'
Abiola Irele — *Présence Africaine*[4]

[1] vol. 60, no. 241, Oct. 1961
[2] no. 8, 1966
[3] no. 1, Sept. 1965
[4] vol. 24, no. 52

*223 **Achebe, Chinua**
A Man of the People
London, Heinemann, 1966. 166 pp. £1.05
London, Heinemann Educ. Books, 1966 (African
Writers Series, 31). 176 pp. 40p
New York, John Day, 1966. 167 pp. $3.95
New York, Doubleday, 1967 (Anchor Book, A
594: with an introduction by Kenneth Post). 141
pp. $1.95
A satirical farce and *exposé* of a corrupt government and the cult of personality in an African
state after four years of independence, once described by Achebe himself as 'a rather serious
indictment — if you like — on post-independence Africa'. The novel revolves around the
affable Chief, the Honourable M. A. Nanga, and
Odili, a former pupil of Nanga's. A 'bush' politician, semi-literate and half-witted, Nanga suddenly finds himself elevated to the new post of
Minister of Culture while Odili, a young intellectual, is a member of the country's new élite.
Odili, who serves as the narrator of the story,
possesses a strong sense of idealism and hopes to
create a better way of life for his country's people.
However, he is soon introduced to the manipu-
lations of power and fraudulent government;
after accepting an invitation to be Nanga's guest
in the capital city he himself enjoys the luxurious
life lived by senior members of government. In
the denouement of the novel, Odili becomes
Nanga's political and social rival and his op-
ponent for election as a member of parliament.
The story climaxes in a military coup, now reminiscent of the army take-over in Nigeria in
January 1966.
'... a vivid, free-moving, agressive, partly impres-
sionistic satirical comedy on contemporary Nigeria ...
the novel beautifully dramatises the multiple conflict
[of] the intemperate intellectual idealism of a young
college graduate ... a most enjoyable novel.'
Joseph Okpaku — *Journal of the New African
Literature and the Arts*[1]

'... does not have the poise of Achebe's earlier novels.
It has the necessary stridency of a tract. The fact is
that Africa needs this kind of novel at this time as
much as Victorian England needed* Hard Times. *
Yet take it out of its immediate environment, retain-
ing the essential message, and its general applicability
is frightening.'
                                    Eldred Jones — *The Journal
                                 of Commonwealth Literature*[2]

Achebe, Chinua
See also 682

224 **Agunwa, Clement**
More than Once
London, Longmans, 1967. 220 pp. £1.05 (45p
pap.)
New York, Humanities Press, distr. $1.50 pap.

The tragi-comic story of Nweke Nwakor, a strug-
gling, illiterate businessman in Onitsha — the
book itself is perhaps reminiscent of Onitsha
market literature — who almost achieves the
opulence of his dreams and ambitions.

225 **Akiga, Benjamin**
*Akiga's story: the Tiv tribe as seen by one of its
members*
(Trans. from the Tiv by Rupert East)
London, Oxford University Press, 1939. 436 pp.
out-of-print

226 **Akpabot, Samuel**
Masters of the Music
Ilfracombe, Devon, Stockwell, 1958. 28 pp. out-
of-print
Poetry.

227 **Akpan, Ntieyong Udo**
The Wooden Gong
London, Longmans, 1965. 118 pp. 27½p
This narrative of life in a village in Ibibioland,
Eastern Nigeria, describes the life of its inhabitants, a people living in scattered huts covering
an area of five square miles.
'... Akpan's story brings in social change, the
mushroom of growth of new churches, local custom,
the clash with the colonial administration and,
guiding everything, the tradition and power of the
tribal secret society. At times the story reads rather
like a simpler version of Achebe's* Arrow of God *but
it has its own interest.'
                                Edgar Wright — *Transition*[3]

Akpan, Ntieyong Udo
See also 690

228 **Aluko, Timothy Mofolorunso**
One Man, One Wife
Lagos, Nigerian Printing and Publ. Co., 1959.
200 pp. out-of-print
London, Heinemann Educ. Books 1967 (African
Writers Series, 30). 208 pp. 45p
New York, Humanities Press, distr. $1.25
Set in a Yoruba village, Aluko's satirical novel
tells of how a large proportion of Isolo's
populace becomes disillusioned with missionary
Christianity, and of their return to the worship
of the old gods.

229 **Aluko, Timothy Mofolorunso**
One Man, One Matchet
London, Heinemann Educ. Books, 1965 (African
Writers Series, 11). 208 pp. 35p
New York, Humanities Press, distr. $1.00

[1]no. 2, Fall, 1966
[2]no. 3, July 1967
[3]vol. 5, no. 25, 1966

A story taking place in a cocoa community in Western Nigeria's Yorubaland. It tells of the conflict between a zestful, greenhorn district officer and a 'black whiteman', the unscrupulous and conceited politician, journalist and agitator Benjamin Benjamin, who stirs up a land dispute between two Yoruba communities.
'For another conflict story, full of a clear and objective understanding of the problems of the period, written with marvellous lucidity, and full of humour without irritating belaboured flowery language, I recommend One Man, One Matchet.'
Nuhasu Amosu — *Black Orpheus*[1]

*230 Aluko, Timothy Mofolorunso
Kinsman and Foreman
London, Heinemann Educ. Books, 1966 (African Writers Series, 32). 208 pp. 90p (45p pap.)
New York, Humanities Press, distr. $1.25
In this novel Titus Oli, a recent engineering graduate from the University of London, returns home to his family in a small town in Western Nigeria to take up a post in the public works department. Here he clashes with his shrewd and corrupt kinsman, the P.W.D. foreman Simeon, who has been with the department for many years, a pillar of society and now head of the family.
'. . . an amusing but penetrating vignette of modern life in a Yoruba village written lightly, in a simple polished style, by one who understands his people well.'
M. N. — *West Africa*[2]

'. . . I strongly recommend this book; it is very eventful and well written with economy of style and a great sense of the ridiculous.'
Anne-Louise Edwards — *The New African*[3]

231 Aluko, Timothy Mofolorunso
Chief the Honourable Minister
London, Heinemann Educ. Books, 1970 (African Writers Series, 70). 160 pp. 60p
New York, Humanities Press, distr. $1.50
A satirical study of a schoolmaster turned government minister; and of his somewhat embarrassing political career.

*232 Amadi, Elechi
The Concubine
London, Heinemann Educ. Books, 1966 (African Writers Series, 25). 288 pp. £1.05 (45p pap.)
New York, Humanities Press, distr. $1.50
The fatal loves of a woman in an Eastern Nigerian village. Its heroine, the remarkable widow Inuoma, is a virtuous, beautiful, gentle, near-perfect woman, respected by the entire village community, but one who brings suffering and death to all her lovers.
'. . . by any account it is a most accomplished first performance . . . Amadi's style is lucid, unpretentious

and direct. He writes with the ease and assurance of a man who enjoys writing. It is difficult to find flaws in this small masterpiece.'
Eustace Palmer — *African Literature Today*[4]

233 Amadi, Elechi
The Great Ponds
London, Heinemann Educ. Books, 1969 (African Writers Series, 44). 224 pp. £1.50 (40p pap.)
New York, Humanities Press, distr. $4.50
A battle between two village groups in Eastern Nigeria waged over the ownership and fishing rights of the pond of Wagaba, provides the focus of this novel.
'Elechi Amadi's achievement in the book consists . . . that he depicts the naivety and superstition of a simple community without making the community in any way look ridiculous.'
Davis Sebukima — *Mawazo*[5]

234 Amali, Samson Onyilokwu Onche
The Downfall of Ogbuu; a play
Ibadan, Author, 1967[?], 43 pp.

235 Amali, Samson Onyilokwu Onche
Selected Poems
Ibadan, University Bookshop Nigeria Ltd, 1968. 129 pp. 6s. 6d. [Nigeria]

236 Amali, Samson Onyilokwu Onche
Onugbo Mloko; a play (parallel texts in English and Idoma)
Ibadan, Author, 1968. Out-of-print?

237 Balewa, Alhaji Sir Abubakar Tafawa
Shaihu Umar.
(Trans. from the Hausa by Mervin Hiskett)
London, Longmans, 1968. 80 pp. 32½p
New York, Humanities Press, distr. $1.00
A novel by the first Federal Prime Minister of Nigeria, who was killed during the military coup of January, 1966. The book tells the story of a distinguished teacher, Shaihu Umar, and is a portrayal of a Hausa family in an Islamic society. It is set at the end of the last century, at a time when civil war and slave-trading plagued the country.

238 Clark, John Pepper
Poems
Ibadan, Mbari, 1962. 51 pp. out-of-print
'. . . poetry that makes heavy reading, but which is moving because it is always nourished by immediate experience and because the author's har-

[1] no. 19, Mar. 1966
[2] Apr. 22, 1967
[3] no. 51, 1968
[4] no. 1, 1968
[5] vol. 2, no. 3, June 1970

rassed, tormented and irrepressible personality is present in every line.'

Ulli Beier — *Black Orpheus*[1]

239 Clark, John Pepper
Song of a Goat
Ibadan, Mbari, 1962. 43 pp. out-of-print
A play. See 241

*240 Clark, John Pepper
America, their America
London, Deutsch, 1964. 221 pp. out-of-print
London, Heinemann Educ. Books 1969 (African Writers Series, 50). 224 pp. 40p
New York, Africana Publishing Corp. 1969. 224 pp. $1.95
A sharp indictment of the sins of American society against John Pepper Clark, who spent the academic year 1962–3 as a Parvin Fellow at Princeton University.
'. . . the strength lies in the message. Clark disagrees with the values of American society — the brazen capitalism, the exploitation of the Negroes, the power of the all-conquering dollar that forces a playwright to mutilate his plays to get financial backing . . . the Negro is not spared either. The Afro-American who has suddenly discovered his Africanness and goes for the ostentatious displays of African masks, imitations or originals, is called to order.'

A. Bolaji Akinyemi — *West Africa*[2]

241 Clark, John Pepper
Three Plays
London and New York, Oxford Univ. Press, 1964 (Three Crowns Book). 134 pp. 42½p/$1.35
Three verse plays: *Song of a Goat* (previously published separately by Mbari, see 239); *The Masquerade*; and *The Raft* — its characters, four lumbermen adrift on the river Niger.

*242 Clark, John Pepper
A Reed in the Tide
London, Longmans, 1965. 40 pp. 30p
A collection of thirty-three poems. Clark says in a personal note on 'the poet presenting himself':
'For me, the feeling is not unlike that of undergoing surgery — and surgery at my own hands too! What to cut, and what to save out of a body of poems that has come to represent more or less part of my own self, will always remain with me an unsettled issue.'

243 Clark, John Pepper
Ozidi
London and New York, Oxford Univ. Press, 1966. 128 pp. 37½p/$1.15
Taking place in the Ijaw region of Nigeria, this play is based on the Ijaw saga of Ozidi, which used to be told in seven days to dance, music and mime. The myth — here recreated by

Clark — tells the tale of a posthumous son, Ozidi, born and raised to avenge his father's murder, and killed in a war by his own comrades.
'Clark has remained true to his source and set down for a much wider audience a most remarkable dramatic experience . . . has offered to the theatre one of the most fascinating works to have been created in Nigeria in recent years.'

Martin Banham — *Journal of Commonwealth Literature*[3]

*244 Clark, John Pepper
Casualties: poems 1966/68
London, Longmans, 1970. 62 pp. £1.05.
New York, Africana Publishing Corp., 1970. 62 pp. $2.75
A new collection of verse from the 1966–68 period, largely concerned with the Nigerian civil war. It is a lament for the casualties, living and dead, of a war that has bewildered the world.

245 Echeruo, Michael J. C.
Mortality
London, Longmans, 1968. 66 pp. 47½p
A volume of poetry.
'It is refreshing to encounter a new poet with as firm a sense of his own possibilities as Michael Echeruo. His gifts are for relaxed irony and the more concentrated expression of his own identity in opposition to a sordid generation . . . he displays most clearly the influence of the late Christopher Okigbo.'

Gerald Moore — *The Conch*[4]

246 Egbuna, Obi B.
Wind versus Polygamy
London, Faber, 1964. 128 pp. 80p
The story is concerned with the beautiful nubile orphan Elina in a village of a small newly independent African nation, who becomes the subject of a marriage dispute.
'. . . entertains immensely . . . Mr Egbuna has written a remarkable novel.'

Mbella Sonne Dipoko — *Présence Africaine*[5]

247 Egbuna, Obi B.
The Anthill
London and New York, Oxford Univ. Press, 1965 (Three Crowns Book). 60 pp. 22½p/$0.75
Only the apex of an anthill can be seen above the ground: its foundations lie several layers deeper. The plot of this play is built to the same plan. It

[1] no. 12, 1963
[2] no. 2722, 2, Aug. 1969
[3] no. 7, July 1969
[4] vol. 1, no. 2, Sept. 1969.
[5] vol. 25, no. 53, 1965

centres on an African art student with an obsession for painting anthills, his English friend
and their Cockney landlady.

248 Ekwensi, Cyprian
When Love Whispers
Yaba, Nigeria, Chuks, 1947. 44 pp. out-of-print
This short novel recounts various mishaps to
Ashoka, a young lady in distress.

*249 Ekwensi, Cyprian
People of the City
London, Dakers, 1954. 237 pp. out-of-print
London, Heinemann Educ. Books 1963 (African
Writers Series, 5). 156 pp. 35p
Evanston, Northwestern Univ. Press, 1967.
156 pp. out-of-print
Greenwich, Conn., Fawcett, 1969 (Premier
Book, T 454). 207 pp. 75c
City life in Lagos today is viewed through the
eyes of a young crime reporter and dance-band
leader, with the action of the book centring
round the three women in his life. It is a social
commentary, in which Ekwensi portrays the
many problems – corruption, bribery and
despotism – that face a large and overcrowded
West African city. Simultaneously, the novel
also presents an attack on the government, the
politicians and the landlords.
'... Posterity will thank Tutuola for recording a
phase of West African life before it disappears for
ever. Judgement may be harsher on Mr. Ekwensi in
the final analysis, but now, in this day and age, he
has something important to contribute ... This is
the first time that we have seen life in the Big City
from the West African point of view ... no European
could have quite the same spontaneous affection for
the warm teeming mass of humanity spilling out into
the city streets.'
Elizabeth Bevan – *Black Orpheus*[1]

*250 Ekwensi, Cyprian
Jagua Nana
London, Hutchinson, 1961. 192 pp. out-of-print
London, Panther Books, 1963. 144 pp. 17½p
Greenwich, Conn., Fawcett, 1969 (Premier
Book, T 455). 159 pp. 75c
Chronicles life in the city of Lagos – its night-
clubs with their high-life music, its bars, its
political intrigue. The heroine is Jagua Nana,
described as 'an ageing African beauty'. Jagua
is a former market woman from Onitsha, but
now of independent means. She is a shrewd and
colourful prostitute who, despite her advancing
age, manages to hold her own against her
younger rivals.
'... conveys an excellent picture of Lagos ... Jagua
is a magnificent woman. She may be a harlot, but
she is also an impressive woman full of warmth and
charm ... The ending rings false, but it should not
blind us to the considerable talent of the author.

This book is infinitely more successful than People
of the City.'
Ulli Beier – *Black Orpheus*[2]

251 Ekwensi, Cyprian
Yaba Roundabout Murder
Lagos, Tortoise Series book [?], 1962. 55 pp.
illus. out-of-print
A detective story that tells how a smart inspector
of police catches a murderer by pretending to
make advances to the murderer's wife.

252 Ekwensi, Cyprian
Burning Grass
London, Heinemann Educ. Books, 1962 (African
Writers Series, 2). 160 pp. 35p illus.
New York, Humanities Press, distr. $1.00
A story of the Fulani, a nomadic tribe in Northern Nigeria. When the grass is burnt on the
plains, the cattlemen move south towards the
banks of the Niger. An old man, Mai Sunsaye
is afflicted with 'sokugo', the wandering sickness, and his experiences involve him with those
of the herdsmen.

253 Ekwensi, Cyprian
Beautiful Feathers
London, Hutchinson, 1963. 159 pp. out-of-print.
London, Heinemann Educ. Books, 1970 (African
Writers Series, 84). 159 pp. 40p
Ekwensi's fourth major novel, again set in Lagos,
concerns Wilson Iyari, a young druggist, married
and the father of three children. He attempts to
found a political party – the Nigerian Movement for African and Malagasy Solidarity – to
assert a desire for Pan-Africanism. Iyari is a
successful man in politics, renowned throughout the city and popular with the girls, but his
marriage is a failure.
'... an excellent document on the Nigeria of today;
one can compare it with the famous Mister
Johnson by Joyce Cary ...'
Michel Ligny – *Présence Africaine*[3]

254 Ekwensi, Cyprian
Lokotown and other stories
London, Heinemann Educ. Books, 1966 (African
Writers Series, 19). 160 pp. 35p
New York, Humanities Press, distr. $1.00
These nine short stories reflect the glitter,
bustle, gaiety and seediness of Nigerian city
life.

255 Ekwensi, Cyprian
Iska
London, Hutchinson, 1966. 222 pp. £1.25

[1]no. 4, Oct. 1958
[2]no. 10, 1961
[3]vol. 23, no. 51, 1964

London, Panther Books, 1968. 208 pp. 25p

The heroine of this novel is Filia Enu, a beautiful Ibo girl brought up in Northern Nigeria, who marries a Hausa civil servant, despite objections from both families. In Lagos she becomes a successful model and attracts the attention of a lecherous and unscrupulous politician as well as that of a young journalist. A conflict ensues and ultimately Filia Enu dies tragically of a mysterious sickness.

Ekwensi, Cyprian
See also 704—713

*256 Equiano, Olaudah
Equiano's travels: his autobiography. The interesting narrative of the life of Olaudah Equiano or Gustavus Vassa the African
Abridged and edited by Paul Edwards
London, Heinemann Educ. Books, 1966 (African Writers Series, 10). 192 pp. £1.05 (50p pap.)
New York, Praeger, 1967, 196 pp. $4.95 illus.

First published in 1789, this autobiography by an African slave is a pioneering work. It is a tale of high adventure and exploration: describing Equiano's first encounter with the white man, the terrors of the slave ships, cruelty and injustice, and the constant dangers and humiliations that made up the life of a slave. But he also writes of his friendships with English ladies, who taught him, of shipmates who cared for him, and of a master who valued his intelligence and integrity. Paul Edwards has provided an introduction on Equiano as a writer and personality, and adds comprehensive explanatory notes to the text.

'... important as an attempt to foster an informed pride in the origins of an increasingly productive literature in English ... a sensitive abridged edition of an historically interesting, often compelling narrative ...'

Peter Young — *African Literature Today*[1]

*257 Fagunwa, D. O.
The Forest of a Thousand Daemons: a hunter's saga
(Trans. from the Yoruba by Wole Soyinka)
London, Nelson, 1968. 160 pp. 30p illus.
New York, Humanities Press, distr. $1.25.

A free translation of the late Chief D. O. Fagunwa's novel *Ogboju Ode Ninu Igbo Irunmale*, which has gone into many editions in its original Yoruba. It is an adventurous tale with a strong element of 'quest', and sheds light on the myths of the Yoruba people of Western Nigeria, whose culture has a very long history. Wole Soyinka, who is responsible for this translation, supplies some introductory notes and a glossary of Yoruba and unfamiliar words.

'Fagunwa's tale is allegorical and as in all allegory the intention is both to teach and to entertain ...

each daemon represents a combination of three levels of comprehension: a realistic figure, a supernatural entity and an allegorical emblem ... Fagunwa's action is rendered by Soyinka with such effectiveness that the novel often comes alive to sweep us into its dance.'

R. W. Noble — *West Africa*[2]

258 Henshaw, James Ene
This is Our Chance: plays from West Africa
London, University of London Press, 1964. 95 pp. 17½p

This is our chance, The jewels of the Shrive (awarded the Henry Carr Memorial Cup in the All Nigeria Festival of the Arts in Lagos, 1952), and *A man of character*, the three plays appearing in this volume, are based on different aspects of African culture and tradition. Written in simple style and with equally simple plots, in one or two acts, these plays are primarily intended for secondary schools and training colleges in West Africa. There is a preface by the author, and notes on production are given.

259 Henshaw, James Ene
Children of the Goddess, and other plays
London, Univ. of London Press, 1964. 128 pp. 22½p

Three plays for reading and production by schools, amateur and professional groups. *Children of the Goddess*, a three-act play in a nineteenth-century setting, tells the story of the establishment of Christianity in a Nigerian village, and the struggles between the local ju-ju priest and the Reverend Donald McPhail and his wife. The other two are one-act plays: *Companion for a Chief*, a melodrama, and *Magic in the Blood*, a comedy, centring round the drunken, inefficient members of a local village court at Udura. Details on stage direction are included.

260 Henshaw, James Ene
Medicine for Love: a comedy in three acts
London, Univ. of London Press, 1964. 108 pp. 22½p

Monogamy, polygamy, medicine-men, tradition and the African are the subjects of this play. Ewia, the central character, is a local election candidate whose committee is attempting to secure his unopposed return by bribing rival candidates into withdrawing their nominations. The second motif concerns Ewia's troubles with three prospective wives sent to him by relatives.

'... a spirited and highly amusing satire which

[1] no. 1, 1968
[2] no. 2727, Sept. 6, 1969

touches on more serious matters . . . an excellently constructed play.'

> Peter Kennard — *Bull. of the Assoc.
> for African Literature in English*[1]

261 Henshaw, James Ene
Dinner for Promotion
London, Univ. of London Press, 1967. 103 pp.
25p
A three-act comedy about an ambitious young man-about-town, a newly rich and touchy businessman, and a quarrelsome sister-in-law. James Henshaw includes notes on production and an introductory article entitled 'The African writer, the audience and the English language'.

262 Ijimere, Obotunde
The Imprisonment of Obatala, and other plays
(Trans. from the Yoruba by Ulli Beier)
London, Heinemann Educ. Books, 1966 (African Writers Series, 18). 124 pp. 35p New York, Humanities Press, distr. $1.00
Three verse plays from Western Nigeria originally written and performed in Yoruba and translated into English blank verse by Ulli Beier. Contains *The imprisonment of Obatala*, based on a Yoruba myth; *Everyman*, an adaption of Hugo von Hoffmannsthal's version; and *Woyengi*, founded on an Ijaw tale.

*263 Ike, Vincent Chukwuemeka
Toads for Supper
London, Harvill Press, 1965. 192 pp. out-of-print
London, Collins (Fontana Books), 1966. 192 pp.
17½p
The severe setbacks and complications in the life of an undergraduate, engaged to three girls simultaneously. He is accused by one of being the father of her child, and is expelled by the university authorities. How Amadi, the hero of this story, got himself into this situation, and his efforts to extricate himself from it, provide the subject of this novel.
'Mr Ike not only has a fine comic touch, but a talent for invoking interesting details and the right metaphor. Authentic African imagery and sayings add to the richness of his prose.'

> Lewis Nkosi — *Africa Report*[2]

'Perhaps the most redeeming thing about this novel is that it has no axe to grind. It is just a book — a look at life. No message . . . At once sad and frequently more than a little humorous, Toads for Supper *is excellent fare.'*

> O. R. Dathorne — *Black Orpheus*[3]

264 Ike, Vincent Chukwuemeka
The Naked Gods
London, Harvill Press, 1970. 288 pp. £1.50
Ike's second novel satirically views the attempts made by British and American expatriates to gain control of an African university. At the centre of this campus comedy are Toogood, the honest and diligent British registrar of Songhai University; Professor Brown, his friend; and Julie Toogood, the registrar's frustrated wife, who falls into the clutches of a ruthless and ambitious West African, Dr Okoro. The latter, sporting a worthless Ph.D. from an American university, aims at becoming vice-chancellor of Songhai upon retirement of the reigning vice-chancellor, an American, bewildered by Africa. He is challenged for the post by another African professor who, however, wishes to develop the university along ancient Oxbridge-type lines.

265 Ladipo, Duro
Three Yoruba Plays: Ọba koso, Ọba mọrọ, Ọba waja
(English adaption by Ulli Beier)
Ibadan, Mbari, 1964. 75 pp. 6s. 0d. [Nigeria]
London, Heinemann Educ. Books (publ. as *Three Plays*: African Writers Series, 65), 1970. 120 pp. 40p
New York, Humanities Press, distr. $1.25
The texts of three popular Yoruba folk operas, here translated by Ulli Beier.

266 Ladipo, Duro
Selections from Ọba koso
(Trans. by Robert Armstrong)
Ibadan, Univ. of Ibadan, Inst. of African Studies, 1966, 39 pp. 6s.6d. [Nigeria]

*267 Munonye, John
The Only Son
London, Heinemann Educ. Books, 1966 (African Writers Series, 21). 202 pp. 90p (35p pap.)
New York, Humanities Press, distr. $1.25 pap.
Nnanna, the only son of a possessive widow, is taken away from her to become the servant of a white priest, who arranges for his education in Mission school. The mother, entirely devoted to bringing him up in the traditions of their people in Eastern Nigeria, despairs when her son is taken away from her by something she is unable to combat.
'. . . Munònye has, to begin with, offered the reader an immediately compelling relationship, that of a mother — a widowed mother — with her only son . . . an altogether successful first novel.'

> Don Carter — *African Literature Today*[4]

268 Munonye, John
Obi
London, Heinemann Educ. Books, 1969 (African

[1]no. 2, 1965
[2]vol. 11, no. 9, Dec. 1966
[3]no. 20, Aug. 1966
[4]no. 3, 1969

Writers Series, 45). 224 pp. £1.05 (45p pap.)
New York, Humanities Press, distr. $1.25
An 'obi' is the equivalent of a house or home-
stead in Ibo. This novel narrates the return of
a young couple, Joe and Anna, from the city to
their native village to set up a new home amidst
their families and relatives. Problems and
conflicts arise as Anna appears to be unable to
have a baby even after three years of marriage.

269 Nwankwo, Nkem
Danda
London, Deutsch 1964. 208 pp. out-of-print
London, Panther Books, 1967. 154 pp. out-of-
print
London, Heinemann Educ. Books 1969 (African
Writers Series, 67). 208 pp. 50p
New York, Humanities Press, distr. $1.50
Described as an 'alakalogholi', a good-for-
nothing, Danda lives in the Ibo village of
Aniocha, in Eastern Nigeria. He travels about
the villages, playing his flute, shocking the
'establishment', charming the women and out-
raging his patriarchal father.
*'. . . Nwanwo's gift for dramatic dialog, his ability
to capture atmosphere and idiom, as well as his
warmth and talent for sketching humorous scenes,
leads one to look for the second novel in preparation.'*
Thomas Cassirer — *African Forum*[1]

270 Nwanodi, Okogbule Glory
Icheke and other poems
Ibadan, Mbari, 1965. 31 pp. 25p
A poetry collection in which the major poem,
'Icheke', derives its name from a local bird,
symbolically interpreted as seer or prophet.

271 Nwapa, Flora
Efuru
London, Heinemann Educ. Books, 1966 (African Writers Series, 26). 288 pp. £1.05 (50 p
pap.)
New York, Humanities Press, distr. $3.000
$1.50 pap.)
Efuru is a beautiful and respected woman. However, she has been chosen by the goddess of the
lake, Uhamiri, to be one of her worshippers. In
effect, this means that although she will be rich,
she will never be able to marry or have children
successfully. This novel was the first to be
published by a woman writer in Nigeria.

*272 Nwapa, Flora
Idu
London, Heinemann Educ. Books, 1969 (African
Writers Series, 56). 218 pp. £1.05 (60p pap.)
New York, Humanities Press, distr. $3.00
A woman's desire for having children is the
basic theme of this novel, set in a small Nigerian
town, where the life of an individual is intri-
cately involved with that of the entire com-

munity. After she finally succeeds in giving
birth to a boy, she becomes much closer to her
husband, Adiewere. When the latter dies
mysteriously she follows his death with her
own suicide.

273 Nzekwu, Onuora
Wand of Noble Wood
London, Hutchinson, 1961. 208 pp. out-of-print
New York, New American Library 1966 (Signet
books D 2788). 142 pp. 60c
London, Heinemann Educ. Books, 1970 (African
Writers Series, 85). 268 pp. 45p
Peter Obiesie, a Lagos magazine-editor, aims to
strike a balance between his traditional society
and the Western civilization in which he was
brought up and educated. Searching for a wife,
he decides to marry a schoolteacher from his
own tribe. However, Nneka, his bride-to-be,
is under the curse of 'iyi ocha', said to bring
doom to anyone under its spell. Although the
two of them perform lengthy and costly rites
to absolve the girl from this curse, Nneka
discovers that a vital white stone was missing
in the ceremony. This causes her to commit
suicide before the wedding.

274 Nzekwu, Onuora
Blade among the Boys
London, Hutchinson, 1962 (pap. edn 1964). 191
pp. 80p (17½p pap.) out-of-print.
London, Heinemann Educ. Books, 1970
(African Writers Series, 91). 192 pp. 45p.
A religious dilemma occurs when Patrick
announces his intention to become a Catholic
priest. His decision horrifies his mother, who
wants him to get married and raise a family
and considers his decision an insult to his
ancestors. In addition to the opposition within
his family, another obstacle to Patrick's path to
holy orders is the pigheadedness of the missionaries who run the church he is about to
join.

275 Nzekwu, Onuora
Highlife for Lizards
London, Hutchinson, 1965. 192 pp. £1.05
Set in the Onitsha area of Eastern Nigeria, this
novel tells how Agom, daughter of a priest,
decides to marry Udezue, a young farmer, in an
effort to escape the toilsome life she has been
sharing with her three sisters. She manages to
keep her husband under her control for five
years, until he introduces a second wife into the
household in the person of her old friend,
Nwadi. The lizards of the title proverbially
flourish in the home of the negligent wife.

[1]vol. 1, no. 4, Spring 1966

Nzekwu, Onuora
See also 747.

276 Ogieriaikhi, Emwinma
Oba Ovonramwen, and Oba Ewuakpe
London, Univ. of London Press, 1969. 92 pp.
17½p
Two short historical plays based on the history
of the Benin Empire, which fell in 1897. The
first play is set in Benin City, when it was
invaded by the British in the late nineteenth
century. The second play, *Oba Ewuakpe*, characterizes the famous Oba, who reigned from
A.D. 1700 to 1711 in a time of social unrest
when the people revolted at the sacrifice of
human beings for the purpose of giving fitting
burial for Ewuakpe's dead mother.

277 Ojike, Mbonu
Portrait of a Boy in West Africa
New York, East and West Assoc., 1945. 36 pp.
illus. out-of-print

278 Ojike, Mbonu
My Africa
New York, John Day, 1946. 350 pp. illus. out-of-
print
London, Blandford Press, 1947. 237 pp. illus.
out-of-print
An early autobiographical sketch of childhood
and life in Nigeria. Ojike recounts stories of his
father — how he found happiness among his ten
wives and how he attempted to prevent young
Mbonu from going to school and gaining an
education.

279 Ojike, Mbonu
I have two countries
New York, John Day, 1947. 208 pp. out-of-print
Written as a sequel to *My Africa*, this volume
tells of Ojike's experiences and observations
in the United States, where he found considerable contrasts in friendliness and hostility.

*280 Okara, Gabriel
The Voice
London, Deutsch, 1964. 157 pp. out-of-print
London, Panther Books, 1969. 107 pp. 25p
London, Heinemann Educ. Books, 1970 (African
Writers Series, 68: with an introduction by
Arthur Ravenscroft). 127 pp. 40p
New York, Africana Publishing Corp., 1970. 127
pp. $1.50
The first novel from the pen of Gabriel Okara,
The Voice is an experiment in translating
Okara's Ijaw dialect, its idioms and forms, into
English. Poetic in structure, it is the story of
Okolo's search for 'it'. Okolo's quest brings him
into contact with hostile antagonists as well as
empathetic allies; he is pitted against the apathy
of the ordinary people as he tries to jolt them

with the question 'have you got "it"?' Essentially a political parable, the complex meaning
of 'it' is arrived at through a cumulative process
as each individual encountered by Okolo adds a
new dimension of meaning to the cryptic
question. Arthur Ravenscroft, in his introduction to this new edition, provides the reader
with a cogent analysis.
'*... ranks among the best of new African novels.*'.
Wilfred Cartey — *African Forum*[1]

'*... an interesting and imaginative piece of writing ...*
Mr Okara has considerable narrative skill: his story
has the simplicity of a parable and the poignancy
of an epitaph. Much of the effect of the language
derives from his use of vernacular English and from
the interplay of vernacular English and standard
English.'
M. Macmillan — *The Journal of Commonwealth*
Literature[2]

281 Okigbo, Christopher
Heavensgate
Ibadan, Mbari, 1962. 39 pp. out-of-print
Poetry.
'*Okigbo is chiefly a poet for the ear and not for the*
eye. We cannot see much of his poetry ... But we can
hear *his verse, it fills our mind like a half forgotten*
tune returning to memory. Everything he touches
vibrates and swings and we are compelled to read
on and to follow the tune of his chant, hardly worried
about the fact that we understand little of what he
has to say.'
Ulli Beier — *Black Orpheus*[3]

282 Okigbo, Christopher
Limits
Ibadan, Mbari, 1964. unpaged. out-of-print
Contains two long poems, 'Siren limits', and
'Fragments out of the deluge', both of which
originally appeared in *Transition* magazine.
'*Christopher Okigbo's poetry is all one poem; it is the*
evolution of a personal religion.'
O. R. Dathorne — *Black Orpheus*[4]

*283 Okigbo, Christopher
Labyrinths with Path of Thunder
London, Heinemann Educ. Books, 1971 (African
Writers Series, 62). 88 pp. 45p
New York, Africana Publishing Corp., 1971.
88 pp. $1.75
This posthumous collection brings together
Okigbo's verse collections *Heavensgate* (1962),
Limits (1964), and *Silences* (1965) — originally
published separately by Mbari — together with

---

[1] vol. 1, no. 2, Fall 1965
[2] vol. 1, no. 1, Sept. 1965
[3] no. 12, 1965
[4] no. 15, Aug. 1964

Distances (1964), and a postscript, *Path of Thunder*. In his introduction the poet states that 'Although these poems were written and published separately, they are, in fact, organically related.'

284 Okogie, M. O
Songs of Africa
Ilfracombe, Devon, Stockwell, 1961. 47 pp. out-of-print.
Poetry.

285 Okpewho, Isidore
The Victims
Harlow, Longmans, 1970. 200 pp. £1.25 (75p pap.)
New York, Doubleday, 1971. (in preparation)
This novel presents a study of the tensions in a present-day Nigerian household between a man, his two wives and their children.

286 Rotimi, Ola
The Gods are Not to Blame
London and New York, Oxford Univ. Press, 1971 (Three Crowns Book). 60 pp. 50p/$1.25
A play that transplants the Oedipus theme to an African setting.

287 Sofola, Samuel Adeniyi
When a Philosopher Falls in Love
New York, Comet Press, 1956. 200 pp. out-of-print
A play.

288 Solarin, Tai
Thinking with you
Ikeja, Longmans of Nigeria, 1965. 100 pp. out-of-print
Essays.

289 Soyinka, Wole
Three Plays
Ibadan, Mbari, 1963. 118 pp.
Contains *The Swamp-Dwellers*, *The Trials of Brother Jero*, and *The Strong Breed*. See *Five plays*, 292.

290 Soyinka, Wole
The Lion and the Jewel
London and New York, Oxford Univ. Press, 1963 (Three Crowns Book). 70 pp. 35p/$1.15
Rivalry in a polygamous marriage is the theme behind this comedy set in the Yoruba village of Ilunjinle. The main characters are Sidi (the jewel), the village belle; Baroka (the lion), the crafty and powerful 'Bale' or chief of the village; Lakunle, a western-influenced modern young teacher; and Sadiku, the eldest of Baroka's wives.
'The play is Soyinka's most fully realized as far as dramatic effectiveness and poetic evocativeness

are concerned and his most delightful in characterization.'
> Susan Yankowitz — *African Forum*[1]

'... might almost be outrageous if it were not so healthily sensual and amoral! The play is full of fresh and vivid imagery ... this is a thoroughly enjoyable play.'
> Peter Nazareth — *Transition*[2]

*291 Soyinka, Wole
A Dance of the Forests
London and New York, Oxford University Press, 1963 (Three Crowns book). 89 pp. 37½p/$1.35
First performed as part of the Nigerian Independence Celebrations, October 1960, this play is generally considered to be Soyinka's most complex and difficult to understand. The play takes place on the eve of a great festivity as the mortals of a tribe gather and call up ancestral spirits, who prove entirely unworthy of the great occasion.

292 Soyinka, Wole
Five Plays
London and New York, Oxford Univ. Press, 1964. 248 pp. out-of-print
Contains *A Dance of the Forests* (see 291), *The Lion and the Jewel* (see 290) and the three plays earlier published in the Mbari collection (see 289). Of the latter three, *The Swamp-Dwellers* contrasts the superstitions and archaic traditions in the backward swamplands with the evils, corruption and exploitation of life in the big city of Lagos. *The Trials of Brother Jero*, a short, light-hearted comedy, satirizes the way of life of certain sectarian cultists in Nigeria. Lastly, *The Strong Breed* centres upon a New Year's celebration in a small village; a time at which traditional custom dictated the villagers' selection of an outsider as carrier of their sins — to carry away last year's sins in order to pave the way for a new year of purity and peace.
'Wole Soyinka is a highly accomplished playwright... My only criticism of his dramatic technique concerns his somewhat overfree, and somewhat confusing, use of flashback scenes ... But this is a minor technical criticism of Soyinka's work. I have no doubt whatever that he is a master-craftsman of the theatre and a major dramatic poet.'
> Martin Esslin — *Black Orpheus*[3]

*293 Soyinka, Wole
The Road
London and New York, Oxford Univ. Press, 1965 (Three Crowns Book). 101 pp. 37½p/$1.15
The 'road' is a highway in Nigeria near its

[1] vol. 1, no. 4, Spring 1966
[2] vol. 4, no. 10, Sept. 1963
[3] no. 19, Mar. 1966

capital city, Lagos. The chief characters in this play are the people who live and work on the road — truck drivers, mammy-wagon drivers, their passengers, touts and corrupt policemen.

*294 Soyinka, Wole
The Interpreters
London, Deutsch, 1965. 251 pp. out-of-print
London, Panther Books, 1967. 254 pp. out-of-print
London, Heinemann Educ. Books 1970 (African Writers Series, 76, with an introduction and notes by Eldred Jones). 45p
New York, Macmillan, 1970. (With an introduction by Leslie Alexander Lacy). 276 pp. $1.50
Soyinka's first novel spotlights a small circle of young Nigerian intellectuals — a journalist, a lecturer, an engineer, a civil servant and an artist — living in present-day Lagos, trying to come to terms with themselves. They have grown up together as close friends, and after leaving the university, they still meet from time to time in university common-rooms, at parties, and above all, in night-clubs and bars, in an effort to 'interpret' themselves and the society of traditional and modern Nigeria.
'The quality of writing is very high. Soyinka has an extraordinarily strong visual imagination. He has the ability to see things superimposed on one another ... a really brilliant novel in which Soyinka's talents as a poet, playwright and an extraordinarily sensitive writer of prose, are all fused.'
Eldred Jones — *Bull. of the Assoc. for African Literature in English*[1]

*295 Soyinka, Wole
Kongi's Harvest
London and New York, Oxford University Press, 1967 (Three Crowns Book). 96 pp. 37½p/$1.15
Soyinka's most recent play deals with the conflict between the cunning President Kongi of Isma, a fictitious West African nation, and its spiritual leader King Danlola. It is set during a harvest festival arranged as the official start of a five-year plan.
' ... a hugely entertaining piece ... Soyinka writes with ease and wit ... the play consolidates Soyinka's position as one of the most promising talents of the contemporary theatre.'
Martin Banham — *Journal of Commonwealth Literature*[2]

*296 Soyinka, Wole
Idanre, and other poems
London, Methuen, 1967. 88 pp. 80p (42½p pap.)
New York, Hill and Wang, 1968. 88 pp. $3.95
This poetry collection features the long poem 'Idanre', written especially for the Commonwealth Arts Festival of 1965; it is a creation myth of Ogun, the Yoruba god of iron. The other poems range from a meditation on the news of the October massacres in Northern Nigeria in 1966, to love poems and a self-mocking lament 'To my first white hairs'.
' ... he displays here a prodigal command of language which one sees seldom; successions of brilliant images disciplined with the lyric form ... the whole is strikingly relevant to the present fortunes of the society in which he lives.'
Elizabeth Isichei — *African Affairs*[3]

297 Soyinka, Wole
Three Short Plays
London and New York, Oxford Univ. Press, 1969 (Three Crowns Book). 128 pp. 37½p/£1.25
The Swamp-Dwellers, The Trials of Brother Jero and *The Strong Breed*, previously included in *Five Plays*, now out of print.

298 Soyinka, Wole
Poems from Prison
London, Rex Collings Ltd, 1969. 4 pp. 7½p
Soyinka managed to smuggle two poems out of prison in Nigeria: 'Live Burial' and 'Flowers for my Land'. The poems arrived in London with a letter to his publisher-friend, Rex Collings, in which Soyinka wrote: 'I've written a few of these, about the only creative writing that successfully defies philistinic strictures. And nihilistic moods.'

299 Soyinka, Wole
The Trials of Brother Jero, and *The Strong Breed*: two plays
New York, Dramatists' Play, 1969. 67 pp. illus. $1.50
A special acting edition with notes on production.

*300 Tutuola, Amos
The Palm-wine Drinkard, and his dead palm-wine tapster in the Deads' Town
London, Faber, 1952. 125 pp. out-of-print
New York, Grove Press, 1953. 130 pp. out-of-print
London, Faber, 1962. 125 pp. 30p
Westport, Conn., Greenwood Press, 1970. (Reprint of ed. New York, 1953) 130 pp. $8.25
'I was a palm-wine drinkard since I was a boy of ten years of age. I had no other work more than to drink palm-wine in my life. In those days we did not know other money, except cowries, so that everything was very cheap, and my father was the richest man in town. My father got eight children and I was the eldest among them, all of the rest were hard workers, but I myself

[1] no. 4, Mar. 1966
[2] vol. 68, no. 271, Apr. 1969
[3] no. 7, July 1969

was an expert palm-wine drinkard. I was drinking palm-wine from morning till night and from night till morning. By that time I could not drink ordinary water at all except palm-wine. But when my father noticed that I could not do any more work than to drink, he engaged an expert palm-wine tapster for me; he had no other work more than to tap palm-wine every day.' Thus begins this adventurous and folkloristic tale by Amos Tutuola, the first West African writer whose work was published in London by a major British publisher. Heavily influenced by Yoruba oral tradition, *The Palm-wine Drinkard* is a journey of the imagination into 'Deads' Town' — a never-never land of magic, ghosts and demons, unknown creatures and supernatural beings. The book might well have gone by unnoticed but for a rave review entitled 'Blithe Spirits' by Dylan Thomas, who had this to say:

' ... *a brief, thronged, grisly and bewitching story ... written in English by a West African ... nothing is too prodigious or too trivial to put down in this tall, devilish story.*'

Dylan Thomas — *The Observer (London)*[1]

301 **Tutuola, Amos**
My Life in the Bush of Ghosts
London, Faber, 1954. 174 pp. out-of-print
London, Faber, 1964. 174 pp. 32½p
New York, Grove Press, 1970 (Evergreen Book, E-559). 174 pp. $1.95
An African fantasy — the people's beliefs about the spiritual world and what happens to a mortal who wanders into the 'bad bush' and the world of ghosts. The American paperback re-issue has an introduction by Geoffrey Parrinder.
' ... *is the expression of ghosts and of African terror, alive with humanity and humility, an extraordinary world where the mixture of Western influences are united, but one always without the least trace of incoherence.*'

Oumar Doduo Thiam — *Présence Africaine*[2]

302 **Tutuola, Amos**
Simbi and the Satyr of the Dark Jungle
London, Faber, 1955. 136 pp. 62½p
This is the fairy tale of Simbi, a rich girl and only child, and the most beautiful girl in the village. Despite the warnings of her over-possessive mother, Simbi escapes from her home only to experience poverty, punishment, and starvation. After a great many misfortunes she finally manages to return to her mother and finds that life at home is better after all.

303 **Tutuola, Amos**
The Brave African Huntress
London, Faber, 1958. 150 pp. illus. out-of-print
New York, Grove Press, 1970 (Evergreen Book, E 560). 150 pp. illus. $1.95

Narrates a brave huntress's search for her four brothers, kept imprisoned by the hostile pigmies.

304 **Tutuola, Amos**
Feather Woman of the Jungle
London, Faber, 1962. 132 pp. out-of-print
London, Faber, 1968. 132 pp. 32½p
An old chief reminisces and entertains the people of a Yoruba village with tales of his adventures for ten memorable nights; notable characters in these stories include the Feather Woman, the Queen of the River, the Goddess of the Diamonds, and the Hairy Giant and Giantess.

305 **Tutuola, Amos**
Ajaiyi and his Inherited Poverty
London, Faber, 1967. 235 pp. £1.25
Again strongly influenced by Nigerian folklore, this story recounts the tale of Ajaiyi and his loyal sister Aina, who set out after the death of their parents to make a living on their own. In his effort to get out of debt, Ajaiyi seeks the help and counsel of an assortment of witches, witch-doctors and wizards.

306 **Tutuola, Amos**
The Palm-wine Drinkard: opera by Kola Ogunmola, after the novel by Amos Tutuola
Transcribed and translated by R. G. Armstrong, Robert L. Awujoola, and Val Olayemi
(Institute of African Studies, occas. publ., 12)
Ibadan, Inst. of African Studies, Univ. of Ibadan, 1968. 118 pp. 35s. 0d. [Nigeria]
The stage version of *The Palm-wine Drinkard* in the original Yoruba, with parallel English translation, as first performed in the Arts Theatre of the University of Ibadan, in April 1963, with Kola Ogunmola taking the leading role as the Drinkard. The Yoruba text here is keyed to R. C. Abraham's *Dictionary of Modern Yoruba*, and words and usages that do not appear in it are explained in notes, unless the English translation makes their meaning sufficiently clear.

307 **Ulasi, Adaora Lily**
Many Thing you no Understand
London, Michael Joseph, 1970. 189 pp. £1.50
This novel set in 1935 is a kind of West African detective story. Its main characters are Mason, the local D.O., an old coaster with many years behind him in West Africa, and his assistant district officer, a young, naïve and zestful Scotsman. The older and experienced Mason, who after his numerous years in Africa has become almost totally assimilated to an African way of life and standards, tries to prevent his assistant from starting an embarrassing investigation into local customs.

[1] 6 July, 1952
[2] vol. 23, no. 51

308 **Umeasiegbu, Rems Nna**
The Way We Lived
London, Heinemann Educ. Books, 1969 (African Writers Series, 61). 139 pp. 45p illus.
New York, Humanities Press, distr. $1.00
An anthology of Ibo customs and stories, grouped under two major themes: *Customs* covers such stories as 'Breaking a kola nut', 'Circumcision', 'Hunting', 'Marrying a new wife', 'Naming a new-born baby'. *Folklore* covers a further fifty-five tales, including 'How the dog became a domestic animal', 'A palm-wine tapper's song', 'Sharing the booty', 'The penalty of pride', 'The result of envy', and 'How man lost his tail'.

309 **Uzodinma, Edmund Chukuemeka Chieke**
Brink of Dawn: stories of Nigeria
Ikeja, Longmans of Nigeria, 1966. 120 pp. illus.

310 **Uzodinma, Edmund Chukuemeka Chieke**
Our Dead Speak
London, Longmans, 1967. 135 pp. 32½p
New York, Humanities Press, distr. $1.25
A series of mysterious events threatens a village in Eastern Nigeria in this tale of murder and revenge.

Sierra Leone

ANTHOLOGIES

311 **Finnegan, Ruth** ed. and trans.
Limba Stories and Storytelling
London and New York, 1967. 364 pp. £3.00./ $9.60
The Limbas are rice farmers living in the hills of northern Sierra Leone. This volume is devoted to certain aspects and examples of Limba oral literature. The stories are treated as a form of literature in their own right, worthy of study in literary terms. In her introduction to this collection, Dr Finnegan comments: '. . . they have no one simple message — there is after all, no reason to assume that the Limba, any more than we ourselves, see life as a simple matter. The stories are a complex medium through which comments can be variously expressed or implied.'
'. . . outstanding quality . . . Dr Finnegan lived and worked among the Limba and collected her impressions in situ. Her comments reflect her understanding of the total situation.'
Eldred Jones — *Sierra Leone Studies*[1]

WORKS
*312 **Cole, Robert Wellesley**
Kossoh Town Boy
London and New York, Cambridge Univ. Press 1960. 190 pp. illus. 62½p (32½p pap.)/$2.75
A memoir of childhood days in Freetown sixty years ago. The first African to be elected a Fellow of the Royal College of Surgeons in London, Dr Cole tells of his own arrival into the world, his upbringing and home surroundings in a mid-Victorian Freetown, his schooling and his teachers.
'This is an altogether charming book which does not invite literary criticism and can be read with pure enjoyment.'
Mercedes Mackay — *African Affairs*[2]

*313 **Conton, William**
The African
London, Heinemann, 1960. 244 pp. out-of-print
Boston, Little Brown, 1960. 244 pp. out-of-print
New York, New American Library (Signet Books D 1906), 1961 out-of-print
London, Heinemann Educ. Books, 1964 (African Writers Series, 12) 224 pp. 35p
New York, Humanities Press, distr. $1.00
One of the earlier West African novels. Writing in the first person, Conton tells the story of Kisimi Kamara, who is awarded a scholarship by his government to study in England. While exploring the Lake District, he meets a white South African girl whom he falls in love with. However, colour prejudice puts an end to their affair. Shocked and embittered, Kisimi returns home to dedicate his energies to the struggles for independence of his country, and eventually rises to power as a nationalist leader.
'. . . a very promising first novel . . . perhaps the best thing about the book is that the author has a rich sense of humour, and is also a fine philosopher.'
Mercedes Mackay — *African Affairs*[3]

'. . . Mr Conton is such an excellent writer . . . that overall faults must be forgiven. This is a delightful book to read and Conton's feel for language is charming.'
Erisa Kironde — *Black Orpheus*[4]

314 **Easmon, R. Sarif**
Dear Parent and Ogre
London, Oxford Univ. Press, 1964. 108 pp. 27½p
A 'drawing-room' three-act play about the conflicts between the old generation and the young, between traditional class distinction and modern classlessness.
'. . . peaches from Lake Como, moonlight on the Riviera, raffish Frenchmen and confetti, champagne and joloff rice on a moon-lit beach — these are the

[1]no. 22, Jan. 1968
[2]vol. 59, no. 239, Apr. 1961
[3]vol. 60, no. 240, July 1961
[4]no. 10, 1962

stock-in-trade of this rather slick, West Endish play, yet there is no denying that the characters not only fit into it, but they would be inconceivable in any other setting.'

Elow Gabonal — *Black Orpheus*[1]

315 **Easmon, R. Sarif**
The New Patriots
London, Longmans, 1965. 90 pp. 30p
New York, Humanities Press, distr. $1.25
A modern comedy and morality play in three acts concerning the relationship between two political leaders and a powerful, well-bred widow with a heart of gold, whom they both wish to marry,

*316 **Easmon, R. Sarif**
The Burnt-out Marriage
London, Nelson, 1967. 240 pp. 30p
New York, Humanities Press, distr. $1.00
Against a background of village life a progressive chief and his even more progressive wife struggle to assert themselves. However, they conflict with one another and with the traditional framework of tribal society.

317 **George, Crispin**
Precious Gems unearthed by an African
Ilfracombe, Devon, Stockwell, 1952. 63 pp. out-of-print
Poetry.

318 **King, Delphine**
Dreams of Twilight
Apapa, Nigerian National Press, 1962, 71 pp. out-of-print
A verse collection, introduced by Chinua Achebe.

*319 **Nicol, Abioseh** (pseud. for **Nicol, Davidson**)
Two African Tales
London and New York, Cambridge Univ. Press, 1965. 75 pp. illus. 62½p (25p pap.)/$2.75
In the 'The Leopard Hunt' a white European officer puts pressure on a local subordinate to take part in a hunt. The African gets killed and local agitation results. The second story, 'The Devil at Yolahun Bridge', concerns Sanderson, a district officer posted near the Kissy hills in Sierra Leone, and his encounter with the visiting engineer from headquarters, who turns out to be an African, Olayemi Egbert Jones, the builder of a Yolahun Bridge.

'[the tales] *... reveal an abundance of what William Dean Howells called the "cheerful realism of the common place". In doing so, they provide insights which are rare and which are to be cherished.'*

Robert F. Cobb — *African Forum*[2]

*320 **Nicol, Abioseh** (pseud. for **Nicol, Davidson**)
The Truly Married Woman, and other stories
London and New York, Oxford Univ. Press, 1965 (Three Crowns Book). 128 pp. illus. 32½p/ $1.05
'Most of these stories are placed in colonial pre-independence Africa with its emphasis on pensionable jobs in Government service, official decoration, and black and white keeping their distance,' writes the author. The two tales in the preceding entry are included, together with the title story, 'The Judge's son', 'Love's own tears', and 'Life is sweet at Kusmansenu'.

Nicol, Davidson
See also 662

321 **Rowe, Ekundayo**
No Seed for the Soil and other stories
New York, Vantage Press, 1968, 67 pp. $2.75
A collection of five short stories, all set in Freetown.

---

[1] no. 11, 1962
[2] vol. 2, no. 2, Fall 1966

CENTRAL AFRICA

322 **Evans-Pritchard, E. E.** ed.
The Zande Trickster
London and New York, Oxford Univ. Press,
1967 (Oxford Library of African Literature).
240 pp. pl. £2.10/$6.75
These tales from the Azande people of the
Central African Republic all concern a character
called Ture. Ture is a trickster and tries to fool
everybody, but often only succeeds in fooling
himself. Chapter I gives a brief account of the
Azande. Chapter II outlines when, how, and
where the tales were collected, and finally,
Chapter III contains the stories themselves.

Sudan

WORKS
323 **Fadl, El Sir Hassan**
Their Finest Days
London, Rex Collings, 1969. 122 pp. £1.00
This book consists of two long short stories.
The first, *Their Finest Days*, is based on the
Sudanese revolution of 1964, when the military
régime in Khartoum was overthrown and the
country returned to civilian rule. The second
story, *Barabbas down the Cross*, portrays the
revolutionary period through the eyes and
personal experiences of a young partisan.

324 **Salih, Tayeb**
The Wedding of Zein, and other stories
(Trans. from the Arabic by Denys Johnson-
Davies)
London, Heinemann Educ. Books, 1968 (African
Writers Series, 47: pap. edn 1969). 120 pp. 90p
(40p pap.)
New York, Humanities Press, distr. $3.00
A translation of 'Urs az-Zain wa sab'qisas', three
traditional stories about the people in the
remote Sudanese villages along the banks of the
Niger. Zein is a modern-age, monstrously ugly
buffoon, an object of both ridicule and affection.
The story opens with the astounding news of
his forthcoming marriage to the most sought-
after girl of the village. The two other stories
are 'The doum tree of Wad Hamid' and 'A handful of dates'.

325 **Salih, Tayeb**
Season of Migration to the North
London, Heinemann Educ. Books, 1969 (African
Writers Series, 66). 169 pp. $1.25 (40p pap.)
New York, Humanities Press, distr. $3.75
Narrates the life of Mustafia Sa'eed, who returns
from a sordid environment in London to a
village near the river Nile.

EAST AFRICA

326 **Andrzejewski, B. W.** and **Lewis, I. M.**
comps.
Somali Poetry
London and New York, Oxford Univ. Press, 1964
(Oxford Library of African Literature). 178 pp.
£1.75/$4.80
Texts and translations illustrating different styles
of verse, song and the works of the greatest
Somali poets. The editors, a linguist and an
anthropologist, aim to provide a true image of
Somali pastoral life and oral tradition.
'... their task has not been to recreate an oral
tradition dependent on sounds extremely stylized
and alien to unacquainted ears, but to introduce
and describe the poetry in its cultural setting. The
great value of this book is the success with which it
accomplishes just that.'
Ellen Conroy Kennedy — *Africa Report*[1]

*327 **Cook, David,** and **Lee, Miles** eds.
Short East African Plays in English
London, Heinemann Educ. Books, 1968 (African
Writers Series, 28). 148 pp. 37½p
New York, Humanities Press, distr. $1.25
In this collection of ten plays by a number of
lesser-known dramatists from East Africa, there
are five short plays, one adaptation, and four
sketches — three of them translations from East
African vernacular languages. Several have been
successfully performed by the Makerere Travelling Theatre and have been broadcast by a
number of radio stations in East Africa.

328 **Cook, David** ed.
Origin East Africa — a Makerere anthology
London, Heinemann Educ. Books, 1965 (African
Writers Series, 15). 200 pp. 40p
New York, Humanities Press, distr. $1.00
Short stories, one-act plays, poetry and articles
by a group of young East Africans who were all,
at one time or another, students at Makerere
University College. The material is drawn from
seventeen issues of *Penpoint*, the journal of the
English Department in the University, which
commenced publication in 1958. Most of the
contributions come from Kenya, Tanzania,
Uganda and Malawi, but there are also writings
by a Nigerian, an Englishman and two Americans.
'... what appeals most in all these works is a
"naturalness" which is not a free gift but the
result of awareness ... this is an excellent selection.'
Michel Ligny — *Présence Africaine*[2]

[1] vol. 11, no. 1, Jan. 1966
[2] vol. 27, no. 55

329 **Fox, Doreen C.** ed., with **Lijembe, Joseph A.**, **Apoko, Anna**, and **Nzioki, J. Mutuku**
East African Childhood: three versions
London and New York, Oxford Univ. Press, 1967. 139 pp. 67½p/$1.80
Originally written for a course in the three-year Bachelor of Education programme at Makerere University College, during 1963—66, these are three versions of childhood days in East Africa, written by members of three different tribes. Each of these biographical sketches throws light on the author's birth and birth-place, traditional upbringing, education and schooling, and adolescent years.

330 **Green, Robert** ed.
Just a Moment, God! An anthology of prose and verse from East Africa
Nairobi, East African Literature Bureau, n.d. (1970) 206 pp. illus. EAsh. 11.00
The first efforts of a group of young and as yet inexperienced writers from Eastern Africa, most of them students from the University College in Nairobi are brought together in this collection. The book takes its title from the opening poem, which explores the theme of God's inhumanity. The volume is the first book in the East African Literature Bureau's 'Students' Bookwriting scheme', which sponsors the work of students with a flair for writing.

331 **Harries, Lyndon**
Swahili Poetry
London and New York, Oxford Univ. Press, 1962. 326 pp. £2.50/$8.00
A descriptive survey illustrating the themes and prosodic forms of early Swahili poetry, with texts transliterated from the adapted form of the Arabic script. The content is grouped around 'The technique of composition', 'The linguistic medium', 'The Utenzi verses', 'Long-measure verse', 'The quartain', 'Miscellaneous verse', and 'Hotuba juu ya Ushairi', and concludes with textual notes.

332 **Harries, Lyndon** ed.
Swahili Prose Texts
London and New York, 1962. 142 pp. out-of-print
A collection of Swahili narrative prose, with translations, and explanatory notes on some of the more difficult Swahili words. The first part of the book deals with Swahili customs; the second contains accounts of a journey from the East African coast to Bemba country, and of the journey made by Salim B. Abakari to Russia and Siberia.

333 **Knappert, Jan**
Traditional Swahili Poetry: an investigation into the concepts of East African Islams as reflected in the Utenzi literature
Leiden, Brill, 1967. 264 pp. Dfl. 45.-
The author aims to reconstruct Swahili concepts of life and death, their outlook on the world and other aspects of their ideology, as seen in their literature.

334 **Knappert, Jan** ed.
Myths and Legends of the Swahili
London, Heinemann Educ. Books, 1970 (African Writers Series, 75). 212 pp. 50p
New York, Humanities Press, distr. $1.50
A sampling from the great wealth of Swahili writing, both secular and religious. In this collection 'an attempt has been made in each case to tell the story in such a manner that is meaningful to an English-reading public, without losing in any way the typical Swahili flavour of the narrative.'

335 **Okola, Lennard** ed.
Drum Beat: East African poems
Nairobi, East African Publ. House, 1967. 160 pp. EAshs. 14.00/$2.00
Evanston, Ill. Northwestern Univ. Press, distr. $1.25
'A modest attempt to bring out in its full freshness and flavour a representative collection of contemporary East African poetry.' The anthology includes verse not only by East African indigenous writers but also poetry by non-African authors who were either born in East Africa or have lived there at one time or another. Mr Okola provides brief biographical notes and an introduction, and there is an index of titles and first lines.

Ethiopia

ANTHOLOGIES
336 **Huntingford, G. W. B.** trans. and ed.
The Glorious Victories of 'Amda Seyon, King of Ethiopia', together with the history of the Emperor and Ceôn, otherwise called Gâbra Mazcâl
London and New York, Oxford Univ. Press, 1965 (Oxford Library of African Literature). 186 pp. pl. £2.25/ $7.20
Specimens of early Ethiopian literature. The text translated here is part of a royal chronicle written in the ancient Ge'ez language in the fourteenth century A.D. The editor supplements the text by explanatory notes and commentaries.

WORKS
337 **Gabre-Medhin, Tsegaye**
Oda-Oak Oracle: a legend of black peoples, told of gods and God, of hope and love, and of fear and sacrifices

London and New York, Oxford Univ. Press, 1965 (Three Crowns Book). 54 pp. 22½p/75c
Based partially on traditional Ethiopian sources, this play develops the theme of fear in the conflict between superstition and reason. Ukutee, betrothed to Shanka, is under a curse, interpreted by the oracle of the sacred Oda Oak to mean that her first-born son should be sacrificed to the ancestral spirits.

338 Sellassie, Sahle
Shinega's Village: scenes of Ethiopian life
(Trans. from the Chaha by Wolf Leslau)
Berkeley, Univ. of California Press, 1964. 112 pp. illus. $3.95
The first work written in Chaha, a heretofore unwritten Ethiopian dialect, and translated into English. It is in the form of autobiographical sketches — a fictionalized memoir of village life in Ethiopia during the past two decades.

339 Sellassie, Sahle
The Afersata
London, Heinemann Educ. Books, 1969 (African Writers Series, 52). 96 pp. 35p illus.
New York, Humanities Press, distr. $1.00
The inhabitants of the thirty villages of Wudma had no police force to investigate the burning down of Namaga huts. But the villagers had their own way of finding out — through their ancient institution of the 'Afersata', the traditional Ethiopian way of investigating crimes.

Kenya

ANTHOLOGIES
340 Mbiti, John ed.
Akamba Stories
London and New York, Oxford Univ. Press, 1966 (Oxford Library of African Literature). 250 pp. £2.25/$7.20
A selection of fables and tales representing the rich oral tradition of the Akamba people that make up one ninth of Kenya's total population. The editor has selected 78 from his collection of some 1,500 stories. It is socially compulsory among the Akamba to learn the art of story-telling; anyone who cannot narrate stories is ridiculed and considered a 'good-for-nothing', since he is unable to do what is considered the most elementary thing on earth. The editor describes this sociological background in an extensive introduction.
'... very *good bed-time reading. But of course they are much more than that. Ethnologists, and those who study the structure of myth, will find plenty to engage their interest.'*
F. B. Welbourn — *African Affairs*[1]

341 Njururi, Njumbu
Agikuyu Folk Tales
London and New York, Oxford Univ. Press, 1966. 120 pp. 75p/$2.40
Twenty-five stories and legends from the Agikuyu people of Kenya, now more commonly known as Kikuyu.

WORKS
342 Asalache, Khadambi
A Calabash of Life
London, Longmans, 1967. 166 pp. 37½p
New York, Humanities Press, distr. $1.50
A story of love, intrigue and war, set in a royal village in the land of the Vatirichi in Western Kenya in pre-colonial days. Its hero Shiyuka, whose family has lost the chieftainship, narrates the novel.

343 Bhalo, Ahmad Nassir bin juma
Poems from Kenya
(Trans. and ed. by Lyndon Harries)
Madison, Univ. of Wisconsin Press, 1966. 244 pp. $5.00/£1.87½
The poems of a young Swahili poet in the original Swahili, with English translations. In his introduction, the translator outlines the complex traditions which form a framework for the poetry.

344 Boruett, William Kibiegon
Give the Devil his Due
Nairobi, East African Publ. House, 1969. 92 pp. EAshs. 3.00/$0.90
Short stories and tales narrated to the author by his Kalenjin elders in Kenya.

345 Gatanyu, James
The Battlefield
Nairobi, East African Publ. House, 1967. 52 pp. EAshs. 14.00
Evanston, Ill., Northwestern Univ. Press, distr. $2.00
A play that deals with the political situation just before Kenya's independence, and portrays the hopes and the intrigues of rival politicians.

*346 Gatheru, Reuel John Mugo
Child of Two Worlds
London, Routledge and Kegan Paul, 1964. 215 pp. illus.
New York, Praeger, 1964. 216 pp. illus. $5.95
New York, Doubleday, 1965 (Anchor Book A 468). 222 pp. $1.25
London, Heinemann Educ. Books, 1965 (African Writers Series, 20). 230 pp. 45p
'This is the story' writes Professor St Clair Drake in his introduction (to the American edition) 'of a young African for whom the dream of an

[1]vol. 68, no. 272, July 1969

education in America became a compelling desire'. Mugo Gatheru's autobiography describes his tribal upbringing in Kikuyu country, his encounter with the West, and then his experience in schools in India, Lincoln University in Pennsylvania, and New York University, where he obtained the degree of Master of Arts, and finally in London, where he went to study law. '. . . this extraordinary sensitive book could well become required reading in introductory courses in African culture.'

Mary H. Lystad — Africa Report[1]

347 Kibera, Leonard and Kahiga, Samuel
Potent Ash
Nairobi, East African Publ. House, 1968. 160 pp. EAshs. 14.00
Evanston, Ill., Northwestern Univ. Press, distr. $2.00
A collection of eighteen short stories.
'The stories in Potent Ash which I have most admired are those in which the inherent conflicts are least clouded by an over-sophisticated sensibility. These reveal two talented young writers who one hopes will now experiment in longer forms of fiction, especially perhaps in a couple of fully contemporary novels.'

Arnold Kettle — East Africa Journal[2]

348 Mbiti, John S.
M. and His Story
London, Nelson, 1954. 60 pp. out-of-print
Short stories.

349 Mbiti, John S.
Poems of Nature and Faith
Nairobi, East African Publ. House, 1969 (Poets of Africa series). 92 pp. EAshs. 4.00
John Mbiti is the author of several books and articles on African religion. This is his first poetry collection.

350 Ng'Ombo, C.
Road to Murugwanza
Nairobi, East African Publ. House, 1967. 150 pp. EAshs. 14.00
Evanston, Ill., Northwestern Univ. Press, distr. $2.00

*351 Ngugi, James
Weep Not, Child
London, Heinemann Educ. Books, 1964 (African Writers Series, 7). 160 pp. 35p
London, Heinemann Educ. Books, 1966 (Students' edn, with an introduction and notes by Ime Ikiddeh) 162 pp. 30p
Evanston, Ill., Northwestern Univ. Press, 1967. 175 pp. out-of-print
New York, Macmillan Co., 1969 (with an introduction by Martin Tucker), 184 pp. $1.25

The first novel in English to be published by an East African writer. Weep Not, Child won a special award at the Festival of Negro Arts in Dakar in 1965, and is now one of the most popular of African novels. Divided into two parts, the first is set in the period just before the emergency in Kenya and the rise of Mau Mau; the second deals with the Emergency itself in the life of a Kenyan family. Its central figure is Njoroge, whose dream of an education is destroyed when his father, Ngotho, a traditional Kikuyu, is arrested as a Mau Mau suspect and tortured by his former employer. Young Njoroge finds himself drawn into the struggle for Kenyan independence and the tragedies that are involved. The title of the novel is from Walt Whitman's poem 'On the beach at night'.
'. . . worth reading for its picture of African family life in Kenya, for its insight into, for instance, the ordinary African's bewilderment and indifference to the great European wars.'

D. E. S. Maxwell — Black Orpheus[3]

'. . . important for three reasons: its historical place — the first novel in English by an East African; its setting or subject — Kenya during the Emergency; and its treatment of that subject or setting.'

M. M. Carlin — Transition[4]

*352 Ngugi, James
The River Between
London, Heinemann Educ. Books, 1965 (African Writers Series, 17). 174 pp. 35p
New York, Humanities Press, distr. $1.00
Evanston, Ill. Northwestern Univ. Press, 1967. 175 pp. out-of-print
A novel of conflict between old and new, between Christianity and African traditional religion. Set in pre-independence Kenya, it tells the story of Waiyake and his love Nyambura, separated by the different beliefs and backgrounds of their families, living in two villages separated by 'the river between' — the river Honia.
'. . . seems to suggest that the solution to the problem of African versus European culture might not at all be synthesis, but rather a return to older values. The author seems to be arguing that evolution of the culture, rather than revolution, is the preferred method of change. This novel can be read as an interesting source-book on this one aspect of culture change, as well as a literary work more notable for its structuring images than for its story.'

Austin Jesse Shelton, Jr. — Africa Report[5]

[1]vol. 10, no. 9, Oct. 1965
[2]vol. 6, no. 1, Jan. 1969
[3]no. 18, Nov. 1965
[4]vol. 4, no. 16, Oct 1964
[5]vol. 11, no. 5, May 1966

'... the conclusion is vague, giving the impression that the author is not certain how to gather together neatly the threads of plot in relation to his theme. But one can point out these limitations because the novel will stand criticism; it is a successful one that makes a striking impression by its sincerity and ability.'

Edgar Wright — Transition[1]

*353 Ngugi, James
A Grain of Wheat
London, Heinemann Educ. Books, 1967 (African Writers Series, 36). 280 pp. £1.25 (40p pap.)
New York, Humanities Press, distr. $4.00 ($1.25 pap.)
Ngugi takes us back to the days immediately preceding Kenya's independence in 1963. The action centres around five main characters: Mugo, a local farmer and a hero in the eyes of the villagers, Mumbi and her carpenter husband Gikonyo, John Thompson, a British district officer, and the local petty clerk Karanja. Mugo is asked to deliver the main speech during the local Uhuru celebrations to be held in honour and memory of his friend Kihika, who was hanged by the colonial administrators. He refuses to make the speech, and though this is interpreted as an act of modesty, he turns out to be a traitor — the man who betrayed Kihika to his death. It is an attempt to identify, in terms of its characters, the racial, moral and social issues that made up pre-independence Kenya.

354 Ngugi, James
The Black Hermit
London, Heinemann Educ. Books, 1968 (African Writers Series, 51). 96 pp. 35p
New York, Humanities Press, distr. $1.00
The published version of a play first produced by the Makerere College Students Dramatic Society at the Uganda National Theatre in November 1962. Its central character is Remi, termed a 'black hermit' because he leaves his village tribe for the university.
'... probably the best of James Ngugi's published writings; and this is saying a great deal. The contrast between Country and City is effectively symbolised by the free verse spoken in the former and the prose of the latter.'

F. B. Welbourn — African Affairs[2]

355 Ogot, Grace
The Promised Land
Nairobi, East African Publ. House, 1966. 194 pp. illus. EAshs. 14.00
Cleveland, World Publ. Co. (Meridian Books), 1970 192 pp. $2.25
Subtitled 'a true fantasy', this novel is the story of Luo pioneers in Tanzania, and portrays the atmosphere and social tensions of rural life in Western Kenya.

*356 Ogot, Grace
Land without Thunder
Nairobi, East African Publ. House, 1968. 204 pp. EAshs. 14.00
Evanston, Ill. Northwestern Univ. Press, distr. $2.00
Short stories of traditional life in the rural areas of East Africa — the villagers' life, fears, superstitions, and customs.
'... undoubtedly, a remarkable contribution to East African literature.'

Neera Kent — Busara[3]

'... By any standards, Grace Ogot is a very good writer of short stories; and her themes range from traditional occasions, through mission hospitals in colonial days, to the problems of sophisticated Africans at an Egyptian airport and the tragedy of young girls in contemporary Nairobi ... she manages to write from the inside of traditional Luo society, so that it comes to life in a wholly new way.'

F. B. Welbourn — African Affairs[4]

357 Wachira, Godwin
Ordeal in the Forest
Nairobi, East African Publ. House, 1967. 200 pp. EAshs. 17.50
Evanston, Ill., Northwestern Univ. Press, distr. $2.50
Describes the effects of the Mau Mau emergency in Kenya on the social structure of the Kikuyu people. The story deals with four young Kenyans whose education abruptly ends with the outbreak of the emergency. Nundu, its principal character, is transformed from a mischievous schoolboy to a courageous and dedicated forest fighter.

358 Waciuma, Charity
Daughter of Mumbi
Nairobi, East African Publ. House, 1969. 96 pp. EAshs. 14.00
Evanston, Ill., Northwestern Univ. Press, distr. $2.00
Describes the seven years emergency period in Kenya through the eyes of an adolescent Kikuyu girl, and her reactions to the chaos that surrounds her.

[1]vol. 5, no. 25, 1966
[2]vol. 69, no. 275, Apr. 1970
[3]vol. 2, no. 1, 1969
[4]vol. 69, no. 275, Apr. 1970

Tanzania

CRITICAL WORKS

359 ten Raa, Eric
Society and Symbolism in Sandawe Oral Literature
London, Cass, 1971 (in preparation)
The Sandawe are a small aboriginal tribe of central Tanzania whose language is not related to that of any other living people in East Africa, although it bears affinities to that of the Hottentot and Bushmen of South Africa. Their stories, collected and interpreted here, reveal much about witchcraft beliefs and the role of natural phenomena in popular imagery.

WORKS

360 Palangyo, Peter
Dying in the Sun
London, Heinemann Educ. Books, 1969 (African Writers Series, 53). 136 pp. 90p (40p pap.)
New York, Humanities Press, distr. $1.25
The story of a man's love-hate relationship with his dying and unloved father, of a family struck by death in a village in the arid interior. The son, Ntanya, goes through a difficult personal time trying to resolve the hatred for his father, the man who killed his mother.
'Peter Palangyo has written the most profound description I have yet read of an African man's journey into the world of hallucinations and mental torture ... moreover there is an awareness of place, of the valley and the fields and the colours of things; and the story is set in a family and a village where daily affections and tensions realistically surround Ntanya's crisis.'
Patricia Howard — *Mawazo*[1]

361 Lienhardt, P. A. ed. and trans.
The Medicine Man
London and New York, Oxford University Press, 1968 (Oxford Library of African Literature). 216 pp. £2.10/$6.75
A translation of Hasani Bin Ismail's 'Swifa Ya Nguvumali', a modern Swahili ballad, which gives an account of a murder investigation in Tanzania, in the poet's own neighbourhood. The villagers summoned not only the police but also the 'medicine man' Nguvumali, whom some regarded as a fraud and others as possessed of magical powers. The editor provides an introduction and discusses the social and cultural background of the poem.

362 Ruhumbika, Gabriel
Village in Uhuru
London, Longmans, 1969. 202 pp. £1.05 (37½p pap.)
New York, Humanities Press, distr. $1.45
Tells what 'Uhuru' — freedom and independence — meant to the people in a remote village in Tanzania accustomed to the immediate authority of their tribal chief and village headman. A glossary of East African words used in the story is included in an appendix.

Uganda

ANTHOLOGIES

363 Morris, Henry ed.
The Heroic Recitations of the Bahima of Ankole
London and New York, Oxford Univ. Press, 1964 (Oxford Library of African Literature). 160 pp. £1.75/$5.00
A study of the heroic poetry of a pastoral people of Uganda. The recitations are praise poems describing — in highly exaggerated terms — the composer's heroism in battle and the beauty of his cattle. An introductory essay on the Bahima and their poetry precedes the recitations.

WORKS

364 Buruga, Joseph
The Abandoned Hut
Nairobi, East African Publ. House, 1969. 112 pp. EAshs. 6.00
A long poem in the p'Bitek style written by the author as 'a reaction to a common belief among some of the educated men and women that all that is traditional is bad'.

365 Kimenye, Barbara
Kalasanda
London and New York, Oxford Univ. Press, 1965 (Three Crowns Book). 110 pp. illus. 30p/$1.00
A collection of short stories telling of incidents in the life of a typical Buganda village.
'... as a documentary account of village life it contains much that is vividly true ... provides an entertaining diversion for anyone who enjoys village gossip.'
Hebe Welbourn — *Transition*[2]

366 Kimenye, Barbara
Kalasanda Revisited
London and New York, Oxford Univ. Press, 1966 (Three Crowns Book). 110 pp. 27½p/$1.00
A further collection including tales of characters familiar from *Kalasanda*, and introducing some new arrivals.

367 Kironde, Erisa
Four Plays for Schools
Kampala, Uganda Publishing House, 1967. 91 pp. illus. EAshs. 9.55

[1]vol. 2, no. 1, June 1969
[2]vol. 5, no. 24, 1966

School drama festivals and competitions inspired the writing of these four short plays, two of which are adaptations from Chekov plays.

*368 Liyong, Taban lo
Fixions and other stories
London, Heinemann Educ. Books, 1969 (African Writers Series, 69). 76 pp. 35p
New York, Humanities Press, distr. $1.00
'Fixions', the short story that supplies the title to this collection, is a satirical tale on the subject of foreign aid. The additional eight stories provide a combination of parables, moral tales, folk-lore, satire, and literary innovations.

369 Liyong, Taban lo
Eating Chiefs. Lwo culture from Lolwe to Maikal
London, Heinemann Educ. Books, 1960 (African Writers Series, 74). 128 pp. 45p
'Forty five bits and pieces' — a representative collection of Lwo (or Luo) verse and folk literature, with an introduction and a series of explanatory notes. The author says of it 'I have been not so much interested in collecting traditions, mythologies or folktales. Anthropologists have done that. My idea has been to create literary works from what anthropologists collected and recorded. It is my aim to induce creative writers to take off from where the anthropologists have stopped.'

370 Massiye, A. Sylvester
The Lonely Village
London, Nelson, 1951 (Eagle Fiction Library). 48 pp. illus. out-of-print

371 Oculi, Okello
Prostitute
Nairobi, East African Publ. House, 1968. 132 pp. EAshs. 30.00 (14.00 pap.)
Evanston, Ill., Northwestern Univ. Press, distr. $4.50 ($2.00 pap.)
A novel, part literary, part social commentary. It portrays the life of a prostitute in a squalid environment.

372 Oculi, Okello
Orphan
Nairobi, East African Publ. House, 1968. 104 pp. EAshs. 12.60
Evanston, Ill. Northwestern Univ. Press, distr. $1.80
'You are going to watch a village opera performed. You will see each character walking along a path. All paths crisscross at a junction. An orphan boy is seated crosslegged at the junction, writing pictures of animals in the sand. Today the people who talk in these pages all pass through this junction. Each of them notices the orphan boy,' writes the author in his prologue.

*373 p'Bitek, Okot
Song of Lawino
Nairobi, East African Publ. House, 1966. 216 pp. illus. EAshs. 30.00 (14.00 pap.)
Evanston, Ill. Northwestern Univ. Press, distr. $4.50 ($2.00 pap.)
Cleveland, World (Meridian Books M. 285), 1969. 216 pp. illus. $2.25
One of the first major poetry collections to come from East Africa. 'Translated from the Acoli by the author who has thus clipped a bit of the eagle's wings and rendered the sharp edges of the warrior's sword rusty and blunt, and also murdered rhythm and rhyme,' writes p'Bitek.
'. . . a powerful impression of richness and plenty, after the thin lyrics and slender short stories which East African English so often produces. Mr Okot has so much more to say, and the reason, surely, is that he said it first in the language which most perfectly expresses it . . . the publishers have produced an attractive volume, sure to be dog-eared or purloined before long.'
Gerald Moore — *Transition*[1]

374 P'Bitek, Okot
Song of Ocol
Nairobi, East African Publ. House, 1970 (in preparation).
A further verse collection.

375 Seruma, Eneriko (pseud. for **Kimbugwe, Henry S.**)
The Experience
Nairobi, East African Publ. House, 1970. 96 pp. EAshs. 8.50
This first novel has certain sociological undertones, and the author describes it as 'an expressionistic painting of contemporary Africa'.

376 Serumaga, Robert
A Play
Kampala, Uganda Publ. House, 1968. 56 pp. EAshs. 3.80
A short one-act play set in contemporary Uganda, first performed by the National Theatre at Kampala in October 1967.

377 Serumaga, Robert
Return to the Shadows
London, Heinemann Educ. Books, 1969 (African Writers Series, 54). 176 pp. £1.25 (45p pap.)
New York, Atheneum, 1970. 176 pp. $4.95
A novel that deals with political realities in an independent African nation. Joe Musizi, lawyer and businessman, a member of the upper class, and his servant Simon, are forced to flee their home after a military take-over.

[1]vol. 6, no. 31, June—July 1967

'Return to the Shadows *is not an exceptionally brilliant novel; nor is the writer wholly unique. But there are traits which reveal that soon the author will come out with a fine masterpiece.'

Pat Abisodu Maddy — *West Africa*[1]

378 **Wegesa, Benjamin S.**
Captured by Raiders
Nairobi, East African Publ. House, 1969. 89 pp. EAshs. 4.50
The plight of a young Bukusu girl is the subject of this short novel. Nanjala is captured by a group of Tondo warriors in a raid upon her village and taken with them to their mountain home.

SOUTHERN AFRICA

ANTHOLOGIES AND CRITICAL WORKS
379 **Schapera, I.** ed. and trans.
Praise Poems of Tswana Chiefs
London and New York, Oxford Univ. Press, 1965 (Oxford Library of African literature). 256 pp. map £2.25/$7.20
This collection of poems in Tswana (using Sotho orthography with parallel English translations), are traditional eulogies of the rulers of four Tswana chiefdoms in the former Bechuanaland protectorate, now Botswana. The Bantu themselves consider these poems as the greatest achievement of their literary art.
'. . . this book is more than a sampling of archaic tradition interesting only to the anthropologist; it is a living record of the Tswana people.'

John Povey — *Africa Report*[2]

Lesotho

CRITICAL WORKS
380 **Guma, S. M.**
The Form, Content and Technique of Traditional Literature in Southern Sotho
Cape Town, Balkema, 1967 (Hiddingh-Currie Publ., no. 8). 215 pp. R. 3.50
A systematic review of traditional literature in Southern Sotho. It provides a detailed analysis of the various *genres*, with a view to establishing their form and technique.

381 **Kunene, Daniel P.**
The Works of Thomas Mofolo: summaries and critiques
Los Angeles, African Studies Center, Univ. of Calif., 1967 (Occas. Papers, no. 2). 28 pp. 50c
A critical appreciation of Mofolo's writings. *Moeti oa Bochabela* (East-Bound Traveller), *Pitseng*, and his most significant piece, *Chaka*, are reviewed in some detail.

WORKS
*382 **Mofolo, Thomas**
Chaka: an historical romance
(Trans. from the Sesuto by F. H. Dutton)
(Reprint of edn London, 1931)
London and New York, Oxford Univ. Press, 1967. 214 pp. £1.50/$5.40
(English Reader's Library) Abridged ed. 1949. 125 pp. 25p
Recreates the career of Chaka, chief and founder of the Zulu nation. The author, Thomas Mofolo, born about 1875, is a Musuto, a native of

Basutoland, and wrote in Sesuto, the language of his people.

'*This reissue of F. H. Dutton's translation of Thomas Mofolo's famous novel is doubly welcome, both as a contribution to the growing volume of African literature and as an insightful description of Zulu culture and values.*'

Sylvia Moeno —*African Studies*[1]

383 Mopeli-Paulus, Atwell Sidwell, and **Lanham, Peter**
Blanket Boy's Moon: based on an original story by A. S. Mopeli-Paulus, chieftain of Basutoland
London, Collins, 1953. 320 pp. out-of-print
New York, Crowell (published as *Blanket boy*) 1953. 309 pp. out-of-print
The story of Monare, who leaves his native Basutoland to work in the mines of Johannesburg. After his return home he becomes a fugitive from justice after having been involved in a ritual murder.

384 Mopeli-Paulus, Atwell Sidwell, and **Basner, Miriam**
Turn to the Dark
London, Cape, 1956. 287 pp. out-of-print

Malawi

WORKS
385 Kachingwe, Aubrey
No Easy Task
London, Heinemann Educ. Books, 1966 (African Writers Series, 24). 240 pp. 90p (45p pap.)
New York, Humanities Press, distr. $3.00 ($1.50 pap.)
A story that tells of the political struggles of a British colony with a white minority, moving towards independence. It focuses around the emotional and political awakening of a young journalist, the son of a village pastor, who is offered a job on a newspaper in Kawacha, the capital of the colony.
'*Mr. Kachingwe writes in an easy style with a remarkable power to create lively and dramatic scenes ... I enjoyed very much reading this first novel from a Malawi writer.*'
Sunday O. Anozie —*Présence Africaine*[2]

386 Kayira, Legson
I Will Try
London, Longmans, 1965. 251 pp. £1.05
New York, Doubleday, 1965. 251 pp. $4.50
New York, Bantam Books (Bantam SP 188), 1967. 216 pp. 75c
London, Longmans, 1969 (abridged edn). 192 pp. 45p
The autobiography of a determined young man who walked 2500 miles across Africa in pursuit of an American education. The major part of the book recounts his experiences during the first two years it took him to travel from Nyasaland (now Malawi) to Khartoum in the Sudan. When he finally reached the U.S. he attended Skagit Valley Junior College in Washington, and later the University of Washington.

387 Kayira, Legson
The Looming Shadow
London, Longmans, 1968. 143 pp. £1.05 (40p pap.)
New York, Doubleday, 1969. 143 pp. $4.50
New York, Macmillan, 1970. 143 pp. $1.50
A novel of village life in Central Africa some thirty years ago. A feud between Musyani and Matenda, two villagers, erupts into accusations of witchcraft and attempted murder.
'*... Mr Kayira adopts no particular attitude towards his story of village intrigue, but handles everyone with detached amusement and considerable felicity of style.*'
Gerald Moore —*African Literature Today*[3]

388 Kayira, Legson
Jingala
London, Longmans, 1969. 160 pp. £1.25 (50p pap.)
New York, Doubleday, 1969. 160 pp. $4.95
The name given this novel is that of its principal character, an elderly widower and retired tax-collector whose son wishes to become a priest. In the ensuing conflict, Jingala totally opposes this plan as he wants his son to continue to belong to himself and to the remote village in which they live. The story revolves around this conflict.

389 Rubadiri, David
No Bride Price
Nairobi, East African Publ. House, 1967. 180 pp. EAshs. 4.50
Evanston, Ill., Northwestern Univ. Press, distr. $2.00
The story of Lombe, a young, ambitious and promising civil servant, just promoted to the rank of Principal Secretary in a government department. He moves about in his new world with uncertainty, and falls foul of his Minister, who has him framed on a false charge. The novel also attempts to present some of the conflicts arising between the East African Indian and the indigenous population.

[1]vol. 29, no. 2, 1970
[2]no. 62, 1967
[3]no. 2, 1968

Rhodesia

CRITICAL WORKS

390 Krog, E. W.
African Literature in Rhodesia
Gwelo, Rhodesia, Mambo Press, 1966. 236 pp.
5s. 9d. [Rhodesia]
The papers from the National Creative Writers Conference, held at Ranche House College, Salisbury, in 1964, on the topic of the vernacular literature of Rhodesia. In addition to a series of critical essays on a variety of subjects, there are detailed analyses of major Shona novels and poems, and novels in Ndebele.

South Africa

ANTHOLOGIES, CRITICAL WORKS AND
BIBLIOGRAPHIES

391 Cope, Trevor ed.
Izibongo: Zulu praise poems
Collected by James Stuart and translated by Daniel Malcolm
London and New York, Oxford Univ. Press, 1968 (Oxford Library of African Literature). 240 pp. £2.75/$8.80
These Zulu eulogies or praise poems resemble odes in that they praise important persons, and epics in that they record great events. The poems in this selection cover the period from 1750 to 1900, and record the growth of the Zulu state from numerous independent tribes, and its subsequent disintegration. An introduction and annotations are provided for each poem, as well as a short account of Zulu history, social and cultural life, traditional literature, and the function, nature and content of praise poems. The Zulu originals are faced by English translations.
'. . . Dr Cope's literary analyses are detailed and informative . . . printed as parallel Zulu and English texts, the poems themselves are most impressive; the startling imagery, imaginative wordplay and deliberate alliteration, together with such devices as understatement and the "contrary twist" at the end of stanzas, all effectively heighten the emotional content.'

J. M. Guy — *African Affairs*[1]

392 Gordimer, Nadine, and **Abrahams, Lionel** eds.
South African Writing Today
Harmondsworth, England, Penguin Books, 1967. 264 pp. 30p
A collection of recent South African poetry, prose and drama, by both white and black South African writers. Among the latter are Dennis Brutus, Alex La Guma, Todd Matshikiza, Ezekiel Mphahlele, Nathaniel Nakasa, Lewis Nkosi, and Can Themba. There is an introduction by Anthony Sampson.

393 Gresshof, N. M.
Some English Writings by South African Bantu
Cape Town, University School of Librarianship, 1943. 11 pp. out-of-print

394 Krige, Uys, and **Cope, Jack** eds.
The Penguin Book of South African Verse
Harmondsworth, Penguin Books, 1968. 331 pp. 50p
Baltimore, Penguin Books, 1968. 331 pp. $1.95
The first section of this anthology covers original writing in English by white South Africans; the second, translations from the Afrikaans; and the third section presents translations from African languages — Bushman, Hottentot, Sotho, Xhosa and Zulu — both traditional and contemporary verse. S. D. R. Sutu, S. E. K. Mqhayi and B. W. Vilakazi are some of the contributions. The editors provide an introduction and biographical notes on the authors.

394 Nyembezi, C. L. S.
A Review of Zulu Literature
Pietermaritzburg, Univ. of Natal Press, 1961. 10 pp. R 0.20

395 Pieterse, Cosmo ed.
Seven South African Poets: poems of exile
London, Heinemann Educ. Books, 1970 (African Writers Series, 64). 96 pp. 45p
New York, Humanities Press, distr. $1.75
A collection of verse by politically committed South African poets. Includes poems by Dennis Brutus, Dollar Brand, Timothy Holmes, Keorerepatse Kgositsile, Arthur Nortje, C. J. Driver and Ismail Choonara.

396 Rive, Richard ed.
Quartet: new voices from South Africa
New York, Crown, 1963. 223 pp. $2.50 (this edition now exclusively distributed by Humanities Press, New York)
London, Heinemann Educ. Books 1964 (African Writers Series, 14). 150 pp. 40p
A collection of sixteen stories by Alex La Guma, James Matthews, Richard Rive and a white South African writer, Alf Wannenburgh. The stories are arranged around four central themes, on which each author contributes a story: 'Without Justice', 'The Dispossessed', 'The Possessed', and 'The Outsider'. There is an introduction by Alan Paton, who considers this anthology 'a milestone in the history of South African literature'.

[1]vol. 68, no. 272, July 1969

397 **Shepherd, Robert Henry Wishart**
Lovedale and Literature for the Bantu: a brief history and a forecast
Lovedale, South Africa, Lovedale Press, 1945. 111 pp. out-of-print
Westport, Conn., Negro Universities Press (Reprint), 1970. 111 pp. $6.50

*398 **Shore, Herbert I.**, and **Shore-Bos, Megchelina** eds.
Come Back, Africa: fourteen stories from South Africa
Berlin, Seven Seas Books, and New York, International Publishers, 1968. 202 pp. $1.50
A panorama of the South African way of life seen through the stories of fourteen South African writers. Among the contributors are: Alex La Guma, William Modisane, Ezekiel Mphahlele, Lewis Nkosi, Alan Paton and Richard Rive. Herbert Shore provides an introduction; 'A note on South African life and letters'.

399 **Wilkov, A.** comp.
Some English Writings by Non-Europeans in South Africa, 1944–1960
Johannesburg, Univ. of the Witwatersrand, Dept. of Librarianship, 1962. 36 pp. R 1.10
Pages 13–20 cover literature, largely being contributions that appeared in *Zonk* and *Drum* magazine during the period covered.

WORKS
400 **Abrahams, Peter**
Dark Testament
London, Allen and Unwin, 1942. 160 pp. out-of-print
Nendeln, Liechtenstein, Kraus Reprint, 1970. 160 pp. $12.00
A volume of short stories that were the first published works of Peter Abrahams.

401 **Abrahams, Peter**
Song of the City
London, Crisp, 1945. 180 pp. out-of-print
A novel.

*402 **Abrahams, Peter**
Mine Boy
London, Crisp, 1946. 183 pp. out-of-print
London, Faber, 1954. 252 pp. out-of-print
New York, Knopf, 1955. 252 pp. out-of-print
London, Heinemann Educ. Books 1963 (African Writers Series, 6). 252 pp. illus. 40p
New York, Macmillan, 1970. 250 pp. $1.50
This early novel of Peter Abrahams relates the story of Xuma, the boy from the country thrown into a large South African industrial city, and the impact on him of the new ways and values of the radically different world he encounters there. It was one of the first books that drew

attention to the condition of black South Africans under a white régime, and the dehumanizing machinery of apartheid.

403 **Abrahams, Peter**
The Path of Thunder
New York, Harper, 1948. 278 pp. out-of-print
London, Faber, 1952. 262 pp. out-of-print
Set in lovely and tranquil Quiet Valley, this is the story of a romance between Lanny, a 'coloured' South African, and Sarie, a white South African girl, a couple who dared to love each other despite the menacing shadow of the South African government's racial policy of segregation.

404 **Abrahams, Peter**
Wild Conquest
New York, Harper, 1950. 309 pp. out-of-print
London, Faber, 1951. 382 pp. 75p
Harmondsworth, Penguin Books, 1966. 252 pp. 30p
New York, Doubleday, 1971. (in preparation)
A novel about the Great Trek of the Boers to the land of the Matabele – their struggles, their motives, and their hopes and fears.
'...the most competent piece of literary craftmanship that one has seen come out of Africa in the last six years.'
H. V. L. S. – *African Affairs*[1]

405 **Abrahams, Peter**
Return to Goli
London, Faber 1954. 224 pp. out-of-print
Essay.

*406 **Abrahams, Peter**
Tell Freedom
London, Faber, 1954. 311 pp. 62½p
New York, Knopf, 1954. 370 pp.
New York, Macmillan, 1970. 304 pp. $1.50
Subtitled 'Memories of Africa', this autobiographical novel narrates the first twenty-two years of a talented boy who grows up in the slums of Johannesburg. It tells of his childhood, of his striving for an education, and his desperate attempts to escape from South Africa to the United Kingdom. The American paperback edition has an introduction by Wilfred Cartey.

*407 **Abrahams, Peter**
A Wreath for Udomo
London, Faber, 1956. 309 pp. out-of-print
New York, Knopf, 1956. 356 pp. out-of-print
London, Faber, 1965. 309 pp. 32½p
San Francisco, Transatlantic Arts, distr. $1.50
A novel that deals with nationalism and poli-

[1]vol. 50, no. 201, Oct. 1951

tics in West Africa; a novel about African leaders – revolutionaries one moment and government ministers the next. Udomo, the hero of the novel, newspaper man and nationalist leader of his people of 'Panafrica', is imprisoned for sedition, yet elected whilst in prison, and then leads his people into independence. However, his position as a nationalist leader is not an entirely easy one: he is betrayed and accused of trying to do away with traditional ways of life, and of bringing more expatriates into the country than there had been during his country's days under colonial rule.

*408 Abrahams, Peter
A Night of their Own
London, Faber, 1965. 269 pp. £1.05
New York, Knopf, 1965. 236 pp. $4.95
A story about the motives and tensions within the racial struggle in South Africa; about the role played by Indians in the underground resistance movement, and their fight against apartheid.
'. . . although unnecessarily long discussions about South African problems sometimes slow down the pace of the narrative A night of their own comes off as an exciting, suspenseful story which gathers momentum as it proceeds. A large measure of the success of the novel is due to Abrahams' clear understanding and sympathetic depiction of the plight of the Indian community in South Africa.'
Bernth Lindfors – *Africa Report*[1]

'Peter Abrahams' narrative power and superb sensitivity bring out so vividly the characters, individually and collectively.'
Nunasu Amosu – *Black Orpheus*[2]

*409 Abrahams, Peter
This Island Now
London, Faber, 1966. 255 pp. £1.05
New York, Knopf, 1967. 305 pp. $5.95
During his term of office, President Moses Joshue so altered the political structure of the Caribbean island he led to independence that his death produced a crisis. This novel reveals the various elements – money, colour, family and custom – underlying the political conflicts and power struggles that follow.

410 Boetie, Dugmore with Simon, Barney
Familiarity is the Kingdom of the Lost
London, Cresset Press, 1970. 189 pp. £1.50
New York, Dutton, 1970. 189 pp. $4.95
This novel, autobiographical in nature, recounts the story of a one-legged, black South African ex-convict in a small African town near Johannesburg. The author, Dugmore Boetie, who died of lung cancer in 1966, was persuaded to produce this book by Barney Simon, Editor of the South African magazine *The Classic* (see p. 109).

Nadine Gordimer provides a preface to the book.

411 Brutus, Dennis
Sirens, Knuckles and Boots
edited by Dennis Williams
Ibadan, Mbari, 1963. unpaged [43 pp.] out-of-print
Dennis Brutus was awarded a Mbari prize for poetry in 1962. This is his first collection, published while he was imprisoned in South Africa. Inevitably, many of the poems are protest literature, but there are also love poems, erotic poetry, and poems on other subjects.
'Dennis Brutus' language and themes are almost prosy. But there is a maturity of feeling and above all a precision of phrase, that lifts this verse far above the common protest cry coming from South Africa.'
Ulli Beier – *Black Orpheus*[3]

*412 Brutus, Dennis
Letters to Martha, and other poems from a South African prison
London, Heinemann Educ. Books, 1969 (African Writers Series, 46). 57 pp. 35p
New York, Humanities Press, distr. $1.00
Poems chiefly of Brutus's experiences as a political prisoner on Robben Island off Cape Town. On release from prison Dennis Brutus was served with banning orders which made it criminal to write anything, including poetry, which might be published. To avoid the banning orders these poems were written as 'letters' to his sister-in-law Martha, after his brother had been sent to Robben Island prison.
'Letters to Martha is a handful of poems which are artistically competent and intellectually meaningful . . . sharply descriptive, these short poems bring out the horror, the misery, the loneliness, the humiliation – but above all, the horror of the South African prison cell . . . Brutus is dignified, self-controlled, almost urbane even when the pain is at its worst . . . many poems and political statements have been written in our time and before: Brutus' poems are among the best, the most important.'
Sam C. Nolutshungu – *The New African*[4]

413 Dhlomo, Herbert
The Girl who Killed to Save
Lovedale, South Africa, Lovedale Press, 1935. 46 pp. out-of-print
A play.

[1]vol. 10, no. 10, Nov. 1965
[2]no. 22, Aug. 1967
[3]no. 12, 1965
[4]no. 53, Nov. 1969

414 **Dhlomo, Herbert**
Valley of a Thousand Hills
Durban, Knox, 1941. 42 pp. out-of-print
A long poem, in praise of the magnificent scenery in the Natal province of South Africa.

415 **Dhlomo, Rolfes, Reginald**
An African Tragedy
Lovedale, South Africa, Lovedale Press, 1928. 40 pp. out-of-print

416 **Head, Bessie**
When Rain Clouds Gather
London, Gollancz, 1969. 188 pp. £1.50
Harmondsworth, Penguin Books, 1971. 30 p.
This novel follows the life of a black South African nationalist and idealist who – after serving two years in a South African prison for alleged subversive activities – flees his native country and escapes across the border into Botswana. Here, in the company of an English agricultural expert, he seeks to revive the poverty stricken village of Golema Mmidi, by introducing modern methods of farming techniques, despite heavy opposition from a local chief who wants to preserve the old system.

417 **Hutchinson, Alfred**
Road to Ghana
London, Gollancz, 1960. 190 pp. out-of-print
New York, John Day, 1960. 190 pp. out-of-print
An autobiographical account that tells of the treason trials, Alfred Hutchinson's attempts to escape from South Africa, and the travelogue of his flight by train and by plane that eventually brought him to Ghana, by way of Zambia, Malawi, and Tanzania. Doris Lessing has described the book as 'a record of brutality and stupidity' and 'also one of the most exciting and moving adventure stories'.

418 **Hutchinson, Alfred**
The Rain-Killers
London, Univ. of London Press, 1964. 80 pp. 22½p
The tensions between the traditional and new ways of thought in a small village community form the core of this four-act play set in Swaziland.

419 **Jabavu, Noni**
Drawn in Colour: African contrasts
London, John Murray, 1963. 261 pp. £1.05
New York, St Martin's Press, 1962. 208 pp. out-of-print
This is a picture of the life the author lived among her Xhosa people in South Africa, and her visit to a sister in Uganda. She says, 'It is a personal account of an individual African's experiences and impressions of the differences between East and South Africans in their contact with Westernisation.'

420 **Jabavu, Noni**
The Ochre People: scenes from South African life
London, John Murray, 1963. 261 pp. £1.05
New York, St Martin's Press, 1963. 261 pp. out-of-print
The author returns home to her Xhosa people in this autobiographical account of her visits to her family at Middledrift, to an uncle at Confluence farm in Pondoland, and to 'Big mother' in Johannesburg.

421 **Kunene, Mazisi**
Zulu Poems
London, Andre Deutsch, 1970. 96 pp. £1.50 (90p pap.)
New York, Africana Publishing Corp., 1970. 96 pp. $4.95 ($1.95 pap.)
A collection of poems – with accompanying notes – several of which the author originally wrote in Zulu. In his introduction Kunene stresses that 'these are not English poems, but poems directly evolved from a Zulu literary tradition.'

422 **La Guma, Alex**
A Walk in the Night
Ibadan, Mbari, 1962. 90 pp. out-of-print
A short story. See 424.

*423 **La Guma, Alex**
And a Threefold Cord
Berlin, Seven Seas Books, 1964. 173 pp.
New York, Jefferson Bookshop, distr. $1.00
A grim presentation of the degradation of human life under apartheid in the slums of a South African city, a ghetto perched on the edge of Cape Town. The community is depicted through the story of one family, the Pauls, and we follow them in their struggle to keep alive. The book was written during the author's house arrest in 1963.
'. . . La Guma's work is a considerable achievement.'
Robert McDowell – *Africa Today*[1]

*424 **La Guma, Alex**
A Walk in the Night
London, Heinemann Educ. Books, 1967 (African Writers Series, 35). 144 pp. 90p (40p pap.)
Evanston, Ill., Northwestern Univ. Press, 1967. 136 pp. $2.00
A new version of the original Mbari edition, now expanded to include six additional short stories. The feature story, 'A walk in the night', follows Michael Adonis, a coloured boy fired from his job for talking back to his white foreman. The story is set in Cape Town's toughest

[1]vol. 14, no. 3, June 1967

quarter, District Six, with its spivs, thugs, whores and derelicts 'doomed for a certain term to walk in the night'.

'... *although the story is both sordid and tragic, it makes refreshing reading after the revolving-door discussions of "what is African literature" that are unavoidable among those who care about literature in Africa ... A walk in the night is truly a slice of life.'*

Anthony M. Astrachan — *Black Orpheus*[1]

'... *the book is short, the story is moving and readable, Alex la Guma's effort is well worth a large circulation. It should take its place on the shelves along with Alan Paton's* Cry the beloved country *and Doris Lessing's* Five.'

Joseph Muwanga — *Transition*[2]

425 **La Guma, Alex**
The Stone Country
Berlin, Seven Seas Books, 1967. 169 pp. DM. 3.00
New York, Jefferson Bookshop, distr. $1.00
Dedicated 'to the daily average of 70,351 prisoners in South African gaols in 1964', La Guma's third novel presents another phase of life in South Africa, based on his experiences in prison, when he was jailed for illegal activities against the state.

426 **Matshikiza, Todd**
Chocolates for my Wife: slices of my life
London, Hodder and Stoughton, 1961. 128 pp. 62½p
An autobiographical account by Matshikiza — who won fame through his successful musical *King Kong* — of his life in London.
'... *a marvellous book; its spontaneous inspiration and deep originality have immediately placed it well above those written by story-tellers or professional novelists.'*

Salem Okonga — *Présence Africaine*[3]

427 **Modisane, Bloke** (pseud. for **Modisane, William**)
Blame me on History
London, Thames and Hudson, 1963. 311 pp. out-of-print
New York, Dutton, 1963. 311 pp. out-of-print

428 **Mphahlele, Ezekiel**
Man Must Live, and other stories
Cape Town, African Bookman, 1947. 60 pp. illus. out-of-print
Ibadan, Ministry of Education, 1958. 60 pp. out-of-print

429 **Mphahlele, Ezekiel**
The Living and the Dead, and other stories

Ibadan, Ministry of Education, 1961. 66 pp. out-of-print

*430 **Mphahlele, Ezekiel**
Down Second Avenue
London, Faber, 1959. 222 pp. out-of-print†
Berlin, Seven Seas Books, 1962. 222 pp. out-of-print
New York, Jefferson Bookshop, distr. $1.00
London, Faber, 1965. 183 pp. out-of-print
Both an autobiographical novel and a social commentary on a childhood in the crowded back streets of a ghetto area in Pretoria, South Africa.
'... *is at once a personal anecdote and a social comment, a factual statement, and a cry from the heart ... as a tale of childhood and of a unique society in Africa* Down Second Avenue *makes fascinating reading; as a measure of human being outraged it cannot fail to move the least committed reader to compassion and a deep and lasting anger and a thankfulness that he was not born into that part of Africa where, by the chance of birth, he is either oppressed or oppressor.'*

Diana Speed —*Black Orpheus*[4]

'... *a brilliant contribution to what is a new genre of our intensely race-conscious century — the autobiography as a vehicle of protest ... Mr Mphahlele shows himself in this work to be master of literary montage.'*

Robert McDowell —*Africa Today*[5]

431 **Mphahlele, Ezekiel**
In Corner B
Nairobi, East African Publ. House, 1967. 208 pp. EAshs 8.50
Evanston, Ill., Northwestern Univ. Press, distr.
A collection of twelve short stories capturing the atmosphere and tensions that make up life in present-day South Africa. The lead story, 'Mrs Plum in Corner B', portrays a 'liberal' white woman and her obscure physical attachment to her dogs, amidst a world of iniquities.

432 **Mphahlele, Ezekiel**
The Wanderers
New York, Macmillan, 1970. 320 pp. $5.95
This four-part novel revolves around Timi, a black South African journalist who seeks to expose South African injustice; around the narrative of a liberal white South African journalist, his friend; around the political

[1]no. 14, Feb. 1964
[2]vol. 4, no. 10, Sept. 1963
[3]vol. 11, no. 39
[4]no. 6, Nov. 1959
[5]vol. 14, no. 3, 1967

†to be reissued in Faber's Papercovered Editions, and by Doubleday, New York

situation in Africa observed by Timi in exile in Nigeria; and around Timi's frustration, as an exile teaching in Kenya, with his life, with Africa, and with his son.

433 Murray, A. A.
The Blanket
New York, Vanguard Press, 1958. 192 pp. out-of-print

434 Nkosi, Lewis
The Rhythm of Violence
London and New York, Oxford Univ. Press, 1964 (Three Crowns Book). 76 pp. 27½p/$1.00
A three-act play set in Johannesburg in the early 1960's, dealing with the personal and ideological struggles between black and white South Africans, the brutality of the police and the problems arising from attempts at racial co-operation.

*435 Nkosi, Lewis
Home and Exile
London, Longmans, 1965. 136 pp. 90p (37½p pap.)
A collection of essays on three major themes: 'Home', meaning South Africa; 'Exile' and Nkosi's encounter with New York; and 'Literary'. The latter covers essays on Africa in Negro-American poetry; 'Black power or Souls of Black Writers'; a survey of modern African drama; an account of the African writers' conference in Kampala in 1962; a review of Mphahlele's *The African Image*; and an article on fiction by black South Africans.
'... Lewis Nkosi has produced a slim but superb book.'
William A. Payne — *Africa Report*[1]

436 Plaatje, Solomon Thekisho
Mhudi: an epic of South African native life a hundred years ago
Lovedale, South Africa, Lovedale Press, 1930. 225 pp. out-of-print
New York, Negro Univ. Press, 1970 (Reprint). 225 pp. $9.50

437 Rive, Richard
African Songs
Berlin, Seven Seas Books, 1963. 149 pp. out-of-print
A collection of short stories.

438 Rive, Richard
Emergency
London, Faber 1964. 251 pp. 90p
New York, Macmillan, 1970. 250 pp. $1.50
The main action of this novel takes place in and

around Cape Town between the 28th and the 30th of March, 1960. Through a series of flashbacks it traces the events that led to the shootings in Sharpeville and Lange, the growing conflict that culminated in the day a state of emergency was declared, and how the situation affects the life of Andrew Dreyer, a young coloured school teacher, who is having an illegal affair with a white girl in violation of the immorality act. Ezekiel Mphahlele adds an introduction to the American paperback reissue.

Zambia

WORKS
439 Mulikita, Fwanyanga M.
Shaka Zulu
London, Longmans, 1967, 74 pp. 25p illus.
New York, Humanities Press, distr. $1.25
A play about the great Zulu leader, Shaka (or Chaka), who, with his predecessor Dingiswayo, was the founder of the Zulu nation. The events of the play cover many years and are linked by chroniclers, who also serve to give accounts of battles and events that cannot be shown on stage.

440 Mulikita, Fwanyanga M.
A Point of No Return
London, Macmillan, 1968. 112 pp. £1.05
Lusaka, National Educational Co. of Zambia Ltd, 1968. 112 pp. 80N
'Human caterpillars were eating away the leaves of his family', 'A Doctor of Philosophy changes his mind', 'A baby reforms a notorious thief' are some of the eleven short stories in this collection. The author was Zambia's first Ambassador to the United Nations.

[1]vol. 11, no. 6, June 1966

PART II: WRITINGS IN FRENCH AND IN ENGLISH TRANSLATION

WEST AFRICA

Cameroon

ANTHOLOGIES AND CRITICAL WORKS

441 **Fouda, Basile-Juleat**, *et al.*, ed.
Littérature camerounaise
Cannes, Imp. Aegitna, 1961. 175 pp. illus. out-of-print.
(Reprinted in *African poems in French*. Nendeln, Liechtenstein, Kraus Reprint, 1970. $27,00)

442 **Lagneau, Lilyan** ed.
Neuf poètes camerounais
Yaoundé, Ed. C.L.E., 1965. 112 pp. out-of-print
A poetry collection of works by Désiré Essama, Mbida, Elolongué Epanya Yondo, Nyunai, Charles Ngandé, Jean-Louis Dongmo, Okala Alene, Ernest Alima, René Philombe, and Léon-Marie Ayissi. The editor provides a brief introduction.

443 **Melone, Thomas**
The Novels of Mongo Beti
London, Heinemann Educ. Books, 1971 (in preparation)

*444 **Mercier, Roger**, and **Battestini, M** and **S.** eds.
Mongo Beti: écrivain camerounais
Paris, Nathan, 1964 (Littérature africaine, 5). 64 pp. F3.00
A critical appreciation and analysis of Beti's work. Includes a bibliography and extracts from reviews.

*445 **Mercier, Roger**, and **Battestini, M.** and **S.** eds.
Ferdinand Oyono: écrivain camerounais
Paris, Nathan, 1964 (Littérature africaine, 8). 64 pp. F3.00
A critical appreciation and analysis of Oyono's work, supplemented by a bibliography and extracts from reviews.

WORKS

446 **Ayissi, Léon-Marie**
Contes et berceuses Beti
Yaoundé, Ed. C.L.E., 1966 (Collection Abbia). 94 pp. CFA 210
New York, Africana Publ. Corp.; distr. $1.75
The author's childhood memories are reflected in this small collection of traditional tales and lullabies.

447 **Ayissi, Léon-Marie**
Les innocents
Yaoundé, Ed. C.L.E., 1969 (Collection C.L.E. Théâtre, 2). 48 pp. CFA 150
New York, Africana Publ. Corp., distr. $1.25
A tragedy in five acts centring around a conflict between the clan and the idea of romantic love.

*448 **Bebey, Francis**
Le fils d'Agatha Moudio
Yaoundé, Ed. C.L.E., 1967 (Collection Abba). 208 pp. CFA 330
New York, Africana Publ. Corp. distr. $2.75
The hero of this novel (or fable) is Mbenda, a young man from a fishing village at the mouth of the Wouri river. In obedience to local tradition, he marries the girl his father chose for him on his deathbed, though his heart longs for another, Agatha Moudio. The novel won the Grand Prix Littéraire de l'Afrique Noire 1968, awarded by the Association des écrivains de langue française (mer et outre-mer); English, German, Italian and Dutch translations are now in preparation.
'... un authentique roman, avec des personnages bien vivants pris dans le mouvement alerte d'une action méticuleusement construite; et surtout le sourire qui plane sur les lèvres de Bebey, la malice qui brille dans ses yeux, sa plume, tres efficace, les restitue fidèlement.'
Abbia[1]

'... du début au coup de théâtre de la fin, se fablieu camerounais est un petit chef-d'oeuvre de burlesque tendre.'
Revue française d'études politiques africaines[2]

*449 **Bebey, Francis**
Embarras et Cie: nouvelles et poèmes
Yaoundé, Ed. C.L.E., 1968 (Collection Abbia). 117 pp. CFA 240
New York, Africana Publ. Corp., distr. $1.75
A collection of eight short stories, each of which is supplemented by a poem.
'... Francis Bebey a donné a ce nouvel ouvrage un rythme a la fois concerté et naturel ... chacun des poèmes est une respiration, une variation lyrique sur

[1]no. 17–18, June/Sept. 1967
[2]no. 32, Aug. 1968.

un thème plus ou moins clairement évoqué par l'anecdote précédente.'
Revue française d'études politiques africaines[1]

450 **Bengono, Jacques**
La perdrix blanche: trois contes moraux
Yaoundé, Ed. C.L.E., 1966 (Collection Abbia).
92 pp. CFA 180

*451 **Beti, Mongo** (pseud. for **Biyidi, Alexandre**)
Le pauvre Christ de Bomba
Paris, Laffont, 1956. 371 pp. out-of-print
Nendeln, Liechtenstein, Kraus Reprint, 1970.
371 pp. $19.00
Written in the form of a diary by the 'boy' of Reverend Father Superior Drumont, this novel centres around the work of a Catholic mission in a remote district of Cameroon in 1938. It is a sharp indictment of white missionary activities in Africa. An English translation by Gerald Moore will be published in 1971.

452 **Beti, Mongo** (pseud. for **Biyidi, Alexandre**)
Mission terminée
Paris, Corrêa, 1957. 255 pp. F5.40
In English *translation*, see 453

*453 **Beti, Mongo** (pseud. for **Biyidi, Alexandre**)
Mission Accomplished
(Trans. from the French by Peter Green)
New York, Macmillan, 1958. 200 pp. out-of-print.
London, Muller, 1958 (publ. as *Mission to Kala*)
207 pp. out-of-print
London, Heinemann Educ. Books 1964 (African Writers Series, 13). 183 pp. 35p
New York, Humanities Press; distr. $1.00
Awarded the Prix Sainte-Beuve, this is Mongo Beti's second novel. Jean-Marie Medza, a young student who has failed his exams, returns to his native village in Southern Cameroon. Despite his academic failure, he finds his prestige and standing among the village community is considerable on account of the mere fact that he has been to College. He becomes involved in a delicate task — to retrieve and bring back a villager's wife who has run off with a man from another tribe and fled to her relatives at Kala. When Jean-Marie reaches Kala he is well received by the villagers, but the woman he seeks is away: he is generously entertained and loaded with gifts, whilst patiently waiting for the woman's return from her adventure. His mission is eventually successful, and he returns home. But he finds himself unable to come to terms with his family, their way of life, and the degenerate state of their society, and he leaves home for good.

454 **Beti, Mongo** (pseud. for **Biyidi, Alexandre**)
Le roi miraculé
Paris, Corrêa, 1958. 255 pp. F6.50
In English *translation*, see 455.

*455 **Beti, Mongo** (pseud. for **Biyidi, Alexandre**)
King Lazarus
(Trans. from the French by Peter Green)
London, Muller, 1960 (reprinted 1969). 191 pp. £1.05
London, Heinemann Educ. Books, 1970 (African writers series, 77). 190 pp. 40p
New York, Macmillan, 1970. 256 pp. $1.50
The Chief of Essazam, a powerful pagan king and spiritual leader of his people, is miraculously saved from a severe sickness, ostensibly by being 'baptized' by his old aunt with the aid of several jugs of water. The local missionary Le Guen is quick to put the King's recovery to use for his own purposes, and persuades the Chief to let it be believed that he has returned from the dead, to renounce his tribal ways and adopt Christianity. The repercussions that ensue are highly complicated.

Biyidi, Alexandre
See **Beti, Mongo,** and **Boto, Eza**

456 **Boto, Eza** (pseud. for **Biyidi, Alexandre**)
Ville cruelle
Paris, Les editions africaines, 1964. 221 pp. F7.70
A novel set in Tanga, Southern Cameroon, in the nineteen-thirties.

457 **Dervain, Eugène**
La reine scélérate, suivi de *La langue et le scorpion*
Yaoundé, Ed. C.L.E., 1968 (Collection Abbia).
106 pp. CFA 300
New York, Africana Publ. Corp., distr. $2.25
Two historical legendary plays set in the kingdom of Ségou in ancient Mali during the latter part of the eighteenth century.

458 **Dervain, Eugène**
Abra Pokou
Yaoundé, Ed. C.L.E., 1969 (Collection C.L.E. Théâtre, 3). 15 pp. CFA 150
New York, Africana Publishing Corp., distr. $1.25
This short one-act play — inspired by a short story by Bernard Dadié — centres around Abra Pokou, chief of the Amansi tribe.

Dipoko, Mbella Sonne
See 131, 132

---

[1]no. 32, Aug. 1968.

459 **Ewandé, Daniel**
Vive le Président: la fête africaine
Paris, Albin Michel, 1968. 224 pp. out-of-print

460 **Evembe, François**
Sur la terre en passant
Paris, Présence Africaine, 1966. 122 pp. F6.00

461 **Ikelle-Matiba, Jean**
Cette Afrique-là
Paris, Présence Africaine, 1963. 241 pp. out-of-print
Recounts the life of Franz Momha during the German colonial days in the Cameroons in the late nineteenth century. The book was awarded the Grand Prix Littéraire de l'Afrique Noire in 1963.
'. . . un document de premier ordre qui fera date.'
Afrique Contemporaine[1]

462 **Isaak, Tchoumba Ngouankeu**
Autour du lac Tchad (contes)
Yaoundé, Ed. C.L.E., 1969 (Collection Abbia). 181 pp. CFA 450
New York, Africana Publ. Corp., distr. $2.75
Folk tales from the diverse ethnic groups of Cameroon and Tchad, which the author wrote during his time in jail as a political prisoner.

463 **Matip, Benjamin**
A la belle étoile. Contes et nouvelles d'Afrique
Paris, Présence Africaine, 1962. 93 pp. F5.50
Short stories and tales from Africa.
'. . . elle fait appel à des ressources verbales et poétiques d'une très rare qualité. Le style est sobre, l'écriture rapide, émaillée de notations d'une précision foudroyante. N'oublions pas, enfin, l'humour de Matip, un humour acide qui atteint parfois les sommets de l'ironie . . .'
Jeune Afrique[2]

464 **Mohamadou, Eldridge**, and **Mayssal, Henriette**
Contes et poèmes Foulbés de la Bénoué
Yaoundé, Ed. C.L.E., 1965 (Collection Abbia). 84 pp. illus. out-of-print
Folk stories and traditional poems – in the original Foulbe text with parallel French translation – collected by students in the northern areas of Cameroon, and here translated by a Cameroon linguist.

465 **Mvomo, Remy Medou**
Africa ba'a
Yaoundé, Ed. C.L.E., 1969 (Collection Abbia). 181 pp. CFA 450
New York, Africana Publ. Corp., distr. $2.75
Set in an imaginary village in South Cameroon, the core of this novel centres around a young man's striving for an education, and a government post.

466 **Ngo Mai, Jeanne**
Poèmes sauvages et lamentations
Monte Carlo, Palais Miami, 1967 (Coll. Les cahier des poètes de notre temps, 362). 111 pp. out-of-print [?]
Poetry collection.

467 **Nyunai, Jean-Paul**
La nuit de ma vie
Paris, Debresse, 1961. 48 pp. F4.80
(Reprinted in *African poems in French*. Nendeln, Liechtenstein, Kraus Reprint, 1970. $27.00)
Poems.

468 **Nyunai, Jean-Paul**
Pigments sang
Paris, Debresse, 1963. 31 pp. F4.50
(Reprinted in *African poems in French*. Nendeln, Liechtenstein, Kraus Reprint, 1970. $27.00)
Poems.

469 **Nyunai, Jean-Paul**
Chansons pour Ngo Lima
Monte Carlo, Palais Miami, 1964 (Coll. Les cahier de poètes de notre temps, 251). 29 pp. out-of-print. (?)

470 **Nzouankeu, Jacques Mariel**
Le souffle des ancêtres: nouvelles
Yaoundé, Ed. C.L.E., 1965. 107 pp. CFA 200
New York, Africana Publ. Corp., distr. $1.75
Four short stories around the theme of human clashes with mystic forces.

471 **Oyono, Ferdinand**
Une vie de boy
Paris, Juillard, 1956. 183 pp. (New edn 1969) 160 pp. F15.70
In English *translation*, see 472

*472 **Oyono, Ferdinand**
Houseboy
(Trans. from the French by John Reed)
London, Heinemann Educ. Books, 1966 (African Writers Series, 29). 144 pp. 90p (35p pap.)
New York, Macmillan (published as *Boy*), 1970. 150pp. $1.25
Written in the form of a diary, this novel describes Toundi Joseph's experiences as a steward in the household of a French District Commissioner in Cameroon, the 'Commandant du Cercle' Robert Decazy, and his wife Madame Decazy. It presents a critical and satirical view of colonial administrators and Christian missionaries. To the new American edition Edris Makward contributes an introduction.
'. . . humour and brutality are depicted with the

[1]Nov., 1963
[2]Dec., 1963 [?]

same simplicity and unpretentiousness which give the reader of this novel a feeling that the author's description has been faithful to his observation.'
Eldred Jones — *Bull. of the Assoc. for African Literature in English*[1]

'. . . John Reed's English translation — with which I have nothing at all to quarrel — will surely enable non-French speaking readers to come to terms good humouredly with this masterpiece of anti-colonialist satire.'
Sunday O. Anozie — *Présence Africaine*[2]

473 Oyono, Ferdinand
Le vieux nègre et la médaille
Paris, Juillard, 1956. 211 pp. out-of-print
In English *translation, see 474.*

*474 Oyono, Ferdinand
The Old Man and the Medal
(Trans. from the French by John Reed)
London, Heinemann Educ. Books, 1967 (African Writers Series, 39). (pap. edn 1969) 167 pp. $1.05 (37½p pap.)
New York, Humanities Press, distr. $3.25 ($1.50 pap.)
This satire on colonialism is viewed through the eyes of Meka, an old cocoa farmer in the village, a devoted Christian and God-fearing man. His two sons have died fighting for the white man, and the Catholic mission has taken his land. He has always been loyal to the white man, and is, in their eyes 'un bon Nègre', a 'good native'. As compensation for his services to France he is to receive a medal, awarded by the French administration. When the great day of his decoration, 14th July, arrives, Meka is early but the Governor General is late. Waiting in the hot sun for the ceremony to commence, Meka's attitude towards the Europeans, influenced by his urgent need to relieve himself and the excruciating pain caused by his new shoes, is somewhat modified. The events following the ceremony confirm Meka's revised estimation of the white man. Politely ignored at the reception, he gets dead drunk, staggers back to his village in a violent tropical storm, loses his medal and is arrested and imprisoned for vagrancy. Eventually recognized and released he returns home cursing the Europeans, his attitute to the colonial administrators vastly changed.
'. . . a devastating indictment of colonialism in fictional terms . . . the point is that Oyono's critique of the colonial set-up is made a hundred times more effective by its brilliance as literature.'
K. W. — *West Africa*[3]

'. . . has the quality, so rare in modern African writing, of bringing together both the comic and the sad elements in the situation of preindependence Africa . . . makes thoroughly enjoyable reading . . .

the translation from the original French by John Reed is excellent.'
Jeanette Kamara — *African Literature Today*[4]

475 Oyono, Ferdinand
Chemin d'Europe
Paris, Juillard, 1960. 196 pp. out-of-print
The hero of Oyono's third novel, Aki Barnabas, is the 'aboyeur' or watchdog in the boutique of a Greek trader in an imaginary place south of Yaoundé. He is haunted by a strong desire for a white bourgeois Frenchwoman to an extent that becomes near obsession.

476 Oyono-Mbia, Guillaume
Trois prétendants, un mari
Yaoundé, Éd. C.L.E., 1964. 128 pp. CFA 170
New York, Africana Publ. Corp., distr. $1.75
A light-hearted play, with music and dancing, that tells of the efforts of a father to obtain the best bride-price for his educated daughter. In English *translation, see 477.*

477 Oyono-Mbia, Guillaume
Three Suitors: One Husband; and *Until Further Notice*
London, Methuen, 1968. 100 pp. 37½p
A translation of the preceding entry plus *Until further notice*, a play written *in English.* The action focuses on a group of villagers waiting in vain for the triumphal return of an educated daughter of the village, who has married an important government official. The play won first prize in the 1967 BBC African Service Drama competition.

478 Oyono-Mbia, Guillaume
Jusqu'à nouvel avis
Yaoundé, Ed. C.L.E., 1970 (Collection C.L.E. Théâtre). 48 pp. CFA 150
New York, Africana Publishing Corp., distr. $1.50
Prompted by the success of the English edition of this comedy (*Until further notice*), Oyono-Mbia here presents an adaptation in French.

479 Philombe, René (pseud. for Ombede, Phillipe Louis)
Lettres de ma cambuse
Yaoundé, Ed. C.L.E., 1965 (Collection Abbia). 64 pp. illus. CFA 140
New York, Africana Publ. Corp., distr. $1.25
Not originally intended for publication, this series of 'letters' or short stories was written whilst René Philombe was in seclusion in a

[1]no. 4, Mar. 1966
[2]no. 62, 1967
[3]no. 2672, Aug. 17. 1968
[4]no. 3, 1969

small Cameroonian village, recovering from an illness. The book was awarded the Prix Mottart de l'Académie Française.

480 Philombe, René (pseud. for **Ombede, Phillipe Louis**)
Sola ma chérie
Yaoundé, C.L.E., 1966 (Collection Abbia). 124 pp. CFA 240
New York, Africana Publ. Corp., distr. $1.75
A novel with an underlying social theme.

481 Philombe, René
Un sorcier blanc à Zangali
Yaoundé, Ed. C.L.E., 1969 (Collection Abbia). 187 pp. CFA 450
New York, Africana Publishing Corp., distr. $2.25
A new white missionary arrives in the Beti village of Zangali, and this novel recounts the stir this causes among the villagers and the events that follow.

482 Towo-Atangana, Gaspard, and **Towo-Atangana, Françoise**
Nden-bobo, l'araignée toilière (conte béti)
Yaoundé, Ed. C.L.E., 1966 (Collection Abbia). 36 pp. CFA 150
New York, Africana Publ. Corp., distr. $1.25
Nden-Bobo, the name given to a spider's web, plays an important role in the daily life of a people living in the Béti region of Cameroon. This volume presents a transcription and translation from an original chant in the Eton language. The authors also provide an introduction and explanatory notes.

483 Epanya Yondo, Elelongue
Kamerun! Kamerun!
Paris, Présence Africaine, 1960. 96 pp. out-of-print
Poems, appearing in vernacular Cameroon languages, each with a French translation.

484 Tatti-Loutard, J. B.
Poèmes de la mer ·
Yaoundé, Ed. C.L.E., 1969 (Collection Abbia). 64 pp. CFA 150
New York, Africana Publishing Corp., distr. $2.25

Dahomey

***485 Mercier, Roger,** and **Battestini, M.** and **S.** eds.
Olympe, Bhêly-Quenum: écrivain dahoméen Paris, Nathan, 1964 (Littérature africaine, 4). 64 pp. F3.00
A critical presentation and appreciation of Bhêly-Quenum's writings, with extracts from his works and biographical details, as well as extracts from book reviews, and a glossary of vernacular terminology.

WORKS
486 Bhêly-Quenum, Olympe
Un piège sans fin
Paris, Stock, 1960. 255 pp. out-of-print
This novel, psychological in nature, is set among planters and stock-breeders in the north of Dahomey under colonial rule, and describes the events in the life of one of them, the farmer Ahouna Bakari.
'. . . a fresco from Dahomey, full of reality and lyricism.'
         Andree Clair — *Présence Africaine*[1]

***487 Bhêly-Quenum, Olympe**
Le chant du lac
Paris, Présence Africaine, 1965. 155 pp. F9.90
'. . . portrays on African community held in the grip of animism . . . Bhêly-Quenum combines humour and psychological penetration with a talent for evocative description; and the extraordinary richness of levels in this novel — its blending of folk legend, social criticism, symbolism, and allegory — makes it stand out among modern African fiction.'
         Thomas Cassirer — *African Forum*[2]

488 Dogbeh, Richard
Les eaux du Mono
Vire, Lec-Vire, 1963. 59 pp. out-of-print
(Reprinted in *African poems in French.* Nendeln, Liechtenstein, Kraus Reprint, 1970. $27.00)
Poems.

489 Dogbeh, Richard
Voyage au pays de Lénine
Yaoundé, Ed. C.L.E., 1967 (Collection Abbia). 96 pp. CFA 270
New York, Africana Publishing Corp., distr. $2.25
Richard Dogbeh visited Russia in 1966 at the invitation of the Union of Soviet Writers. This is his account of his impressions of that visit.

[1]vol. 8, no. 36, 1962
[2]vol. 2, no. 4, Spring 1967

490 **Dogbeh, Richard**
Rives mortelles
Porto-Novo, Silva, 1964. 36 pp. out-of-print
(Reprinted in *African poems in French*. Nendeln,
Liechtenstein, Kraus Reprint, 1970. $27.00)
Poems.

491 **Dogbeh, Richard**
Cap liberté
Yaoundé, Ed. C.L.E., 1969 (Collection Abbia).
76 pp. CFA 300
New York, Africana Publishing Corp., distr.
$1.75
A verse collection.

492 **Hazoumé, Paul**
Doguicimi
Paris, Larose, 1935. 511 pp. out-of-print
Drawing heavily upon traditional and oral
literature, this historical novel — set in pre-
colonial Dahomey — narrates the events of an
expedition of the kings of Abomey against the
Mahi tribe, through the adventures of a
Dahoman princess.

493 **Joachim, Paulin**
Anti-grâce
Paris, Presence Africaine, 1967. 64 pp. F8.10
A poetry volume.

Guinea

CRITICAL WORKS
*494 **Mercier, Roger,** and **Battestini, M.**
and **S.** eds.
Camara Laye: écrivain guinéen
Paris, Nathan, 1964 (Littérature africaine, 2).
64 pp. F3.00
A critical appreciation and presentation of
Camara Laye's writings, with extracts from
his works, a bibliography, extracts from reviews,
and a biographical feature.

WORKS
495 **Camara, Sikhe**
Poèmes de combat et de vérité
Honfleur-Paris, Oswald, 1967. 85 pp. F15.00

496 **Fodeba, Keita**
Aubé africaine
Paris, Séghers, 1965. 85 pp. F9.90
Poetry.

497 **Fodeba, Keita**
Le mâitre d'école, suivi de *Minuit*

Paris, Séghers, 1952. out-of-print
Plays.

498 **Laye, Camara**
L'enfant noir
Paris, Plon, 1953, 1965 (new illus. ed 'Coll.
Super', 1967). 256 pp. F15.00 illus. (Livre de
poche, 2699) 1970. 190 pp. F3.50
In English *translation*, see 499.

*499 **Laye, Camara**
The Dark Child
(Trans. from the French by James Kirkup)
New York, Noonday Press, 1954. 188 pp. out-of-
print
London, Collins, 1955 (publ. as *The African
Child*: Fontana Books, 1236). 159 pp. 22½p
New York, Farrar, Straus and Giroux, 1969
(Noonday paperbacks, N. 365: with an introduc-
tion by Philippe Thoby-Marcelin) 188 pp. $1.95
Camara Laye's autobiographical recollections of
childhood days in Guinea are recreated with
nostalgia. He describes his life in chronological
order: his early childhood days, portraying his
father with great respect and his mother with
love and tenderness, his attainment of manhood,
his initiation and circumcision ceremonies.
After finishing primary school he entered a
Technical College in Conakry, and four years
later was offered a scholarship to study engineering in Argenteuil near Paris. In France
Camara Laye's funds soon ran out. Confronted
with serious financial difficulties, he was obliged
to interrupt his studies and seek work in the
Simca car factories. Lonely and unhappy, he was
spurred to put down on paper these vivid memories of an African childhood, which he dedicated to his mother.
'It is not often that any reviewer gets the chance to
read a simple and natural work of art like this
work ... this book is high art, springing straight
from first sources, and woven instinctively into a
flowing pattern of deeply poetic prose. The book has
rightly made a sensation in France and it is hoped
that every encouragement will be given to this
young writer to enable him to continue a literary
career.'
                    Mercedes Mackay — *African Affairs*[1]

500 **Laye, Camara**
L'enfant noir
Edited by Joyce Hutchinson
London and New York, Cambridge Univ. Press,
1966. 196 pp. 62½p/$1.75
Another edition, presented here in the original
French, with an introduction, a bibliography,
and notes in English.

[1]vol. 55, no. 219, April 1956

501 **Laye, Camara**
Le regard du roi
Paris, Plon, 1965. 255 pp. out-of-print
In English *translation*, see 502.

•502 **Laye, Camara**
The Radiance of the King
(Trans. from the French by James Kirkup)
London, Collins, 1956. 318 pp. out-of-print
London, Collins, 1965 (Fontana Books, 1208).
284 pp. pap. 32½p
New York, Macmillan, 1970. 256 pp. $1.50
Clarence, the white hero of this symbolic novel,
is in search of the briefly glimpsed king whom he
wishes to serve. Having lost all his money at
cards, his financial resources exhausted, the
bankrupt Clarence is thrown out of his hotel.
Without any support from his fellow white men,
he is forced to beg for help and sustenance.
Clarence pins his hopes on the African king in
whose service he hopes to find peace. The novel
follows his search for the king, his gruelling
trek through the forest, his companions – the
beggar, the eunuch, the blacksmith and the
fortune-teller – to his life in Anzia, where
Clarence ultimately sees the full radiance of the
King and has his long-awaited encounter with
him. A great many interpretations have been
offered of *The Radiance of the King*. The English
publishers claim that the book is an allegory
of 'Man's search for God', while critics have
interpreted it as 'a search for identification'
(Gerald Moore), 'a tentative approach to the
mystery of our being – an approach which
suggests that a journey into the primitive, and
apparently utterly strange, can result in a self-
discovery altogether startling but none the less
illuminating' (John Ramsaraan), or, 'a lesson
in African wisdom' (Janheinz Jahn). The
American paperback reissue has an introduction by Albert Gérard.

503 **Laye, Camara**
Dramouss
Paris, Plon, 1966. 253 pp. F12.00
In English *translation*, see 504.

•504 **Laye, Camara**
A Dream of Africa
(Trans. from the French by James Kirkup)
London, Collins, 1968. 191 pp. £1.05
In this translation of Laye's third novel,
Dramouss, the narrator returns from six arduous
years in Paris, where he had fought poverty and
hunger, to his homeland in Africa, now on the
verge of independence. Through his family, his
friends and his new wife, he rediscovers his
own country, and sees its magic, religion and
the ancient skills of his people replaced by
political violence. A vision reveals to him a
terrifying period of unrest in the immediate

future. The novel is dedicated to the young
people of Africa in general, and of Guinea in
particular; it is a call to them to revive and
restore 'native ways of thinking'.
'... as with Laye's other works, one is struck by
the beauty of this poetic prose which loses nothing
in Mr Kirkup's admirable translation from the
French.'
S. K. Dabo – *African Affairs*[1]

Ivory Coast

CRITICAL WORKS

•505 **Mercier, Roger**, and **Battestini, M.
and S.** eds.
Bernard Dadié: écrivain ivoirien
Paris, Nathan, 1964 (Collection Littérature
africaine, 7). 64 pp. F3.00
A critical presentation and appreciation of
Dadié's work, with extracts from his writings
and from book reviews. Includes biographical
details and a bibliography.

506 **Quillateau, C.**
Bernard Binlin Dadié: l'homme et l'oeuvre.
Paris, Présence Africaine, 1967 (Coll. Approche).
176 pp. F12.00 illus.
In this critical study of Dadié's work, there is
a detailed introduction, excerpts from his poetry
and prose, an interview, quotations from book
reviews, and a bibliography.

WORKS

507 **Bognini, Joseph-Miezan**
Ce dur appel de l'espoir
Paris, Présence Africaine, 1960. 127 pp. F5.50
A volume of poetry.
'... shows all the virtues of true simplicity ... the
controlled fervour, quality of melody and innocence
of language give Bognini's poems great depth and
significance.'
Jacques Howlett – *Présence Africaine*[2]

508 **Dadié, Bernard**
Afrique debout!
Paris, Séghers, 1950. 43 pp. out-of-print
Poems.

509 **Dadié, Bernard**
Climbié
Paris, Seghers, 1953. 191 pp. out-of-print
Dadié's first novel is largely autobiographical
in content, reminiscent of Camara Laye's *African
child* (see 499). It recounts the childhood, upbringing, daily life and social environment of a

[1]vol. 69, no. 275, April 1970
[2]vol. 8, no. 36

boy living in pre-independent Ivory Coast. In its later chapters it is also concerned with the struggle of African trade unionists and nationalists under the French colonial administrators, with their determined assimilation policies. (An English translation will be published in 1971.)

510 **Dadié, Bernard**
Légendes africaines
Paris, Séghers, 1954. 127 pp. out-of-print
Alioune Diop has provided a preface to this collection of folk tales.

*511 **Dadié Bernard**
Le pagne noir: contes africains
Paris, Présence Africaine, 1955 (Collection Contes africains). 173 pp. F5.65
Another volume of African legends and fables.

512 **Dadié, Bernard**
La ronde des jours
Paris, Séghers, 1956. 59 pp. out-of-print

513 **Dadié, Bernard**
Un nègre à Paris
Paris, Présence Africaine, 1959. 219 pp. out-of-print
A satirical view of Paris and Parisians, seen through the eyes of an African student. In this novel Dadié makes repeated comparisons between his own culture and customs and those of the French people.

*514 **Dadié, Bernard**
Patron de New York
Paris, Présence Africaine, 1964 (Collection Chronique). 311 pp. F12.90
Dadié's personal and satirical account of life and society in New York in particular, and of American civilization in general. The book is the result of the author's four-month stay in the U.S., and is perhaps the francophone equivalent to John Pepper Clark's *America their America*, see 240.

*515 **Dadié, Bernard**
Légendes et poèmes: Afrique debout!; Légendes africaines; Climbié; La ronde des jours
Paris, Séghers, 1966. 260 pp. F13.50
An anthology of previously published poetry and folk tales, together with the novel *Climbié* in its entirety.

516 **Dadié, Bernard**
Hommes de tous les continents
Paris, Présence Africaine, 1967. 103 pp. F12.30
A new book of poetry.

517 **Dadié, Bernard**
La ville où nul ne meurt

Paris, Présence Africaine, 1969. 212 pp. F12.00
A sequel to *Patron de New York,* presenting Dadié's view of Rome, and the way of life in contemporary Roman society.
'. . . c'est un recit agréable et bien enlevé par un écrivain doué et qui a le don de raconter, la grace d'observer et de rendre, ce qui n'est pas donné a tout le monde.'
Paulin Joachim — *Bingo*[1]

518 **Dadié, Bernard**
Sidi Maitre Escroc; Situation difficile; Serment d'amour
Yaoundé, Ed. C.L.E., 1969 (Collection C.L.E. Théâtre, 4). 32 pp. CFA 150
New York, Africana Publishing Corp., distr. $1.25
Three short plays.

519 **Dadié, Bernard**
Monsieur Thogo-Gnini
Paris, Présence Africaine, 1970. 115 pp. F9.60
A satirical play that was first performed — with considerable success — at the First Pan-African Cultural Festival in Algiers in 1969.

520 **Koné, Maurice**
La guirlande des verbes
Paris, Grassin, 1961 (Collection Poésie nouvelle, 22). 32 pp. out-of-print
(Reprinted in *African poems in French.* Nendeln, Liechtenstein, Kraus Reprint, 1970. $27,00)

521 **Koné Maurice**
Le jeune homme de Bouaké
Paris, Grassin, 1963. 64 pp. F8.00
A novel.

522 **Koné, Maurice**
Au seuil du crépuscule: poèmes
Rodes, Subervie, 1965. 40 pp. out-of-print [?]

523 **Kourouma, Ahmadou**
Les soleils des indépendances
Montreal, Les Presses de l'Université de Montréal, 1968. 171 pp. Can. $2.50
A deposed chief has to adjust himself to living among the proletariat. It is the story of Fama, the last legitimate ruler of Horodougou in the Malinke region, exiled after losing his chieftaincy to his cousin Lacina, who proved to be more acceptable to the colonial administrators.
'. . . a variation of the familiar "things fall apart" theme . . . Kourouma manages to create an atmosphere of intimacy . . . he does not hesitate to let the images, the rhythms, the words of his mother tongue pierce the polished surface of polite prose . . . the author, an Eburnean working as an actuary in

[1]no. 200, Sept. 69

Algiers, his adopted home, has presented us with an exciting first novel.'

Willfried Feuser — *The New African*[1]

524 **Loba, Ake**
Kocoumbo, l'étudiant noir
Paris, Flammarion, 1960. 269 pp. F12.00
An African student thrust into a working-class environment in Paris.
'... profoundly original and of considerable significance.'

Guy de Bosschère — *Présence Africaine*[2]

525 **Nokan, Charles**
Le soleil, noir point
Paris, Présence Africaine, 1962. 71 pp. F5.20
Autobiographical in nature, this novel introduces a new genre of literature. A succession of over sixty brief *tableau* are presented, centring around the major themes of love, rebellion, despair and hope.

526 **Nokan, Charles**
Violent était le vent
Paris, Présence Africaine, 1966. 181 pp. F10.80
Novel.

527 **Nokan, Charles**
Les malheurs de Tchakô: pièce en cinq tableaux
Honfleur-Paris, Oswald, 1968 (Collection Théâtre africain, 3). 98 pp. F9.00
A play.

Mali

CRITICAL WORKS
528 **Mercier, Roger,** and **Battestini, M.** and **S.** eds.
Seydou Badian: écrivain malien   ·
Paris, Nathan, 1968 (Collection Littérature africaine, 10). 64 pp. F3.00
A critical study and appreciation of Badian's writings, with extracts from his works and from book reviews. Includes biographical details and a bibliography.

WORKS
529 **Ba, Amadou-Hampate**
Kaidara
Paris, Juillard, 1969 (Collection Classiques africains). 179 pp. F25.00
This piece of oral literature is a long allegorical poem transcribed into French from the Peul; the original text accompanies the translation. The author is a prominent historian.

530 **Badian, Seydou**
La mort de Chaka: pièce en cinq tableaux
Paris, Présence Africaine, 1962. 61 pp. F5.00

A historical play based on Thomas Mofolo's *Chaka*, which narrates in dramatic form the death, by assassination at the hands of his brothers, of Chaka, the chief who founded the Zulu nation.

530a **Badian, Seydou**
The Death of Chaka. A play in five tableaux (Trans. from the French by Clive Wake)
Nairobi, Oxford Univ. Press, 1968 (New Drama from Africa, 1). 52 pp. 55p
An English translation of the preceeding entry.

531 **Badian, Seydou**
Sous l'orage
Paris, Présence Africaine, 1963. 155 pp. F6.50
A novel with pre-independence Sudan as a setting.

532 **Niane, Djibril Tamsir**
Soundjata ou l'épopée mandique
Paris, Présence Africaine, 1960. 156 pp. F5.00
In English *translation*, see 533

*533 **Niane, Djibril Tamsir**
Sundiata: an epic of old Mali
(Trans. by G. D. Pickett)
London, Longmans, 1965 (Forum series). 96 pp. map 30p
New York, Humanities Press; distr. $1.50
The preservers and 'archivists' of historical oral tradition in French West Africa are the griots. This faithful translation of a griot's tale belongs to the sphere of historical novels. It tells the story of Sundiata, founder and hero of the medieval Mandingo empire, one of the great Negro kingdoms of the late middle ages. 'The griot,' as Niane explains in his preface, 'who occupies the chair of history of a village and who bears the title 'Belen-Tigui', is a very respectable gentleman and has toured Mali. He has gone from village to village to hear the teaching of great masters; he has learnt the art of historical oratory through long years.'

*534 **Ouologuem, Yambo**
Le devoir de violence
Paris, Seuil 1968. 208 pp. F24.00 (F15.00 pap.)
Yambo Ouologuem, the first African writer to receive a major French literary award, won the Prix Renaudot 1968 for this first novel. It is a kind of epic of a fictitious Sudanese empire. His main thesis is that the black man has been created and formed by violence, and that three forces in his history are largely responsible for the Negro's 'slave' mentality and character: first,

---

[1]no. 52, 1969
[2]no. 30, 1950

the ancient African emperors and notables; then the Arabs; and lastly, since the mid-nineteenth century, the European colonial administrators. English translations are in preparation, see 536.

Like Orwell, who in Burmese Days *exposed the essential weakness of colonial rule, the young Malian Yambo Ouologuem in his fascinating first novel,* Le Devoir de violence, *presents the white colonialist as a mere pawn of the native potentate... Yambo Ouologuem has succeeded in blending the legendary and the real without ever lapsing into pomposity or sentimentality.'*

Hena Maes-Jelinek — *African Literature Today*[1]

535 Ouologuem, Yambo
Lettre à la France Nègre
Paris, Edmond Nalis, 1968 (Collection Le document du Mois). 220 pp. F15.00
Contains 'Lettre au Président de la République Française', 'Lettre aux couples mixtes', 'Lettre à tous ceux qui fréquentent les Nègres', 'Lettre aux femmes nègrement seules', 'Lettre à tous les racistes', and several others.
'... the essays are primarily addressed to Europeans, especially bogus liberals and paternalists, and probe in particular the seamy side of the noble sentiments sometimes expressed in France about Africa. I am told even to a French reader he is sometimes obscure and convoluted, but the brilliance of his style, his verbal acrobatics and brazen handling of language illuminates the occasional profundities.'
K. W. — *West Africa*[2]

536 Ouologuem, Yambo
Bound to Violence
(Translated from the French)
London, Secker and Warburg, 1971. *ca.* £1.50 (in preparation)
London, Heinemann Educ. Books, 1971 (African Writers Series, 99). (in preparation)
New York, Harcourt, Brace, World, 1971 (in preparation)

537 Sissoko, Fily-Dabo
Crayons et portraits
Mulhouse, Imprimerie Union, 1953. 79 pp. out-of-print

538 Sissoko, Fily-Dabo
Harmakhis: poèmes du terroir africain
Paris, Éd. de la Tour du Guet, 1955 (Collection Poétique). 80 pp. out-of-print
Poems from the treasures of 'the soil', inspired by oral traditions.

539 Sissoko, Fily-Dabo
Sagesse noire, sentences et proverbes malinkes
Paris, Éd. de la Tour du Guet, 1955. 63 pp. F6.00
A collection of Malinke proverbs, sayings and stories.

540 Sissoko, Fily-Dabo
La passion de Djimé
Paris, Éd. de la Tour du Guet, 1956. 115 pp. out-of-print.

541 Sissoko, Fily-Dabo
La savane rouge
Avignon, Les Presses Universelles, 1962. 141 pp. F6.15
Recounts the story of French repression of a Tuareg rising during the first world war.

542 Sissoko, Fily-Dabo
Poemes de l'Afrique noire: Feux de brousse Harmakhis; Fleurs et chardons
Paris, Debresse, 1963. 171 pp. out-of-print
A collection of poetry.

Nigeria

543 Balogun, Ola
Shango, suivi de *Le roi-eléphant*
Honfleur-Paris, Oswald, 1968 (Collection Théâtre africain, 4). 96 pp. F9.00
These two short three-act plays are the only writing in French to have so far come from Nigeria. *Shango* is a historical play based on a Yoruba myth; and *Le roi-eléphant* takes place in the animal world, with an elephant and a cock confronting each other.

Senegal

ANTHOLOGIES AND CRITICAL WORKS
544 Copans, Jean
Contes Wolof du Baol
Dakar-Hann, Centre O.R.S.T.O.M., 1968. 184 pp. Traditional Wolof tales.

545 Guibert, Armand
Léopold Sédar Senghor: l'homme et l'oeuvre
Paris, Présence Africaine, 1968 (Collection Approches). 180 pp. illus. F12.00
A critical study of Senghor's work, in which, after a detailed introduction, there are extracts from his poetry, prose and political writings, an interview with Senghor, quotations from book reviews, and a bibliography.

[1]no. 4, 1970
[2]no. 2729, Sept. 20, 1968

*546 Mercier, Roger, and **Battestini, M.** and **S.** eds.
Birago Diop: écrivain sénégalais
Paris, Nathan, 1964 (Collection Littérature africaine, 6). 64 pp. F3.00
A critical presentation and appreciation of Diop's writing, together with a biography, a bibliography, and extracts from book reviews.

*547 Mercier, Roger, and **Battestini, M.** and **S.** eds.
Cheikh Hamidou Kane: écrivain sénégalais
Paris, Nathan, 1964 (Collection Littérature africaine, 1). 64 pp. F3.00
A critical commentary on Kane's writing, including biographical details, a bibliography and glossary, and extracts from book reviews.

*548 Mercier Roger, and **Battestini, M.** and **S.** eds.
Léopold Sédar Senghor: poète sénégalais
Paris, Nathan, 1964 (Collection Littérature africaine, 3). 64 pp. F3.00
A critical analysis of Senghor's writing, with a biography, a bibliography and a glossary, as well as extracts from book reviews.

549 Mezu, S. Okechukwu
Léopold Sédar Senghor et la défense et illustration de la civilisation noire
Paris, Didier, 1968. 232 pp. F30.00
This study traces Senghor's life from his birth in 1906 to his present position as President of Senegal. It evaluates his contribution as the driving force behind the negritude concept, and examines both Senghor the man and Senghor the writer, following his literary career from the publication of his first volume of verse to the award-winning *Nocturnes.* An extensive bibliography is included.

WORKS
550 Cissoko, Siriman
Ressac de nous-mêmes
Paris, Présence Africaine, 1968. 50 pp F12.20
Poetry.

551 Diakhate, Lamine
La joie d'un continent
Alès, Ed. P.A.B., 1954. 57 pp. out-of-print

552 Diakhate, Lamine
Primordiale du sixième jour
Paris, Présence Africaine, 1963. 61 pp. F6.00
Poetry.

553 Diakhate, Lamine
Temps de mémoire
Paris, Présence Africaine, 1967 (Collection Poésie). 64 pp. F14.20 illus.
A further volume of poetry.

554 Diallo, Bakary
Force bonté
Paris, Rieder, 1926. 211 pp. out-of-print

555 Diop, Birago
Contes et lavanes
Paris, Présence Africaine, 1963 (Collection Contes africains). 257 pp. F7.70
Diop's first rendering of folk tales, collected from the rich oral tradition and literary heritage of his ancestors.

556 Diop, Birago
Les contes d'Amadou Koumba
Paris, Présence Africaine, 1965 (Collection Contes africains). (New edn) 191 pp. F7.30
A collection of traditional folk tales from Senegal, awarded the Grand Prix Littéraire d'Afrique Noire in 1964. These stories were told to Diop by Amadou, his family griot, the traditional story-teller and keeper of oral tradition. Amadou had first heard them at his grandmother's hut, told in the original Wolof of Senegal.
' ... B. Diop joue ses personnages avec une grande sûreté des gestes et d'intonation Il s'agit de véritables spectacles aux dialogues animés.'
Léopold Sédar Senghor — *L'Afrique et l'Asie*[1]

*557 Diop, Birago
Tales of Amadou Koumba
London and New York, Oxford Univ. Press, 1966 (Trans. from the French by Dorothy S. Blair). 134 pp. 87½p/$2.60
Amadou's tales presented in English, fourteen of them from the original collection, and five translated from *Les nouveaux contes d'Amadou Koumba.* Dorothy Blair has provided a foreword and a glossary of local terms.

*558 Diop, Birago
Les nouveaux contes d'Amadou Koumba
Paris, Présence Africaine, 1967 (Collection Contes africains). (3rd edn) 176 pp F5.65
Diop's second collection of traditional folk stories, handed down by word of mouth and inspired by his household 'griot'. This edition has a foreword by Léopold Senghor.
' ... everything in this very delicate work is marvellous ... must it be repeated for the benefit of those who have not yet understood, that the significance of Negro-African literature lies in the disinterment of abolished Negro cultural values.'
Olympe Bhêly-Quenum — *Présence Africaine*[2]

[1]vol. no. 32/33, 1960
[2]vol. 8, no. 36

559 **Diop, Birago**
Leurres et lueurs: poèmes
Paris, Présence Africaine, 1967 (2nd edn). 87 pp.
F5.50
An anthology of Diop's verse, presenting poems
written as early as 1925, and as recently as
1966.

' ... *the style is rhythmical and perfectly in tune
with the climates of expression ... Birago Diop is by
temperament a lyric poet: this meets a deep personal
need and is in keeping with his African nature ...
Leurres et Lueurs is an important contribution
to contemporary African poetry.*
Guy de Bosschère — *Présence Africaine*[1]

*560 **Diop, Birago**
Contes choisis
Ed. by Joyce A. Hutchinson.
London and New York, Cambridge Univ. Press,
1967. 176 pp. 55p/$2.50
A school edition, including stories from both
collections of the Amadou Koumba tales, in the
original French, with extensive footnotes in
English. In the introduction there is an analysis
of the 'conte' in African literature, and Diop's
treatment of it, together with an appreciation of
his work. The introduction stresses that the
'conte' or folk tale is a vital part of the oral
tradition of African peoples, and fundamental to
an understanding of African literature.

'... *a useful introduction to Birago Diop's short
stories which are part of the drive to help restore the
African's self-confidence by bringing to light a glorious
past which had either been denigrated or overlooked.
Diop achieves these objectives by his qualities as a
story teller.*'
S. K. Dabo — *African Affairs*[2]

*561 **Diop, David**
Coups de pilon
Paris, Présence Africaine, 1961. 40 pp. out-of-
print
This slim volume of poems of protest in the
negritude vein, and poems of love, is the only
material Diop left behind him, though several
of his earlier poems appeared in the Senghor
anthology (see 113), and in the journal *Présence
Africaine*. David Diop died tragically young in an
air-crash over the Atlantic near Dakar, in
September, 1960. This small book of verse, however, roughly translated as 'Pounding', was
enough to establish him as one of the major new
African poets. Paradoxically, though, the
publishers have allowed the book to go out-of-
print.

' ... *David Diop's poetry ... is difficult to analyse
by reason of its singular poetic compactness and its
high content of poetry. The work is complete in itself
and perfectly impervious. It is like those works of art*

*whose beauty is beyond question but defies explana-
tion.*'
Guy de Bosschère — *Présence Africaine*[3]

Diop, Ousmane Socé
See **Socé, Ousmane**

562 **Fall, Malick**
Reliefs
Paris, Présence Africaine, 1964. 103 pp. F12.00
A volume of poems, with an introduction by
Léopold Senghor.

563 **Fall, Malick**
La plaie
Paris, Albin Michel, 1967, 253 pp. F13.50
In this symbolic novel a social outcast, suffering
from a huge festering sore on his foot, becomes
isolated from the world around him.

564 **Faye, N. G. M.**
Le débrouillard
Paris, Gallimard, 1964 (Souvenirs, l'air du temps,
187). 224 pp. F12.00
The adventures of a carefree and cunning young
boy in Dakar as a porter, cocoa-vendor, photo-
grapher, and poster-hanger.

565 **Kane, Cheikh Hamidou**
L'aventure ambiguë
Paris, Juillard, 1961. 211 pp. F15.00
In English translation, see 566.

*566 **Kane, Cheikh Hamidou**
Ambiguous adventure
New York, Walker, 1963 (Trans. from the
French by Katherine Wood). 178 pp. out-of-
print
New York, Macmillan, 1969. 166 pp. $1.25
An autobiographical novel that tells of the conflict in Samba Diallo, the son of a Fulani noble-
man, living in Paris; he is caught between his
belief in the traditional Islamic faith, and the
Western European culture and life encountered in his new environment. The original
French edition won the Grand Prix Littéraire
d'Afrique Noire in 1962. The Macmillan paperback re-issue has an introduction by Wilfred
Cartey.
'... *In some ways this is the most powerful statement of the complexity of the cultural 'ambiguity'
of the French assimilé ... Diallo faces the most
acute of cultural divisions, between his tradition
and the new Western imposition of values.*'
John Povey — *African Studies Review*[4]

[1]Feb., 1966 [?]
[2]vol. 67, Oct. 1968
[3]no. 32/33, 1960.
[4]vol. 12, no. 1, Apr., 1970

567 Ndao, Cheik A.

L'exil d'Albouri, suivi de *La décision*
Honfleur-Paris, Oswald, 1967 (Collection
Théâtre Africain, 1). 134 pp. F12.00
Two plays: the first one, a historical play, is set
in the middle ages in the old empire of Mali; *La
décision* is set in the American south. Bakari
Traoré has contributed a foreword.

568 Niang, Lamine

Négristique
Paris, Présence Africaine, 1968, 86 pp. F18.80
A personal philosophy of negritude is expressed
in this volume of verse.

569 Ousmane, Sembène

Le docker noir
Paris, Nouvelles Éditions Debresse, 1956. 223 pp.
out-of-print
In the early nineteen-fifties Sembène Ousmane
found employment as a docker in the Marseille
harbour. An accident there forced him to leave
work for several months, during which time he
put down on paper his personal experiences as
a docker, resulting in this, his first (autobiographical) novel.

570 Ousmane, Sembène

O pays, mon beau peuple
Paris, Amiot-Dumont, 1957. 236 pp. out-of-print.
After serving in the French army, Faye returns
to his home in Senegal, accompanied by a white
European wife. Difficulties ensue as Faye's
community objects to the white woman and
Faye's newly acquired progressive ideas, the
model farm he initiates for one. When Faye
is ultimately killed by African mercenaries hired
by the white men, he is seen as a hero.
*'... there is much in it that is worth our attention
and the author shows ability and promise'.*
Ulli Beier — *Black Orpheus*[1]

571 Ousmane, Sembène

Les bouts de bois de Dieu
Paris, Le Livre contemporain, 1960. 383 pp.
out-of-print
In English *translation*, see 572.

*572 Ousmane, Sembène

God's bits of wood
(Trans. by Francis Price)
Garden City, N.Y., Doubleday, 1962. 333 pp.
out-of-print
London, Heinemann Educ. Books, 1969 (African
Writers Series, 63). 288 pp. 60p
New York, Doubleday, 1971 (Anchor Books).
(In preparation)
From October 1947 through to March 1948 the
workers on the Dakar-Niger railway were out
on strike. Sembène Ousmane has utilized this
historical event in a novel which follows the
struggles of the strikers in Dakar, Thiès and

Bamako. In this fictionalized account he parti-
cularizes the problems connected with the
workers' movement by concentrating on the
hardships and struggles encountered by individual families — largely as a result of their
own actions — in these three towns.

573 Ousmane, Sembène

Voltaïques: nouvelles
Paris, Présence Africaine, 1962. 210 pp. F7.50
Short-story collection.

574 Ousmane, Sembène

L'harmattan. Vol. I: Référendum
Paris, Présence Africaine, 1964. 302 pp. F10.80
This political novel, the first volume of an en-
visaged trilogy on contemporary Africa, takes as
its theme the national referendum of 28
September, 1958. The vote asked for a 'oui' or
'non' for De Gaulle's French community, the
'yes' meaning the continued presence of the
colonial administrators, the 'no' deciding for
total independence.

*575 Ousmane, Sembène

Véhi Ciosane ou blanche genèse, suivi du *Mandat*
Paris, Présence Africaine, 1965. 221 pp. F10.80
Paris, Présence Africaine, 1969 (reissued as *Le
Mandat et Véhi Ciosane*), 192 pp. F5.85
The two short novels in this book —awarded the
literature prize at the first Festival of Negro
Arts in Dakar, 1966 — are set in contemporary
Senegal. *Le Mandat* has recently been adapted for
the screen and was presented for the first time at
the Venice Film Festival of 1968.

576 Sadji, Abdoulaye

Maimouna
Paris, Présence Africaine, 1965 (2nd edn). 253
pp. F9.30
Chronicles the life of a beautiful, naïve young
village girl in a working-class environment.
Living in the city of Dakar she meets with ultimate disgrace.

*577 Sadji, Abdoulaye

Nini, mulâtresse du Sénégal
Paris Présence Africaine, 1965 (2nd edn). 189 pp.
F7.80
Nini is a young half-caste who little resembles
the African woman she is. Despising her African
heritage, Nini searches for a new life, for total
assimilation in European society. This in the end
results in her downfall.

578 Sadji, Abdoulaye

Tounka; nouvelle
Paris, Présence Africaine, 1965. 95 pp. F4.00

[1]no. 6, Nov. 1959

'... *combines an epic account of the settlement of Cap Vert by the Lebou tribe with an African version of the Undine theme, in which a hero marries a sea nymph and then makes her the laughing-stock of the village by revealing her frigidity ... the reader's interest is held by the rapidity and economy of narrative, as well as by Sadji's success in recreating the style of the African epic in French.*'

Thomas Cassirer — *African Forum*[1]

Sembène, Ousmane
See **Ousmane, Sembène**

579 Senghor, Léopold Sédar
Chants d'ombre
Paris, Seuil, 1945. 78 pp. out-of-print
Senghor's first volume of poetry.

580 Senghor, Léopold Sédar
Hosties noires
Paris, Seuil, 1948. 86 pp. out-of-print
Senghor resided in Paris at the outbreak of World War II. *Black Victims*, his second verse collection, contains the poems both written in and concerned with these war years. They substantially reflect the impact the war had on Senghor and his personal reactions to the conflict.

581 Senghor, Léopold Sédar
Chants pour Naett
Paris, Séghers, 1949. 49 pp. out-of-print
'Songs for Naet' — a set of love poems.

*582 Senghor, Léopold Sédar
Nocturnes
Paris, Seuil, 1961. 94 pp. F6.00
This collection contains Senghor's 'Elegies', a series of poems that deal with the nature of poetry and the role of the poet himself. An English version is about to appear as this book goes to press (see 583).
'... *the poetry of Léopold Sédar Senghor is an exclusive gathering place of words ... the theme of the poet is sumptuously African ... his poetry is not one of dispute, or even of discussion, but one of taking root.*'

Guy de Bosschère — *Présence Africaine*[2]

*583 Senghor, Léopold Sédar
Nocturnes: love poems
(Trans. from the French by Clive Wake and John Reed)
London, Heinemann Educ. Books, 1970 (African Writers Series, 71). 64 pp. 50p

584 Senghor, Léopold Sédar
Chants d'ombre, suivis de *Hosties noires*
Paris, Seuil (2nd edn) 1956. 157 pp. out-of-print
A new edition combining the first two published verse collections.

585 Senghor, Léopold Sédar
Éthiopiques
Paris, Seuil, 1956. 126 pp. out-of-print
A further volume of poetry by the chief exponent of negritude. This book includes his long dramatic poem 'Chaka', Senghor's adaption of Thomas Mofolo's historical novel (see 382).

586 Senghor, Léopold Sédar, and Sadji, Abdoulaye
La belle histoire de Leuk-le-Lièvre
Paris, Hachette, 1953. 176 pp. F8.70
A collection of short folk tales. They are aimed primarily at younger readers, featuring Leuk the hare as the main character in all the stories.

*587 Senghor, Léopold Sédar
Poèmes
Paris, Seuil, 1964. 255 pp. F24.00
A comprehensive collection that contains *Chants d'ombre*, *Hosties noires*, *Éthiopiques*, *Nocturnes*, and *Poèmes divers*

588 Senghor, Léopold Sédar, and Sadji, Abdoulaye
La belle histoire de Leuk-le-Lièvre
Edited by J. M. Winch
London, Harrap, 1965. 154 pp. 52½p
An English edition with an introduction, notes and a vocabulary. Difficult and unusual points of grammar and syntax are noted and explained.

*589 Senghor, Léopold Sédar
Selected Poems
(Trans. from the French and introduced by John Reed and Clive Wake)
London, Oxford Univ. Press, 1964. 120 pp. £1.25
New York, Atheneum, 1964. 99 pp. $3.95
A selection of the outstanding poems from each of Senghor's five volumes of verse, with an introduction by the translators, who also provide a glossary defining African words frequently used by Senghor.
'... *the sights, sounds, smells, motions, music and texture of tropical landscapes populated with creatures living and dead, present and familiar, distant and mysterious; the sensuous maternal warmth, the loving sternness of father and uncle; the proud heritage of forbears, these are the Africa his poems evoke. Senghor's genius and what will make his poetry endure is his extraordinary lyric and imaginative power.*'

Ellen Conroy Kennedy and Paulette J. Trout — *Africa Report*[3]

---

[1]vol. 2, no. 4, Spring 1967
[2]vol. 9, no. 37
[3]vol. 10. no. 4, Apr. 1965

*590 Senghor, Léopold Sédar
Prose and Poetry
(Selected and trans. by John Reed and Clive
Wake.
London, Oxford Univ. Press, 1965. 192 pp.
37½p [not available in U.S.]
The English-speaking reader is here presented
with a wide range of Senghor's writings. A
detailed introduction by the translators discusses
Senghor's achievements and his career as a
politician. There are translations from Senghor's
scattered prose writings and speeches and from
his book *Nation et voie africaine du socialisme.*
These are arranged in such a fashion as to
show in outline his thinking on cultural, political and artistic matters. The second part of the
book consists of a selection of his poetry. A
glossary of African names often used by Senghor
and a bibliography complete the volume.

*591 Socé, Ousmane
Karim, roman Senégalais, suivi de *Contes et légéndes
d'Afrique noire*
Paris, Nouvelles éditions latines, 1948. 239 pp.
F7.70
Karim is an early African novel originally
published in 1935 and now in its third edition. It
is the story of a young man attracted by the
prospects of big-city life in Dakar, its pleasures
and fascinations, who eventually returns to his
village up-country and his traditional garb. The
second part of the book consists of traditional
folk tales and legends. It has a foreword by
Robert Delavignette (See also 593).

592 Socé, Ousmane
Mirages de Paris, suivi des *Rhythmes du khalam*
Paris, Nouvelles éditions latines, 1956. 283 pp.
out-of-print
Socé's second novel followed by a collection of
verse.

593 Socé, Ousmane
Contes et légéndes d'Afrique noire
Paris, Nouvelles éditions latines, 1962. 157 pp.
F7.70
A volume of folk tales and legends, here publish-
ed separately (see also 591).

594 Socé, Ousmane
Rhythmes du Khalam
Paris, Nouvelles éditions latines, 1962, 61 pp.
F5.00
Poetry.

595 Socé, Ousmane
Mirages de Paris
Paris, Nouvelles éditions latines, 1965. 189 pp.
F7.70

Tchad

WORKS
596 Seid, Joseph Brahim
Au Tchad sous les étoiles
Paris, Présence Africaine, 1962. 103 pp. F4.50
A collection of folk stories, fables and legends
based on local oral traditions and set in the
Kotoko-Kanem area to the west and south of
Lake Chad.

597 Seid, Joseph Brahim
Un enfant du Tchad: récit
Paris, Éd. S.A.G.E.R.E.P., 1967 (Dossiers littér-
aires de l'Afrique Actuelle, no. 1). 112 pp. F8.00

CENTRAL AFRICA

Congo-Brazzaville

WORKS

*598 Menga, Guy
La palabre stérile
Yaoundé, Éd. C.L.E., 1968 (Collection Abbia).
138 pp. CFA300
New York, Africana Publ. Corp., distr. $2.25
'Fruitless palavers' retraces the changes and
events in the life of a young Congolese who
decides to leave his native village on the brink
of his country's independence. The book was
awarded the Grand Prix Littéraire de l'Afrique
Noire for 1969.

599 Ndebeka, Maxime
Soleils neufs
Yaoundé, Éd. C.L.E., 1969 (Collection Abbia).
107 pp. CFA300
New York, Africana Publishing Corp.; distr.
$1.75
Poetry.

600 Tchicaya U Tam'si, Gérald Félix
Le mauvais sang
Paris, Caracteres, 1955. 45 pp. out-of-print
U Tam'si's first volume of poetry.

601 Tchicaya U Tam'si, Gérald Félix
Feu de brousse
Paris, Caracteres, 1957. 86 pp. out-of-print
In English *translation*, see 602

*602 Tchicaya U Tam'si, Gérald Félix
Brush Fire
(Trans. from the French by Sangodare Akanji;
pseud. for Ulli Beier)
Ibadan, Mbari, 1964. unpaged [96 pp.] 6s. 0d.
The first volume of verse by U Tam'si available
in English, translated from *Feu de brousse* above.

603 Tchicaya U Tam'si, Gérald Félix
À triche coeur
Paris, Éd. Hautefeuille, 1958. 82 pp. out-of-print
A volume of poetry. As this bibliography goes to
press, Pierre Jean Oswald, publisher, Honfleur-
Paris, has announced that this and the previous
two poetry collections are to be reissued by
them.

604 Tchicaya U Tam'si, Gérald Félix
Le ventre
Paris, Présence Africaine, 1964 (Collection
Poésie). 136 pp. F12.00
A further collection of verse. U Tam'si was
awarded first prize for poetry at the first World
Festival of Negro Arts held in Dakar in 1966.

605 Tchicaya U Tam'si, Gérald Félix
Epitomé
Paris, Oswald, 1968 (2nd edn), 137 pp. F9.75
A fourth book of poetry, with an introduction by
Léopold Senghor.

*606 Tchicaya U Tam'si, Gérald Félix
Légendes africaines
Paris, Séghers, 1969. 264 pp. F12.00
Extracts from fourteen African legends and folk
tales, with an introduction and explanatory
notes on each passage. U Tam'si provides the first
story, and this is followed by extracts from the
works of Thomas Mofolo (*Chaka*), Djibril Niane
(*Soundjata*), Ousmane Socé (*Karim*), Blaise
Cendrar from France, and five passages from the
writings of the ethnologist Leo Frobenius, all
originally published in German. Mercer Cook
provides a preface.
' . . . *Empreintes tantot de poésie, tantot de violence,
tantot de fantaisie, tantot de mystère, ces legendes sont
vivantes et variées. Leur principal merite est surtout
leur caractère original.*'
C. J. — *L'Afrique Littéraire et Artistique*[1]

*607 Tchicaya U Tam'si, Gérald Félix
Poems
(Trans. from the French by Gerald Moore)
London, Heinemann Educ. Books, 1970 (African
Writers Series, 72). 96 pp. 55p
Includes poems written both before and after U
Tam'si's first English volume *Brush Fire* was
published by Mbari in 1964.

Congo-Kinshasa

WORKS

608 Bolamba, Antoine-Roger
Esanzo: chants pour mon pays
Paris, Présence Africaine, 1955. 45 pp. out-
of-print
Verse. With a preface by Léopold Senghor.

609 Lukumbi, Etienne Thsinday
Marché, pays des espoirs
Paris, Présence Africaine, 1967 (Collection
Poésie). 55 pp. F13.20
Poems. André Terrisse contributes a foreword.

[1]no. 5, June 1969

EAST AFRICA

Malagasy Republic

CRITICAL WORKS
610 **Valette, Paul**
Jean-Joseph Rabéarivelo
Paris, Nathan, 1967 (Collection littérature malgache). 64 pp. F3.00
A critical introduction to Rabéarivelo's writings.

WORKS
611 **Rabéarivelo, Jean-Joseph**
La coupe de cendres
Tananarive, Pitot de la Beaujardière, 1924.
The first book of poems by the man who is considered to be the father of modern literature in Madagascar.

612 **Rabéarivelo, Jean-Joseph**
Sylves
Tananarive, Imp. de l'Imerina, 1927. 103 pp. out-of-print
Verse. Contains 'Nobles dédains', 'Fleurs mêlées', 'Destinée', 'Dixains', and 'Sonnets et poèmes d'Iarive'.

613 **Rabéarivelo, Jean-Joseph**
Volumes
Tananarive, Imp. de l'Imerina, 1928. 108 pp. out-of-print
This third collection of poetry includes 'Vers le bonheur', 'La guirlande à l'amitié', 'Interlude rythmique', 'Sept quatrains', 'Arbres', 'Au soleil estival', and 'Coeur et ciel d'Iarive'.

614 **Rabéarivelo, Jean-Joseph**
Imaitsoanala — Fille d'oiseau — Cantate
Tananarive, Imp. Officielle, 1935. 236 pp. out-of-print
Poems.

615 **Rabéarivelo, Jean-Joseph**
Traduit de la nuit
Tunis, Éd. de mirages, 1935. 69 pp. out-of-print
Poems transcribed from the Hova.

616 **Rabéarivelo, Jean-Joseph**
Vieilles chansons du pays Imerina
Tananarive, Imp. Officielle, 1939. out-of-print
This is a posthumous collection of love poems. Rabéarivelo committed suicide in 1937 at the age of only thirty-six.

617 **Rabéarivelo, Jean-Joseph**
Des stances oubliées
Tananarive, Imp. Live, 1959. 24 pp.
Poems.

618 **Rabéarivelo, Jean-Joseph**
Presques-Songes et Traduit de la nuit
Tananarive, Imp. Officielle, 1960. 221 pp.
Two reissues of previously published verse.

*619 **Rabéarivelo, Jean-Joseph**
24 Poems
(Trans. from the French by Ulli Beier and Gerald Moore)
Ibadan, Mbari, 1962. unpaged [40 pp.] 7s. 6d. illus. [Nigeria]
Contains 'The white bull', 'Three birds', 'Valiha' 'Cactus', 'Birth of day', 'Zebu', and several others

620 **Rabémananjara, Jacques**
Sur les marches du soir
Gap, Éd. Ophrys, 1942. 76 pp. illus. out-of-print
Verse.

621 **Rabémananjara, Jacques**
Rites millénaires
Paris, Séghers, 1955 (Collection cahiers bi mensuels, 55). 33 pp. out-of-print
Verse.

*622 **Rabémananjara, Jacques**
Les boutriers de l'Aurore
Paris, Présence Africaine, 1957. 232 pp. F7.70
A three-act historical play set in Madagascar

*623 **Rabémananjara, Jacques**
Antidote
Paris, Présence Africaine, 1961. 48 pp. F5.00
For actively partaking in the national liberation movement in Madagascar, Rabémananjara was imprisoned from 1947 to 1950. The poems were written during this time; their central themes are negritude, ancestry, and Rabémananjara's political hopes.

624 **Rabémananjara, Jacques**
Antsa
Paris, Présence Africaine, 1962. 70 pp. F5.00
A further collection of verse.

625 **Rabémananjara, Jacques**
Agapes des dieux: Tritiva — tragédie malgache
Paris, Présence Africaine, 1962. 266 pp. F7.70
Set in the ancient kingdom of Ambohimena, this historical play tells the tragic story of two young lovers, Hanta and Ratrimo.

626 **Rabémananjara, Jacques**
Les dieux malgaches (version destinée à la scène
Paris, Hachette, 1964. 165 pp. F9.00
A reissue of a play first published in Paris in 1947.

*627 **Rabémananjara, Jacques**
Lamba

Paris, Présence Africaine, 1966. 85 pp. F5.00
A new edition of a book of poems, with a foreword by Aimé Césaire.

628 Ranaivo, Flavien
L'ombre et le vent
Tananarive, Imp. Officielle, 1947. 30 pp. illus.
out-of-print
Antananarivo, 1967 (new edn) 32 pp. illus.
(Reprinted in *The poetic works of Flavien Ranaivo*.
Nendeln, Liechtenstein, Kraus Reprint, 1970.
$7.50)
Verse.

629 Ranaivo, Flavien
Mes chansons de toujours
Paris. Author, 1955. 31 pp. out-of-print [?]
(Reprinted in *The poetic works of Flavien Ranaivo*.
Nendeln, Liechtenstein, Kraus Reprint, 1970.
$7.50)
Ranaivo's second book of poems. There is a fore-
word by Léopold Senghor.

630 Ranaivo, Flavien
Le retour au bercail
Tananarive, Imp. Nationale, 1962. 36 pp. out-of-
print [?]
(Reprinted in *The poetic works of Flavien Ranaivo*.
Nendeln, Liechtenstein, Kraus Reprint, 1970.
$7.50)

Rwanda

CRITICAL WORKS
631 Coupez, A. and **Kamanzi, Thomas** eds.
Littérature courtoise du Rwanda
London and New York, Oxford Univ. Press,
1969 (Oxford Library of African Literature).
238 pp. £3.00/$9.95
The complex and refined poetry of Rwanda has
been transmitted orally since the seventeenth
century. The editors of this volume have recorded much of this heritage, and it is presented
here in the original Rwanda and in French
translation. The introduction and notes are also
in French.

632 Kagame, Alexis
Bref aperçu sur la poésie dynastique du Rwanda
Bruxelles, Éd. Universitaires, 1950. 30 pp. out-of-
print

633 Kagame, Alexis
La poésie dynastique au Rwanda
Bruxelles, Inst. Royal Congo Belge, 1951. 240
pp. out-of-print

634 Kagame, Alexis
Introduction aux grands genres lyriques de l'ancien Rwanda
Butare, Rwanda, Éd. Universitaires du Rwanda
(B.P. 117), 1969 (Collection 'Muntu', 1). 324 pp.
map F600 [Rwanda]/$6.00
A collection of traditional verse from Rwanda,
in Kinyarwanda and parallel French translation,
with commentary and explanatory notes.

WORKS
635 Naigiziki, J. Saverio
Escapade ruandaise: journal d'un clerc en sa trentième année
Bruxelles, G. A. Deny, 1949. 210 pp. out-of-
print
A narrative of life in Rwanda.

636 Naigiziki, J. Saverio
L'optimiste: pièce en trois actes
Astrida, Rwanda, Groupe scolaire, 1954. 59 pp.
out-of-print

637 Naigiziki, J. Saverio
Mes transes à trente ans, 2 vols.
Astrida, Rwanda, Groupe scolaire, 1955. 483
pp. out-of-print
A reissue of *Escapade ruandaise* in an expanded
form, here published in two volumes as *De
mal en pis* and *De pis en mieux*.

Somaliland

WORKS
638 Syad, William
Khamsine
Paris, Présence Africaine, 1959. 72 pp. out-of-
print
Love poems. With a foreword by Léopold
Senghor.

POLITICALLY COMMITTED LITERATURE IN ENGLISH: A SELECTION

GIDEON-CYRUS M. MUTISO

The following selection provides details of works by Africans who are, or have been, politically active. Some of their works are entirely creative in nature. However, the literature included in this section contains autobiographical accounts, speeches and theoretical works. They are works which are partisan and by their nature draw attention to the major intellectual positions in African political and social thought. This selection is concerned primarily with the writings of recent activists, and the works of earlier authors such as Blyden, Horton or Danquah have, therefore, been excluded. Other writers like Ojike Mbonu or Bloke Modisane have also been excluded as they tend to fall within the creative literature or academic category. All contemporary academics in their disciplines as they relate to Africa have been omitted, since they are scholarly analyses of Africa and are not as clearly partisan as the writings of the activists. My only exception in this instance is W. E. Abraham's *The Mind of Africa*, which I feel is basic to the understanding of the other materials.

639 **Abraham, W. E.**
The Mind of Africa
London, Weidenfeld, 1962. 208 pp. £1.05
Chicago, Univ. of Chicago Press, 1963. 208 pp. $5.00 ($1.95 pap.)
London, Weidenfeld (Goldbacks series), 1967. 206 pp. 62½p
Starting with the proposition that there is a unique African culture, and using the Akan peoples' society as a paradigm of this culture, Professor Abraham discusses the nature of African philosophical, political, and social systems, as well as methods of social control and distribution of goods and services. In the process, he rejects the idea that black African culture has Egyptian (therefore Indo-European) origins. He evaluates slavery and colonialism and their role in the development of Europe, pointing out that the gross effect was to industrialize Europe at the price of depopulating Africa. Abraham further discusses the forces contributing to African nationalism.

640 **Afrifa, A. A.**
The Ghana Coup, 24th February 1966
London, Cass, 1966. 144 pp. illus. £1.25 (62½p pap.)
New York, Humanities Press, distr. $5.00 ($2.00 pap.)
In this volume Afrifa describes the actual military movements that brought about the Ghana coup. He includes some autobiographical material, a criticism of Ghanaian developments from 1957–1966, and an account of hopes of

the military regime. There is an appendix covering a variety of subjects.

641 **Armah, Kwesi**
Africa's Golden Road
London, Heinemann, 1965. 304 pp. £1.50
New York, Humanities Press, distr. $6.00
This book is an attempt to theorize about the immediate past — the nationalist era and the forces that led to the challenging of imperial power. It also argues for the political unification of Africa and the one-party state as a model for state organization based on the principle of centralized power. In terms of international relations and ideology, non-alignment is stressed.

642 **Awolowo, Obafemi**
Awo: the autobiography of Chief Obafemi Awolowo
London and New York, Cambridge Univ. Press 1960. 316 pp. £1.25/$4.75 ($2.45 pap.)
Though the political careers of Nnamdi Azikiwe and Obafemi Awolowo merged in the Nigerian Youth Movement, later they both developed separate political organizations: the National Council of Nigeria and the Cameroon and Action Group. They disagreed on the issue of federation and the Northern Peoples Congress. This autobiography illustrates the effects of these conflicts.

643 **Awolowo, Obafemi**
Path to Nigerian Freedom
London, Faber and Faber, 1966. 137 pp. 47½p
Written in 1945, this work argues for the creation of a Federal Nigeria, establishment

of local self-government, and constitutional progress towards independence.

644 Awolowo, Obafemi
Thoughts on the Nigerian Constitution
London and New York, Oxford University Press, 1967. 208 pp. £1.10/$2.35
These thoughts took shape while Awolowo was in prison following the constitutional crisis of Western Nigeria. In part, it is a defence of his position in the crisis, and also a proposal for a radical restructuring of the Nigerian Federal constitution, by breaking up the three component regions into eighteen states on the basis of language. There are also specific proposals for sharing the revenue among states as well as for reorganizing the civil service and public corporations.

645 Azikiwe, Nnamdi
Renascent Africa
Lagos, Author, 1937. Out-of-print
London, Cass, 1969 (Reprint). 313 pp. £3.25
New York, Negro Univ. Press, 1970 (Reprint). 313 pp. $11.00
This book, like Kenyatta's *Facing Mount Kenya*, documents the concerns of the first generation of nationalists. *Renascent Africa*, according to Azikiwe, is the transitional period between the old Africa and the future. The future, as he predicted, would be dominated by Africans. Azikiwe lists five principles as the prerequisites for the new Africa: (1) Tolerance of diversity, (2) Social regeneration, accentuating pan-tribal organizations and loyalties, (3) Economic development, (4) Mental emancipation, (5) Creation of nation states.

646 Azikiwe, Nnamdi
Zik: a selection from the speeches of Nnamdi Azikiwe
London and New York, Cambridge Univ. Press, 1961. 244 pp. 75p/$2.45 ($1.35 pap.)
This collection of speeches covers the following topics: American interlude, education, liberty, Africa's natural rulers, democracy, Nigerian constitutional development, the colour bar, colonialism, the National Council of Nigeria and Cameroon, finance and banking, press and broadcasting, the Ibo people, moral rearmament, local government, the University of Nigeria, the development of political parties in Nigeria, and the Church Missionary Society. The speeches are selected from Zik's long career in public life, from 1927 to 1960. As an educator, newspaper publisher, politician and head of state, he was given unique opportunities to comment upon the nature and directions of African intellectual development, nationalism and race.

647 Balewa, Alhaji Sir Abubakar Tafawa
Nigeria Speaks: speeches made between 1957 and 1964
Ikeja, Nigeria, Longmans of Nigeria, 1964. 178 pp. illus. £1.50 (62½p pap.)
New York, Humanities Press, distr. $6.00 ($2.50 pap.)
These speeches begin with Balewa's appointment as Federal Prime Minister. They deal with the establishment of an African Government and the major crises that followed. Among them are the Cameroon referendum, the constitutional crisis of Western Nigeria, constitutional amendments, the general election, and proposals for the Mid-Western State and development. On major international events, he commented on the Congo crisis (in which Nigeria took the conservative African position), the O.A.U., and related African unity problems (in which Nigeria stressed the regional-economic approach), and Nigeria's links with the European Common Market.

648 Busia, Kenneth A.
The Challenge of Africa
London, Pall Mall, 1962. 156 pp. out-of-print
New York, Praeger, 1962. 156 pp. out-of-print
Busia, writing in 1962, seeks to refute the idea of an African personality, by arguing that culturally Africa is very diverse. He further contends that all in all colonization bestowed benefits, particularly order and technology, which are an integral part of present-day African culture. He feels that industrialization would lead to structural changes in culture, the implications of which have not been completely thought through by rulers preoccupied with nationalism. Busia is critical of the one-party systems, the personality cults of most leaders, and, in general, of political developments in Africa.

649 Busia, Kenneth A.
Africa in Search of Democracy
London, Routledge, 1967. 192 pp. £1.00
New York, Praeger, 1967. 192 pp. $4.25
Dr Busia's study of democracy in Africa begins with a discussion of Africa's religious heritage and its bearing upon social institutions. The traditional rulership systems and present-day one-party systems are then examined in the light of 'democratic' definitions. The concept 'African socialism' is explained as basically a social system where there is popular participation. In his discussion of tribalism, Busia suggests methods of integrating different tribes into a modern nation within a democratic framework. In the final chapter, he considers the Marxist and western views of democracy, and closes with a call to free the African continent from oppressive government.

650 **Dia, Mamadou**
The African Nations and World Solidarity
(Trans. from the French by Mercer Cook)
New York, Praeger, 1961. 145 pp. out-of-
print
This work was written before the break-up of
the Mali Federation. It seeks to define a 'nation',
operationally, within the African situation
in the twentieth century. Mamadou Dia de-
nounces local élites, African governments
and foreign governments for failing to re-
cognize technological development and culture
as the two priorities in bringing about social
change. Both legal independence and economic
dependence are examined, particularly with
regard to Middle East and North African
economies. The volume concludes with an
evaluation of the failure of the Mali Federation.

651 **Kariuki, Josiah Mwangi**
*Mau Mau Detainee: the account by a Kenyan
African of his experiences in detention camps 1953–
1960*
London, Oxford Univ. Press, 1963. 212 pp. illus.
£1.05/$3.40
Harmondsworth, Middx., and Baltimore,
Penguin Books (Penguin African Library AP
15), 1965. 224 pp. 22½p/$1.25
Kariuki was a student in Uganda during the
four years prior to the declaration of the
Emergency in 1952. However, he returned
to Kenya and became involved in the activities
of the Nakuru Branch of the Kenya African
Union, and later in Mau Mau. The major body
of the book is an account of his experience in
a detention camp.

652 **Kaunda, Kenneth** and **Morris, Colin**
*A Humanist in Africa: letters to Colin Morris from
Kenneth Kaunda, President of Zambia*
London. Longmans, 1966. 136 pp. 80p (42½p
pap.)
New York, Abingdon Press, 1968. 136 pp. $3.50
This book is compiled from communications —
not strictly letters — between President Kaunda
and Colin Morris, a Christian minister at
Chigola, Zambia. President Kaunda writes of
his philosophical and political positions.
It emerges that he is a humanist in the Teilhard
de Chardin vein, deeply religious, and a believer
in African psychology — the unity between
'the natural and the supernatural'. President
Kaunda also touches on the psychology of
colonialism, with its heightened sense of
loneliness and insecurity for the Africans. Other
subjects commented on are African nationalism
and African unity. African nationalism is seen
as a force that is rising with the intellectuals
and spreading to the urban élites and the rural
people.

653 **Kaunda, Kenneth**
Zambia Shall be Free: an autobiography
London, Heinemann Educ. Books 1962 (African Writers series, 4). 208 pp. illus. 40p
New York, Praeger, 1963. 202 pp. illus. out-of-
print
This autobiography documents the rise of
Zambian nationalism and the major issues involved, which were race, the unequal funding
of the Federation, and political repression
of the African political parties.

654 **Kenyatta, Jomo**
Facing Mount Kenya
London, Secker and Warburg (Mercury
Books), 1953 (New edn). 356 pp. £1.80 (62½p
pap.)
New York, Vintage, 1962. 327 pp. $2.29 ($1.65
pap.)
Nairobi, Heinemann Educ. Books, 1971
(Abridged students' edn, ed. Joe Kariuki) *ca.*
200 pp. *ca.* 50p
Facing Mount Kenya was first issued in the year
1938. It was a rejection of the European stereo-
typed view about the natives of Africa. It particularly dealt with the Kikuyu, and their traditional social structures and institutions; significantly among them the role of initiation as
a system of establishing social and rulership
groups. This was misunderstood particularly by
the missionaries, who nearly precipitated a
war in Kenya on the issue. Other issues discussed are the roles of magic, ancestor-
worship, and separatist churches. Kenyatta
makes a distinction between Western education, which is designed primarily for individual instruction, and African education,
which is geared basically toward community
learning. *Facing Mount Kenya* summarizes the
major issues responsible for the rise of Kenyan
nationalism.

655 **Kenyatta, Jomo**
*Harambee: The Prime Minister of Kenya's speeches
1963–1964*
Nairobi and London, Oxford Univ. Press, 1964.
115 pp. illus. 45p/95c
This collection of speeches covers the first
year of Kenya's independence — a period of
setting new direction. The speeches, therefore,
reveal the new Africanization policy, the re-
current theme of national unification, and
the problems of establishing the East African
Federation. Kenya's diplomacy at the Organization of African Unity, attempts by the government to turn the tide of migration to the cities,
the new socio-economic plans, and the beginnings of the Kenya-Somali conflict are covered
in other speeches.

556 Kenyatta, Jomo
Suffering Without Bitterness: the founding of the Kenya nation
Nairobi, East African Publishing House, 1968.
348 pp. illus. EAshs. 49.00 (21.00 pap.)
Evanston, Northwestern Univ. Press, distr.
$7.00 ($3.00 pap.)
Part one of this book describes the roots of Kenyatta's politics, going back to the nineteen-twenties. It traces his involvement in Kenya up to 1929 and his European sojourn between 1929 and 1946. Part two describes the post-war period: his activities before Mau Mau, his imprisonment, and eventual freedom. An appendix gives President Kenyatta's speeches from 1963–1967, and there is a commentary on their background. The speeches reveal Kenyatta's views on the diplomacy of the Congo crisis, the primacy of agriculture, and the essence of African socialism.

557 Lumumba, Patrice
Congo, my Country
London, Pall Mall Press and Barrie and Rockiff, 1962. 195 pp. illus. out-of-print
New York, Praeger, 1962. 224 pp. illus. $6.50
Lumumba sent the original manuscript of this book to a Belgian publisher in 1956. As it was not published until 1962, some questions were raised as to its authenticity. A more important problem however is that because of the delay in publication the book does not really reflect the prevailing image of the Congo, i.e. that of the days of independence and civil war. Rather, it is an intellectual critique of the colonial system, with specific recommendations on how to avoid the holocaust. In 1956 Lumumba was apparently still looking for avenues through which Africans could participate in the colonial government, and on the evidence of this book he was not advocating independence. Assuming the book to be authentic, one may conclude that the nationalist revolt for independence did not begin in the Congo until some time after 1956, because Lumumba's view throughout is that the Belgian régime must change to allow the Congolese to participate in colonial government.

558 Luthuli, Albert
Let My People Go
New York, McGraw-Hill, 1962. 256 pp. $5.95
London, Collins, 1963 (Fontana series) 256 pp. illus. £1.25 (25p pap.)
Cleveland World Pub., (Meridian Books), 1969.
$2.65
Nobel Peace Prize-winner Albert Luthuli, grandson of a Zulu chief, was President of the African National Congress from 1952 until 1962, when he was imprisoned on political grounds. Here he writes about the attempts by the A.N.C. to participate in normal democratic politics under a racist régime. His positions and those of his party on non-violence, and co-operation with the Indian National Congress and several left-wing 'white' parties, were under challenge in the Congress during his entire tenure. An open split came after the repression that followed the mass protests of 1960 and the Sharpeville massacre. Throughout the book there is the implication that reason and interracial peace can come to South Africa only by outside influence and pressure.

659 Mandela, Nelson
No Easy Walk to Freedom: articles, speeches and trial addresses
Edited by Ruth First
London, Heinemann Educ. Books, 1965. 196 pp. illus. £1.05 (52½p pap.)
New York, Basic Books, 1965. 189 pp. illus.
$4.95
This is a collection of Mandela's articles, a conference speech, and his testimony and addresses at three trials, during the years 1953–1963. Mandela is the son of a Tembu chief (from the Transkei), correspondence-school educated, and a lawyer. At the time of going to press he is a political prisoner interned on Robben Island, South Africa. As an organizer of the youth wing of the African National Congress in the 1952 selective defiance campaign, he was banned from public speaking. This moved him toward activism – the M. plan, which staged a series of public demonstrations and strikes. After 1960, when he and others were acquitted at the Treason Trials, and South Africa moved toward a Republic, there was an increase in the tempo of repression. The May 1961 call for a general strike led to Mandela's theories about the use of propaganda by the government to subvert such an attempt. His tactics therefore moved toward sabotage, and though by 1962 he was travelling (secretly) to Addis Ababa as a delegate of the African National Congress, his tactics and attitudes now rejected the mass non-violent approach. Mandela lived underground for seventeen months. On capture, he was charged with inciting the 1961 stay-at-home strike and leaving South Africa without a valid visa. His statements and cross-examination of witnesses are considered key documents in the rejection and opposition of apartheid policies. There are extensive introductory notes to each speech.

660 Mboya, Tom
Freedom and After
Boston, Little Brown, 1963. 288 pp. illus. $5.95
London, Deutsch, 1963. 272 pp. £1.50 (42½p pap.)

This book outlines the politics during Kenyatta's imprisonment, a period that later led to independence for Kenya. The late Tom Mboya, after being elected as one of the first African members of the Legislative Council in 1957, soon emerged as the political strategist of the group. He writes about the organization of his Nairobi party — Peoples' Convention Party — and the eventual co-ordination of this and other parties into the Kenya African National Union, which constituted the majority party of Kenya's first independent government. There are accounts of the constitutional conferences and the famous student air-lifts to the United States; there are definitions of African socialism, neo-colonial interferences, and the role of Africa in international affairs. Tom Mboya died tragically in late 1969 at the hands of an assassin.

661 Mphahlele, Ezekiel
The African Image
London, Faber, 1962. 246 pp. £1.25
New York, Praeger, 1962. 240 pp. out-of-print
These essays are grouped around four main themes: the African personality, which Mphahlele views as both political slogan and reality; the philosophy of negritude, of which he is critical; nationalism as seen by African and European; and lastly the literary image created by black and white alike. In the latter two groups, he quotes extensively from and comments on the literary achievements of Africans and Europeans.

662 Nicol, Davidson
Africa: a subjective view
London, Longmans, 1965 (Forum series). 88 pp. 62½p (37½p pap.)
New York, Humanities Press, distr. 1964. $2.25 ($1.50 pap.)
This collection presents the five lectures given at the Fourth Aggrey-Fraser-Guggisberg Lecture series at the University of Ghana in 1963. Dr Nicol comments on five significant areas of African development, under the themes 'Our Politicians', 'Our Critics and Lovers', 'Our Universities', 'Our Public Services', and 'Our Writers'. The second lecture is an examination of the writings of three Europeans who have concerned themselves with Africa and Africans — Albert Schweitzer, Joyce Cary, and Graham Greene.

663 Nkrumah, Kwame
I Speak of Freedom: a statement of African ideology
London, Heinemann, 1961. 291 pp. out-of-print
New York, Praeger, 1961. 291 pp. out-of-print
This selection of Nkrumah's speeches outlines the later years of Ghana's pre-independence

history. He begins here to define a major thesis in his quest for an ideology. In early 1958 Ghana was host to the conference of all independent African states. From this point on the thesis of all-Africa political unity under imperial conditions is stressed in his thought. Nkrumah is speaking of the freedom of the non-independent African countries, and the need to co-ordinate decolonization and political programmes among all African countries.

664 Nkrumah, Kwame
Towards Colonial Freedom
London, Heinemann Educ. Books, 1962. 64 pp. out-of-print. 1967 (paperback edn) 17½p
Originally written during the years 1942—1947, when Nkrumah was a student in the U.S.A. and in Britain, though not published until 1962, this is an attack against the colonial exploitation and political oppression of the African people. They are the early thoughts of Nkrumah, as he sees the newly independent countries of Africa threatened by a new phase of colonialism, which he terms *neo-colonialism*.

665 Nkrumah, Kwame
Africa Must Unite
London, Heinemann Educ. Books, 1963. 248 pp. out-of-print. 1965 (Mercury Books). 62½p (pap.)
New York, Praeger, 1963, 242 pp. $5.95
Affirming Nkrumah's firm belief in African unity, this book is designed as a call to the world's developing countries to work for their potentially rich and prosperous future. Nkrumah argues that it is important for each country to establish strong self-government. He discusses the case for Ghana and the role of the one-party system in unification. This, he feels, is a prerequisite to good administration and planning for economic development. On the point of priorities Nkrumah advocates the creation of political institutions rather than economic relationships.

666 Nkrumah, Kwame
Consciencism: Philosophy and Ideology for De-Colonization and Development with particular reference to the African Revolution
London, Heinemann Educ. Books, 1964, 128 pp. 75p
Nkrumah, after looking at the historical Euro-Christian and Islamic thinkers, and traditional African philosophy, tries to synthesize a working philosophy of his own, related to the revolutionary process. Most important in his philosophical scheme is the idea that there is 'absolute and independent existence of matter' as well as 'capacity of matter for spontaneous self-motion' — impulses which he claims are found in many traditional African societies to accentuate the natural forces existing in tension.

These two ideas are used by Nkrumah in analysing the economic role of a colony and the dependency situation of the African, which must come to an end through the politics of the mass party, which heightens the 'consciousness' of the masses. All this is used to illustrate what he calls the positive approach to African revolution.

667 Nkrumah, Kwame
Ghana: the autobiography of Kwame Nkrumah
London, Nelson, 1965. 320 pp. illus. £1.50 (25p pap.)

This book was completed in 1956, just before Ghana's independence and in it Nkrumah discusses in detail the ten years leading to self-rule. He had returned to Ghana in 1946 as an unknown university graduate. In six years he had taken over the old United Gold Coast Convention, a party dominated by civil servants and closed to the masses. He was detained, but later founded his own political party, the Convention People's Party, and began the mass action programme that ultimately led him to become Prime Minister in 1952. Until independence he ran the government in the name of the Queen.

668 Nkrumah, Kwame
Neo-colonialism: the last stages of imperialism
London, Nelson, 1965. 280 pp. illus. £2.10
London, Heinemann Educ. Books, 1968 (African Writers Series, 49). 180 pp. 50p.
New York, International Publishers, 1969. illus. $7.50 ($2.85 pap.)

Neo-colonialism involves balkanization, which according to Nkrumah leads to total dependence. This work supplies data on international financial holdings in Africa, and reaches the conclusion that until such time that the ownership and profits of these companies are channelled into African development, African independence remains meaningless. The companies studied by Nkrumah are basically those involved highly profitably in mining and investment banking.

669 Nkrumah, Kwame
Axioms of Kwame Nkrumah
London, Nelson, 1967. 85 pp. 52½p

A collection of significant short extracts from Nkrumah's previously published works, articles and speeches.

670 Nkrumah, Kwame
Challenge of the Congo
London, Nelson, 1967. 304 pp. £2.10
New York, International Publishers, 1967 and 1969. 304 pp. $7.50 ($2.65 pap.)

Several important themes emerge from this book, which deals with the crisis of Congo independence and the ensuing civil war. The major point made is that the mining interests in the Congo were opposed to Congolese independence. It is further argued that they precipitated the Katangese split. The United Nations force in the Congo is seen as basically incompetent and working for American ends. Ghana's army contingent under the U.N., Nkrumah feels, was used ineffectively, because of the expatriate commanders who did not agree with Ghana's diplomatic positions. Underlying these arguments is the implicit theme that crises such as the one in the Congo can be handled better by agreements between African countries — consequently Nkrumah proposes an all-African force.

671 Nkrumah, Kwame
Dark Days in Ghana
London, Panaf Books, 1968. 227 pp. 37½p
New York, International Publishers, 1969. 227 pp. $1.25

In this work Nkrumah is concerned with the legitimacy of the Ghanaian coup of Feb. 24, 1966, the forces that caused it, the people involved in it, and the reaction of his advisers and other politicians who went over to the National Liberation Council. Nkrumah places blame for the organization of the coup on Colonel Kotoka and Major Afrifa of the Army, and John Willie Kofi Harley, Commissioner of Police. He then discusses the relationship between the new military régime and the old opposition groups.

672 Nkrumah, Kwame
Handbook of Revolutionary Warfare: a guide to the armed phase of the African revolution
London, Panaf Books, 1968. 128 pp. 37½p
New York, International Publishers, 1969. 128 pp. illus. $1.50

Nkrumah here reveals that he had written some notes about guerrilla warfare before he was overthrown, and this book is an extension of his radical pan-Africanist position. He argues that guerrilla warfare should be directed against the remnants of colonial territories, Portuguese Guinea, Angola, Mozambique, and South Africa. This book sets up rules for the guerrillas and the All Africa Peoples' Revolutionary Party, which he sees as bearing the responsibility for continuing the revolution on a continental scale.

673 Nyerere, Julius K.
Uhuru na Ujamaa: Freedom and Socialism
London and New York, Oxford Univ. Press, 1968. 422 pp. £2.50/$9.50 ($3.25 pap.)

This is Nyerere's most extensive collection of public speeches (and therefore, official government statements) for the 1965–1967 period. These were the crucial years when Tanzania (1) moved towards a militant posture on decolonization; (2) established a rigorously neutral diplomatic position, unlike other African governments; (3) dissolved the independence parliament and held model elections in which some key ministers lost their posts; (4) rode the crisis of the East African Common Market; (5) reorganized the Civil Service. These speeches established Nyerere as one of the most innovatory African presidents as regards theories about the nature of the governmental process and its relationship to the people, particularly the peasants.

674 Nyerere, Julius K.
Ujamaa: essays on socialism
London and New York, Oxford Univ. Press, 1968. 186 pp. £1.07½/$3.40
The speeches drawn together in this collection present President Nyerere's theories on socialism. Among the several major points which emerge are that socialism represents the traditional African socio-politico-legal system, as stated in the now famous Arusha declaration; and the idea that Tanzania is committed to the preservation of those individual rights associated with the European enlightenment. He further argues for an economy controlled by workers and peasants through governing structures. To the extent that Tanzania is short of monetary resources, developmental capital was to be human investment, particularly through education of the population, since foreign aid would ultimately mean dependence. He also emphasizes the role of agriculture and the rights of a rural populace in a modern society.

675 Odinga, Oginga
Not yet Uhuru: an autobiography
London, Heinemann Educ. Books, 1967 (African Writers Series, 38). 340 pp. illus. £1.75 (55p pap.)
New York, Hill and Wang, 1967 and 1969. 324 pp. illus. $7.50 ($2.45 pap.)
Odinga, as a member of the Legislative Council, was one of the first people to publicly call for the release of Jomo Kenyatta and other nationalist leaders from prison in 1958; a call which united all other politicians in pledging allegiance to the released leader's party. When this was achieved, Kenyatta's Kenya Africa National Union organized the first government with Odinga as Vice-President. In 1966 came the split from KANU and Odinga's founding of the Kenya Peoples' Union. He argues that the break was caused by the failure of Kenya's ruling party to redistribute the country's resources to the people. Odinga's position is that the KANU Government had become unresponsive to the

masses and that the 'party bosses', led by Mboya, engineered a campaign to discredit him in the eyes of President Kenyatta. This political autobiography recounts the rise of Odinga from his birth, through his education, his political career, his drive for independence, and ultimately his split with Kenyatta.

676 Quaison-Sackey, Alex
Africa Unbound: reflections of an African statesman
New York, Praeger, 1963. 174 pp. $4.95 ($1.95 pap.)
Starting with an evaluation of the nature and causes of African independence and the African personality, Quaison-Sackey aims to chart a path for African diplomacy in its relations with the United States. Emphasis, he believes, should be placed on multi-lateral diplomacy, animated by the desire for positive neutrality. Quaison-Sackey illustrates his theories from the diplomatic record of Ghana. He makes a case for a reorganization of the United Nations, in which greater representation would be given to the Afro-Asian bloc.

677 Senghor, Léopold Sédar
Nationhood and the African Road to Socialism
(Trans. from the French)
Paris, Présence Africaine, 1962. 135 pp. F15.00
Written in 1959 before the break-up of the Mali Federation, the first part of this work, *Report on the Party's Doctrine and Programme*, is an attempt to define the nationality of the then emerging nation. Senghor does this persuasively in spite of the eventual failure of the Federation. He presents here his concepts of nation, fatherland and state, and his views on how to strengthen the Federation along democratic lines. In part two, *The African Road to Socialism*, President Senghor stresses the need for a culture emancipated from colonial values. Such, he states, will stress the 'emotive' tradition of Africa and synthesize it with the scientific method of Europe.

678 Senghor, Léopold Sédar
On African Socialism
(Trans. from the French by Mercer Cook)
London, Pall Mall Press, 1965. 173 pp. 80p
New York, Praeger, 1965. 173 pp. $5.00
The first two parts of this work originally appeared in French and were published by Présence Africaine. The third part, concerned with the theory and practice of Senegalese Socialism, is a speech delivered at a Seminar for Political Cadres of the Senegalese Progressive Union in December 1962. Senghor here denies the applicability of Marxian economics, but not the dialectic method. He assigns the state the duty of planning and executing social and economic change. Senghor borrows from

Teilhard de Chardin in his concept of the growing complexity and universalization of man's quest for the biological and psychological base of society.

679 **Sithole, Ndabaningi**
African Nationalism
New York and London, Oxford Univ. Press, 1968 and 1969 (2nd edn). 200 pp. illus. £1.75 (75p pap.)/$5.00 ($1.95 pap.)
Major themes in African political evolution are discussed in this partly autobiographical, partly political work. The causes behind African nationalism are identified as (1) the World War II experience, (2) United Nations' concern with decolonization, (3) Pan-African sharing of culture, (4) colonial racism, (5) the traditional heritage of democracy, (6) the egalitarian ideology of Christianity, (7) the positive aspects of European colonialism, such as the ending of *Mfecane*, and the coming of education and communication systems, and (8) new economic relationships. Sithole sees race as a major factor in the continued presence of colonial rule in Rhodesia, Mozambique, Angola and South Africa. He feels that the present debate on what form of political organization nations should adopt ignores the fact that ultimately different party organizations suited to individual situations must evolve.

680 **Touré, Sékou**
General Congress of the U.G.T.A.N. (G.U.N.A.W., General Union of Negro African Workers) held at Conakry, 15th to 18th January 1959: Report of policy and doctrine
(Trans. from the French)

Paris, Présence Africaine, 1959. 80 pp.
Sékou Touré, the President of Guinea, here presents a statement on the role of African trade unionism. He rejects unity among workers of the world when it comes to decolonization problems, since he sees metropolitan workers as benefiting from colonial exploitation. The realization of this, he states, will move African trade unionism from major international concerns, and will enable it to fight against balkanization of the continent. Touré argues that by unifying the various trade unions will become an instrument of the decolonization of society, rather than merely being an organization catering for the economic betterment of individual sectors of society.

681 **Touré, Sékou**
Guinean Revolution and Social Progress
Cairo, Societé Orientale de Publicité, 1963 [?]. 448 pp. out-of-print
The introduction to this work is an extract from the Report on Policy and Orientation submitted to the sixth Partie Démocratique de Guinée Congress, held at Conakry from 27 December 1962 to 1 January 1963. The President of Guinea evaluates the significance of World War Two, and the evolution of Guinean nationalism from that point on. He comments on the significance of the colonial party splits, its regrouping during the fifties, and the policies followed by independent Guinea under the leadership of Touré. Touré, goes on to discuss the important P.D.G. issues of non-alignment, African unity, the primacy of party control over the bureaucracy, and the reorganization of the mass party.

CHILDREN'S BOOKS

The following section presents a *selection* of books for children written by African authors. In most cases the illustrations are contributed by African artists. For some time African teachers and educators rightly complained that African children were forced to read books with an alien background, including those drab European classics and 'Jack-and-Jill'-type material, in lieu of books written by Africans with a familiar African setting.

The African Universities Press in Lagos (originally an associate company of André Deutsch) set out to remedy the situation in 1962 with the publication of its first titles in their *African Junior Library* and *African Readers Library* series. The latter, now consisting of eighteen titles, has made an important contribution to the literature for young people in Africa. Most of the books were written by Nigerian authors and, inevitably, provided a West African scenario; but in 1966 the East African Publishing House in Nairobi introduced its own series, the *East African Readers Library* and later the *East African Junior Library*.

These four series form the nucleus of the selection that follows, together with the titles in the *Rapid Reading Series* published by Thomas Nelson and Sons, London. The majority of all these simple readers contain lively and exciting adventure stories, often copiously and attractively illustrated. Several of them were produced by such prominent African novelists as Chinua Achebe, Cyprian Ekwensi and Onuora Nzekwu. Just as these books have been enthusiastically welcomed in Africa, they are similarly becoming increasingly popular outside the African continent, especially in the U.S.A., where the output of the African Universities Press is now exclusively distributed by Africana Publishing Corporation of New York, and that of the East African Publishing House by Northwestern University Press, Evanston, Illinois. In Britain, A.U.P. is distributed by Ginn and Co. and the E.A.P.H. list by Heinemann Educational Books Ltd. When local publishers are given, local prices are quoted.

Approximate age-groups are indicated in parentheses following prices, though it is stressed that these should *not* be interpreted too rigidly.

For a useful and informative survey of African juvenilia we recommend an article by Lalage Bown entitled 'Children's Books from Africa', published in Spring 1970 in *Interracial Books for Children*[1].

Abbs, Akosua
Ashanti Boy
See 143

682 **Achebe, Chinua**
Chike and the River
London and New York, Cambridge Univ. Press, 1966. 64 pp. illus. 15p/75c (11–14)
A first children's book by the prominent Nigerian novelist. It recounts Chike's adventure on the river Niger that 'brought him close to danger and then rewarded him with good fortune'.

683 **Ajose, Audrey**
Yomi's Adventures
London and New York, Cambridge Univ. Press, 1964. 90 pp. illus. 20p/75c (13–15)
An adventure story set in Nigeria and London by a Nigerian journalist.

684 **Ajose, Audrey**
Yomi in Paris
London and New York, Cambridge Univ. Press, 1966. 92 pp. illus. 20p/75c (12–15)
Yomi, the heroine of Audrey Ajose's previous story, goes to Paris and becomes involved in

[1] *Interracial Books for Children*, vol. 2, no. 4, Spring 1970, various pp., Council on Interracial Books for Children, Inc. 9 East 40th Street, New York, N.Y. 10016.

a mystery. Includes a list of French words used in the dialogue.

685 **Akinsemoyin, Kunle**
Stories at Sundown
London, Harrap, 1965. 71 pp. illus. 17½p (11–14)
Stories of 'Simple, the Elephant', 'Ika, the Ungrateful Lion', 'Slaka, the Poet', and other folk tales.

686 **Akinsemoyin, Kunle**
Twilight and the Tortoise
Lagos, African Univ. Press, 1963 (African Readers Library, 3). 80 pp. illus. 4s.0d./95c (12–15)
The author conveys the village atmosphere in a prelude: twilight is story-time in Nigeria. In those last rays of daylight the village children gather round the feet of the story-teller, begging for a tale before bedtime. These are the stories of the wily Tortie the tortoise, a not unfamiliar figure in African folk-lore.

687 **Akinsemoyin, Kunle**
Twilight Tales
Lagos, African Univ. Press, 1965 (African Readers Library, 10). 80 pp. illus. 4s.0d./95c (12–15)
More traditional stories, simply told.

688 **Akpabot, Anne**
Aduke Makes her Choice
London, Nelson, 1966 (Rapid Reading series, higher level, 4). 57 pp. illus. 20p (13–15)
The dreams and ambitions of a young Nigerian girl.

689 **Akpabot, Anne**
Sade and her Friends
London, Nelson, 1967 (Rapid Reading series, higher level, 6). 62 pp. illus. 20p (13–15)
Sade is a young Yoruba girl whose parents neglect her education, but she finally succeeds in obtaining one after many setbacks.

690 **Akpan, Ntieyong Udo**
Ini Abasi and the Sacred Ram
London, Longmans, 1966. 26 pp. illus. 5p (8–11)
Ini Abasi, son of Okon and Nko, is an incredibly strong champion wrestler, who apparently was born dumb. He miraculously recovers his voice when falsely accused of killing the village's sacred ram.

691 **Anizoba, Rose**
The Adventures of Mbugwe the Frog
London and Ibadan, Oxford Univ. Press, 1965 (The Little Bookshelf series). 94 pp. illus. 37½p
The many adventures of an enterprising frog from Enugu in Eastern Nigeria, in search of an education.

692 **Asheri, Jedida**
Promise
Lagos, African Univ. Press, 1969 (African Readers Library, 17). 96 pp. illus. 5s.6d./95c (13–15)
The story of a girl growing up thirty years ago in rural Cameroon. It tells of her family and her friends, her schooling, and her training in teaching and nursing, and depicts the influence of environment on an adolescent girl.

693 **Beier, Ulli,** and **Gbadamosi, Bakare** eds.
The Moon Cannot Fight
Ibadan, Mbari, 1964. Unpaged, illus. [46 pp.] out-of-print (13–15)
Yoruba childrens' poems, with explanatory notes.

694 **Blay, J. Benibengor**
Coconut Boy
Accra, Author (P.O. Box M12), 1970. 134 pp. N₵1. 25 (13–15) A story from Ghana

695 **Cartey, Wilfred** ed.
Palaver. Modern African Writings
Camden, N.J., Nelson, 1970. 224 pp. illus. $4.95 (13–15).
This anthology for young readers is an invitation to *palaver*, a getting together to chat, to discuss things, to confer, or to argue. Twenty-six African authors are represented with selections from poetry, drama, folk myths, and the novel. Each of the six parts is introduced by the editor with background information on the authors and the selections.

696 **Chibule, Anderson**
The Broken Branch
Nairobi, East African Publ. House, 1968. 48 pp. EAshs. 2/50 (13–15)
A young East African boy caught in the midst of conflict between the traditional views of his parents and those he has assimilated at school.

697 **Clinton, J. V.**
The Rescue of Charlie Kalu
London, Heinemann Educ. Books, 1970 (Heinemann Secondary Reading Scheme, 2). 64 pp. 20p (13–15)
The story of the rescue of a kidnapped boy in the creeks of Nigeria.

698 **Cole, Aaron**
Animal Palaver
London, Nelson, 1965 (Rapid Reading series, lower level, 5). 48 pp. illus. 12½p (13–15)
The animals meet to elect their king, but events take an unexpected turn. A story from Sierra Leone.

Cole, Robert Wellesley
Kossoh Town Boy
See 312

699 **Dahal, Charity**
The Orange Thieves, and other stories
Nairobi, East African Publ. House, 1966 (East African Readers Library, 5). 76 pp. illus. EAshs. 3.50/90c (11—14)
Stories of magic, mystery and adventure with one thing in common — they are all about giants.

700 **Decker, Thomas**
Tales of the Forest
London, Evans, 1968. 72 pp. illus. 22½p (11—14)
Twenty-six stories, simply told, based on traditional West African folk tales.

De Graft-Hanson, J. O.
The Secret of Opokuwa
See 165

701 **Dickson, Timothy**
David and the Gangsters
London, Nelson, 1965 (Rapid Reading series, lower level, 1). 80 pp. illus. 19p (13—15)
An adventure story.

702 **Doob, Leonard W.**
A Crocodile has me by the Leg; African poems
New York, Walker, 1967. unpaged $2.95 illus. (10—12)
A collection of proverbs, songs, chants and poems of traditional and modern Africa.

703 **Dzovo, E. V. K.**
Salami and Musa
London, Longmans, 1967. 72 pp. 25p (13—15)
The story of Salami, a Northern Ghanaian boy, who against his family's advice leaves home to seek his fortune.

704 **Ekwensi, Cyprian**
Ikolo the Wrestler, and other Ibo tales
London, Nelson, 1947. out-of-print
Reissued as *The Great Elephant-Bird* in 1965, see 710

705 **Ekwensi, Cyprian**
The Leopard's Claw
London, Longmans, 1950. 90 pp. out-of-print

706 **Ekwensi, Cyprian**
The Drummer Boy
London and New York, Cambridge Univ. Press, 1960. 88 pp. illus. 20p/$0.75 (13—15)
Tells the story of Akin, a blind beggar boy, who is a superb drummer.

707 **Ekwensi, Cyprian**
The Passport of Mallam Ilia
London and New York, Cambridge Univ. Press, 1960. 80 pp. illus. 20p/75c (13—15)
A tale of intrigue and revenge.

708 **Ekwensi, Cyprian**
An African Night's Entertainment
Lagos, African Univ. Press, 1962 (African Readers Library, 1). 96 pp. illus. 5s.6d./95c (13—15)
An adventure story of betrayal and vengeance, by a prominent Nigerian novelist, which centres on the African custom of betrothing girls when they are very young.

709 **Ekwensi, Cyprian**
The Rainmaker and other stories
Lagos, African Univ. Press, 1965 (African Readers Library, 6). 80 pp. illus. 4s. 0d./95c (13—15)
A collection of adventure stories and tales featuring schoolboys of Nigeria as its heroes.

710 **Ekwensi, Cyprian**
The Great Elephant-Bird
London, Nelson, 1965 (Rapid Reading series, lower level, 2). 80 pp. illus. 19p (11—14)
A collection of Nigerian folk tales, 'to be told only at night, for it was believed that the narrator's mother would die if they were told by day.'

711 **Ekwensi, Cyprian**
The Boa Suitor
London, Nelson, 1966 (Rapid Reading series, lower level, 6). 64 pp. illus. 19p (11—14)
A sequel to *The Great Elephant-Bird:* more popular tales.

712 **Ekwensi, Cyprian**
Trouble in Form Six
London and New York, Cambridge Univ. Press, 1966. 76 pp. illus. 17½p/75c (13—15)

713 **Ekwensi, Cyprian**
Juju Rock
Lagos, African Univ. Press, 1966 (African Readers Library, 11). illus. 110 pp. 4s.6d/95c (11—14)
Rikku Sansaye's adventures when he joins in the search for the missing Captain Plowman, lost in an expedition to find gold at Juju rock.

714 **Gichuru, Stephen**
The Fly Whisk, and other stories
Nairobi, East African Publ. House, 1968 (East

African Readers Library, 10). 72 pp. illus. EAshs. 3.50/50c (11–14)

An anthology of stories and folk tales from Masailand, Kenya.

715 **Gwengwe, J. W.**
Sulizo Achieves Greatness
London, Evans, 1968. 62 pp. 21p illus. (11–13)
The adventures of young Sulizo, from his school-days to early manhood.

716 **Hoh, I. K.**
Prodigal Brothers
London, Evans, 1968 (Plays for African Schools) 48 pp. 15p (13–15)
The reverend Doe and his wife have two trouble-some sons. This play tells the story of their many adventures and misfortunes.

717 **Hunter, Cynthia**
The Speck of Gold
Nairobi, East African Publ. House, 1968 (East African Readers Library, 20). 52 pp. illus. EAshs. 2.00 50c (11–13)
Eight stories from East Africa.

718 **Ibongia, John M.,** and **Bobrin, M.**
The Magic Stone and other stories
Nairobi, East African Publ. House, 1967 (East African Readers Library, 12). 50 pp. illus. EAshs. 2.50/75c (11–13)
Stories told by a grandmother from the high-lands in western Kenya.

719 **Irungu, Daniel**
The Powerful Magician, and other stories
Nairobi, East African Publ. House, 1969 (East African Readers Library, 24). 46 pp. illus. EAshs. 3.00/90c (11–13)
Daniel Irungu recounts the stories told to him by his grandmother.

720 **Japuonjo, Roeland**
Mzee Nyachote
Nairobi, East African Publ. House, 1967 (East African Readers Library, 6). 56 pp. illus. EAshs. 2.50/75c (10–12)
Told as a series of anecdotes, these are tales of the adventures of a mischievous boy in Kenya.

721 **Kala, John**
The Adventures of Musa Kaago
Nairobi, East African Publ. House, 1968 (East African Readers Library, 8). 99 pp. EAshs. 4.00/$1.50 (10–12)
An attempt by Musa Kaago's stepmother to do away with him brings tragedy and the death of her own daughter.

722 **Kawegere, Fortunatus**
Inspector Rajabu investigates

Nairobi, East African Publ. House, 1968 (East African Readers Library, 15). 36 pp. illus. EAshs. 2.00/50c (11–13)
Set in Tanzania, an inspector of police on leave in Mwanza gets onto the trail of a gang of bank robbers.

723 **Kay, Kwesi**
The Treasure Chamber
London, Heinemann Educ. Books, 1970 (Heine-mann Secondary Reading Scheme, 6). 96 pp. illus. 20p (11–13)
A historical play about Egypt, written by a Ghanaian.

724 **Kimenye, Barbara**
The Smugglers
London, Nelson, 1968 (Rapid Reading series, lower level, 9). 64 pp. illus. 19p/95c (11–13)
An eventful adventure awaits three African boys who stray across the Congo-Uganda border.

Kimenye, Barbara
Kalasanda
See 364
Kalasanda revisited
See 365

Kironde, Erisa
See 367

725 **Kuguru, Peter**
The Tales of Wamugumo
Nairobi, East African Publ. House, 1968 (East African Readers Library, 7). 73 pp. illus. EAshs. 4.00/$1.50 (11–13)
The stories of Wamugumo, retold by a young Kenyan. Wamugumo was one of the most famous story-tellers among the Kikuyu people of Kenya.

726 **Kyendo, Kalondu**
Cock and Lion
Nairobi, East African Publ. House, 1969 (East African Junior Library, 9). 32 pp. illus. EAshs. 1.70/50c (10–12)
Seven stories from central Kenya.

727 **Lantum, Daniel** ed.
Tales of Nso
Lagos, African Univ. Press, 1969 (African Readers Library, 18). 80 pp. illus. 5s.0d./95c (13–15)
A number of tales from the Nso area of Cameroon, primarily evolving around a wicked character named Wanyeto.

728 **Leshoai, B. L.**
Masilo's Adventures
London, Longmans, 1968. 48 pp. 21p (11–13)
Four tales from Lesotho concerning giants,

monsters, warriors and a beautiful princess, as told to the author by his grandmother.

729 Manley, Deborah ed.
Growing Up
Lagos, African Univ. Press, 1967 (African Readers Library, 15). 80 pp. illus. 4s.6d./95c (13—15)
West African childhood memories. Includes extracts from the writings of Adelaide Casely-Hayford, Prince Modupe, Camara Laye, William Conton, Mabel Segun and others.

730 Makumi, Joel
The Children of the Forest
Nairobi, East African Publ. House, 1968 (East African Readers Library, 18). 42 pp. illus. EAshs. 2.50/75c (10—12)
A shepherd finds two little children abandoned in a deserted hut in a forest, and he and his wife decide to bring them up as part of their family.

731 Matindi, Anne
The Lonely Black Pig
Nairobi, East African Publ. House, 1968 (African Junior Library, 5). 30 pp. illus. EAshs. 1.70/50c (8—10)
Stories and folk tales from East Africa.

732 Matindi, Anne
The Sun and the Wind
Nairobi, East African Publ. House, 1968 (East African Junior Library, 7). 28 pp. illus. EAshs. 1.65/50c (9—11)

733 Muffett, D. J. M.
The Story of Sultan Attahiru
Lagos, African Univ. Press, 1968 (African Readers Library, 16). 112 pp. illus. 5s.6d./95c (13—15)
An account of Sultan Attahiru's courageous fight against the British in 1902.

734 Mukunyi, Dickson
The Pet Snake and other stories
Nairobi, East African Publ. House, 1968 (East African Readers Library, 19). 47 pp. illus. EAshs. 2.50/75c (9—11)
Ten short stories.

735 Mukunyi, Dickson
Kikuyu Tales
Nairobi, East African Publ. House, 1969. 100 pp. illus. EAshs. 3.50/$1.40 (9—11)
Tales from Kenya's Kikuyu country.

736 Murphy, M., Maley, A., and Onadipe, Kola
The Chief's Counsellors, with other plays
Lagos, African Univ. Press, 1971. (in preparation)

Contains plays to act and plays for puppets, with instructions on how to produce plays and how to make puppets and a puppet stage in the classroom.

737 Nagenda, Musa
Dogs of Fear
London, Heinemann Educ. Books, 1970 (Heinemann's Secondary Reading Scheme, 1). 96 pp. illus. 20p (13—15)
A short story of a boy who, having failed his initiation rites, finds school a more hospitable place than home.

738 Ndoro, Joyce
The Hare's Horns
Nairobi, East African Publ. House, 1968 (East African Readers Library, 16). 36 pp. illus. EAshs. 2.00/50c (9—11)
Six stories from the Baringo district in Kenya.

739 Ngibuini, Peter Kuguru
Tales of Wamugumo
Nairobi, East African Publ. House, 1967 (East African Readers Library, 7). 70 pp. illus. EAshs. 4.00/$1.40 (10—12)
Traditional tales of a giant named Wamugumo, a man of fantastic strength and an enormous appetite.

740 Ndungu, Frederick
Beautiful Nyakio
Nairobi, East African Publ. House, 1968 (East African Readers Library, 17). 34 pp. illus. EAshs. 2.00/50c (10—12)
The main story in this collection centres around the ugliest man in the village, who very nearly succeeds in winning the hand of the beautiful Nyakio, a girl who has refused to speak to any man.

741 Ng'osos, David
The Man who Stopped Hunting, and other stories
Nairobi, East African Publ. House, 1968 (East African Readers Library). 100. pp. EAshs. 4.50/$1.70 (10—12)
Stories of the Tugen people of the Baringo district in Kenya.

Nicol, Abioseh
Two African tales
See 319

742 Njoroge, J. K.
The Greedy Host and other stories
Nairobi, East African Publ. House, 1968 (East African Readers Library, 11). 36 pp. illus. EAshs. 2.00/50c (10—12)
Stories of zebras, tortoises and hyenas, simply told.

743 Njoroge, J.K.
The Proud Ostrich and other tales
Nairobi, East African Publ. House, 1968 (East African Readers Library, 9), 49 pp. illus. EAshs. 2.00/50c (9—11)
Six simple folk tales from East Africa.

744 Njoroge, J. K.
Tit for Tat
Nairobi, East African Publ. House, 1969 (East African Senior Library). 101 pp. illus. EAshs. 4.50/$1.70 (11—13)
Traditional folk tales from Kenya. 'These stories deal with human beings and animals in all their glory, folly, agony and wisdom,' writes the author.

745 Nwankwo, Nkem
Tales out of School
Lagos, African Univ. Press, 1963 (African Readers Library, 2). 80 pp. illus. 4s.0d./95c (13—15)
The adventures of two Nigerian schoolboys, Bayo and Ike — two great friends although of different tribes — during their first term of grammar school.

746 Nwankwo, Nkem
More Tales out of School
Lagos, African Univ. Press, 1965 (African Readers Library, 7). 80 pp. illus. 4s.0d./95c (13—15)
In this sequel to *Tales out of School* Bayo becomes an amateur detective.

747 Nzekwu, Onuora, and Crowder, Michael
Eze Goes to School
Lagos, African Univ. Press, 1963 (African Readers Library, 4). 80 pp. illus. 4s.6d./95c (13—15)
The trials of an Ibo boy determined to go to school and get an education, despite all the odds against him.

748 Ogot, Pamela
East African How Stories
Nairobi, East African Publ. House, 1968 (East African Junior Library, 2). 44 pp. illus. EAshs. 1.70/50c (9—11)
A collection of traditional tales, containing 'How the hawk and the crow came to hate each other', 'How the leopard got his spots', 'How the hyena got an ugly coat', and other stories.

749 Ogot, Pamela
East African When Stories
Nairobi, East African Publ. House, 1968 (East African Junior Library, 8). 35 pp. illus. EAshs. 1.70/50c (9—11)

This book includes 'When death began', 'When people stopped killing twin girls', 'When the guinea-fowl stopped living with people', and other tales.

750 Okoro, Anezi
New Broom at Amanzu
Lagos, African Univ. Press, 1967 (African Readers Library, 14). 96 pp. illus. 4s.6d./95c (13—15)
The village school gets a new headmaster, and his methods arouse strong feelings locally.

751 Okoro, Anezi
The Village School
Lagos, African Univ. Press, 1966 (African Readers Library, 13). 112 pp. illus. 4s.6d./95c (13—15)
A picture of life in a primary school in Nigeria. A soccer match between the school's first and second elevens is of particular importance.

752 Olagoke, D. Olu
The Incorruptible Judge
London, Evans, 1967 (Plays for African Schools). 48 pp. 15p (10—12)
A judge withstands all temptations of bribery.

753 Olagoke, D. Olu
The Iroko-man and the Wood-carver
London, Evans, 1963 (Plays for African schools). 44 pp. 15p (10—12)
A play based on a local Nigerian legend that a wood-carver can never get rich through such a trade. The play, taking this superstition into account, gives it a happy turn by making a wood-carver prosper.

754 Olela, Henry and Neuendorffer, Mary Jane
Beyond Those Hills
London, Evans, 1966 (Evans Children's Library). 134 pp. 22½p illus. (10—11)
Jumu is a young boy who lives with his family on Rusinga Island in Lake Victoria. He has great dreams of going to Kisii on the mainland to further his education and to see more of the world. The story tells how he achieves this. The late Tom Mboya contributes a foreword, in which he says 'this is a book that will contribute much to our efforts in education.'

755 Omolo, Leo Odera
Onyango's Triumph
Nairobi, East African Publ. House, 1968 (East African Readers Library, 14). 47 pp. illus. EAshs. 3.00/90c (13—15)
A Kenyan schoolboy's adventurous career, from new boy to senior prefect.

756 **Onadipe, Kola**
The Adventures of Souza
Lagos, African Univ. Press, 1963 (African
Readers Library, 5). 80 pp. illus. 4s.0d./95c
(11—13)
The adventures, deeds and misdeeds of a
Nigerian boy in his home village, told by Souza
himself.

757 **Onadipe, Kola**
Koku Baboni
Lagos, African Univ. Press, 1965 (African Junior
Library, 3). 80 pp. illus. 3s.0d./80c (8—10)
A brave woman and a little boy bring to an end
the fear of twin births in their community.

758 **Onadipe, Kola**
Sugar Girl
Lagos, African Univ. Press, 1964 (African Junior
Library, 1). 72 pp. illus. 3s.0d./80c (8—10)
A kind of West African *Little Red Riding Hood*,
this is the story of Ralia, the 'sugar girl' who
follows a little bird and finds herself lost in the
forest.

759 **Onadipe, Kola**
The Boy Slave
Lagos, African Univ. Press, 1966 (African
Readers Library, 12). 112 pp. illus. 4s.6d./95c
(8—11)
The life story of a Nigerian boy taken as a slave
by Sheik Maitama's men to the edge of the
Sahara in the mid-nineteenth century.

760 **Oppong-Affi, A. M.**
Powers of Darkness
London, Heinemann Educ. Books, 1970 (Heinemann Secondary Reading Scheme, 4). 96 pp.
illus. 20p (13—15)
A Ghanaian Roman Catholic schoolboy is
attracted by a Muslim magician, and this leads
to conflicts with his teachers.

761 **Owosu, Martin**
The Story Ananse told
London, Heinemann Educ. Books, 1970 (Heinemann Secondary Reading Scheme, 5). 64 pp.
20p (13—15)
A play about Ananse the spider, one of the
central figures of West African folk-lore.

762 **Redford, William**
The Elephant's Heart and other stories
Nairobi, East African Publ. House, 1968 (East
African Junior Library, 6). 38 pp. illus. EAshs.
2.00/50c (8—10)
East African stories of elephants, giraffes,
donkeys and other animals.

763 **Redford, William**
Game Park Holiday
Nairobi, East African Publ. House, 1967 (East
African Readers Library, 13). 38 pp. illus. EAshs.
2.00/50c (9—11)
John's adventures during his holiday with his
uncle, a game warden in the National Park.

764 **Segun, Mabel**
My Father's Daughter
Lagos, African Univ. Press, 1965 (African
Readers Library, 8). 80 pp. illus. 4s.6d./95c
(10—12)
Portrays the experiences of a young Kenyan girl,
the daughter of a versatile father, a doctor, judge
and postal agent.

765 **Sutherland, Efua Theodora**
Playtime in Africa
Photographs by Willis E. Bell
New York, Atheneum, 1962. 58 pp. illus. $3,50
(11—13)
A picture essay combining rhythmic verse with
photographs depicting playtime activities of
children in Ghana.

Sutherland, Efua Theodora
See also 187

766 **Taiwo, Oladele**
The King's Heir
London, Nelson, 1965 (Rapid Reading series,
lower level, 4). 80 pp. illus. 19p (10—12)
A collection of stories, riddles and proverbs
from Nigerian folk-lore, reflecting the traditional
beliefs, customs and attitudes of Nigerians.

767 **Taiwo, Oladele**
The Hunter and the Hen
Lagos, African Univ. Press, 1965 (African Junior
Library, 2). 80 pp. illus. 3s.0d./80c (8—10)
Twenty-four stories and folk tales from Nigeria.

768 **Tetteh-Lartey, A. C. V. B.**
The Schooldays of Shango Solomon
London Cambridge Univ. Press, 1965. 80 pp.
illus. 20p (10—12)
A school story set in Ghana.

769 **Ukoli, Neville M.**
The Twins of the Rain Forest
London, Longmans, 1968. 64 pp. 25p (10—12)
New York, Humanities Press, distr. $1.00
This story is set in an imaginary village in the
Niger delta. The events take place in an era long
past when the birth of twins was considered
an evil omen to the local community.

770 **Uwemedimo, Rosemary**
Akpan and the Smugglers
Lagos, African Univ. Press, 1965 (African
Readers Library, 9). 78 pp. illus. 4s.6d./95c
(13—15)

A detective-type story involving Akpan Bassey in an attempt to foil a smugglers plot.

771 **Waciuma, Charity**
Mweru the Ostrich Girl
Nairobi, East African Publ. House, 1966 (East African Readers Library, 1). 48 pp. illus. EAshs. 2.50/75c (13—15)
Mweru, the ostrich girl, runs away from home into a world of magic, alien creatures and strange adventures.

772 **Waciuma, Charity**
The Golden Feather
Nairobi, East African Publ. House, 1966 (East African Readers Library, 4). 48 pp. illus. EAshs. 2.50/75c (11—13)
A search for a lost cow leads little Keru to the home of the great giant after a series of exciting adventures.

Wegesa, Benjamin S.
Captured by raiders
See 378

773 **When I awoke**
Nairobi, East African Publ. House, 1968 (East African Senior Library). 69 pp. illus. EAshs. 3.50/$1.70 (10—12)

A collection of stories by young East African school children, this is the outcome of a literary competition sponsored by the Associated Tea Growers of East Africa and the Brooke Bond Tea Company. One of the rules of the competition stated that all essays had to begin with 'When I awoke . . .'

774 **Wimbush, Dorothy**
The Man with the Matchet
London, Nelson, 1965 (Rapid Reading series, lower level, 3). 87 pp. illus. 19p (10—12)
Four tales from Northern Nigeria. How police Corporal Shehu solves a murder case is the subject of the first of them.

775 **Wimbush, Dorothy**
The Road Raiders
London, Nelson, 1967 (Rapid Reading series, lower level, 10), 84 pp. illus. 19p (10—12)
A tale of robbery and detection in Nigeria today.

776 **Yassin, Mohammed**
Tales from Sierra Leone
London, Oxford University Press, 1967. 55 pp. illus. 22½p (11—13)
These stories from Sierra Leone in West Africa were collected over a long period from different people of various dialects.

STOP PRESS ADDENDUM

At the time of writing, the following titles have been announced for publication late in 1970, or during the course of 1971. (All prices and bibliographical details are subject to change.)

BIBLIOGRAPHIES

777 **Jahn, Janheinz,** and **Dressler, Claus Peter**
Bibliography of Creative African Writing
Nendeln, Liechtenstein, Kraus, 1971. $25.00

CRITICAL WORKS

778 **Anozie, Sunday O.**
Sociologie du roman Africain. Realisme, structure et détermination dans la roman moderne ouest-Africain
Paris, Aubier, 1970 (Coll. Tiers-Monde et Developpment). 268 pp. F12.00

779 **Anozie, Sunday O.**
Christopher Okigbo
London, Evans, 1971 (African Writers and their Work). 160 pp. £1.25 (60p pap.)

780 **Awoonor, Kofi**
The Breast of the Earth. A study of the cultures and literature of Africa
New York, Doubleday, 1971.

781 **Carroll, David**
Chinua Achebe
New York, Twayne, 1970 (Twayne's World Authors, 101). 156 pp. $5.50

782 **Finnegan, Ruth**
Oral Literature in Africa
London, Oxford Univ. Press, 1970 (Oxford Library of African Literature), 580 pp. map £5.00

783 **Goodwin, K. L.** ed.
National Identity. Papers delivered at the Commonwealth literatue conference, University of Queensland, Brisbane, 9th—15th August, 1968
London, Heinemann Educ. Books, 1970. 219 pp. £3.00

784 **King, Bruce** ed.
Introduction to Nigerian Literature
London, Evans (with the University of Lagos), 1971. 224 pp. £2.50 (£1.00 pap.)

785 **Klimá, Vládimir**
Modern Nigerian Novels
London, C. Hurst, distr., 1970 (Dissertationes orientales, vol. 18). 204 pp. £2.25

786 **Moore, Gerald**
Wole Soyinka
London, Evans, 1971 (African Writers and their Work). 112 pp. £1.25 (60p pap.)

787 **Wade, Michael**
Peter Abrahams
London, Evans, 1971 (African Writers and their Work). 112 pp. £1.25 (60p pap.)

ANTHOLOGIES

788 **Cazziol, Roger J.**
Douze auteurs Africains. A direct method reader with oral practise
London, Nelson, 1971. 88 pp. 40p

789 **Cook, David,** and **Rubadiri, David**
Poems from East Africa
London, Heinemann Educ. Books, 1971 (African Writers Series, 96). 240 pp. 55p

790 **Knappert, Jan**
A Choice of Flowers. Swahili love poems with translations
London, Heinemann Educ. Books, 1971 (African Writers Series, 93). 300 pp. 60p

791 **Knappert, Jan**
Myths and Legends of the Congo
London, Heineman Educ. Books, 1971 (African Writers Series, 83). 224 pp. 75p

792 **Kunene, Daniel P.**
Heroic Poetry of the Basotho
London, Oxford Univ. Press, 1971 (Oxford Library of African Literature). 240 pp. £3.50

793 **Okeke, Uche**
Ibo Folktales
New York, Doubleday, 1971. illus.

794 **Soyinka, Wole** ed.
Plays from the Third World. An anthology
New York, Doubleday, 1971.

FICTION

795 **Achebe, Chinua**
Girls at War and other Stories
London, William Heinemann, 1971 (cloth ed)
London, Heinemann Educ. Books, 1971 (African Writers Series, 100) 50p

796 **Armah, Ayi Kwei**
Why Are We So Blest?
New York, Doubleday, 1971.
London, Heinemann, 1971.

797 **Awoonor, Kofi**
This Earth, my Brother
New York, Doubleday, 1971.

798 **Bebey, Francis**
Agatha Moudio's Son
(Trans. from the French by Joyce Hutchinson)
London, Heinemann Educ. Books, 1971 (African
Writers Series, 86). 160 pp. 50 p.

799 **Beti, Mongo**
The Poor Christ of Bomba
(Trans. from the French by Gerald Moore)
London, Heinemann Educ. Books, 1971 (African
Writers Series, 88). 256 pp. 60p

800 **Blay, J. Benibengor**
Alomo
Accra, West African Publ. Co. (Box 40), 1970.
72 pp. 35Nc

801 **Dadié, Bernard B.**
Climbié
(Trans. from the French by Karen C. Chapman)
London, Heinemann Educ. Books, 1971 (African
Writers Series, 87). 196 pp.
New York. Africana Publishing Corp., 1971.
196 pp.

802 **Head, Bessie**
Maru
London, Gollancz, 1971. 127 pp. £1.20

803 **Kayira, Legson**
The Civil Servant
London, Longman, 1971. 216 pp. £1.75

804 **Mezu, S. Okechukwu**
Behind the Rising Sun
London, Heinemann, 1971. 241 pp. £2.10

805 **Mazrui, Ali**
The Trial of Christopher Okigbo
London, Heinemann Educ. Books, 1971
(African Writers Series, 97). 160 pp. 50p.

806 **Mphahlele, Ezekiel**
Down Second Avenue (New impr.)
London, Faber, 1971. 60p
New York, Doubleday, 1971 (with a new intro-
duction by the author).

807 **Mulaisho, Dominic**
The Tongue of the Dumb
London, Heinemann Educ. Books, 1971 (African
Writers Series, 98). 280 pp. 60p

808 **Munonye, John**
The Oil Man of Obange
London, Heinemann Educ. Books, 1971 (African
Writers Series, 94). 224 pp.

809 **Ousmane, Sembene**
The Money Order
(Trans. from the French by Clive Wake)
London, Heinemann Educ. Books, 1971 (African
Writers Series, 92). 160 pp. 40p

POETRY
810 **Awoonor, Kofi**
Night of my Blood
New York, Doubleday, 1971.

811 **Kgositsile, Keroapetse**
My name is Afrika
New York, Doubleday, 1971.

812 **Lo Lyiong, Taban**
*Franz Fahon's Uneven Ribs and Poems More and
More*
(African Writers Series, 90). 160 pp. 60p
London, Heinemann Educ. Books, 1971.

813 **p'Bitek, Okot**
Song of a Prisoner
New York, The Third Press, 1971 (With an
introduction by Edward Blishen). $5.00

DRAMA
814 **Carlin, Murray**
Not so Sweet Desdemona
Nairobi, Oxford Univ. Press, 1970 (New Drama
from Africa, 2). 68 pp. 50p

815 **Carlin, Murray**
The Thousand
Nairobi, Oxford Univ. Press, 1970. (New Drama
from Africa, 3). 86 pp. 50p

816 **Egbuna, Obi B.**
The Gods are not to Blame
London, Oxford Univ. Press, 1970 (Three
Crowns Book). 60 pp. 50p

817 **Lemma, Menghista**
The Marriage of Unequals: a comedy
London, Macmillan, 1970. 96 pp. 30p

818 **Maddy, Pat**
Obasai and Other Plays
London, Heinemann Educ. Books, 1971 (African
Writers Series, 89) 240 pp. 55p

POLITICALLY COMMITTED LITERATURE
819 **Mboya, Tom**
The Challenge of Nationhood
London, Deutsch, 1970. 288 pp. £2.10
New York, Praeger, 1970. 288 p. $7.50

CHILDREN'S
820 **Onadipe, Kola**
Magic Land of the Shadows
Lagos, African Univ. Press, 1971.

SOME ARTICLES ON AFRICAN LITERATURE

BARBARA ABRASH

This is an annotated list of select articles that have appeared in magazines and periodicals on creative African literature in the European languages. I should stress that it is a *selection* only.

The articles presented deal with African literature *in general*. Specialized papers analysing the work of a single author have not been included.

Special emphasis has been placed on critical writings by Africans writing on their own literature.

All the articles are in English and may be found in periodicals available in academic libraries.

BIBLIOGRAPHIES
Periodicals

African Literature Today regularly includes bibliographies of new and recently published creative writing by African authors. Related critical and reference works are also listed.

The Journal of Commonwealth Literature has comprehensive annual bibliographies of creative African writing in English.

The annual *MLA International Bibliography* gives extensive coverage of *scholarship* on African literature.

Articles

East, N. B., 'African theatre: a checklist of critical materials', *Afro-Asian Theatre Bulletin*, IV, 2 (Spring 1969), N3—N17.

Graham-White, Anthony 'A bibliography of African drama', *Afro-Asian Theatre Bulletin*, III, 1 (October 1967), 10—22.

Lindfors, Bernth 'Additions and corrections to Janheinz Jahn's *Bibliography of Neo-African Literature* (1965)', *African Studies Bulletin*, XI, 2 (September 1968), 129—148.

Lindfors, Bernth, 'A preliminary checklist of Nigerian drama in English', *Afro-Asian Theatre Bulletin*, II, 2 (February 1967), 16—21.

Lindfors, Bernth, 'American university and research library holdings in African literature', *African Studies Bulletin*, XI, 3 (December 1968), 286—311.

Lindfors, Bernth, 'Nigerian drama in American libraries', *Afro-Asian Theatre Bulletin*, III, 2 (February 1968), 22—27.

Lindfors, Bernth, 'Addenda to a preliminary checklist of Nigerian drama in English', *Afro-Asian Theatre Bulletin*, III, 1 (October 1967), 22—25.

Páricsy, Paul, 'A supplementary bibliography of J. Jahn's Bibliography of Neo-African Literature from Africa, America and the Caribbean', *J. of the New African Literature and the Arts*, 4 (Fall 1967), 70—82.

GENERAL

Achebe, Chinua, 'Where angels fear to tread', *Nigeria Magazine*, no. 2 (1962), 61—62.
The problem of European and American critics validly analysing and judging African fiction is raised. The conclusion is that no man can understand another whose language and world-view he does not share.

Achebe, Chinua. 'The novelist as teacher', *New Statesman*, 29 Jan. 1965, 161—2.
Achebe's thesis is that art and education need not be mutually exclusive in Africa. His role as a novelist is to help his people regain their belief in themselves after years of degradation.

Achebe, Chinua, 'English and the African writer', *Transition*, IV, 18 (1965), 27—30.
The use of the English language by African writers has been questioned. This author feels that the African writer can effectively adapt and use English to bear the burden of African experience.

Crowder, Michael, 'Tradition and change in Nigerian literature', *Triquarterly*, 5 (1966), 117—128.
Nigerian writers, 'popular' and intellectual, their themes, their audiences, and their links with the past. Ekwensi, J. P. Clark, Tutuola, Soyinka, and others.

Dipoko, Mbella Sonne, 'Cultural diplomacy in African writing', *Africa Today*, XV, 4 (August/September 1968), 8—11.
French-African writing has been a response to the colonial experience, idealizing the past and addressing itself to a European audience. This author suggests that this produces cultural alienation, and that African writers should find a new realism. Discusses Senghor, Césaire, Oyono, and U Tam'si.

'First word', *African Arts/Arts d'Afrique*, I, 4 (Summer 1968), 2, 7, 111.
General introduction to the role of African literature and the African writer.

Hendrickse, Begum, 'The Mbari story', *African Forum*, I, 1 (Summer 1965), 109—111.
An account of the Mbari Club, founded by Ulli Beier in 1961, which supported and publicized the work of writers and artists, providing stimulus to the creative arts in Nigeria.

Jahn, Janheinz, 'African literature', *Présence Africaine*, Eng. ed., XX, 48 (1963), 47—57.
States the view that there is a distinct 'African' literature, possessing a unique style embedded in African culture, which may express itself in whatever language the African author chooses to use.

Jones, Eldred D., 'African literature 1966—1967', *African Forum*, III, 1 (Summer 1967), 5—25.
An evaluation of J. P. Clark's *Ozidi*, Lenrie Peters' *Satellites*, James Ngugi's *A Grain of Wheat*, and several other works.

Jones, Eldred D., 'Jungle drums and wailing piano: West African fiction and poetry in English', *African Forum*, I, 4 (Spring 1966), 93—106.
West African writers, subject both to traditional African and modern influences, who are creating a unique new literature. Achebe, Okara, Soyinka, and Ekwensi are discussed.

Larson, Charles, 'The search for the past: East and Central African writing', *Africa Today*, XV, 4 (August/September 1968), 12—15.
East and Central African writers are preoccupied with themes of the past. Kayira's *A Looming Shadow*, Samkange's *On Trial for my Country*, Asalache's *A Calabash of Life*, and Ngugi's novels are discussed.

Lindfors, Bernth, 'A decade of *Black Orpheus*', *Books Abroad*, XLII, 4 (Autumn 1968), 509—516.
An account of a literary magazine, begun in 1957, which was a primary influence in stimulating and publicizing African literature.

Moore, Gerald, 'African writing seen from Salisbury', *Présence Africaine*, Eng. ed., III, 31 (1960), 87—94.
A short review of the influences which caused African writing in French to develop differently from African writing in English.

Moore, Gerald, 'Towards realism in French African writing', *J. of Modern African Studies*, I, 1 (March 1963), 61—73.
The 'négritude' of early French-African writing had a rhetorical and sentimental quality. In the novels of Mongo Beti, Ferdinand Oyono, and Cheikh Hamidou Kane this author sees a trend toward a more searching realism.

Moser, Gerald M. 'African literature in Portuguese: the first written, the last discovered', *African Forum*, II, 4 (Spring 1967), 78—96.
The literatures of Angola, Mozambique, the Cape Verde Islands, and the Islands of São Tomé and Príncipe — their sources, themes, and writers.

Mphahlele, Ezekiel, 'African literature for beginners', *Africa Today*, XIV, 1 (January 1967), 25—31.
An outline of African literature in terms of its dominant themes (the colonial experience, the black-white encounter, the erosion of traditional values, etc.) and key writers.

Nicol, Davidson, 'The soft pink palms', *Présence Africaine*, Eng. ed., 8—10 (1956), 107—121.
On British West African writers — historical, political, and literary — from the seventeenth century to the 1950's, with emphasis on the twentieth century.

Nkosi, Lewis, 'African fiction: Part I — South Africa: protest', *Africa Report*, VII, 9 (October 1962), 3—6.
The moods and themes of South African writing. Rive, Modisane, Mphahlele, and others are discussed.

Nkosi, Lewis, 'African literature: Part II — English-speaking West Africa', *Africa Report*, VII, 11 (December 1962), 15—17, 31.
An early survey of literature in Nigeria and Ghana. Tutuola, Soyinka, Achebe, Okigbo, Okara, Ekwensi, Nzekwu, Parkes, Dei-Anang, and others are discussed.

Nkosi, Lewis, 'Fiction by black South Africans', *Black Orpheus*, 19 (1966), 48—54.
A summary of black South African writers, their themes and styles. Includes Modisane, Mphahlele, and La Guma.

Nkosi, Lewis, 'Some conversations with African writers', *Africa Report*, IX, 7 (July 1964), 7—21.
Interviews with Amos Tutuola, Ulli Beier, Ezekiel Mphahlele, David Rubadiri, Willie Abraham, and Chinua Achebe.

Nkosi, Lewis, 'Where does African literature go from here?' *Africa Report*, XI, 9 (December 1966), 7—11.
A review of some English-language fiction by Africans, published in 1966. Includes Soyinka's *The Interpreters*, Achebe's *A Man of the People*,

Okara's *The Voice*, Dipoko's *A Few Nights and Days*, and others.

Obiechina, Emmanuel N., 'Transition from oral to literary tradition', *Présence Africaine*, 63 (1967), 140—161.
Asserts the view that the oral tradition informs the writing of West African authors, because it 'best expresses the West African consciousness and sensibility'.

Obiechina, Emmanuel N., 'Growth of written literature in English-speaking Africa,' *The Conch*, I, 2 (September 1969), 3—21.
The central proposition is that the introduction of Western-oriented literacy (accomplished mainly by Christian missionaries) caused the growth of written literature in West Africa as well as in Europe.

Obumselu, Ben, 'The background of modern African literature' *Ibadan*, 22 (June 1966), 46—59.
African epic poetry and vernacular literature, their themes and language. The author suggests that contemporary African writing in English and French is essentially European, incorporating traditional motifs only selectively.

Povey, John, 'How do you make a course in African literature?' *Transition*, IV, 18 (1965), 39—42.
An approach to the principles underlying an African literature course, with a list of suggested titles.

Povey, John, 'The First World Festival of the Negro Arts at Dakar', *J. of the New African Literature*, 2 (Fall 1966), 24—30.
Impressions of the art, dance, and literature represented at this festival, which brought together black artists from across the world.

Povey, John, 'The quality of African writing today', *Literary Review*, XI, 4 (Summer 1968), 403—421.
A survey of African literature, with its double heritage of colonialism and negritude, as an assertion of the validity of African culture.

Shelton, Austin J., 'The articulation of traditional and modern in Igbo literature', *Conch*, I, 1 (March 1969).
Contemporary Igbo writers, such as Ekwensi, Achebe, Nzekwu, Okigbo, and Egbuna, although clearly influenced by European literature, incorporate stylistic elements and themes from the oral tradition. This article contends that there is a close relationship between modern literature by Igbo writers and Igbo oral tradition.

Soyinka, Wole, 'From a common back cloth: a reassessment of the African literary image', *American Scholar*, XXXII, 3 (Summer 1963), 387—396.
The African writer asserts the integrity of the

African as a creature of sensibilities. The works of Beti, La Guma, Achebe, and Tutuola are discussed.

Stuart, Donald, 'African literature III: the modern writer in his context', *J. of Commonwealth Literature*, 4 (December 1967), 113—129.
A consideration of some of the oral literatures that form part of the context of modern African literature. References to the *Oxford Library of African Literature*.

DRAMA

Banham, Martin, 'African literature II: Nigerian dramatists in English and the traditional Nigerian theatre', *J. of Commonwealth Literature*, 3 (July 1967), 97—102.
Yoruba folk opera and contemporary drama. Discussion of the work of Duro Ladipo and Wole Soyinka, among others.

Clark, John Pepper, 'Aspects of Nigerian drama'. *Nigeria Magazine*, 89 (June 1966), 118—126.
A discussion of the various types of traditional and modern drama in Nigeria, and the relationships between them.

Jones-Quartey, K. A. B., 'Problems of language in the development of the African theatre', *Okyeame*, IV, 1 (December 1968), 95—102.
The African playwright lacks a homogeneous audience — that is, one with a common language and culture. This article discusses problems in language communication, and possible alternatives for writers and producers of drama.

Mahood, M. M., 'Drama in new-born states', *Présence Africaine*, Eng. ed., XXXII, 60 (1966), 23—39.
A survey of drama in West Africa, East Africa, and South Africa, respectively.

Povey, John, 'West African drama in English', *Comparative Drama*, I, 2 (1967), 110—121.
Modern African drama in European languages falls into two categories: realistic prose plays, such as those of R. Sarif Easmon, and the poetic plays of Wole Soyinka and J. P. Clark. This article suggests that the poetic form allows greater experimentation and the incorporation of traditional elements, and will develop into a distinctly African drama.

Shore, Herbert, 'Drums, dances, and then some', *Texas Quarterly*, VII, 2 (Summer 1964), 225—231.
An introduction to modern African drama, indicating its traditional and contemporary sources, and its rich variety.

FICTION

Brench, A. C., 'The novelist's background in

French colonial Africa', *African Forum*, III, 1 (Summer 1967), 34—41.
Trends in the development of the French African novel, as a response to political and geographical influences. Includes Malonga, Dadié, Ousmane, Sadji, and others.

Dathorne, O. R., 'The African novel — document to experiment', *Bulletin of the Association for African Literature in English*, 3 (1965), 18—39.
The ways in which African writers express various experiences of cultural conflict, in novels ranging from flat reportage to imaginative experiments in language and form.

Dathorne, O. R., 'The beginnings of the West African novel', *Nigeria Magazine*, 93 (June 1967), 168—170.
Reviews two early works of fiction by Ghanaians: R. E. Obeng's *Eighteenpence*, published in 1943, and E. Casely-Hayford's *Ethiopia Unbound*, published in 1911.

Gleason, Judith, 'The African novel in French', *African Forum*, I, 4 (Spring 1966), 75—92.
An examination of some African novels that express the impact of the colonial experience upon the cosmogonies of traditional cultures. Includes Sadji's *Tonka*, Laye's *L'Enfant Noir*, and Kane's *L'Aventure Ambiguë*.

Kane, Mohamadou, 'Naissance du roman africain francophone', *African Arts/Arts d'Afrique*, II, 2 (Winter 1969), 54—58.
French African novelists have written in a realistic mode, which this author believes is too limited to alone convey the richness and complexity of the African experience.

Larson, Charles R., 'The search for the past: East and Central African writing', *Africa Today*, XV, 4 (August/September 1968), 12—15.
The novels of Legson Kayira, Stanlake Samkange, Khadambi Asalache, and James Ngugi — all concerned with themes of the past.

Povey, John, 'Changing themes in the Nigerian novel', *J. of the New African Literature*, 1 (Spring 1966), 3—11.
Early African novels in English concentrated on the theme of culture conflict. This article discusses the broadening range of themes, and the gradual emergence of a specifically 'African' English literary language.

Ravenscroft, Arthur, 'African literature V: novels of disillusion', *J. of Commonwealth Literature*, 6 (January 1969), 120—137.
Reviews several novels that deal with the political problems of independence. Includes *A Man of the People*, *The Voice*, *A Grain of Wheat*, and *The Interpreters*.

Reed, John, 'Between two worlds: some notes on the presentation by African novelists of the individual in modern African society',

Makerere J., 7 (1963), 1—14.
Mentions novels by Chinua Achebe, Mongo Beti, Cheikh Hamidou Kane, Camara Laye, Onuoro Nzekwu, and Ferdinand Oyono.

Wali, Obiajunwa, 'The individual and the novel in Africa', *Transition*, IV, 18 (1965), 31—33.
The African novelist faces the dilemma of delineating individual characters in traditional societies that reject the notion of individualism. Discusses Achebe's *No Longer At Ease*, Laye's *The Radiance of the King*, and Okara's *The Voice*.

POETRY

Beier, Ulli, 'Some Nigerian poets', *Présence Africaine*, Eng. ed., IV/V, 32/33 (1960), 50—63. Nigerian poetry in the 1950's: Adeboye Babalola, Dennis C. Osadebay, Mabel Imoukhuede, Grabiel Okara, J. P. Clark, and Wole Soyinka.

Beier, Ulli, 'Three Mbari poets', *Black Orpheus*, 12 (1963), 46—50.
A discussion of three volumes of verse presented by Mbari Publications: Okigbo's *Heavensgate*, Clark's *Poems*, and Brutus' *Poems*.

Clark, J. P., 'The communication line between poet and public', *African Forum*, III, 1 (Summer 1967), 42—53.
Nigerian poets are consciously attempting to speak directly to their public. This article traces communication between poet and public from Osadebay to Soyinka.

Clark, J. P., 'Themes of African poetry of English expression', *Présence Africaine*, Eng. ed., XXVI, 54 (1965), 70—89.
Themes of African poetry are diverse, reflecting the experiences and talents of individual poets. West African, South African, and East African poetry are discussed.

Melone, Thomas, 'New voices of African poetry in French', *African Forum*, I, 4 (Spring 1966), 65—74.
A discussion of changing themes of French African poetry in the post-independence period. Malick Fall, Lamine Diakhaté, and Tchicaya U Tam'si are included.

Moore, Gerald, 'Time and experience in African poetry', *Transition*, VI, 26 (1966), 18—22.
An article suggesting that traditional and modern African poetry convey a unique concept of man's experience of space and time. The poetry of George Awoonor-Williams, Tchicaya U Tam'si, Lenrie Peters, and J. P. Clark appears, along with traditional verse.

Nicol, Davidson, 'West African poetry', *Africa South in Exile*, V, 3 (1961), 115—122.
An introduction to French and British West African poetry, both modern and traditional.

Reed, John, 'Poetry in East Africa', *Mawazo*, I, 4 (December 1968), 31–36.
A discussion of East African poetry, taking as its point of reference *Drum Beat: East African Poems*, edited by Lennard Okola.

Theroux, Paul, 'Voices out of the skull: a study of six African poets', *Black Orpheus*, 20 (August 1966), 41–58.
An analysis of the poetry of Christopher Okigbo, George Awoonor-Williams, Dennis Brutus, Lenrie Peters, Okogbule Wonodi, and J. P. Clark.

AFRICAN PERSONALITY AND NEGRITUDE

Beier, Ulli, 'In search of an African personality', *Twentieth Century*, CLXV, 986 (April 1959), 343–349.
This article describes the reactions – particularly of French West Africans – against cultural assimilation, and their search for an African personality.

Furay, Michael, 'Negritude – a romantic myth?' *New Republic*, CXLV, 1 (1966), 32–35.
The search for a black identity involves similar questions in the Western world (Baldwin, Ellison, etc.) and in Africa (Senghor, U Tam'si).

Irele, Abiola, 'In defence of negritude', *Transition*, III, 13 (1964), 9–11.
An article, *à propos* of Sartre's *Black Orpheus*, describing the aims of negritude, as the revolt of the black man and his search for self-identity.

Irele, Abiola, 'Negritude – literature and ideology', *J. of Modern African Studies*, III, 4 (December 1965), 499–526.
An essay on negritude as a literary and ideological movement, with its themes of alienation, revolt, and rediscovery.

July, Robert W., 'African literature and the African personality', *Black Orpheus*, 14 (1964), 33–45.
Insights into African personality found in *L'Aventure Ambiguë, Blade Among the Boys, Jagua Nana*, and *A Walk in the Night*.

lo Liyong, Taban, 'Africans, stretch your minds', *Africa Report*, XIII, 7 (October 1968), 17–20.
An article opposing negritude as essentially parochial, and urging African students to contribute to their cultural development by opening themselves to Western culture.

Makward, Edris, 'Negritude and the new African novel in French', *Ibadan*, 22 (June 1966), 37–45.
A summary of the historical development of negritude and its significance. Several novels by French West African authors are discussed.

Mohome, Paulus M., 'Negritude: evaluation and elaboration', *Présence Africaine*, 68 (1968), 122–140.
The philosophy of negritude, which this author sees as a civilizing force, having a significance far beyond that of a literary movement.

Mphahlele, Ezekiel, 'The cult of negritude', *Encounter*, XVI, 3 (March 1961), 50–52.
A questioning of the concept of negritude, as a limitation on literary development and expression.

Obiechina, E. N., 'Cultural nationalism in modern African creative literature', *African Literature Today*, 1 (1968), 24–35.
The imaginative insight of African writers contributes to the growth of cultural identity and pride. Discusses negritude, African personality, and other manifestations of cultural nationalism.

Senghor, Léopold Sédar, 'Negritude and the concept of universal civilization', *Présence Africaine*, Eng. edn, XVIII, 46 (1963), 9–13.
A statement of the view that the literature of negritude in French contributes a new kind of rhythmic imagery and 'integral humanism' to universal literature.

Thomas, L. V., 'Senghor and negritude', *Présence Africaine*, Eng. edn, XXVI, 54 (1965), 102–132.
An analysis of the evolution of Senghor's philosophy of negritude, the influences upon it, and its cultural, economic, and psychological significance.

LITERARY CRITICISM

Green, Robert, 'Under the mango tree: criticism of African literature', *J. of the New African Literature and the Arts*, 3 (Spring 1967), 25–30.
Contemporary African writers, strongly influenced by the oral tradition, experiment with forms and styles in ways that distinguish their work from Western writing. Their work, according to this article, should therefore not be judged by the same critical criteria as Western writing.

Okpaku, Joseph, 'Let's dare to be African', *Africa Report*, XIII, 7 (October 1968), 13–16.
This author contends that African intellectuals, by accepting the standards and values of Western culture, have been alienated from their own culture. He asserts the validity of African art, communicating with an African audience, and subjected to African critical standards.

Okpaku, Joseph, 'Tradition, culture, and criticism', *Présence Africaine*, 70 (1969), 137–146.
An article suggesting that African literature should be addressed to an African, not a European audience, and that it should be judged according to African aesthetic standards.

Wake, Clive H., 'African literary criticism', *Comparative Literature Studies*, I (1964), 197—205.
Issues of literary criticism by Africans, from Senghor to Mphahlele.

Wright, Edgar, 'African literature I: problems of criticism', *Journal of Commonwealth Literature*, 2 (December 1966), 103—112.
A consideration of four books that raise the question of whether the critical standards applied to world literature in English are appropriate to African literature in English: Tibble's *African/English Literature*, Gleason's *This Africa: Novels by West Africans in English and French*, Ramsaran's *New Approaches to African Literature*, and Jahn's *Bibliography of Neo-African Literature*.

MARKET LITERATURE

Beier, Ulli, 'Public opinion on lovers', *Black Orpheus*, 14 (1964), 4—16.
An examination of several Onitsha novels.

Nwoga, Donatus I., 'Onitsha market literature', *Transition*, IV, 19 (1965), 26—33.
The popular penny novels of Onitsha have a vitality and style of their own. This article discusses the themes and characteristics of the literature, and offers many sample passages.

Young, Peter, 'A note from Onitsha', *Bulletin of the Association for African Literature in English*, 4 (March 1966), 37—40.
An article conveying the flavour of the Onitsha market and the popular novelettes of such authors as Highbred Maxwell, which are published and sold at Onitsha.

ROLE OF THE WRITER

Achebe, Chinua, 'The African writer and the Biafran cause', *Conch*, I, 1 (March 1969), 8—14.
For 400 years African writers have been concerned with the effects of European domination and themes of racial inequality. Achebe con-

tends that the political and social issues of independent African countries now provide the relevant themes of African literature.

Achebe, Chinua, 'The black writer's burden', *Présence Africaine*, Eng. edn, XXXI, 59 (1966), 135—140.
Whether the writer finds himself in a colonial or an independent state, his primary task is that of defending freedom of expression.

Cassirer, Thomas, 'Politics and mystique — the predicament of the African writer', *African Forum*, III, 1 (Summer 1967), 26—33.
During the period of colonialism and early independence, the African writer was the voice of freedom. The article surveys varying opinions on the writer's changing role in independent Africa.

Kane, Mohamadou, 'The African writer and his public', *Présence Africaine*, Eng. edn, XXX, 58 (1966), 10—32.
Suggests that African writers should return to traditional themes.

lo Liyong, Taban, 'The role of the creative artist in contemporary Africa', *East Africa Journal*, VI, 1 (January 1969), 29—39.
A rejection of negritude and traditionalism, as responses of a suppressed and powerless culture. Urges Africans to pragmatically borrow from the West in order to develop an assertive African culture.

Soyinka, Wole, 'And after the narcissist?' *African Forum*, I, 4 (Spring 1966), 53—64.
The writer is necessarily self-involved, but the good writer transcends himself in expressing his experience and vision of truth. Discusses Laye, Senghor, La Guma, and others.

Soyinka, Wole, 'The writer in an African state', *Transition*, VI, 31 (June/July 1967), 11—13.
The writer must not divert himself from the urgent issues of the present by becoming too concerned with the past. He should assume a leadership role in the modern African state.

PERIODICALS AND MAGAZINES

This section is divided into two parts: (I) features major literary and cultural periodicals, and (II) lists *little magazines*, as well as general Africanist periodicals, which frequently include creative writing from Africa, and essays, book reviews, bibliographies, etc. on African literature.

Complete availability data is provided, and information on back numbers and reprints is given in some instances. Prices quoted — which are of course subject to change — cover *annual* subscriptions (by surface mail) unless otherwise specified.

(I) Literary and cultural periodicals:

Abbia

Centre de Littérature Evangelique, B.P. 4048, Yaoundé, Cameroon
1964 — quarterly
Subscription rate: CFA 1200
Back numbers: all available, except vol. 1, no. 4, at CFA 200 per vol.

This bilingual journal is published by Éditions C.L.E., the pioneering Cameroon publishers of francophone African writing, and is issued under the auspices of the Cameroon Ministry of National Education. Articles appear both in English and in French, covering a wide variety of cultural activities. There are frequent essays on both traditional and modern African literature, supplemented by short stories, plays, poetry and book reviews. *Abbia*'s aim is reflected in its editorial policy:

> Not merely to recount
> What has been
> But to share in moulding
> What should be

The journal is edited by Bernard Fonlon, with Marcien Towa, Eldridge Mohamadou and Gregory Tanyi.

African Arts/Arts D'Afrique

African Studies Center, University of California, Los Angeles, Calif. 90024
1967 — quarterly
Subscription rate: $10.00 (Student rate: $8.00)
Back numbers: all available at $3.00 per copy

A lavishly produced and scholarly journal, edited by Paul O. Proehl and John Povey, which is aimed at both general and academic audiences. Its subject area spans the entire field of the African arts — drama, pure and applied art, sculpture, cinema, literature, literary criticism, music and dance, and each issue is richly illustrated with many full-colour plates. The journal

aims to record Africa's traditional art and stimulate its contemporary art. African arts are thus viewed from a dual perspective, i.e. their origins and their directions. '*African Arts/Arts d'Afrique* has a double mission — to act as a catalyst to the contemporary African artist and to gain a wider audience for the arts of all of Africa *in* Africa and *beyond* Africa.' In pursuance of the first part of this objective, it sponsors competitive contests each year in which successful entrants receive substantial awards: in 1968 it was the literary, graphic and plastic arts and in 1969 the fields of drama, film, music and dance. Articles are in English and French and some of them have parallel texts. (As from volume 3, no. 4, in English only.)

African Literature Today. A Journal of Explanatory Criticism

Heinemann Educational Books Ltd, 48 Charles Street, London W.1
U.S.: Africana Publishing Corporation, 101 Fifth Avenue, New York, N.Y. 10003. [supersedes Bulletin for the Association for African Literature in English]
1968 — twice yearly [no issues published in 1970; as from June 1971, no. 5 — annually]
Subscription rate: (issues nos. 1–4 inclusive) £1.60/$8.00
Back numbers: all available at 40p/$2.00 per copy

Professor Eldred Jones, Head of the Department of English at the University of Sierra Leone, edits this journal of explanatory criticism. '*African Literature Today* aims at providing analyses of the works of African authors, not to save readers from making their own judgements, but to provide starting points for personal appreciation and evaluation.' It 'is intended to be a forum for the examination of the literature of Africa.' The majority of articles closely analyse individual novels or poems or the entire opus of a particular writer. By offering different and sometimes opposing interpretations, the editor hopes 'it will be possible to see our authors from many angles and elicit more complete responses to them.' In addition, each issue contains a book-review section and a current bibliography of new African literature, covering both books and periodical articles.

Black Orpheus

Longmans of Nigeria Ltd (in association with Mbari Club)
Ikeja, Nigeria. (Nos. 1—22) (U.S.: Northwestern University Press, Evanston, Ill.)
Daily Times of Nigeria Ltd, 3 Kakawa Street, P.O. Box 139, Lagos (vol. 2, no. 1 —)
1957 — 3 times yearly (vol. 2, no. 1, February 1968—)
Subscription rate: £1.25./$6.00
Back numbers: Nos. 1 — 3 out-of-print; nos. 5 —12 32½p each; nos. 13—22 8s. 6d. each.
In reprint: nos. 1—22, clothbound $190.00. Kraus Reprint, FL 9491 Nendeln, Liechtenstein.

Black Orpheus has had a chequered career. As the name suggests, it was adopted from Sartre's article 'Orphée Noire' and Jahn's anthology *Schwarzer Orpheus*. 'The magazine owed its birth to the stimulus of *Présence Africaine* and to the first Congress of African Writers in Paris (1956); in particular,' writes Ulli Beier, the founding editor and stalwart supporter of this magazine. It was established largely 'as a platform for creative writing'.

The first issue of *Black Orpheus*, containing 52 pages, appeared in September 1957. Ulli Beier, together with his German compatriot Janheinz Jahn, edited the first six issues, sponsored by the Nigerian Ministry of Education. Initially Beier hoped that the publicity given to the works of distinguished black writers from the West Indies, French-speaking Africa, and North and South America would act as a creative impetus to the yet-unborn English-speaking African writer. Thus the first numbers featured translations of Léopold Senghor, Aimé Césaire, David Diop, South Africa's Ezekiel Mphahlele, and the poetry of the black Americans Langston Hughes and Paul Vesey among others. Two English-speaking West Africans were discovered in the early years of *Black Orpheus'* history: Gabriel Okara (no. 1) and Wole Soyinka (no. 5), both Nigerians. For the most part, however, this part of the continent was represented largely by articles on their oral and artistic traditions. Contemporary art was frequently contributed by Europeans.

As of issue number seven, Ezekiel Mphahlele and Wole Soyinka co-edited the journal with Beier, and during the years 1961—1963 the focus of the magazine changed as Beier's hope became reality. Contributions by anglophone Africans, predominantly Nigerians and South Africans, gradually outspaced French-speaking African and West Indian writers, though these were still well represented. Christopher Okigbo, John Pepper Clark, Gabriel Okara, Wole Soyinka again, Dennis Brutus, Lenrie Peters, George Awoonor-Williams, Alex La Guma, Christina Aidoo and Grace Ogot were among the new names to grace the pages of *Black Orpheus*. New African artists, too, were featured. Now it was the traditional literature of East and Central Africa that appeared as well.

Soyinka and Mphahlele left the journal's editorial board in 1964 and 1966 respectively. With issue number 12 the Nigerian branch of the English publisher Longman Green and Company began publishing the journal, and the Congress for Cultural Freedom made funds available for payment to contributors.

During 1964—1967 *Black Orpheus* was 'now more cosmopolitan, better balanced, and its contributors more accomplished, more assured . . . The twenty-five writers who published fiction in the late numbers of *Black Orpheus* hailed from 16 different countries and wrote in at least as many different styles.'[1] Literary activity was burgeoning in Nigeria in the early sixties and *Black Orpheus* heavily reflected this. From elsewhere, Mbella Sonne Dipoko, David Rubadiri and Paul Theroux were among the names of contributors. Critics now had a high calibre of material to explain and interpret, and this they did, in the form of book reviews and critical articles. *Black Orpheus* 'continued to draw contributions from throughout the Negro world, publishing in ten years works by 224 writers and artists from 26 African nations, 14 West Indian and Latin American states, England, Germany, Sweden, India, Persia, Indonesia and the United States.'[2]

Editorial control was taken over by J. P. Clark and Abiola Irele in 1968. Issue number 22 was the first of volume two (actually better described as a 'new series') and a further issue has since appeared though publication has been rather irregular during the past two years. However, publication and distribution is now being handled by the *Daily Times of Nigeria*, who promise to recommence regular publication.

Bulletin of the Association for African Literature in English

1964—1967 [ceased, see African Literature Today*]*
Back numbers: available in reprint from Kraus Reprint, FL 9491, Nendeln, Liechtenstein (nos. 1—4, $30.00)

[1]Bernth Lindfors, 'A decade of *Black Orpheus*,' *Books Abroad*, October 1968,
[2]ibid.

Busara

East African Publishing House, P.O. Box 30571, Nairobi, Kenya [supersedes Nexus]

1966 − [as Nexus] 1968 − [as Busara] 3 times yearly

Subscription rate: EAshs. 7.50/£1.30/$3.00

When *Nexus* renamed itself *Busara*, the editor announced the following change in policy: 'As *Nexus*, we dealt mainly in creative writing pieces and book reviews. As *Busara* we shall carry on with this but we shall also go in for more critical factual articles regarding our cultural or social scene.' An English-department publication based at University College, Nairobi, this new journal presents poems, stories and criticism reflecting literary activity predominantly in East Africa. The Kiswahili-named *Busara* was edited in 1968 by Awori Wa Kataka and in 1969 by Richard Gacheche. Its Editorial Board includes Grace Ogot and Taben Lo Liyong, the latter a frequent contributor to the journal as well.

The Conch

c/o Department of English, University of Texas, Austin, Texas 78712

1969 − twice yearly

Subscription rate: $3.50/87½p (Library rate $5.00)

Back numbers: all available except no. 1

Edited by Sunday Anozie of the University of Texas, this journal derives its title from William Golding's novel *Lord of the Flies* − 'Hear him! He's got the conch!' The initial two issues (the first number was devoted 'In Memoriam Chris Okigbo', the late Nigerian poet) were sub-titled 'A Biafran Journal of Literary and Cultural Analysis', but as from volume 2, no. 1 it was changed to 'A Sociological Journal of African Cultures and Literatures'. *The Conch*'s editorial policy 'emphasizes the need for a close analytical study of specific African social and cultural environments in relation to specific African languages and works of art . . . it favours the use of modern structuralist methods and theories.' Emphasis is laid on critical writings and interpretations, but some poetry is also included in each issue, along with a series of book reviews. Chinua Achebe, Gerald Moore and Austin Shelton are among the members of the editorial advisory committee of the journal.

Cultural Events in Africa

The Transcription Centre, 84c Warwick Avenue, London, W.9

1965 − monthly

Subscription rate: £14.00/$30.00

Back numbers: some available, for details apply to publishers

Recent and forthcoming cultural events taking place, whether in Africa or contributed to by Africans in any part of the world, are extensively covered in this news bulletin edited by Dennis Duerden and Maxine Lautré at London's Transcription Centre. 'Cultural events' here signify happenings and general trends in the areas of African art, theatre, film, literature, dance, music, broadcasting and publishing. All these media are comprehensively covered in each issue in the form of short notices, news stories or reviews. Festivals, conferences and exhibitions pertaining to the African arts scene are similarly announced and reviewed. African artists and writers are given an opportunity to speak out freely in interviews, which make up a specially valuable supplementary feature to each number.

Darlite

The University College, P.O. Box 35041, Dar-es-Salaam, Tanzania

1967 − irregular (two or three times a year)

Subscription rate: EAsh. 7.50/62½p/$1.50

'A magazine of original writing from the University College Dar-es-Salaam' and published under the auspices of the Department of Literature. Edited by Ralph Ng'ethe, this journal features poetry, fiction, drama, criticism and book reviews by a host of young creative writers from East Africa.

Dombi: Revue Congolaise des Lettres et des Arts

B.P. 3498, Kinshasa-Kalina, Rep. of the Congo

1970−

Subscription rate: 1 Z (150FB/$3.00) Bi-monthly

Subtitled 'Création et Critique', the maiden issue of this new cultural journal contains poetry, short stories, essays, book reviews, an extract from an unpublished novel by Michel Mwilambe, plus an interview with the Congolese poet Alexis Mwamb'a Musuas. It is edited by Philippe Masegabio.

Journal of Commonwealth Literature

Heinemann Educational Books Ltd, 48 Charles Street, London W.1 (no. 1−8)

Oxford University Press, Ely House, Dover Street, London, W.1 (no. 9−)

(Orders to: Africa Research Ltd, Africa House, Kingsway, London W.C.2)

1965 − twice yearly

Subscription rate: £3.60/$10.50

Back numbers: all available from Swets and Zeitlinger, Heeteweg 347B Lisse, Holland

Intended as a forum for commentary and debate, the aim of this journal 'is to provide information to writers and scholars throughout the world about creative writing in English from all Commonwealth countries, except Great Britain . . .' Within this scope, the journal features critical articles and occasionally lengthy book reviews. An annual bibliography of Commonwealth literature, listing the preceding year's literary output, is included in the January number of each volume. Arthur Ravenscroft of the University of Leeds, England, serves as the editor.

The Jewel of Africa: A Literary and Cultural Magazine from Zambia

Mphala Creative Society, University of Zambia, Box 2379, Lusaka, Zambia
1968 — quarterly
Subscription rate: $1.20

This is the new journal of the MPHALA (music, philisophy, history, art and literary appreciation) Creative Society, and is published by MPHALA with the assistance of the National Educational Company of Zambia Limited. Edited by Steven P. C. Mayo, its contents include short stories, poems, short plays, reviews, criticisms, folk tales and articles. Dr Kenneth Kaunda (President of Zambia and Patron of MPHALA Creative Society) hopes that 'its appearance [may] assist in blazing a trail of enlightenment to all its readers and be a boost to the inchoate literary development in Zambia.'

The Journal of the New African Literature and the Arts

444 Central Park West, New York, N.Y. 10025 [quarterly as from winter, 1970 —]
1966 — twice yearly [no issues published during 1969]
Subscription rate: $3.00

Back numbers: all available at $1.50 per copy (vol. 1, no. 1 in reprint at $2.75 per copy) (nos. 1–3 & 4–6 in reprint. New York, Crowell, 1970, $8.95 ea.)

The stated policy is to publish 'creative works of art, including plays, essays, short stories, poetry and reproductions of art work as well as critiques, criticisms, reviews, and other scholarly articles on African literature, music, fine art, dance and other aspects of African culture.' Editor and publisher Joseph O. O. Okpaku hopes that the journal will serve as a forum for hitherto unknown writers. However, he has also been successful in attracting more prominent writers and critics who have contributed to the journal.

L'Afrique Littéraire et Artistique

32, rue de l'Echiquier, Paris 10
1968 — six times yearly
Subscription rate: F60.00

Back numbers: all available at F10.00, except no. 1, October 1968, which is out-of-point

Written entirely in French, this new cultural magazine surveys literature, drama, art, music and cinema as well as history; it also includes creative writing, essays, and reviews. Considerable attention is devoted to the development of an indigenous African theatre. Tourism, gas-

tronomy and news stories make up additional features. Francis Bebey, Olympe Bhêly-Quenum, Lillyan Kesteloot and Claude Wauthier are among recent contributors in the area of literature.

The New African

2 Arundel Street, London, W.C. 2
1962 — monthly
Subscription rate: £1.00/$3.50 (Africa 75p)
Back numbers: some available, including bound volumes. For details and prices apply to the publishers.

This radical magazine was originally published in Cape Town. It has served as an important voice of opposition to South Africa's apartheid regime, and a great many South African writers, such as Dennis Brutus, Lewis Nkosi and Ezekiel Mphahlele have expressed themselves in its columns. Randolph Vigne was its editor from nos. 1–52 though, since he was banned from South Africa, it appeared for a period under other editor's names. The magazine was harassed by the special branch, and in early 1964 had to change printers five times in two issues. Randolph Vigne, who had been organizing sabotage, fled the country at the same time as other members of the editorial staff. In 1964 too, the journal was punitively fined for mild obscenity. It recommended publication in London, benefiting for a time from a grant from the Congress for Cultural Freedom and set about to change the emphasis from South Africa to Africa as a whole. Lewis Nkosi, also in exile in London, joined *The New African* as literary editor.

From issue no. 53 *The New African* is edited by the Sierra Leonean writer and broadcaster Mukhtar Mustapha. Mr Mustapha, in a recent editorial, said that 'the magazine is to appeal to a whole new generation of Blacks and Whites aspiring to a peaceful co-existence in an age stifled with war, oppression, racism, political and economic enslavement, automation and rising standards.' The journal contains political and social commentary, along with essays on African arts and culture, short stories, poetry and extensive book reviews.

New Writing from Zambia

The New Writers' Group, Box 1889, Lusaka, Zambia
1968 — twice a year
Subscription rate: 15 ngwee

The birth of this new magazine marked what the editors hoped to look upon as a 'major breakthrough in Zambia's efforts to develop a literature of its own'. The first issue was devoted to a literary contest organized as part of the Zambia Festival of Arts, and several of the winning entries appear in this number. Kelvin Mlenga edited the initial issue and Godfrey Kasoma was responsible for no. 2, which contains short stories, poetry, plays and book reviews.

Nexus
1967—1968 [ceased, see Busara*]*

Okyeame
Writers' Workshop; in collaboration with the institute of African Studies, University of Ghana, Legon, Ghana
1964 — quarterly [ceased. Last issue vol. 4, no. 1, December 1968]
Subscription rate: NC 3.00/$3.00
This journal (whose name means 'spokesman' or 'linguist'), now apparently defunct, was edited by the Ghanaian authoress Efua Sutherland. The content of each issue is grouped around the central themes of poetry, fiction, and drama and includes a 'writer's forum'. The latter carries essays on African literature, language, and music. Book reviews and brief news stories supplement each number.

Ozila: Forum littéraire Camerounais (Cameroon Literary Workshop)
B.P. 73, Yaoundé, Cameroon
1970 — monthly
Subscription rate: CFA 200/in U.S. CFA 1,400
Under the editorial direction of Jean-Pierre Togolo, this new magazine aims to be influential in stimulating a dialogue among young and as yet unknown writers in the Cameroons. Contributions are in English and French and each number contains creative writing as well as articles and papers of a critical nature.

Présence Africaine
25 bis, rue des Écoles, 75-Paris V
1947 — quarterly [English version since 1959; bilingual version, no. 61, January 1967 —]
Subscription rate: F25.00 (F35.40 foreign)
Back numbers: English and bilingual versions nos. 8—10, F13.00; 24—25 F20.50, 21; 30—52 F4.90 (some issues double numbers); 53—56 F6.30; 57 F8.00; 58—60 F6.30; 61—70 F7.00
A few numbers of the French version 'Ancienne série' and 'Nouvelle série' are also still available. For details and prices apply to the publishers.
Présence Africaine has undoubtedly been the pioneer among African literary and cultural magazines. It has been published for twenty-three years, first entirely in French and then from 1957 in English also. Since 1965 it has been published as a bilingual magazine. Founded by a Senegalese intellectual, Alioune Diop, with the support of a distinguished group of patrons, the first issue containing 198 pages was launched in November 1947 with very little financial support. Alioune Diop had long advocated a debate between Africa and the West in his contacts with leading French intellectuals. This had attracted the attention of such prominent French men of letters as André Gide, Jean-Paul Sartre and Albert Camus, as well as

the black American Richard Wright, Diop's compatriot Léopold Senghor, and Aimé Césaire from Martinique. With the establishment of *Présence Africaine* Diop aimed to provide a journal open 'to all contributors of good will (White, Yellow or Black) who might be able to help define African originality and to hasten its introduction into the modern world'. Jean-Paul Sartre, too, felt a need for an African presence, 'which would be among us not like that of a child in the family circle but like the presence of a remorse and a hope'. *Présence Africaine* opened its columns not only to black intellectuals but also to religious leaders of both Christian and non-Christian denominations, socialists, communists, historians, anthropologists and political commentators. African students were invited to express their views in a special number.

In the issues of the late forties and early fifties contributions from virtually all leading black intellectuals from Africa, the Americas and the Caribbean had appeared. During 1950—1954 the first in a series of special issues was published. Among these there appeared a volume examining African art, and another containing Cheik Anta Diop's now highly significant essay, 'Nationales Nègres et Culture'.

The 'new series' of *Présence Africaine* was inaugurated in the spring of 1955, followed by two special issues covering the First International Conference of Negro Writers and Artists held in September 1956 in Paris, and the subsequent Second International Conference held in Rome in March/April 1959.

Earlier, in 1956, the Society of African Culture was created, and *Présence Africaine* became its official organ. A separate publishing division was added, which has published over a hundred titles to date.

Since 1965 *Présence Africaine* has been published as a single bilingual review, with articles, poetry, prose, and drama appearing either in English or in French. Occasional special issues on African literature have appeared, for instance number 47 in 1966 on the 'new sum of poetry from the Negro world'.

Research in African Literatures
Bernth Lindfors, English Department, University of Texas, Austin, Texas 78712
1970 — twice yearly
Subscription rate: Gratis on request to individuals; on exchange to libraries
Edited by Bernth Lindfors at the University of Texas, this journal is published as the official organ of both the African Literature Committee of the African Studies Association and the African Literatures Seminar of the Modern Language Association.

The scope of this new journal, 'addressed to the neophyte as well as the initiated', extends to all aspects of the oral and written literatures of Africa. Emphasis is placed on theoretical, historical and biographical articles, surveys of published research on individual topics, bibliographies, discographies and filmographies. Reports on conferences, descriptions of university courses, and book reviews supplement this.

Transition

P.O. Box 20026, Kampala, Uganda [This office closed October 1968]

Paris office: c/o International Association for Cultural Freedom, 104 Boulevard Haussmann, Paris XIII

1961 — six times yearly [Temporarily ceased publication with no. 37, vol. 7, 1968]

Subscription rate: EAshs. 15.00/£1.40/$4.50

Back numbers: a limited number of single issues are available at $1.25—$1.75 per copy; nos. 8, 11—13, 18, 20—25, 29—31, 33—37

In reprint: nos. 1—6/7 paperbound in one volume $24.00 (Johnson Reprint Corp., New York); vols. 1—7 (nos. 1—37), Nov. 1961—Oct. 1968; Clothbound $180.00, paperbound $162.00. Single vols.: 1—2, paperbound, $11.00 per vol. 3—7, paperbound, $28.00 per vol. (Kraus Reprint, FL-9491 Nendeln, Liechtenstein, and New York)

Rajat Neogy, a young Ugandan Indian living in Kampala, published the first number of *Transition* in October 1961. It was started on a shoestring — the first issue was hand-set, two pages at a time, and printed on a flat-bed press.

When the magazine was started (originally under the auspices of the Congress for Cultural Freedom) it had a largely cultural and literary slant, but over the years it has served as a forum for free and outspoken intellectual discussion in the areas of art, politics, literature, sociology and economics. 'Our primary aim', Neogy has said, 'is to discuss matters of African relevance . . . in an African context.' Every point of view was tolerated, as *Transition* reflected the heartbeat of the African continent. Prominent African politicians and statesmen, Julius Nyerere and Kenneth Kaunda among them, contributed articles. Africa's leading literary figures, Christopher Okigbo, Chinua Achebe, Ezekiel Mphahlele, Gabriel Okara, have appeared frequently in the pages of *Transition* (as well as Rajat Neogy himself). Special issues were devoted to particular topics as both African and western intellectuals presented a wide range of scholarly and candid ideas. Contributors represented all parts of the globe. Neogy, however, has stressed that 'we never allow anyone to feel that they were printed just because they were Africans writing. When you are printed in *Transition* you have arrived.' Entire issues have been devoted to

violence in Africa (21); student unrest (37); an account of 'Nkrumah — The Leninist Czar' (26); 'Our Cultures and Loves' (22), analysing the attitudes of Africa held by Graham Greene, Albert Schweitzer and Joyce Cary; 'Why African Literature', and a controversial number interpreting the contemporary African literary scene (18). Another issue that brought forth much debate was entitled 'Is Tarzan an Expatriate?' (32); yet another number was devoted entirely to aspects of sex — sociological, physical and psychological.

Abiola Irele has written in *The Journal of Modern African Studies*: '*Transition* is not merely reporting about Africa or feeling its pulse, but is charting the directions of its mind.' Rajat Neogy has remained Editor-in-Chief since its inception; past associate editors have included Christopher Okigbo, Denis Williams, Ali Mazrui, Raymond Apthorpe and George Awoonor-Williams.

On 18 October 1968 Rajat Neogy was arrested and detained in Kampala, together with Abu Mayanja, a lawyer and M.P., on charges arising out of a letter to the editor that Neogy had printed in issue number 37. Abu Mayanja's letter was written in response to an article printed in an earlier issue by Picho Ali, a young Moscow-educated lawyer and director of research in the office of President Milton Obote. The letter was critical of Ali's contention that the courts in Uganda should not be independent of the views of the ruling party. Rajat Neogy and Abu Mayanja were brought to trial for sedition only after a great deal of pressure, mainly from academic and intellectual groups abroad. The trial, held in February 1969, attracted a great deal of attention both in Uganda and internationally. Both were cleared of sedition, but despite their acquittal, they were rearrested and held in prison under Uganda's detention laws.

On 27 March 1969 Neogy was released, but at the end of 1969 Majanya still remained in prison. During Neogy's detention the journal ceased publication and several issues were confiscated by the Ugandan authorities. Neogy has since communicated to his readers that '*Transition*'s home is . . . all Africa. And it was at home in the world outside. However, I do not know as yet whether magazines can survive transplant . . . and if the magazine can continue to perform usefully from elsewhere, we will resume publication.' Neogy is at present looking toward the more liberal ambience of Ghana as a possible future headquarters for *Transition* and hopes to recommence publication soon.

Zuka. A Journal of East African creative writing

P.O. Box 12532, Nairobi, Kenya

1967 — twice yearly

Subscription rate: EAsh 5.00/35p/$1.00
Back numbers: all available at EAshs 2.50/17½p/
$0.50
The Swahili word Zuka means 'emerge'. In adopting this word for the name of their new journal the editors aim 'to imply the newness and, we hope, the freshness of East African writing.' Their original conviction was 'that we needed an outlet, in the form of a regular magazine, for the great creative upsurge now

sweeping through East Africa.' Initially edite by James Ngugi, now jointly with Jonathan Ka iara (both contributors as well), they have con to realize that their magazine now serves as platform for the wealth of literary activi evident today in East Africa. Though stress placed largely on literature — short storie poems, critical essays and book reviews — the are also occasional articles concerned wit African art.

(II)   Other periodicals and magazines in brief:

Africa Report
Suite 500, Dupont Circle Building, Washington, D.C.
20036
1955 — nine times a year $6.00 ($8.00/£3.35
foreign)
Current events, politics, economics, African arts and literature, 'in-depth' book reviews, interviews. Those back numbers which devote considerable space to African literature include; vol. 7, no. 9, October, 1962; vol. 9, no. 7, 1964; vol. 11, no. 9, December 1966; vol. 13, no. 5, May 1968.

Africa Today
c/o Graduate School of International Studies, University Park Campus, Denver, Colorado 80210
1954 — bi-monthly $6.50 ($8.50 foreign)
Commentary and articles on current affairs, politics, sociology, economics, African international relations. Essays on arts and culture, literature, book reviews. A recent special issue on African literature was vol. 15, no. 4, August/September 1968.

African Affairs
Oxford University Press (for Royal African Society), Press Road, Neasden, London, N.W. 10
1901 — quarterly   £2.00./$5.50
African international relations, politics, social and cultural affairs, economics, anthropology, frequent book reviews of African Literature.

African Forum
American Society for African Culture, 101 Park Avenue, New York, N.Y. 10017
1965 — quarterly [ceased, no issues have appeared since vol. 3, no. 4/vol. 4, no. 1, Spring/Summer 1968] $4.00 (Student rate $2.00)
'A quarterly journal of contemporary affairs'. Articles and bibliographical essays on the arts and literature. Extensive book reviews. Special issues on African literature were: vol. 1, no. 4, Spring 1966; vol. 3, no. 1, Summer 1960.

African Notes
Institute of African Studies, University of Ibadan,

Ibadan, Nigeria (distr. by University Book Sho Nigeria Ltd, Ibadan, Nigeria)
1963 — irregular [quarterly]   27½p (rates to increased shortly)
Political, anthropological, language studie literary and bibliographical essays.

African Studies
Witwatersrand University Press, Jan Smu Avenue, Johannesburg, South Africa.
1941 — quarterly R.4.00
'A quarterly journal devoted to the study (African Anthropology, Government and La guage.' Vernacular language studies, occasion book reviews of African writing, especially or literature.

African Studies Bulletin [African Studies Review (of April 1970 issue]
African Studies Association, Brandeis Universit 218 Shiffman Humanities Center, Waltham, Mas. 02154
1957 — three times a year $20.00/£8.35
Research papers, notes, conference report bibliographies, bibliographic essays.

Africana Library Journal. A quarterly bibliograph and news bulletin
Africana Publishing Corporation, 101 Fifth Avenu New York, N.Y. 10003
1970 — quarterly $20.00 (to Libraries)/$13.5 (to Individuals) ($22.00/$15.00 foreign)
Extensive bibliographic coverage of Africa studies, arts and literature. Book review bibliographical essays. News of bibliograph developments in Africa. 'Bio-bibliographies' c African scholars and literary figures.

Afro-Asian Theatre Bulletin
American Educational Theater Association, In John F. Kennedy Center, 726 Jackson Plac Washington, D.C. 20566
1965 — twice yearly   gratis on exchange
Research reports, conference papers, bibliogr phies and checklists; African and Asian theat news.

fro-Asian Writings
rmanent Bureau of Afro-Asian Writers, 104
asr-el-Aini St., Cairo, United Arab Republic
968 — quarterly $2.00
fro-Asian literature and culture. Fiction, short
ories, critical essays, poetry, book reviews.

a Shiru
epartment of African Languages and Literature,
450 Van Hise Hall, University of Wisconsin,
adison, Wisconsin, 53706
970 — twice a year $2.00
resents facts in terms of the African perspec-
ve, not the European, in terms of the African
terest, not the European.' First issue is strong
1 African literature.

ngo
P. 176, Dakar, Senegal. (French office: 11, rue de
heran, Paris 8)
953 — monthly CFA 1000/F24.00/$4.80
pular illustrated news magazine. Short stories.
eports. Book reviews.

ack Academy Review
ack Academy Press, Inc., 3296 Main Street,
affalo, New York, N.Y. 14214
970 — quarterly $7.00 (Special student rate
4.00)
n interdisciplinary quarterly publication de-
ted to the defense and edification of the black
vilization in all its dimensions and variations.'

oks Abroad
niversity of Oklahoma Press, Norman, Oklahoma
3069
27 — quarterly $4.00
n international literary quarterly'. Critical
says, notes and frequent book reviews on Afri-
n literature. A recent issue, vol. 44, no. 3, Sum-
er 1970, was a special number on African
riting.

Cameroun Littéraire: Journal de l'Association
ationale des poètes et écrivains Camerounais
aoundé
64—1965 [ceased] In reprint: nos. 1—2, $5.00.
raus Reprint, Fl-9491, Nendeln, Liechtenstein
short-lived literary magazine featuring prim-
ily creative writing by Cameroonian authors.
nly two numbers were published.

arimo: a review of poetry
x A 294, Avondale, Salisbury, Rhodesia
68 — three times a year £1.00/$2.90
etry.

e Classic
assic Magazine Trust Fund, Box 23642, Joubert
rk, Johannesburg, South Africa

1964 — quarterly R 1.50/$3.00
Essays, short stories, book reviews. Special
recent issue devoted to new poetry by South
African writers is vol. 3, no. 2, 1969.

Contrast
211 Long Street, Cape Town, South Africa
1960 — quarterly R 2.00
Essays, fiction, poetry. Book reviews in English
and Afrikaans.

A Current Bibliography on African Affairs
Greenwood Periodicals, Inc. (for African Bibliographic Center), 51 Riverside Avenue, Westport,
Conn. 06880
1965 — (New series 1968 —) monthly $25.00
($27.00 foreign)
Bibliographic coverage of new Africana materials. Bibliographical essays. Book reviews.

Drum
Drum Publications (Pty) Ltd, 62 Eloff Street Ext.,
P.O. Box 3413, Johannesburg, South Africa. (Separ-
ate edition for West Africa published by Academy
Press, Lagos)
1951 — monthly £1.25
Popular illustrated news magazine. Short stories,
reports, book reviews.

East Africa Journal
East African Publishing House (for East African
Institute of Social and Cultural Affairs), P.O. Box
30571, Nairobi, Kenya
1964 — monthly EAsh 30.00/£2.10/$5.00
Current events, East African affairs, politics,
economics, sociology, education. Book reviews.
Special 'Ghala' literary issues devoted to East
African writing have been published in January
and July of each year since 1968.

English Studies in Africa
University of the Witwatersrand Press, Milner
Park, Johannesburg, South Africa
1957 — twice a year R 1. 50
English and African literature, critical articles,
book reviews, bibliographical essays.

Ethiopia Observer
P.O. Box 1896, Addis Ababa, Ethiopia
1957 — quarterly Eth. $12.00/U.S. $5.00
'Journal of Independent Opinion, Economics,
History and the Arts'. Poetry, fiction, essays,
book reviews.

Expression
Dept. of English, University of Malawi, Limbe,
Malawi
1968 — irregular 7½p per issue
Short stories, essays, poetry.

Ibadan
Ibadan University, Ibadan, Nigeria
1957 — three times a year $37\frac{1}{2}p$
Cultural and literary journal. Poems, linguistics, politics, anthropology. Book reviews.

Ife-Writing
Writer's Circle, University of Ife, Ile-Ife, Nigeria
1968–irregular 1s. per issue
Essays, fiction, poetry.

Jeune Afrique
51, Avenue des Ternes, Paris 14, France
1947 — weekly   CFA 4000/F100/$30.00
Popular illustrated news magazine. Arts and culture, sociology, education, sports, short stories, reports. Book and record reviews.

Journal of the Language Association of Eastern Africa
East African Publishing House, Uniafric House, Koinange Street, P.O. Box 30571, Nairobi, Kenya
1970 — twice a year   EAsh 15.00/£1.75/$4.00
Language and linguistics, language teaching with special reference to East Africa. Papers on oral literature and contemporary creative writing in Eastern Africa.

Journal of the Nigerian English Studies Association
c/o B. Smith, The British Council, Dugbe, Ibadan, Nigeria
1968 — quarterly subs. rate not known
Language and literature studies. Book reviews.

L'Afrique Actuelle
19 rue Greneta, Paris 2, France
1967 — monthly   F.3.00 per issue
News and cultural magazine, with articles in French and in English. Edited by Dahomean writer Olympe Bhêly-Quenum.

The Literary Review
Farleigh Dickinson University, Teaneck, N.J. 07666
1957 — quarterly $5.00
Essays, drama, fiction, poetry. Summer issue 1969, vol. 11, no. 4, devoted exclusively to African writing.

Literature East and West
Louis Hartley, Carney 446, Boston College, Chestnut Hill, Mass. 02167
1956 — quarterly $8.00
Comparative literature studies. Book reviews. Covers some African writing. The March 1968 issue, vol. XII, no. 1, was a special Africa issue.

Makerere Journal
1958–1967
ceased, see Mawazo

Mawazo
[*supersedes* Makerere Journal]
Makerere University, Box 7062, Kampala, Uganda
1967 — twice a year   EAshs.20.00/£2.00/$6.00 per two year volume
Political, educational and cultural magazine. Frequent book reviews on African literature.

Mila
Cultural Division, Institute for Development Studies University College, Nairobi, Kenya
1970 — bi-annually   gratis on exchange
'A biannual newsletter of cultural research'. Essays, reports, current research projects, fiction.

Moran
Department of Literature, Morogoro's Teachers College, Morogoro, Tanzania
1967 — twice a year
'A magazine of literary writing'. Fiction, poetry, essays.

New Coin
South African Poetry Society, Rhodes University, Grahamstown, South Africa
1965 — quarterly   R 1.00
Poetry in English and Afrikaans, largely by white South Africans.

Nigeria Magazine
Exhibition Centre, Marina, Lagos, Nigeria
1934 — quarterly   40p/$2.00
Popular illustrated magazine published by the Nigerian Ministry of Information. Current events in Nigeria, political and cultural. Special literary issues, poetry, drama.

Odu. A journal of West African Studies (succeeds Journal of Yoruba, Edo and Related Studies)
Oxford University Press Warehouse, State Highway Ilupeju Industrial Estate, P.M.B. 1003, Oshodi Lagos, Nigeria
1955 — (New Series, 1969 —)   Twice a year £1.25p/ $4.00
West African culture and religions, archaeology linguistics; critical essays on African literature.

Ophir
P.O. Box 3846, Pretoria, South Africa
1965 — Three times a year $62\frac{1}{2}p$
'An independent poetry magazine'.

Panafrica. A monthly journal of African life, history and thought
T. R. Nakonnes, 58 Oxford Road, Manchester England
1947 — monthly [ceased]
Ceased publication by early 50's. Contributors and editors included Peter Abrahams, George Padmore, Jomo Kenyatta, Kwame Nkrumah

Penpoint
Dept. of English, Makerere University College, Kampala, Uganda
1967 — Subscription rate not known
Essays, short stories, poetry.

The Purple Renoster
87 Roberts Avenuw, Kensington, Johannesburg, South Africa
1956 — irregular   R 2.00 (covers four issues)
New South African stories, poems, essays, humorous sketches, letters, dramatic excerpts, one-act plays, reviews, serial novels, etc.'

South Africa: Information and Analysis
104 Blvd. Haussmann, Paris VIII, France
1962 — monthly $2.50
Newsletter edited by Lewis Nkosi. Events in South Africa. Some literary commentary and critical studies.

South African Outlook
Box 363, Cape Town, South Africa
1870 — monthly   R.2.00/$3.50/$1.50
'An independent journal dealing with ecumenical and racial affairs.' Also poetry and fiction by South Africans. Book reviews.

Studies in Black L Iterature
Raman K. Singh, Editor, Dept. of English, Mary

Washington College, Fredericksburg, Virginia 22401
1970 — three times a year $3.00
Critical studies of Afro-American and African Literatures. Book reviews, bibliographies — the first issue contains an international bibliography of negritude. Special number on Chinua Achebe to be published in February, 1971.

Ufahamu. Journal of the African Activist Association
African Activist Association, African Studies Center, University of California, Los Angeles, Calif. 90024
1970 — three times a year $5.00 ($3.00 to individuals)
A new interdisciplinary journal, radical in character, run entirely by students. Essays, book reviews. First number had two contributions on African literature.

West Africa
Overseas Newspapers Ltd, 9 New Fetter Lane, London E.C.4
Iliffe NTP Inc., 300 East 42nd Street, New York, N.Y. 10017
1917 — weekly   £5.20/$13.00
Current events in West Africa, political, cultural, economic and social. News, conference reports, portraits, and very frequent book reviews of creative African writing.

BIOGRAPHIES

As a supplement to the bibliographic section, we present here a series of biographies on the most prominent African authors. The immediate question that comes to mind is just *who* are 'the most prominent' or significant writers? Who has established them as such, and what are the criteria? Is it the quantity or the quality of a writer's output? The question is clearly open to debate. Also, why have we devoted considerable space, for instance, to Yambo Ouologuem, who has produced only one novel thus far, whereas the biography of Asare Konadu, who has several novels to his credit, has been somewhat more briefly summarized? There is disparity in length and treatment in some cases, but what we have attempted to do is to present a *cross-section* of Africa's contemporary literary scene. These writers are representative of Africa's geography: their homes are in West, East, Central or Southern Africa. They speak and write English or French. They include both men and women. They write fiction, poetry, drama, children's books, or literary criticism.

We have largely been led by the belief that the writers ought to speak for *themselves*: both about their achievements and ideologies as well as on the subject of African literature — its definition, its validity, its language, and its future. It is through the expression of these views that we have tried to feel the pulse of African writing today. We discovered a wealth of sources on many of the authors, in the form of articles, interviews and speeches. The task that remained in these cases was one of sifting and selecting, and keeping the biographies to manageable proportions. In contrast, however, other writers appear to have been somewhat more reticent. Certainly they do not seem to have voiced their views in print as yet, and even essential data about their lives, birth-dates, family background, education, etc. was hard to come by. Lacking a sufficient amount of such data, we have tried in these instances, to cite what their fellow writers or literary scholars have had to say about them.

It has been somewhat paradoxical to find that on some of the authors there was considerably more written *about* them than the amount of actual creative output *by* them. Another frequent problem we encountered was that of conflicting biographic data. We hope that our portraits are reasonably accurate, but we should be grateful to hear from anybody pointing out any gross inaccuracies, so that these could be taken into account in any future editions of this book.

In preparing these biographies we have relied on a great variety of sources. Some of the interviews that appeared in the pages of *Cultural Events in Africa* were perhaps of particular assistance (see 104).

Peter Abrahams *(1919–   )*   SOUTH AFRICA

From 1930 to 1946 no black South African had a published novel to his credit. Peter Abrahams brought this situation to an end with the publication of his first novel, *Mine Boy*, in 1946. It followed upon the earlier release of his collection of short stories *Dark Testament* (1942), and has since been succeeded by a prolific list of novels published in New York and London: *Song of the City* (1945), *Path of Thunder* (1948), *Wild Conquest* (1950), *A Wreath for Udomo* (1956), *A Night of their Own* (1965), and *This Island Now* (1966) in addition to his autobiographical *Tell Freedom: memories of Africa* (1954), and an essay, *Return to Goli* (1953).

Born Peter Henri Abrahams to a 'Cape Coloured' mother and Ethiopian father in the slums of Vrededorp, Johannesburg, the young Abrahams spent his youth in part with relatives in Elsenburg before returning to live with his brother, sister, and mother in Johannesburg. When he was ten years old and working in an office a 'short-sighted Jewish girl . . . looked at me and then began to read from Lamb's *Tales from Shakespeare*,' Abrahams records in *Tell Freedom*.

> The story of Othello jumped at me and invaded my heart and mind as the young woman read.
>
> I attended school regularly for three years [after that]. I learned to read and write. Lamb's *Tales from Shakespeare* was my favourite reading matter. I stole, by finding, Palgrave's *Golden Treasury*. These two books, and the European edition of John Keats, were my proudest and dearest possessions, my greatest wealth. They fed the familiar craving hunger that awaits the sensitive young and poor when the moment of awareness comes.
>
> With Shakespeare and poetry, a new world was born. New dreams, new desires, a new self-consciousness, were born. I desired to know myself in terms of the new standards set by these books. I lived in two worlds, the world of Vrededorp and the world of these books. And, somehow, both were equally real. Each was a potent force in my life, compelling. My ear and mind were in turmoil. Only the victory of one or the other could bring me peace.[1]

Abrahams continued to attend school sporadically after that. Though he did go to St Peter's College in South Africa, in 1939 he was counted among Durban's unemployed. If 'life had a meaning that transcended race and colour' Abrahams 'could not find it in South Africa'. He felt 'the need to write, to tell freedom and for this I needed to be personally free' he says.[2] So in 1939 he signed up as a stoker, and after two years aboard ship, he decided to settle in Britain. It was in England that Abrahams began to write, and even though he was living abroad, it was his home that he returned to for his plots. When *Mine Boy* was published in 1946, it was one of the first books to draw attention to the blacks' situation in South Africa, and it simultaneously established Abrahams as an important novelist. 'Most of Peter Abrahams' other books [except *A Wreath for Udomo*] recreate the social climate of this country of racial segregation,' Claude Wauthier notes. The exception, *A Wreath for Udomo,* 'caused a considerable stir in the Gold Coast [now Ghana] in 1956. Appearing a few months before independence, it looked like a gloomy prediction since similarities between Udomo's career and the early career of Nkrumah had not escaped notice . . .'[3]

Even now, after having lived abroad for more than thirty years, Abrahams returns to Africa for his settings. In his most recent novel, *This Island Now,* set in the Caribbean (his present home), 'its concerns are those that face most of the states which used to be colonies, the terms in which they are presented (with great emphasis on black-white race relations) remain essentially African', comments Arthur Ravenscroft. Ravenscroft also finds that both *A Wreath for Udomo* and *This Island Now* 'show an extraordinary awareness of personal and public dilemmas in a newly independent country. The central figure in each is a political leader who is fired with an almost impersonal vision of his country's potential greatness, once it is truly free from colonialism.'[4]

Abrahams did return to Africa in 1952 to do a series of articles on Kenya and South Africa for the London *Observer.* They were also printed in the Paris *Tribune* and the European edition of the *Herald Tribune.* In 1957, after he had been to Jamaica to prepare an official report on the British West Indies, Abrahams wrote a travel book, *Jamaica: an island mosaic,* and moved to the island with his wife and family. He thereafter became editor of the *West Indian Economist,* controller of the daily radio news network *West Indian News,* and a commentator on Jamaica's radio and television programmes. In 1964 Abrahams resigned from most of his duties in order to devote himself more fully to writing.

Peter Abrahams is one of the very few black novelists to have emerged from South Africa. His works continue to attract world-wide attention. They have all been translated into numerous languages: *The Path of Thunder* alone is now available in at least twenty-six languages. *Tell Freedom,* also one of his most popular books, appeared in 1970 in Collier's African/American Library with a new introduction by Wilfred Cartey. It has been announced that *Mine Boy* will be published in this series in August 1970; it has been available since 1964 in the African Writers Series.

A study of Abrahams by Michael Wade will be published by Evans in 1971.

¹Peter Abrahams, *Tell Freedom* (New York, 1954), pp. 171—172, 189
²Ibid., p. 370
³Claude Wauthier, *The Literature and Thought of Modern Africa: a survey* (London, 1966), pp. 158—159
⁴Arthur Ravenscroft, 'African literature V: Novels of disillusion', *The Journal of Commonwealth Literature*, no. 6, Jan. 1969, p. 128.

Chinua Achebe *(1930–   )*   NIGERIA

The most prominent novelist writing in Africa today is Chinua Achebe. Born a member of the Ibo tribe in 1930 in the large village of Ogidi in Eastern Nigeria, he grew up in a Christian family, the son of a retired Christian Churchman and the grandson of one of the first men to embrace Christianity. The pre-colonial era of his grandparents' generation had not yet been completely eclipsed during the early years of Achebe's life. He says:

> I think I belong to a very fortunate generation in this respect . . . the old hadn't been completely disorganized when I was growing up . . . it was easy, especially if you lived in a village to see, if not in whole, at least in part, these old ways of life. I was particularly interested in listening to the way old people talked and the festivals were still observed; maybe not in the same force, but they were still there.¹

At six his formal education began. He later attended a leading Government Secondary School in Umuahia, and received a scholarship to pursue

studies in medicine at the University College of Ibadan. After a year, however, he switched his course to literature and received his B.A. in 1953, in one of the first graduating classes. He taught for several months after graduation, and then in 1954 embarked on a career with the Nigerian Broadcasting Company in Lagos, where in 1961 he became Director of External Brodcasting until 1966, when he left to devote himself full-time to writing.

Chinua Achebe is thus the product of three eras. With vestiges of traditional practices still existing in his childhood, Achebe's youth was spent in a predominantly colonized society, in a village where Christians and non-Christians maintained their distance; he reached maturity in a newly independent state (1960) beset by the problems that traditionally accompany liberation. After being a Biafran partisan in Nigeria's civil war, today he is perhaps witnessing the dawn of a new era in a nation almost torn asunder.

His four novels, which have received universal acclaim, are drawn from and reflect this span of history. And this is perhaps deliberate; Achebe says:

> I would be quite satisfied if my novels (especially the ones I set in the past) did no more than teach my readers that their past — with all its imperfections — was not one long night of savagery from which the first Europeans acting on God's behalf delivered them. Perhaps what I write is applied art as distinct from pure. But who cares? Art is important but so is education of the kind I have in mind. And I don't see that the two need be mutually exclusive.[2]

Taking an overall view of his continent's literature, Achebe 'does not see African literature as one unit but as a group of associated units — in the sum total of all the *national* and *ethnic* literatures of Africa.'[3] For him English has become the primary language because it is a medium for international exchange. He feels that the African writer, while respecting and adhering to this attribute of the language, should simultaneously fashion a 'new English, still in full communion with its ancestral home but altered to suit its new African surroundings'.[4]

Achebe's first novel, *Things Fall Apart*, published by William Heinemann in 1958, was reissued four years later in paperback, inaugurating Heinemann Educational Books' African Writers Series. The winner of the Margaret Wrong Prize, in seven years it sold over 300,000 copies in this paperback edition and brought Achebe to Heinemann's as the Editorial Advisor of this pioneering series. A sequel, *No Longer at Ease* (originally conceived as one novel in combination with his first), appeared in 1960 and won the Nigerian National Trophy. This was followed by *Arrow of God* in 1964, the first recipient of the *New Statesman* Jock Campbell award, and in 1966 by *A Man of the People*. The latter, his most recent novel, Achebe considers 'a rather serious indictment — if you like — on post-independence Africa. But I don't despair because I think this is a necessary stage in our growth.'[5] The following year Achebe commented,

> Right now my interest is in politics or rather my interest in the novel is politics. *A Man of the People* wasn't a flash in the pan. This is the begin-

ning of a phase for me in which I intend to take a hard look at what we in Africa are making of independence — but using Nigeria which I know best.[6]

In 1967 Chinua Achebe, together with Christopher Okigbo, Nigeria's foremost poet, launched a publishing company in Enugu. Their initial intention was to feature several outstanding African literary figures; their dominant aim was to publish a relevant African children's literature founded on local thought. However, when the Nigerian civil war broke out Okigbo joined the Biafran army and later that year was killed in action. Achebe subsequently became actively involved in the Biafran cause.

Living in the midst of this conflict Achebe thought, '... even if I felt like seeing my way through to a brilliant novel, I might in fact, not find the emotional or even the physical convenience to do it.'[7] So instead of fiction, he wrote essays and poems, and gave lectures.

On the orientation of his future literary career Achebe has said,

> It is clear to me that an African creative writer who tries to avoid the big social and political issues of contemporary Africa will end up being completely irrelevant — like that absurd man in the proverb who leaves his burning house to pursue a rat fleeing from the flames.[8]

> What is the place of the writer in this movement? I suggest that his place is right in the thick of it — if possible, at the head of it.[9]

When recently asked if he considered himself a protest writer, Achebe replied, 'Well, according to my own definition of protest, I *am* a protest writer. Restraint —well, that's my style, you see.'[10]

Chinua Achebe's four novels have been translated into sixteen languages. His works are the subject of three full-length critical commentaries, G. D. Killam's *The Novels of Chinua Achebe* and Arthur Ravenscroft's *Chinua Achebe*, both published in 1969, and David Carroll's *Chinua Achebe* (1970). In the company of two fellow Biafran writers, Gabrial Okara and Cyprian Ekwensi, Mr Achebe toured the United States in the latter part of 1969, speaking at university and college campuses. Shortly after the termination of the war, he was appointed Research Fellow in the Institute of African Studies at the University of Nigeria in Nsukka. His collection of short stories, *Girls at War*, will be number 100 in the African Writers Series. He is also at work collecting his essays.

[1] 'Conversation with Chinua Achebe', *Africa Report*, vol. 9, no. 5, July 1964, pp. 19—20
[2] Chinua Achebe, 'The novelist as teacher', in *Commonwealth Literature* (London, 1965) p. 205
[3] Chinua Achebe, 'English and the African writer', *Transition*, vol. 4, no. 18, 1965, p. 27
[4] Ibid., p. 30.
[5] 'Chinua Achebe interviewed by Robert Serumaga', *Cultural Events in Africa*, no. 28, Mar. 1967
[6] 'Chinua Achebe talking to Tony Hall', *Sunday Nation* (Nairobi), 15 Jan. 1967, p. 15
[7] 'Chinua Achebe on Biafra', *Transition*, vol. 7, no. 36, 1968, p. 37
[8] Chinua Achebe, 'The African writer and the Biafran cause', *The Conch*, vol. 1, no. 1, Mar. 1969, p. 8
[9] Bernth Lindfors, 'Achebe on commitment and African writers', *Africa Report*, Mar. 1970, p. 16
[10] Ibid., p. 18

Ama Ata Aidoo (1942–   )   GHANA

This young Ghanaian poetess, playwright, and short-story writer, was born Christina Ama Ata Aidoo; in recent years she has purposefully dropped Christina.

Miss Aidoo became seriously motivated to write after winning a prize in a short-story competition organized by Ibadan's Mbari Club. At that time, though she was still an undergraduate reading English at the University of Ghana in Legon, she began to write *The Dilemma of a Ghost*. This, her first play, was initially presented by the Students' Theatre in March 1964 at the Open Air Theatre at the university. Later that year, after its production in Lagos, Eldred Jones wrote,

> Miss Aidoo displays a gift — very useful to a social dramatist — of show-ing both sides of the coin at the same time. She shows the reverence of African village society towards motherhood while at the same time exposing the inherent cruelty of a system which makes the childless woman utterly miserable. . . . This play should be speedily published.[1]

In 1965 Longmans did so.

Ama Aidoo attended Wesley Girls High School and graduated from the University of Ghana in July 1964. Thereafter her poems, short stories, and book reviews began appearing frequently in a variety of African journals, among them *Black Orpheus, Okyeame, The Journal of the New African Literature and the Arts, Zuka, Présence Africaine,* and *The New African.* Her short creative works, in particular the short story 'Cut Me a Drink', were included in numerous anthologies. Her stories 'are written primarily to be heard'. A firm believer in the potency and positive aspects of oral communication, she would like to see a theatre in which stories could just be recited or related to the audience. 'If I have any strong conception of what else could be done in literature today it is this,' she says.[2]

However, Miss Aidoo believes it is also important to cultivate a wider African readership, which she sees as vital to the emergence of a critical audience — 'If you're writing from a certain background, it's only the people from that background can tell the world whether this is good or bad.' She does not see 'any validity in having someone who does not belong to the society from which the literature itself springs telling you how to write.'[3]

The Institute of African Studies at the University of Ghana granted

Ama Ata Aidoo a research fellowship which enabled her to continue writing and to conduct research into contemporary Ghanaian drama, 'a kind of drama in Fanti which has been going on since the '30s. It caters to a clear 80% of the people.'[4] Miss Aidoo feels, regretfully, that her writing can reach perhaps only one-fifth of the people, and she says,

> I feel almost guilty myself writing the type of thing I write, but my own sort of alibi for wanting to continue writing in English is that one gets the chance to communicate with other Africans outside Ghana. Even in Ghana alone, if you are writing in English you are more able to carry yourself over, and if you have a message, to carry your message over to more people outside.[5]

Miss Aidoo's second play, *Anowa*, was originally a story she had heard from her mother in the form of a song. Published in London in 1969, it is a dramatization of an old Ghanaian legend to which she gives her own interpretation. A translation has been started by James Kangwana of the Voice of Kenya into Swahili for a production planned by James Ngugi, Primila Lewis, and Jonathan Kariara. Longmans have scheduled for publication a collection of Ama Aidoo's short stories, to be titled *No Sweetness Here*.

Ama Aidoo spent most of 1967 travelling throughout the United States. In 1969 she returned to Ghana after a two-year trip that had also taken her to London and East Africa. She is now back in East Africa again.

[1] Eldred Jones, 'A note on the Lagos Production of Christina Aidoo's *Dilemma of A Ghost*', *Bulletin of the Association for African Literature in English*, no. 2, no date, pp. 33—34.
[2] Ama Aidoo, Interview in *Cultural Events in Africa*, no. 35, Oct. 1967, p. 1.
[3] Ibid. p. II
[4] Ibid.
[5] Ibid.

Timothy M. Aluko *(1918–   )*   NIGERIA

Timothy Aluko's first novel, *One Man, One Wife*, was the third major novel written by a Nigerian. It appeared originally in 1959, and was

the first novel to be published by a Nigerian publisher, the Nigerian Printing and Publishing Company in Lagos. Mr Aluko has since written three further novels, *One Man, One Matchet* (1964), *Kinsman and Foreman* (1966), and *Chief the Honourable Minister* (1970).

Margaret Laurence says of him, 'Aluko's work as an engineer has enabled him to understand in profound detail the clash between cultures and the difficulties involved in social change. These are the chief themes in his novels.'[1]

A Yoruba born in Ilesha, Aluko studied at Government College, Ibadan, in Lagos, and in 1946 in London, his subjects being civil engineering and town planning. He returned to Nigeria in the 1950's, worked as an engineer, and later accepted an appointment as Director of Public Works for Western Nigeria. He is now on the staff of the University of Lagos.

First achieving prominence in short-story form, Aluko's work appeared in *West Africa Review* and was broadcast by the BBC African Service; some of his stories received awards in contests sponsored by the British Council.

[2]Margaret Laurence, *Long Drums and Cannons* (New York, 1968), p. 170

Elechi Amadi (1934–   )   NIGERIA

Elechi Amadi's first novel, *The Concubine*, published in London in 1966, was greeted as 'a most accomplished first performance'[1] by Eustace Palmer, an 'outstanding work of pure fiction'[2] by Eldred Jones, and as 'a lovely and dignified picture of a society, not only still ruled by gods, but governed by a great delicacy in human relationship full of respect for others' by the *Guardian*.[3]

Elechi Amadi, an Ekwerri, was educated at Government College, Umuahia, and graduated with a degree in mathematics and physics from University College, Ibadan. Employed for a time as a land surveyor and later as a teacher in the Nigerian army at the Military School in Zaria, he attained the rank of captain. In 1965 he left the army and began teaching at the Anglican Grammar School, Igrito, Port Harcourt, where he hoped to have more time to write.

In 1969 Elechi Amadi's second novel appeared. *The Great Ponds*, set in pre-colonial Eastern Nigeria, concerns a battle between two village communities over the possession of a pond.

During the Nigerian civil war, Mr Amadi was twice detained in

Eastern Nigeria. Upon his second release, despite Biafran pressures, he joined the Federal army and was later appointed District Officer in Ahoada. Since the cessation of hostilities he has been living in Port Harcourt, where he is Acting Permanent Secretary at the Ministry of Information. *West Africa* reported early in 1970 that Amadi is currently writing a play, to concern a wrestling champion, entitled *Isiburu*[4], and this will appear in an anthology to be published by Heinemann.

[1]Eustace Palmer, 'Elechi Amadi and Flora Nwapa', *African Literature Today*, no. 1, 1969, p. 56
[2]Eldred Jones, 'African Literature 1966–1967', *African Forum*, vol. 3, no. 1, p. 5
[3]*The Guardian* quoted in *Cultural Events in Africa*, no. 56, 1969
[4]'Matchet's Diary', *West Africa*, Mar. 14, 1970, p. 283

Ayi Kwei Armah (1939–   )   GHANA

Upon the New York publication of his first novel in 1968, *The Beautyful Ones are Not Yet Born*, Ayi Kwei Armah was internationally greeted as an important new writer. The distinguished African literary critic Abiola Irele wrote,

> ... there is enough evidence in the novel of the writer's tremendous talent, of a profound imaginative perception coming through in sensitive language, which is the mark of a great writer.
>
> The novel itself seems to have been meant as a kind of metaphysical novel with which readers of contemporary European fiction have become familiar and in its description of the vague existential *ennui* of his unnamed hero, recalls Sartre's *La Nausée*.[1]

Born in Takoradi, this Ghanaian writer has lived in several areas

within his country. After his education at Ghana's Achimota School, Armah spent one year at Groton School in Massachusetts and afterwards, on a scholarship, majored in social studies at Harvard, from where he graduated *cum laude*. He has been variously employed as a French-English translator in Algiers, in Ghana as a television scriptwriter, an English teacher in Navrongo School, and as an editor-translator for the Paris-based international news magazine, *Jeune Afrique*. Ayi Kwei Armah recently attended Columbia University's Graduate School of Fine Arts. He is at the moment on the staff of the University of Massachusetts.

Before the publication of his first novel, Armah wrote for such magazines as *The New African, Drum Magazine, Atlantic Monthly*, and *The New York Review of Books*. His short stories, 'Asemka', 'Contact', and 'An African Fable' appeared in *Okyeame, The New African*, and *Présence Africaine* respectively.

Armah's second novel, *Fragments*, was released by Houghton Mifflin in 1970. Autobiographical in nature, it concerns a child whose parents are disappointed in him. 'He is like a ripple on the water, spreading further and further out and not bringing back the material possessions that might have been expected from his early promise,' Armah says. 'My family was unhappy because I was too full of ideas, not actions . . . I found it very traumatic writing this book because of my family's attitude.'[2]

Publishers' Weekly called *Fragments* 'powerful and poetic'[3] and Christopher Lehmann-Haupt of the *New York Times* found that,

> Mr Armah's descriptive powers are formidable: There are passages that actually left me feeling nostalgic for Ghana, and I've never even been in Africa. His sense of structure is worthy of a Swiss watchmaker: Near the book's beginning there's a 17-jewel scene describing the slaughter of a mad dog that symbolically foreshadows the action of the novel's mainspring with gleaming precision. He is inventive and perceptive and wickedly satirical. I grant I'll remember many of the scenes and characters in *Fragments* next week, next month, next year.[4]

In March of 1968 it was reported that Armah had plans for his third novel: a story to concern his trip through Africa.

[1] Abiola Irele, 'A new mood in the African novel', *West Africa*, Sept. 20, 1969, p. 1119.
[2] *Cultural Events in Africa*, no. 40, Mar. 1968, p. 5
[3] *Publishers' Weekly*, vol. 196, no. 18, Nov. 3, 1969, p. 48
[4] Christopher Lehmann-Haupt, 'Books of the Times', *The New York Times*, Jan. 16, 1970, p. 45

Kofi Awoonor (George Awoonor-Williams)
(1935–   )   GHANA

Kofi Awoonor's poems are considered to be among the most exciting African verse, and have been extensively anthologized and translated into French, Russian, Chinese, and German. Although his literary achievement thus far lies essentially with the poetry volume *Rediscovery and Other Poems* published by Mbari in 1964, Doubleday and Heinemann now

have in preparation Awoonor's first novel, *This Earth, My Brother*, and his second verse collection, *Night of my Blood*, both scheduled for publication in 1971. In addition, Heinemann Educational Books are soon to release an anthology of Ghanaian poetry edited by Awoonor.

Born in Wheta, he received his education at Achimota Secondary School and the University of Ghana in Legon, where in 1959 he won the university's Gurrey Prize for the best original creative writing and obtained a degree in English language and literature. Following graduation, Awoonor lectured in English at the School of Administration in the University of Ghana (1960—1963) and thereafter became a research fellow and lecturer in African literature at the university's Institute of African Studies.

Kofi Awoonor's activities have also extended far beyond the university campus. Although he resided in Ghana until 1967, his travels took him to the Soviet Union, Cuba, Indonesia, and China, where he was a guest of the Writers Union of the People's Republic of China. He served as managing director of the Ghana Film Corporation, founded and chaired the Ghana Playhouse, where he produced plays for stage and television, was an editor of the Ghanaian literary review *Okyeame*, which published some of his own writings, and in 1967—1968 was an associate editor of *Transition*.

In 1967 Kofi Awoonor left Ghana. A Longmans' fellowship brought him to the University of London, and he began work on his M.A. in modern English (with emphasis on the linguistic features of English in West Africa). He then received a Farfield fellowship, and 1968 saw him at the University of California at Los Angeles. The following year Awoonor broke new ground at the State University of New York at Stony Brook by starting a course in African literature. He is now chairman of their department of comparative literature.

As a participant in the 1967 African-Scandinavian Writers Conference in Stockholm, Kofi Awoonor made clear his view of the writer's role in contemporary African society:

> He is going to provide in his writings a certain articulate vision, which must order his society because otherwise social life would be a very sterile and a very futile exercise. . . . whether he writes poetry or

whether he writes a piece of drama or whether he writes fiction, he must, through his writings, provide a vision for those who are going to order his society. . . . he must be a person who has some kind of conception of the society in which he is living and the way he wants the society to go.[1]

[1]George Awoonor-Williams, quoted in Per Wästberg, ed., *The Writer in Modern Africa* (New York, 1969), p. 31

Francis Bebey *(1929–   )*   CAMEROON

Francis Bebey had attained an international reputation as a guitarist and composer of considerable talent by 1967. He had performed in Paris, New York, and Africa and had recorded *Spirituals du Cameroun, Pièces pour guitare seule, Le chant d'Ibadan/Black Tears* and *Concert pour un vieux mosque.* Then in 1967 the Cameroonian publisher Editions C.L.E. issued *Le fils d'Agatha Moudio.* The following year it won the *Grand Prix Littéraire de l'Afrique Noir* and established Bebey as a writer of note. (Translation rights were obtained by Heinemann's and it will be published in 1971 in a translation by Joyce Hutchinson.) Bebey's first novel was succeeded in 1968 by *Embarras et Cie,* a collection of nine short stories, each one followed by a poem.

Gifted with outstanding abilities in two creative media, Bebey draws a distinction between them:

As far as writing is concerned, I do have a strong feeling that I can write only when I remain an African in the full sense of the word. It's quite different from my feeling about music, really quite different, because the spoken language, or the written language, is much stronger actually than the dream which you have when you think about music. So you remain yourself. At least I remain more personal, more African

if you like, when I tell a story or when I write it down, than if I just let
my memory wander about and find some notes and arrange them in a
melody.[1]

There have been times when Bebey has turned to music when the
literary vision failed to materialize. For example, in reference to *Le chant
d'Ibadan* Bebey has said, 'For me, it is a poem which I failed to write,
because I could not find the words. Perhaps the music will redeem this
original intention.'[2] And words, in the sense that Bebey utilizes the French
language in his work, at one time proved a problem to him, as they have
for many African writers. But he overcame this.

> There are sometimes difficulties in putting the right expressions which
> would correspond exactly to what African expressions would have
> meant. This, to me, was one of the main difficulties when I started,
> but I was lucky because I am a radio man basically and writing for
> radio, is, to me, very African-like. Writing for radio is
> like telling things to the radio, to the microphone, as we tell things
> to other people in Africa. So, little by little, I came to combining
> both media. I found that every time I tried to write what we call 'liter-
> ature' which is very polished, very clean, I couldn't tell my story
> like an African would have told it. But if I considered my reader as a
> listener, then I could tell him the story in a more African way.[3]

Bebey realizes though that it would be 'somewhat dishonest for contemporary African art deliberately to ignore foreign influences, which
are on the other hand changing many aspects of African literature
today.'[4]

Since the early 1960's Francis Bebey has been working in the Paris
office of UNESCO. Employed in its Information Office, he has been concerned with the extension of radio broadcasting, a means of communication which he has been involved with for many years. Bebey began broadcasting in the Cameroon, was later associated with Radio Ghana, broadcast on several French-speaking African radio stations, and is the author
of *La radiodiffusion en Afrique noir*, published in Paris in 1963.

Born in Douala in Cameroon, Bebey learned to play several instruments
even before he learned to read. At the Sorbonne he studied French
literature and musicology. He has produced two books on African music:
one published by Présence Africaine in 1967, *La musique Africaine moderne*,
and in 1969, *Musique de l'Afrique*.

Bebey is also a poet, and his verse has appeared in many reviews and
several anthologies. At the close of 1968, it was reported that Bebey was
working on his third novel to be released by C.L.E., *La poupée ashanti*.

---

[1] Francis Bebey interviewed in *Cultural Events in Africa*, no. 40, Mar. 1968, p. I
[2] Back sleeve of Bebey, *Pièces pour guitare seule*, Disque Ocora Oct. 27 (Paris, 1965)
[3] Francis Bebey interviewed in *Cultural Events in Africa*, no. 40, p. 11
[4] Back sleeve of Bebey, *Pièces pour guitare seule*

Mongo Beti *(1932–   )* CAMEROON

Mongo Beti's literary career reached its prime in the period 1955–1958. During that time he had four novels published: *Ville cruelle* (1955), *Le pauvre Christ de Bomba* (1956), *Mission terminée* (1957), and *Le roi miraculé* (1958). As A. C. Brench points out, they were written 'in the years of greatest confusion in French colonial — and internal — affairs . . . '³ Along with the works of Ferdinand Oyono in particular, they

> reflect very closely the state of mind among Africans at the time when the impetus of nationalist movements was becoming irresistible. There is a ferocious rejection of European ways and ideas and an affirmation of the positive value of African culture. . . . Their novels [Beti and Oyono] have the definite purpose of attacking colonialism as a political force.²

Alexandre Biyidi, who took the pen-name of Mongo Beti, was born some 25 miles south of Yaoundé in Mbalmayo, Cameroon. A Béti, he was educated at the local Catholic mission school until 1945, when he rejected his Christian faith and left the mission. He entered the lycée in Yaoundé and in 1951 at 19 years of age took his *baccalauréat*. Beti obtained a scholarship and left for France to continue his education. Studying first in the Faculty of Letters at the University of Aix-en-Provence, he completed his *licence* at the Sorbonne. Later he received his doctorate and was appointed to Lambelle in western France as a university lecturer in literature.

At 22, while Beti was studying at Aix, a chapter to his first novel was published in *Présence Africaine* under the title 'Sans haine et sans amour'. The novel itself, *Ville cruelle* (written under the pen-name Eza Boto), was released by Présence Africaine in 1954. However, Beti was doubtful of its literary quality. He decided to drop the Boto pseudonym and adopted 'Mongo Beti', the name thereafter affixed to all his novels.

His second novel, *Le pauvre Christ de Bomba*, created something of a furore in Paris, as colonialist France and the Catholic Church's missionary activities in colonial Africa were not portrayed exactly favourably. Gerald Moore says: 'With this book . . . the author emerged as a formidable satirist and one of the most percipient critics of European colonialism. . . . we see the greed, the folly and tragic misunderstandings of a whole epoch in Africa's history.'³ On its publication in Paris, a Russian publisher secured translation rights. Gerald Moore has translated this novel, which many consider to be Beti's best, and it will be published by Heinemann.

In 1957 Beti's reputation was firmly established with his third semi-autobiographical and now most successful novel, *Mission terminée*. '"Here at last is an African novel which has no political motive." This was the sigh of relief of the French publisher who brought [it] out,' says Claude Wauthier.[4] *Mission terminée* received the 1958 *Saint Beuve* literary award and was nominated for the *Prix Renaudot*. *Mission Accomplished* (*Mission to Kala* in the British edition) appeared the following year in New York and London.

Le roi miraculé, translated as *King Lazarus*, is the most recent novel from the pen of Mongo Beti. Long out of print, it was reissued in 1969 and will be released in 1970 as a paperback in Heinemann's African Writers Series and in Collier's African/American Library.

Beti's works have variously been called comedies, humorous, ribald, boisterous, and Rabelaisian; 'Beti was the master of a scalding and amazing comic talent,' wrote Gerald Moore.[5] Underneath these adjectives however, Brench discerned 'this inexpressible sadness, as if a great deception had made life bitter and cynical humour was the only relief'[6] and he found that essentially 'Beti is a pessimist.'[7] In 1962 Gerald Moore wrote that Beti

> seems to have entered a mood of disenchantment with literature and with what it can achieve. He believes that the new nations can only shake free from colonialism by a double revolution; the revolution of formal political independence is now complete in most of tropical Africa, but the more painful and drastic revolution which will produce truly independent societies is only just beginning. Mongo Beti is throwing himself into this second revolution as a publicist through such articles as his *Tumultueux Cameroun* which appeared in the *Revue Camerounaise* in 1960. His conversation, especially since the Congo débâcle, reveals the same restlessness and disquiet.[8]

Mongo Beti resides in France and is now teaching in Brittany. He has remained at least peripherally a publicist. In a recent article in the leftist daily *Combat* — translated in *Peace News* and reported upon in *West Africa* — 'he seems ... to denounce the apostles of négritude, and also the leaders of independent states, who are castigated as "that era of bloody dictatorships which was inaugurated by the independence gained in 1960."'[9]

Heinemann Educational Books has in preparation a students' critical study on Mongo Beti by Thomas Melone to be titled *The Novels of Mongo Beti*; Présence Africaine will publish his full-length study in French.

---

[1] A. C. Brench, *The Novelists' Inheritance in French Africa* (London, 1967), p. 48
[2] Ibid., p. 48
[3] Gerald Moore, *Seven African Writers* (London, 1966), p. 77–78
[4] Claude Wauthier, *The Literature and Thought of Modern Africa* (London, 1966), p. 157
[5] Moore, *Seven African Writers*, p. 91
[6] Brench, *The Novelists' Inheritance*, pp. 66–67.
[7] A. C. Brench, *Writings in French from Senegal to Cameroon* (London, 1967), p. 56
[8] Moore, *Seven African Writers*, p. 91
[9] Griot, 'Mongo Beti's blast', *West Africa*, p. 1506.

Dennis Brutus (1924–   )

Although born in Salisbury, Southern Rhodesia, Dennis Brutus spent his childhood in the township of Dowerville in Port Elizabeth, South Africa. Of mixed descent, a 'coloured' by South African definition, he was one of four children; his parents were both teachers by profession. Engaged in a continuous battle against poverty, Mr Brutus today suggests it was this struggle that forced his father to abandon his family. Though in his child- hood he did not attend school regularly, he did spend much time reading and participating in family poetry recitations led by his mother. Her favourite poems, Tennyson's 'Lady of Shalott' and 'The Round Table' and Wordsworth's narrative poems, were to become his favourites as well. Acknowledging this early influence on his career, Brutus has written:

> . . . I discovered something that linked my adult work with the begin- nings of my literary knowledge; there recur in my poetry certain images from the language of chivalry — the troubadour, in particular. The notion of a stubborn, even foolish knight-errantry on a quest, in the service of someone loved; this is an image I use in my work, because it seems to me a true kind of shorthand for something which is part of my life and my pursuit of justice in a menacing South Africa. But it only made sense to me when in prison another image came to me; of my mother, in the afternoon sunlight, reading of Sir Galahad's search for light and beauty, with the sunlight falling on the page, and on the glowing colours of a picture of a knight entering a dark forest.[1]

An arts graduate from Fort Hare University College, Dennis Brutus taught English and Afrikaans for fourteen years in South African high schools — ten of those years teaching at Government High School in Port Elizabeth. Dismissed from that post in 1962, he moved to Johannes- burg to study law and enrolled in the University of Witwatersrand. Brutus, however, was an activist, a leader in the struggle against racialism in

South African sport, and involved in anti-apartheid campaigns. Because of this, he was arrested early in 1963. He was released on bail, but his activities did not cease and he was soon banned by the South African government from attending social or political meetings. When the No Trial act took effect Brutus moved to Swaziland, where he was ultimately refused a residence permit. On his way to an Olympic committee meeting in Germany he was detained at a Portuguese port in Mozambique, handed over to the South African police, and taken to Johannesburg. A desperate attempt on Brutus' part to escape resulted in his being shot and sentenced to eighteen months' hard labour on Robben Island.

During his imprisonment his first volume of poetry, *Sirens, Knuckles, Boots*, was awarded the 1962 Mbari prize for poetry; the following year it was published by Mbari. Essentially protest poetry, the critic Ulli Beier found it 'transfigured by a quiet fortitude'.[2] Brutus, however, judged the competition as racially discriminatory in that it was open only to black writers, and rejected the money prize.

He was freed from prison in 1965, but new bans prohibited him from writing, from being published, even from being quoted. In 1966 Dennis Brutus obtained a Rhodesian passport and left for England on a one-way exit permit.

His second collection of poetry was published in 1969 under the title *Letters to Martha and Other Poems from a South African Prison*. They are chiefly inspired by his experiences as a prisoner on Robben Island and were originally written as 'letters' — it was a crime for Brutus to write poetry. *Library Journal* notes that,

> They express his fear, loneliness, and deprivation (especially the lack of music), and they are peopled by figures from his nightmares — brutal prison wardens, fellow prisoners, former friends, and so on. A few written earlier in 1962 and 1963, or later in 1966, when the poet was outside South Africa, are somewhat different in tone, but they are equally successful in conveying his feelings — tender, angry, puzzled, mystical.[3]

Even after his oppressive life in South Africa, Dennis Brutus looks back on his home with affection. 'It's a suffering people and a suffering land, assaulted, violated, raped, whatever you will, tremendously beautiful and I feel a great tenderness for it,' he says.[4]

After residing in England for a while, Dennis Brutus spent some time on the staff of the University of Denver, where he is currently teaching. Since leaving South Africa he has remained vigorously involved in anti-apartheid activities, serving as Director of the World Campaign for the Release of South African Prisoners, President of the South African Non-Racial Open Committee for Olympic Sports, and Campaign Director of the International Defence and Aid Fund. It was Dennis Brutus who was largely responsible for South Africa's exclusion from the Olympic Games, and in March of 1970 the United Nations' Special Committee on Apartheid granted him a hearing. His testimony concerned apartheid in sport and the conditions of political prisoners in South Africa; he also spoke of the International Year for Action to Combat Racism and Racial Discrimination, 1971. In order to publicize his statement as widely as possible, the

U.N. Unit on Apartheid has released a pamphlet, available free upon request, entitled *Special Committee on Apartheid hears Mr Dennis Brutus.*[5]

A third collection of his poems is planned which is to be published by Heinemann and Doubleday.

[1] Dennis Brutus, 'Childhood reminiscences' in Per Wästberg, ed., *The Writer in Modern Africa* (New York, 1969), p. 98.

[2] Ulli Beier quoted in Anne Tibble, *African English Literature* (London, 1965), p. 55

[3] *Library Journal*, Aug. 1969, p. 2790

[4] Dennis Brutus, 'New Poems', *African Arts/Arts d'Afrique*, vol. 1, no. 4, Summer 1968, p. 12

[5] United Nations Unit on Apartheid, Department of Political and Security Council Affairs, *Special Committee on Apartheid Hears Mr Dennis Brutus*, 7/70, Mar. 1970

John Pepper Clark *(1935–   )*   NIGERIA

J.P. Clark considers himself

> . . . that fashionable cultural phenomenon they call 'mulatto' — not in flesh but in mind! Coming of an ancient multiple stock in the Niger Delta area of Nigeria from which I have never quite felt myself severed, and going through the usual educational mill with the regular grind of an English school at its end, I sometimes wonder what in my make-up is 'traditional' and 'native' and what 'derived' and 'modern'.[1]

Thus Clark introduced *A Reed in the Tide* (1965), his second volume of verse, in which he also noted his gratitude to his friend and likewise poet, Christopher Okigbo who, he says, 'was the first to take my poetry seriously enough to want to publish a volume of it at a time when I was still at college. His constant encouragement and criticism have been a great help.'[2]

J. P. Clark's first volume of verse was published by Mbari in 1962. Reviewing the collection, simply entitled *Poems*, Ulli Beier found his technique to result in a

> poetry that makes heavy reading, but which is moving, because it is always nourished by immediate experience and because the author's harassed, tormented and irrepressible personality is present in every line. . . . Some of his moving poems are touched off by a specific

moment from the past which is suddenly remembered . . . and very often, as one might expect, it is love. . . . Whatever it is, there is always immediacy, urgency and spontaneity in his work.[3]

Clark's activities as a poet have also included a number of critical articles, among them, 'Poetry in Africa today', and 'Themes of African poetry of English expression'. In 1961 he established himself as a playwright as well, with Mbari's publication of his first drama, *Song of a Goat*. Performed at Ibadan and Enugu the following year, it has since been well received throughout Africa, Europe and at the Commonwealth Festival of the Arts in London in 1965, along with his drama *The Masquerade*. In 1964, Oxford University Press issued Clark's *Three Plays*, which included the two pieces already mentioned, plus *The Raft*. Said one of his fellow Nigerian writers: 'Clark's three plays are tragedies and critics have attempted to show how close to Greek tragedies they are.'[4]

His most recent play, *Ozidi*, based on Nigerian folk-lore, was published in London in 1966. Earlier, in 1964, André Deutsch had released his controversial and satirical *America, their America*. This was 'a kaleidoscope of America as' J. P. Clark says, he 'caught it in one year'.[5] In 1963 he had been a Parvin fellow at Princeton University and, as he writes:

I was determined right from when I jumped on the last plane in Lagos for New York that I would smell things out for myself and made certain I would touch and taste to the full all that my bounteous host had to offer. What follows therefore, the charitable might say is not so much the story of my host and incredibly sumptuous establishment but the jaundiced and unsavoury account of the responses and reactions of one difficult, hypercritical character and palate, who, presented with unusually rich grapes in a dish of silver and gold, took deprecatory bites and churlishly spat everything out on the face of all.[6]

In 1969 the book was reissued in London and also − for the first time − released in the U.S.A.

J. P. Clark received his schooling and education in Okrika and Jeremi, at Warsi Government College in Ughelli, and at the University of Ibadan. In Ibadan, Clark founded the student poetry magazine *The Horn*, which published some of his first verse. After receiving his B.A. Honours degree in English in 1960, he began work in journalism, first as Information Officer for the government of Nigeria for a year; he then joined the staff of the Nigerian *Daily Express* in Lagos, as a features and editorial writer.

Upon returning from a year's study at Princeton, Clark became a research fellow and did work on Ijaw traditional myths and legends at Ibadan's Institute of African Studies. Since 1966 he has been teaching English at the University of Lagos, and recently he became co-editor (with Abiola Irele) of the influential literary magazine *Black Orpheus*.

According to Frederick M. Litto, Clark's current activities − in addition to a great deal of travel − engage him in the compilation of 'A companion dictionary to Nigerian literature'; a monograph entitled 'A writer on writing', and a United Nations report. Litto further reports him to be working on *The Ghost Town*, a documentary film on the Nigerian port

Forcados.[7] Clark had previously produced *The Ozidi of Atazi*, a film based on the ancient Ijaw epic, made under the sponsorship of the University of Ibadan and the Ford Foundation. He has also worked on an English translation of this seven-day song-and-dance drama, a portion of which was recently published in *Black Orpheus*.

In 1970 Longmans in England and Africana Publishing Corporation in the U.S.A. simultaneously released Clark's latest volume, *Casualties: poems 1966/68*, a new collection of verse concerned largely with the Nigerian civil war. Longmans and Northwestern University Press are about to release a collection of Clark's critical writings on African literature, entitled *The Example of Shakespeare*.

[1] John Pepper Clark, *A Reed in the Tide* (London, 1965), from the introduction.
[2] Ibid.
[3] Ulli Beier, 'Three Mbari poets', *Black Orpheus*, no. 12, p. 48
[4] Oladele Taiwo, *An Introduction to West African Literature* (London, 1967), p. 76
[5] John Pepper Clark, *America, their America* (London & New York, 1969), p. 12
[6] Ibid. pp. 11–12.
[7] Fredric M. Litto, *Plays from Black Africa* (New York, 1968), p. 314

William Conton (1925–   )   SIERRA LEONE

Born in Bathurst, The Gambia, William Conton, historian, teacher, and writer, was educated in Sierra Leone and the United Kingdom. From 1947 to 1953 he was Durham University Lecturer in history at Fourah Bay College in Freetown, Sierra Leone. This was followed by appointments as Headmaster of Accra High School, Principal of the Government Secondary School at Bo in Sierra Leone, and Principal of the Prince of Wales School in Freetown in 1960. He is the author of an autobiographical novel, *The African*, published in 1960, extracts from which have been widely anthologized. He has also written a short story, 'The Blood in the Washbasin'. His most recent work for school use is a two-volume history of West Africa.

When asked what the main influence on his writing had been, Conton said '. . . my growing awareness of the sharp conflicts between African and

Western culture, and in particular the frequent triumphing of the material-
ism of the latter over the spiritualism of the former, whenever they
do clash.'[1]

William Conton resides with his wife and five children in Freetown, and
is currently Sierra Leone's Chief Education Officer.

[1] William Conton, quoted in E. N. Obiechina, 'Cultural nationalism in modern African creative
literature', *African Literature Today*, no. 1. 1968, p. 35

Bernard Dadié *(1916–   )*   IVORY COAST

The French West African Bernard Dadié has a long and varied list of
publications to his credit: three volumes of poetry, an equal number of
collections of short stories, four novels, plays, and children's books, in
addition to articles and short stories that have appeared regularly in
Africa periodicals. It is only in recent years, though, that Dadié has become
known to an Anglophone public through translations of his poems appearing in several African anthologies. However, Dadié will soon be available
to an even wider audience, as an English translation of his first novel,
Climbié, has now been prepared by Karen Chapman and will be published
simultaneously in New York and London in 1971.

Before the publication of his second novel, *Un nègre à Paris*, A. C.
Brench recorded that his 'works are set in Africa and the "contes", most
of the poems and the drama are inspired by traditional themes from the
Ivory Coast. Like all other African writers of this period, Dadié consciously uses themes and materials from Africa's past as a protest against

colonial domination and as evidence of the richness of his cultural heritage.'[1] Dadié would undoubtedly agree with this generalization. Speaking at the First International Congress of Africanists in Accra (December 1962), he cogently defended and explained the often criticized unity of themes employed by black writers:

> The titles of most of the works clearly reveal the situation in which the Negroes are placed, and the reason why they take to writing. Certainly they are quite capable of singing of rain and birds. This is a point that has obviously escaped the notice of persons who criticise Negro-African writers for producing far too many works in which a definite stand against the system of government to which they are subjected becomes a constant refrain. Surely these critics forget that Negro writers are men who in fact have lost everything — lands as well as independence... they desire to be genuine producers, convinced ... they are contributing something specific and regenerative. They are in fact defending their right to live, the beauty of life, the excellence of life as compared with death, whether we conceive of death in terms of disease, poverty, injustice, slavery or racial segregation. It is important that this essential aspect of the work of Negro-African writers should be grasped. They impart once more to their people the joy of living, ... their own distinctive qualities, which came very near to being swept away by the wave of imitations. They cease to harbour any sense of shame at being an African and a Negro, but rather they put the word Negro back into its proper perspective.[2]

Dadié's first poetry collection, *Afrique debout*, published in Paris in 1950, launched his literary career. In the field of poetry he has since produced two additional volumes: *Ronde de jours* (1956) and *Hommes de tous les continents* (1967). Of his poems, Clive Wake says that they 'remind one of Reverdy in style, but his themes are all African. They deal very simply and without pretension or anger of Africa and the African's desire to proclaim his equality with other peoples.'[3] Brench finds 'his best equal to Senghor's best' while his marked lyricism is noted by all.[4]

Dadié's *Légendes africaines* (1954), *Le pagne noir* (1955), and *Légendes et poèmes* are collections of the rich and varied oral literature of Africa. The stories, proverbs, and legends that make up this distinct genre are 'a lesson in prudence, generosity, patience and wisdom, indispensable to the guidance of mankind and the stability of society,'[5] according to Dadié; 'these stories and legends are our museums, monuments and street names — our only books, in fact. This is why they have such an important place in our daily lives...'[6]

While *Climbié* is an autobiographical account of Dadié's schooldays, *Un nègre à Paris* was the harbinger of a new type of African novel, written in letter-form. Brench writes:

> Its real significance is that, published in 1959, it is the first example of a novel by a committed writer to be set outside Africa, in which the African hero is not forced to live within the limitations set by colonial domination... colonialism and racial prejudice are hardly present; this is not in character with the novels which precede or follow it. Yet,

it does prelude a new development in the novel. Not only does Paris become the background for later novelists to use but, more important, the African hero becomes an objective observer, freed from the restraint of his inferior position in society. In the novels which follow *Un nègre à Paris*, the hero has, also, to accept the responsibility of his new freedom.[7]

Dadié's third novel, *Patron de New York*, was released in 1965, and his most recent novel, *La ville où nul ne meurt*, was published in 1968.

Born in Assinie, Ivory Coast, Bernard Dadié attended the local Catholic school in Grand Bassam. At the École William Ponty at Gorée (an island off Dakar) he became active in a drama and folk-lore movement, and began writing plays; in 1939 he received his *Diplôme de commis d'Administration*. From 1936 to 1947 he worked at IFAN, the Institut Français d'Afrique Noire. Upon his return to the Ivory Coast in 1947, he began teaching and writing, and later founded a National Drama Studio. For a time he served as Directeur des Arts et de la Recherche. He is presently Minister of Culture.

In 1967 Présence Africaine produced a full-length study of Bernard Dadié by C. Quillateau, entitled *Bernard Binlin Dadié: l'homme et l'oeuvre*.

---

[1] A. C. Brench, *The Novelists' Inheritance in French Africa* (London, 1967), p. 86
[2] Bernard Dadié, 'Folklore and literature', (trans. by C. L. Patterson) in Lalage Bown and Michael Crowder, eds., *The Proceedings of the First International Congress of Africanists* (Illinois, 1964) pp. 215—216
[3] Clive Wake, *An Anthology of African and Malagasy Poetry in French* (London, 1965), p. 19
[4] Brench, p. 86
[5] Bernard Dadié, 'Le rôle de la légende dans la culture populaire des noirs d'Afrique'. *Présence Africaine*, XIV—XV, p. 167, trans. and quoted in Claude Wauthier, *The Literature and Thought of Modern Africa* (London, 1966), p. 67
[6] Ibid., Dadié, p. 165, Wauthier, pp. 64—65
[7] Brench, pp. 90—91

Birago Diop (1906–   )   SENEGAL

Birago Diop was born and raised in Dakar, one of the four 'communes' in Senegal in which the populace was accorded French citizenship. His family were members of the Wolof tribe and the young Birago was brought up in the Islamic faith. A. C. Brench has recorded that 'Islam and French culture are fused in his works but he is first and foremost an African....'[1]

Diop was educated in Dakar and later attended the Lycée Faidherbe in the former capital of Senegal, St Louis. Moving to France, he pursued a course in veterinary medicine at the University of Toulouse until 1933. It was there that Diop met and collaborated with his fellow countryman, Léopold Senghor, in the publication of the single yet highly influential issue of the journal *L'étudiant noir*.

In addition to being a veterinarian, he had studied philosophy for his second *baccalauréat*, and after Toulouse, began writing much of the poetry that was later to appear in *Leurres et lueurs*. Several of his poems were included in Senghor's *Anthologie de la nouvelle poésie nègre et malgache de langue française* (1948), thus introducing him to a wide audience.

Upon his return to Africa, Diop devoted himself to his career as a veterinary surgeon. The years 1937–39 saw him working in the Sudan, and after a brief return to Paris in the early forties, he continued his work in the Ivory Coast, Upper Volta, and in the early fifties, in Mauritania.

Diop tells us that during his travels,

> ... beneath other skies, when the weather was dull and the sun was sick I often closed my eyes and there would arise from my lips the *Kassaks* which used to be sung in the 'Men's Huts'; and I would hear my mother or my grandmother recounting once again the rebuffs of Bouki-the-Hyena, that conceited coward, or the misfortunes of Khary-Gaye, the orphan girl, the tricks of that *enfant terrible* Djabou N'Daw, the triumphs of the diabolical Samba Seytane, and the misadventures of Amary-the-Devout.
>
> This momentary return to my childhood tempered my exile ... On my return to my own country, having forgotten little of what I had learnt as a child, I had the great good fortune to meet by chance old Amadou-Koumba, our family *griot*.
>
> ... Amadou-Koumba recounted to me the tales which had lulled me to sleep as a child. He taught me others, too, studded with maxims and morals, in which can be found all the wisdom of our ancestors.
>
> These same tales and legends — with slight variations — I also heard in the course of my travels along the banks of the Niger and across the plains of the Sudan, far from Senegal.[2]

The first product of such avid and attentive listening was a volume in which Diop rendered these memorable tales into French, *Les contes d'Amadou Koumba*, published in Paris in 1947. This volume (which has been translated into Russian), has since been followed by two more books of *contes* in which Diop renders the 'most traditional form of African literature'.[3] They were *Les nouveaux contes d'Amadou Koumba* in 1958, with a preface contributed by Senghor, and *Contes et lavanes* in 1963.

In these works 'Diop offers the reader the whole canvas of the "comédie humaine" which is to be found in the traditional stories', writes Joyce Hutchinson:

> If his observation of the human comedy is necessarily influenced by his broader knowledge and understanding of humanity, this influence is not obtrusive; he is never patronising. There is nothing artificial about the insistence on respect for tradition which pervades all histories. The other insistent and pervading theme, which is obviously as important for Diop as it was fundamental for the griot, is the belief that everything, elements, spirits, animals, plants, stones as well as human beings, is endowed with life.[4]

Birago Diop has written numerous poems and short stories, both extensively anthologized. A complete volume of his poetry was published by Présence Africaine in 1960, *Leurres et lueurs*.

In *Tales of Amadou Koumba*, published in 1966, Dorothy S. Blair has translated into English nineteen of Diop's traditional folk tales. Joyce Hutchinson has also produced a volume of selected stories from Diop's two volumes, with an introduction in English.

Since Senegal achieved independence in 1960 Birago Diop has been her Ambassador to Tunisia.

---

[1]A. C. Brench, *Writings in French from Senegal to Cameroon* (London, 1967), p. 5
[2]Translated and quoted by Dorothy S. Blair, *Tales of Amadou Koumba* (London, 1966) p. XXII
[3]Ibid., p. XXIII
[4]Joyce Hutchinson, ed., *Birago Diop: contes choisis* (London, 1967), p. 24

David Diop *(1927–1960)*   SENEGAL

David Diop had published only one small verse collection, *Coups de pilon*, in 1956, before his untimely death in 1960. He has nevertheless been called 'the most promising of West Africa's younger French poets'[1] by Gerald Moore and 'a leader of the younger generation of "negritude" writers, those who reached their twenties in the postwar years,' by Paulette Trout and Ellen Kennedy.[2] Moore finds that this one volume 'was enough to establish David Diop as the most interesting and talented new African poet of the fifties.'[3]

Although recognized as a West African poet, Diop was born in Bordeaux, France, to Christian parents, a Cameroonian woman and a Senegalese doctor. After his primary education in Senegal, the remainder of his schooling took place in France, where he earned two *baccalauréats* and a *licence-ès-lettres*. Frequently hospitalized and a semi-invalid for most of his life, Diop passed only a brief time during his childhood in Senegal and Cameroon. Spending most of his life in France, Diop witnessed World War II; he saw many of his compatriots wage and suffer in a European war. Later, in the fifties, he followed the moves for independence in many parts of Africa. His exile from his native country exerted a decisive influence on his work, as did Aimé Césaire (the writer from Martinique). His vehement and critical opposition to European society, its position in and effect on Africa, stood in contrast to his love for Africa and his African brethren, and his vision of a sovereign Africa. These are the dominant motifs in his poetry.

In the latter part of the fifties Diop returned to Senegal. In Dakar he taught for a year at the Lycée Maurice Delafosse, and in 1958 he went to Kindia, Guinea, where he was principal of a secondary school. Two years later, he was killed with his wife in an air crash off Dakar, returning from a vacation in France. Since his manuscripts were destroyed in the crash, Diop left only the volume published by Présence Africaine. During his life, his work had appeared in *Présence Africaine* and had been included in Senghor's *Anthologie de la nouvelle poesie nègre et malgache*.

In a 1968 issue of the *Journal of the New African Literature and the Arts*, Paulette Trout and Ellen Kennedy translated ten of Diop's poems and accompanied them with a short biographical essay.

[1]Gerald Moore, *Seven African Writers* (London, 1962), p. 18
[2] Paulette Trout and Ellen C. Kennedy, 'Profile of an African artist. David Diop: Negritude's angry Young Man', *Journal of the New African Literature and the Arts*, Spring and Fall 1968, p. 77
[3]Gerald Moore, p. 18

Mbella Sonne Dipoko (1936–   )   CAMEROON

To Mbella Sonne Dipoko the position held by French-speaking creative writers in Africa is an anomaly. He is critical of the constant glorification of Africa before colonization:

> It is a search for authenticity in which they get their people's dream of happiness all wrong. For the masses happiness was, as it still is, a dream of better living conditions, greater purchasing power, personal freedom, a share of all the good things of modern life, from industrial products to learning; in short a longing for better days to come.[1]

Although born in Douala, Cameroon, Dipoko was raised for a time by his uncle, a strict Protestant, on a farm in Missaka on the Mungo River. At this time he developed an avid interest in tribal dance and ritual. He obtained his education at schools in both Cameroon and Nigeria,

receiving his secondary-school education during 1952—6 in the eastern part of Nigeria. Returning to Cameroon, he became a clerk with the Development Corporation in Tiko and then joined the staff of the Nigerian Broadcasting Corporation, where he became a news reporter stationed in Lagos. In 1960 Dipoko moved to Paris to write and to read law at the Sorbonne. He also served on the staff of *Présence Africaine.*

The author of two novels, poems, and short stories, this Cameroonian has done all his writing in English. Living in France since 1960, Mbella Sonne Dipoko set his first novel, *A Few Days and Nights,* in Paris, returning only in his second novel to his native country. Of the latter he says, '*Because of Women* is a study in pleasure and change; the story of a womaniser who dreams of founding a large family. The novel tries to show the deep joy there is in women.'[2]

> I want to describe the quintessence of life. . . . I'm not interested in politics, which many other African writers like Achebe have done so well. Only in life — and women. . . . *A Few Days and Nights* was written straight off, very quickly. I had a lot to say then, and I've worked over and rewritten *Because of Women* until I really feel satisfied with it . . . It's about life in an African village . . . there is a woman, a very young woman, very young indeed, but who is just feeling her womanhood — who has just begun to live. It ends tragically — to feel beauty you must have tragedy.[3]

Speaking of African literature Dipoko remarks:

> Too much fuss is made of books from Africa — they're given too much critical attention. If you're an African you can become someone overnight — after one book. This is wrong. Writers should have time to test themselves. . . . I'm not saying that books shouldn't be published, but there shouldn't be such a fuss about them. My first book had too much fuss.[4]

Dipoko's poems have appeared in *Présence Africaine, Transition,* and several other journals, and have been widely anthologized in recent years. Two of his short stories have been published in *Présence Africaine* and one in *The New African.* His literary career has recently extended to radio: his play *Overseas* has been produced by the B.B.C., and is soon to be published in *Eleven Short African Plays* in the African Writers Series.

Mbella Sonne Dipoko is now writing his third novel, as well as doing translations of French writings by Cameroonian authors. Of the novel he says, 'I want it to be a therapy. If it is read by a racialist — either of one extreme or the other — both should finish reading it having come to the same conclusion.'[5]

Mbella Sonne Dipoko, 'Cultural diplomacy in African writing', *Africa Today,* Aug. —Sept. 1968, p. 9

Cultural Events in Africa. no. 56, 1969.

Cultural Events in Africa, no. 40, Mar. 1968.

Ibid

Ibid.

R. Sarif Easmon (1925–   )   SIERRA LEONE

A prominent Sierra Leonean figure, Dr R. Sarif Easmon is a medical prac-
tioner in Freetown, professionally educated in England, and a leading
voice in political matters in Sierra Leone. Half Creole and half Susu (a
people from Guinea), he says, 'I have a very large and interesting family —
I don't need to go outside my family at all to find plots.'[1]

He is the author of two published plays. *Dear Parent and Ogre* was
initially performed in Lagos by the '1960 Masks' in 1961. It was the first
prize-winner in a London playwriting contest organized by *Encounter*
magazine. It was published in 1964, and was followed in 1965 by *The
New Patriots*, a play dealing with corruption in the civil service. This
opened in Ghana in the period following President Nkrumah's des-
position, and after several presentations along the west coast of Africa,
was performed in Sierra Leone in 1968.

Dr Easmon is the author of two further plays: *Mate and Checkmate*,
produced by the Nigerian Television Service, and *Dilys Dear Dilys*. Of his
four plays he has said, 'One tries to write not only of a theme that is of
passing interest but on the basic themes of humanity that interest people
at all times. My plays are wildly different.'[2]

Easmon also has to his credit two novels: *The Burnt-out Marriage*, which
appeared in London in 1967, and *Geneviève*, submitted to the 1968 *African
Arts/Arts d'Afrique* literary competition (excerpted in the winter 1969 issue),
and noted as being a 'close runner up to the prize-winning novel of Ezekiel
Mphahlele'.[3]

[1]*Cultural Events in Africa*, no. 44, 1968
[2]Ibid.
[3]*African Arts/Arts d'Afrique*, vol. 2, no. 2, Winter 1969, p. 30

Cyprian Ekwensi (1921–   )   NIGERIA

To date Cyprian Ekwensi has published six full-length novels (reportedly
with another four as yet unpublished), seven children's books and popular
Onitsha novels, two books of short stories, and numerous articles and
stories that have appeared in newspapers and magazines throughout the
English-speaking world. His works have been translated into several
languages and he himself has toured Africa, Europe, and America extensively. Undoubtedly Cyprian Ekwensi is one of the best-known names
in the field of African writing.

He is a *popular* novelist. He 'prides himself on being a writer for the
masses, a writer who can communicate with any African literate in
English,'[1] writes Bernth Lindfors. Ekwensi tersely summarized his literary
span in 1964. Speaking of himself in the third person he wrote,

> Cyprian Ekwensi's range embraces the Northern Savannah, the Eastern
> Village, Western Nigeria's sophistication and the city's decadence and
> degradation. He has been described as a city novelist, perhaps because

his best-known works *People of the City* and *Jagua Nana* are set in the City of Lagos; but he has also produced *Burning Grass*, a stark novel about the cattlemen of the Northern Savannah.[2]

At the same time Ekwensi defined his understanding of the oft-debated concept 'African literature':

My own definition of African Literature is literature based on African character and psychology. This means that the main theme may be anthropological, traditional or modern, but the traits, temperaments and reactions of the characters will be peculiarly African due to influence of tribe, culture and history.[3]

This Nigerian novelist, an Ibo, was born in Minna in the northern part of his country. Educated in Nigeria, Ghana, and London, he attended Government College, Ibadan; Achimota College in Ghana; the School of Forestry, Ibadan; and on a government scholarship, Chelsea School of Pharmacy, London University, where his interest in writing first developed.

His initial literary encounters were with 'reading Rider Haggard, Edgar Wallace, Dickens, Sapper, Bates. At Government College in Ibadan,' Ekwensi says, 'we could recite whole chunks of *King Solomon's Mines. Nada the Lily* was a favourite; so was *She*, and *Allan Quatermain . . . Treasure Island* [was] unforgettable.'[4] These influences have since been discerned in his writings.

Ekwensi's checkered career has seen him lecture in fields as diverse as English, science, and pharmacy. For a time he was Head of Features at the Nigerian Broadcasting Corporation, and later in Lagos he held the position of Information Officer for the Nigerian government's Information Department, before the outbreak of the Nigerian civil war.

The seeds of Ekwensi's literary career were sown with such titles as the extremely successful *When Love Whispers* (first published in 1947) and *The Leopard's Claw*. These paperback novellas are popularly called Onitsha market literature, Onitsha being a market town in eastern Nigeria with an enormous output of these romantic books, sentimental and moralistic in character. Ekwensi also collected Ibo folk tales, and as early as 1947 *Ikolo the Wrestler and other Ibo tales* was released in London, while his other translations appeared in local magazines and booklets intended for school use.

People of the City, originally published in 1954, was Ekwensi's first full-length novel. It is generally considered to be the first contemporary African novel, and was reissued in Britain in 1963, and more recently as a Fawcett Premier paperback in the U.S. Ekwensi followed this with more novellas, children's stories, and the full-length novels *Jagua Nana* (perhaps his most popular), *Burning Grass*, *Beautiful Feathers*, and *Iska*. Again to quote Professor Lindfors, 'Ekwensi has an uncommonly good ear for narrative style, a gift for mimicry, and a knack for transplanting un-African events onto African soil. . . . His is a literature of imitation and adaptation. . . .'[5]

With the outbreak of the Nigerian war Ekwensi became Chairman of the Bureau for External Publicity in Biafra and a prominent figure on behalf of the Biafran cause. Since the end of the conflict he has been actively involved in reorganizing Biafra's former radio station at Orlu.

[1]Bernth Lindfors, 'Cyprian Ekwensi: an African popular novelist', *African Literature Today*, no. 3. p. 3
[2]Cyprian Ekwensi, 'African literature', *Nigeria Magazine*, no. 83, Dec. 1964, p. 296
[3]Ibid., p. 295
[4]Cyprian Ekwensi, 'Literary influences on a young Nigerian', *The Times Literary Supplement*, 4 June 1964, p. 475, quoted in Bernth Lindfors, 'Cyprian Ekwensi: an African popular novelist', p. 3
[5]Bernth Lindfors, 'Cyprian Ekwensi: an African popular novelist', p. 7

Alfred Hutchinson (1924–   )   SOUTH AFRICA

Author and teacher, Alfred Hutchinson now resides in Brighton, England, an expatriate from South Africa. Hutchinson recently wrote in the London *Observer* of being asked by one of his students what it felt like to be black:

> It was an impossible question. One *lived* blackness. . . . But if I had tried to answer his question where should I have begun? Perhaps I would have had to journey back to my English highwayman grandfather — the notorious pre-Boer War 'Captain Moonlight' — and my maternal grandfather, a Swazi chief of note. I would have had to tell him about my impossible half-caste father and his brother — both DCMs.
>
> But how could I have described life in South Africa: the sweaty humiliations; the heart-tearing rages; the laxative of helplessness . . . ? How could I have told him of pass laws, arrests, prison, high treason; my flight from a treason charge to marry an English woman in Ghana?[1]

Born in Hectorspruit in Eastern Transvaal, Alfred Hutchinson was educated at St Peter's School and Fort Hare University, from which he received a B.A.; he also has an M.A. from the University of Sussex. The treason charge Hutchinson refers to above resulted from his disagreement with apartheid. Freed on bail, he was arrested two days later for failure to carry a pass. Released because he was of mixed blood, Hutchinson escaped from Johannesburg by train for the North. Travelling through Northern Rhodesia (present-day Zambia), through Portuguese East Africa to Nyasaland (now Malawi) to Dar es Salaam, Tanzania, he was once again arrested and jailed for failure to have a permit to enter the country. Unexpected assistance, however, arrived from the local Christian Action Group, and Hutchinson made his way to Ghana.

His experiences on this journey are the basis of his novel *Road to Ghana*, published in England in 1960. Widely praised, this novel has since been translated into French, Russian, German, Swedish, Polish, Arabic, and Roumanian. A fellow South African writer, Dennis Brutus, speaking of 'explicit non-literary or non-creative denunciations of apartheid' has called *Road to Ghana* 'the finest ever to come out of South Africa'. He goes on to say, 'This had pace and momentum, simplicity and directness, and best of all, a freshness of language, a new minting of idiom and of image which I have never seen paralleled in any other writer who came out of South Africa.'[2]

From Ghana Hutchinson left for England in 1960. He is married to an Englishwoman and has three children.

Alfred Hutchinson is also the author of a drama, *The Rain Killers*, published in London in 1964 and included in Frederic Litto's *Plays from Black Africa*, and *Fusane's Trial*, a radio drama appearing in *Ten One-Act Plays* edited by Cosmo Pieterse. Hutchinson has written short stories, articles, and several other plays for radio.

[1]Alfred Hutchinson, 'What's it like to be black, Sir?', *The Observer*, 10 Aug. 1969, p. 9
[2]Dennis Brutus, 'Protest against apartheid', in C. Pieterse and D. Munro, eds., *Protest and Conflict in African Literature* (London & New York, 1969), p. 99

Legson Kayira (19---   )

MALAWI

This young writer from Malawi was born in a village in the bush country of pre-independence Nyasaland (now Malawi). Educated by Presbyterian missionaries in Nyasaland's Livingstonia mission school, Legson Kayira decided that he, like the Abraham Lincoln he had studied, would somehow rise above his childhood penury and serve the interests of his country

and people. Without the financial resources to pursue his education, he decided to go to the United States and work towards an education in America. Lacking funds and passport, but carrying a Bible and a copy of *Pilgrim's Progress*, he set out on foot to journey 2,500 miles across Africa from Nyasaland to Khartoum. Here, with the assistance of the U.S. consul, he was accepted for study at Skagit Valley Junior College in Washington. 'I Will Try', the motto of his Nyasaland secondary school, Legson adopted for the title of his autobiography, a book recounting his determined struggle and his adventurous two-year 2,500-mile trek. The winner of the Northwest Non-fiction Prize, it was initially published in 1965, and has recently been reissued by Longmans in an abridged, simplified edition suitable for lower secondary-school students.

After completing the two-year course at Skagit, Kayira enrolled in the University of Washington, majoring in political science. He obtained his degree here and went on to Cambridge University, where he is currently doing postgraduate work on a two-year scholarship.

Legson Kayira is also the author of two novels: *The Looming Shadow*, published in 1968 and to be reissued in paperback in Collier's African/American Library in 1970, and *Jingala*, released in 1969 in both London and New York. Of *The Looming Shadow*, Kayira says 'it fills up what I probably missed out in *I Will Try*, namely my background. This is a story of a village and its people.'[1] Ezekiel Mphahlele finds it

> ... a tale of scalding malice ... it leaves little or no room for romanticism. ... He [Kayira] captures the quality of village life, a life that is changing even while the shadow of the past lingers. Kayira is good at sketching the surface of things in this village life: the landscape, festivities, physical appearances of people, the ordeal etc.[2]

Kayira would have liked to write this book in his native language, for as he says, 'I was sitting on my mother's verandah for a good part of the writing, looking at the system, and if I had been able to get a publisher to put it out in Timbuka, I would have written it in Timbuka.'[3]

Of *Jingala*, the author notes, 'The story is basically a feud between a 50-year old man and his 18-year old son. The theme is similar — the conflict of old and new.'[4]

When asked his opinion on the role to be played by the writer in Africa, Legson Kayira said:

> Certainly the writer is serving a purpose — books by and about Africans for schools are very important. Now that the way is being opened up for these writers to come up and write their own books, I think that their chances of playing a large role in society have increased, so that a writer has just as much role to play in society as a politician.[5]

In 1971 Longman will publish Kayira's latest novel, *The Civil Servant*.

[4]'Legson Kayira from Malawi, Author of *I Will Try* and *The Looming Shadow*, interviewed by Margaret Henry'. *Cultural Events in Africa*, no. 41, 1968, p. 1
[2] Ezekiel Mphahlele, '*The Looming Shadow*, L. Kayira', *The Jewel of Africa*, vol. 2, no. 1, 1969, p. 40
[3]*Cultural Events in Africa*, no. 41
[4] Ibid.
[5] Ibid.

Asare Konadu *(1932–)* GHANA

On a continent yet relatively devoid of indigenous private publishing houses, Samuel Asare Konadu is today the successful publisher of Anowuo Educational Publishers, a Ghanaian firm established by him in 1965. His initial list of books, many of which have run into several impressions, has been well received.

Konadu himself is the author of *The Wizard of Asaman* (1964) and *The Player who Bungled his Life*, novels published by the Waterville Publishing House in Accra, and *Shadows of Wealth* (1966) and *Night Watchers of Korlebu* (1967), issued under his own imprint. More recently two additional novels of his have been published in Heinemann's African Writers Series: *A Woman in her Prime* in 1967, and in 1969 *Ordained by the Oracle*, which was a new edition of his previous *Come Back Dora*, again originally published by his own company.

A Woman in her Prime was greeted by Douglas Killam as 'a relatively rare thing in modern African writing – a novel by a Ghanaian'. It was further distinguished as being a novel which, according to Killam, avoided the 'thematical material . . . one almost invariably has come to expect or associate with modern African fiction; the theme of conflict resulting from the presence of Europeans in West Africa and the social, cultural and political changes which this presence promotes.'[1] Instead it focuses on life in an Ashanti village, essentially that of a childless woman, a situation considered a misfortune in African society.

Before becoming either publisher or writer, Konadu was associated with the Ghana News Service, which he left in 1963 in order to concentrate more fully on both his writing and his research into Ghanaian traditional practices and customs.

Born in Asaman in Ashanti, Ghana, Konadu attended local schools, and later Abuakwa State College in the south of his country. In 1951 he became a government reporter for the Gold Coast Information Service and the Broadcasting Service. He later went to London, and then studied journalism at Strasbourg University. Asare Konadu has since travelled extensively throughout Africa and Europe.

[1]Douglas Killam, 'Reviews,' *Black Orpheus*, vol. 2, no. 2, p. 43

Alex La Guma (1925–   )

SOUTH AFRICA

Jimmy La Guma was one of the leading figures in South Africa's non-white liberation movement. His son Alex was therefore raised in a politically conscious environment and likewise plotted a politically active course, a dangerous thing for a 'coloured' in South Africa.

As a young man Alex La Guma joined the Communist Party and became a member of its Cape Town District Committee until 1950, when it was banned by the government. The authorities learned of his activities in 1955 when he helped to organize the South African representatives who drew up the Freedom Charter, a declaration of rights. Consequently in 1956 he was among the 156 people accused in the notorious Treason Trial, a charge which was dropped five years later.

His professional career took root in 1960, when he joined the staff of *New Age*, a progressive newspaper for which he wrote until August 1962. Always simultaneously involved in politics, by 1960 he was an executive member of the Coloured People's Congress and thus became one of 2,000 political prisoners detained for five months as a state of emergency was declared by the government after the violent incidents at Sharpeville and Langa. During this imprisonment, La Guma read voraciously and wrote. A year later, he was again arrested, this time for his part in organizing a strike in protest against the Verwoerd Republic. When South Africa's Sabotage Act was passed in the early sixties, it enabled the government to detain its opponents under house arrest without trial: in December 1962, La Guma became its victim. He was confined to his house for twenty-four hours a day, every day, for five years. Nothing he said or wrote was allowed to be quoted or printed in the republic. Before the five years elapsed, however, a No-Trial Act was passed in South Africa and La Guma and his wife were arrested and confined to solitary imprisonment. Though his wife was soon released, a longer time elapsed before La Guma himself was, and then on bail, for he was now charged with possessing ban   literature, and again subjected to 24-hour house arrest.

Though his work was not allowed to be published in South Africa, in 1962 Mbari in Ibadan issued Alex La Guma's first novel, *A Walk in the Night*, It was reissued by Heinemanns and Northwestern University Press simultaneously in 1967 together with six of his short stories, three of which had appeared previously in *Black Orpheus*. This short work 'has distinct Dostoevskian overtones', claims Lewis Nkosi, himself a black South African who finds it 'inexcusable that European and American publishers who are in such indecent haste to put into print any mediocre talent from Africa have ignored this novel'.[1] Robert July describes it as 'a story on which is built a picture of such vividness and verisimilitude that one can almost taste and smell the air, the streets, the buildings against which the characters move in sure and full three-dimensional reality.'[2]

During his initial house arrest La Guma wrote his first full-length novel, *And a Threefold Cord*, published in 1964 in East Germany. While this dealt with events in a ghetto on the periphery of Cape Town, his experiences in prison thereafter prompted him to dedicate his novel *The Stone Country* 'to the daily 70351 prisoners in South African goals in 1964.'[3] This novel was published in 1967, at a time when his East German publishers, Seven Seas Books, were happy to announce that the La Guma family had arrived safely in Britain — where they continue to reside.

'What is African literature, what is its place in the continent and in the world?' La Guma asks, and answers himself:

It is possible that I may oversimplify things by saying that African literature or Scandinavian literature or American or English literature is simply that which concerns itself with the realities of its prospective or appropriate societies. African literature concerns itself with the realities of Africa. And South African literature, I am prepared to say, is that literature which concerns itself with the realities of South Africa.[4]

La Guma first established his literary career as a short-story writer with 'A Glass of Wine' and 'Slipper Satin', which appeared in early issues of *Black Orpheus* (7 and 8 respectively). Later years saw 'At the Portagees', 'Blankets', and 'Tattoo Marks and Nails' appear in its pages. 'A Matter of Honour' was published in *The New African*, and magazines in South America, Germany, the United States, and Sweden have featured his stories as well. They also appear in numerous collections, including Richard Rive's *Quartet*. Bernth Lindfors writes that 'the most accomplished non-white short story writers in South Africa today are Richard Rive and Alex La Guma,' and summarizes the latter's technique and subject matter:

La Guma's style is characterized by graphic description, careful evocation of atmosphere and mood, fusion of pathos and humor, colorful dialogue, and occasional surprise endings. His stories most often concern lawbreakers — criminals, prisoners, prostitutes and apartheid offenders — who possess either an unusual sensitivity or a sense of honor or morality which redeems them as human beings and raises them to heroic stature.[5]

[1] Lewis Nkosi, 'Fiction of black South Africans', in Ulli Beier, ed., *Introduction to African Literature* (Illinois, 1967), p. 127
[2] Robert July, 'The African personality in the African novel', in Ulli Beier, ed., *Introduction to African Literature* (Illinois, 1967), p. 219
[3] Alex La Guma, *The Stone Country* (Berlin, 1967), p. 7
[4] Alex La Guma, 'The writer in a modern African state' in Per Wästberg, ed., *The Writer in Modern Africa* (New York, 1969), p. 22.
[5] Bernth Lindfors, 'Form and technique in the novels of Richard Rive and Alex La Guma', *Journal of the New African Literature and the Arts*, no. 2, Fall 1966, p. 11

Camara Laye (1928–   )   GUINEA

One of the first black African authors to receive world-wide recognition was Camara Laye, a Muslim from upper Guinea.

His childhood was spent in an essentially traditional society in the ancient city of Kouroussa; it was a society in which magic was revered, a familiar part of everyday life. His parents, reputed to possess supernatural powers, were both leading and respected figures.

The young Laye went first to the local Koranic school and then to the Government Primary School before leaving Kouroussa to attend Conakry's technical college, Ecole Poiret, where he received a scholarship to study in France. Against his mother's protestations, he left Guinea for Argenteuil (near Paris) to train as an engineer. Upon finishing his studies there, Laye wanted to carry his education still further, but financially hampered from doing so, he was only able to attend evening classes at the Conservatoire des Arts et Métiers while he worked as a mechanic at the Simca car factory.

At this point in his life Laye says,

Vivant à Paris, loin de ma Guinée natale, loin de mes parents, et y vivant depuis des années dans un isolement rarement interrompu, je me suis transporté mille fois par la pensée dans mon pays, près des miens. ... Et puis, un jour, j'ai pensé que ces souvenirs, qui à l'époque étaient dans toute leur fraîcheur, pourraient, avec le temps, sinon s'effacer — comment pourraient-ils s'effacer? — du moins s'affaiblir. Et j'ai commencé de les écrire. Je vivais seul, seul dans ma chambre d'étudiant pauvre, et j'écrivais: j'écrivais comme on rêve, je me souvenais; j'écrivais pour mon plaisir; et c'était un extraordinaire plaisir, un plaisir dont le coeur ne se lassait pas.[1]

The culmination of this effort established Camara Laye's reputation. When the autobiographical novel *L'enfant noir* was published in Paris in 1953 it was welcomed 'by some as a minor masterpiece' and by others, chiefly African nationalists, as 'a colonialist pot-boiler'.[2] The following year it won for Laye the famed Prix Charles Veillon, and was subsequently published in the United States as the *The Dark Child* (translated by James Kirkup) in 1954, and in Great Britain as *The African Child* in 1955. Janheinz Jahn later wrote:

In *The Dark Child* Camara Laye shows the new spirit of French West Africans towards tradition. He did not consider his African childhood as something remote, primitive, something to be ashamed of. On the contrary: looking back on it from a distance, and having the technical skills European education had to offer, he discovered that these skills had been animated, and had been more closely related to man in his native civilisation.[3]

When it was reissued in the United States late in 1969, Thomas Lask writing in the *New York Times* commented, 'Written for himself for neither show nor consumption *The Dark Child* is a tender re-creation of African life, mysterious in detail but haunting and desirable in spirit.'[4] Laye's first novel continues to be widely read, and remains today the subject of heated literary discussion.

1954 saw the publication of Camara Laye's symbolic novel, 'usually considered as an ingenuous allegory about man's search for God'.[5] *Le regard du roi*, open to widely different interpretations, appeared in English as *The Radiance of the King* in 1956; it is to be released again late in 1970 in Collier's African/American Library.

Camara Laye returned to Guinea in 1956 and for two years worked as an engineer. When Guinea achieved independence in 1958 Laye entered the political arena and was appointed Director of the Centre de Recherches et d'Etudes for the Ministry of Information in Conakry.

Twelve years elapsed between the appearance of *Le regard du roi* and *Dramouss*, his third and latest novel. In the interim he wrote short stories for *Black Orpheus*, *Présence Africaine*, *Paris-Dakar*, and *Bingo*, and a paper, 'L'âme de l'Afrique dans sa partie Guinéenne', contributed to the *Colloque sur la littérature africaine d'expression française*. Returning again to autobiography, in *Dramouss* (long scheduled for publication as *Retour au pays natal*) his 'emphasis changes from fiction narration to direct social comment', notes A. C. Brench.[6] First published in 1966 after Laye had left Guinea for Senegal, it appeared in English in 1968 as *A Dream of Africa*. Laye dedicated this book 'to the young people of Africa. ... I write this book in order that African ways of thinking, re-integrated and restored ... may be a new force — not aggressive but fruitful.'[7] A.C. Brench records that here Laye re-introduces the characters from *L'enfant noir*. 'This time, however, he is a stranger looking at a world he knows imperfectly. His memories are blurred and idealized while the country has changed considerably during his absence. He looks at his country critically and seems to deplore what he sees.'[8]

Since 1964 Camara Laye has lived in exile in Senegal with his wife Marie (his childhood girl-friend in *L'enfant noir*). He is currently a Research Fellow in Islamic Studies at Dakar University.

[1] From a paper read by Camara Laye at the *Colloque sur la littérature africaine d'expression française. Faculté des Lettres de Dakar, 26—29 Mar. 1963*, quoted in Joyce A. Hutchinson, ed., *L'enfant noir* (London, 1966), p. 7
[2] A. C. Brench, 'Camara Laye: idealist and mystic', *African Literature Today*, no. 2, Jan. 1969, p. 11
[3] Janheinz Jahn, 'Discussion on Camara Laye', *Black Orpheus*, no. 6, Nov. 1959, p. 35
[4] *The New York Times*, Sept. 16, 1969, p. 45
[5] Jahn, p. 36
[6] Brench, p. 31
[7] Camara Laye, *A Dream of Africa* (London, 1968), pp. 7—8
[8] Brench, p. 28

Taban lo Liyong (1939–   )   UGANDA

Within the past two years Taban lo Liyong has established himself as one of the most candid, controversial and prolific African men of letters. In 1969 and 1970 no less than three volumes of his appeared in rapid succession: *The Last Word, Fixions*, and *Eating Chiefs*.

The Last Word was the first book of literary criticism to be published in East Africa. Many of its essays originally appeared in African and American journals; their compilation (with five additional articles) provide a

composite picture of lo Liyong's idea of 'cultural synthesism', as he calls it in the collection's subtitle. A review by Basil Busacca in *Africa Report* found *The Last Word* 'a Magna Carta for African greatness', and called lo Liyong 'an East African writer and critic who genuflects before no idols — European, Nigerian or local —and who proves that he is right to exercise the prerogatives of genius. With this slim book of essays he introduces himself as a powerful voice, a spectacular and audacious intelligence.'[1]

One selection in *The Last Word* is autobiographical, others discuss the American Negro and the African in the United States, and the majority of essays concern African literature. Lo Liyong's stimulating commentary have led some to call him 'a *bad African* in the sense that recalls a term like *un-American*',[2] according to Basil Busacca. Lo Liyong is not a chauvinist. He rejects the philosophy of negritude and black mysticism in any form. He also opposes another current trend, in that he feels 'it is folly to imagine that an African, any African, is the best critic of things African . . . it is the height of folly for Africans to declare that African culture or literature is the one branch of knowledge beyond the attainment of all non-Africans'[3] If black people have a monopoly on 'soul' lo Liyong asks, does it follow that only white people can appreciate classical music, art, and literature?

The British, too, do not escape his criticism. In 1965 lo Liyong saw East Africa as a literary wilderness and he wrote:

> I blame the British. The education they came to offer was aimed at recruiting candidates for a Christian Heaven and eliminating others for a Christian Hell; they sought to teach clerks, teachers, servants and administrators. Culturally, they stood aloof. . . . Not only that, the British went about castrating the Africans. Culturally our dances, in- cluding songs became Satanic. . . . Poetry writing and the art of fiction were not taught us though we debated and reasoned. This led directly to early writings which were of a quarrelsome nature; political grievances (about land, mostly) and answering back the white racist charges through pamphlets, and biographies and anthropological works.[4]

However, when lo Liyong returned to East Africa in 1968 after his studies abroad, he found that during his absence the output of literature had proliferated. Now, his previous call for the incorporation of African literature into the curricula could become a reality. But for him the study of the world's literature is vital as well, because 'we need to know how our works stand in relation to other contemporary works throughout the world; we also need to compare our works with those by past societies.'[5]

Although Taban lo Liyong realises that African writers will have to utilize a foreign language to attain a wide readership, he points out that if the language is English, 'we will not have to stick to Queen's English . . . . we have to tame the shrew and naturalize her. . .'[6] 'The new languages such as English and French have to pay a price for their absorption into the African's thought process.'[7]

Eating Chiefs. Lwo culture from Lolwe to Malkal selected, interpreted and trans- muted by Taban lo Liyong was published in the African Writers Series in 1970. Here he utilized Africa's cultural heritage to forge a new literary medium. His aim was to 'induce creative writers to take off from where the anthropologists have stopped. . . . This book is merely an attempt to show what can be done. If it inspires other artists or, better still, provokes them to treat their tribal literature as raw material, or artistic forms for containing their views on the past and the present, then our legacy from the past will have been accepted and our forefathers rewarded by multiplication of their efforts.'[8] *Eating Chiefs* is part of lo Liyong's research at the Cultural Division, Institute for Development Studies, University College Nairobi where he now has a Tutorial Fellowship. He is also a lecturer in the university's Department of English and editor of their new newsletter of cultural research, *Mila.*

Taban lo Liyong was born in northern Uganda. He attended Gulu High School and Sir Samuel Baker School. Upon graduating from National Teachers College, Kampala he was awarded two scholarships. Under the influence of his father, he chose a political science course in the United States where he attended Howard University and Knoxville College. He took his graduate degree at the famed writer's workshop at the University of Iowa, the first African writer to attend this school.

In addition to the two volumes discussed, Taban lo Liyong has produced a collection of short stories entitled *Fixions,* also published in the African Writers Series. Speaking of his future literary career he said, late in 1969:

> I have an idea for a play.... After that I want to write a novel which would be a mirror of East Africa at the moment.... And I think that as East Africa is a political country, a political entity with plenty of political involvement, if I am to address myself to East Africa...it will have to have something to do with politics.[9]

[1]Basil Busacca, Book review of *The Last Word, Africa Report,* Nov. 1970,
[2]Ibid., p. 35
[3]Taban lo Liyong, *The Last Word* (Nairobi, 1969) p. 63
[4]Taban lo Liyong, 'Can we correct literary barrenness in East Africa?', *Transition* no. 19, and *East Africa Journal,* June 1965, and *The Last Word* (Nairobi, 1969) pp. 31–32.
[5]Taban lo Liyong, *The Last Word,* p. 36
[6]Ibid., p. 79
[7]Ibid., p. 81
[8]Taban lo Liyong, *Eating Chiefs* (London, 1970) pp. xi-xii
[9]'Taban lo Liyong, Ugandan writer, interviewed by Heinz Friedlberger', *Cultural Events in Africa,* no. 57, 1969, p. III.

Ezekiel Mphahlele (1919–   )   SOUTH AFRICA

Despite the hardships of poverty and prejudice, Ezekiel Mphahlele has emerged from the slums of Pretoria to become a novelist, essayist, and teacher, and one of the leading voices from South Africa. The hard work and sacrifice of his grandmother and aunt, with whom he lived on Pretoria's Second Avenue, enabled the young Mphahlele to attend primary school and later escape the ghetto to board at Johannesburg's St Peter's Secondary School, an institution noted for its high standards of academic freedom and scholarship, and from there to Adams College in Natal. Having been banned from a teaching career for his outspoken oppo-

sition to the government's Bantu Education Act, Mphahlele worked as a messenger for a while, but then returned to Pretoria. Here he began his literary career as a reporter for *Drum*, a picture magazine designed for a black African audience, while simultaneously studying externally for his B.A. and M.A. from the University of South Africa. However, Mphahlele was not really a journalist; he did not believe in 'a press for whites and a press for non-whites'; he was mostly interested in 'the editing of short stories'.[1]

In 1957, at the age of 37, Ezekiel Mphahlele left South Africa for Nigeria, where he taught at a grammar school; he then lectured in English language and literature in the University of Ibadan's Department of Extra-Mural Studies. In 1959 his first full-length autobiographical work, *Down Second Avenue*, met with critical acclaim. In 1961 his second collection of short stories, *The Living and the Dead*, was published by Mbari. His first such collection, *Man Must Live*, had been published in 1947 in Cape Town, but by 1957 Mphahlele had found that his perspective had changed from escapist to protest writing and, hopefully, he said, 'to something of a higher order, which is the ironic meeting between protest and acceptance in their widest terms.'[2]

From Nigeria Mphahlele went to Paris, where at the Congress for Cultural Freedom he was director of the African programme. In the meantime, together with Wole Soyinka and Ulli Beier, he co-edited issues number seven (June 1960) to 13 (November 1964) of the literary journal *Black Orpheus*. Returning to Africa in 1963, Mphahlele founded Chemchemi, a new cultural centre for writers and artists in Nairobi, and directed its activities up to 1965.

Living his life in exile, Mphahlele described himself as 'the personification of the African paradox, detribalized, Westernized, but still an African'.[3] His outlook toward himself and South Africa was revealed in a 1964 National Educational Television interview:

> These two ways of living, the African and the European, I think in South Africa are much more integrated than you will find outside South Africa ... the black tar has rubbed off on to the white man and ... the stuff of whiteness has rubbed off on to the black ... we have influenced one another so much.... I have reconciled a good number of these disparate elements in me.... My African values continue to remain a top, solid thing inside me, the African humanism ... wanting to be one of a community which is very African; this individualism also ... the

European part of one; but at the same time . . . you get to this middle
point where you can reconcile the disparate elements. And I think I
have done so in me. . . .

I feel very gloomy about the whole situation as far as creative writing
is concerned. I think right now we are being sucked into this battle
between the ruling whites and the Africans . . . our energies go into
this conflict to such an extent that we don't have much left for creative
work. One might ask the question — why could this not be a spur towards creative writing? . . . I think it's a paralyzing spur . . . we get
all involved in it . . . we build up reflexes . . . even as writers . . . ready
and stock responses which . . . always come out in our writing. . . . We
are in two ghettos, two different streams . . . and you can't get really
dynamic art in this kind of society. You won't get a great, white novel,
I don't think, and you won't get a great black novel until we get to a
point where we . . . integrated.[4]

Mphahlele's odyssey took him to the United States in 1967 to lecture
in English at the University of Denver, where he also acted as editor of
Africa Today; then back to Africa in the fall of 1968 to lecture in the English
department at the University of Zambia in Lusaka. In June of 1970 Mphahlele returned to the University of Denver.

The 1968 *African Arts/Arts d'Afrique* literary competition awarded *The
Wanderers* its first prize. Subtitled *A Novel of Africa*, this autobiographical
novel describes Mphahlele's 'experiences as a wanderer with his family,
as he moved across the continent seeking for those essential roots which
a writer must have.'[5] This four-part novel will be released by Collier in
1971.

Ezekiel Mphahlele's output has been considerable: he has written
numerous articles, essays, book reviews, and short stories, including the
volume *In Corner B* published in 1967, and *The African Image*, a collection
of essays growing out of his M.A. thesis. He is the editor of two anthologies,
Writing Today in Africa and *Modern African Stories*, the latter produced in
association with Ellis Komey.

His fellow South African writer Lewis Nkosi esteems him highly:

He differs from other black South African writers in his pre-occupa-
tions. . . . he has been moving in the direction of saying something
positive about black experience in South Africa instead of writing, as
many of our writers do, as though everything the blacks did in the
country was a reaction to white oppression.[6]

[1] Ezekiel Mphahlele. *Down Second Avenue* (German Democratic Republic, 1962), p. 187
[2] Ibid., p. 217.
[3] 'African Writers of Today', National Educational Television, Program no. 3, 1964.
[4] Ibid.
[5] *African Arts/Arts d'Afrique*, vol. 2, no. 2, Winter 1969, p. 12
[6] Lewis Nkosi, 'Fiction by black South Africans' in Ulli Beier, ed., *Introduction to African Literature*
(Illinois, 1967), p. 213

James Ngugi (1938–   )   KENYA

Weep Not, Child was the first English-language novel to be published by an East African writer. James Ngugi won international praise for this work, first published in Heinemann's African Writers Series, and it received awards from both the 1965 Dakar Festival of Negro Arts and the East African Literature Bureau. Written during his student days at Makerere University College in Kampala, Uganda, "*Weep Not, Child* is divided into two parts: the first deals with the period just before the Emergency, the second with the Emergency itself in the life of a Kenyan family.'[1] 'Written in a simple, lyrical style, it creates a song about a society in transition. . . . Like the transition of the hero from youth to adulthood, the movement of society is inevitable. The kind of movement and the direction of the movement are not, however, predetermined. That is in the hands of the people affected . . .'[2] In 1969 *Weep Not, Child* was also published in New York. In actuality, this was Ngugi's second novel, for *The River Between*, although published a year later in 1965, was written first.

When in 1967 his third novel was published, it was generally agreed that *A Grain of Wheat* was 'a great advance in Ngugi's development as a novelist'.[3] Eldred Jones wrote that 'It has a denser texture than either of his earlier novels. . . . He looks at the Kenyan struggle for independence, the emergency, and independence itself with considerable depth and penetration. . . . It is difficult to think the same about Kenyan independence after reading Ngugi's novel, which has the stature of art that changes and transforms our vision.'[4] And this last phrase in Jones's comment sums up Ngugi's goal as a writer. Elaborating on this 'vision', Ngugi has said,

> Today the revolutionary struggle . . . is sweeping through Africa. And Africa is not alone. All over the world the exploited majority, from the Americas, across Africa and the Middle East, to the outer edges of Asia is claiming its own. The artist in his writings is not exempted from the struggle. By diving into the sources, he can give moral direction and vision to a struggle which, though suffering temporary reaction is continuous and is changing the face of the 20th century.[5]

However, after reading all the reviews of *A Grain of Wheat*, Ngugi felt 'a general sense of futility'[6] and has written nothing since. (In 1969 his last novel was translated into French as *Et le blé jaillira*.)

By 1967 Ngugi felt that the African writer had failed and he pointed out a future course for the writer in Africa to take. At the 1967 African-Scandinavian Writers' Conference he said,

When we, the black intellectuals, the black bourgeoisie, got the power, we never tried to bring about those policies which would be in harmony with the needs of the peasants and workers. I think it is time that the African writers also started to talk in the terms of these workers and peasants.[7]

Speaking on the same point in a 1969 interview Ngugi said,

Meanwhile I think the African writers ought to be addressing themselves more and more fully to the present needs, especially what I call the crisis or conflict between the emergent African bourgeoisie and the African masses.[8]

James Ngugi is a Kikuyu, born in Limuru to one of his peasant father's several wives. After graduating with honours in English from Makerere University College in 1964 he worked on Nairobi's *Daily Nation* for several months before he left to do graduate work at the University of Leeds. Upon his return to Africa, Ngugi became a special lecturer in English at Nairobi's University College, a post he held for the year and a half preceding the January 1969 student strike. He resigned from his position in protest following the college's closure on January 27th and the alleged dictatorial attitude taken towards the student body both during and after the strike. He was editor of *Zuka: A Journal of East African Creative Writing*. (During his student days he had edited *Penpoint*, a periodical published by the Department of English at Makerere.) Ngugi is engaged in writing a book on his impressions of East Africa.

Ngugi's literary career has also extended itself to playwriting, short-story writing, and journalism. *The Black Hermit*, his first play, was expressly written for the Uganda National Theatre as part of the 1962 Independence celebrations and has since been published in the African Writers Series. His second play, *This Time Tomorrow*, will be included in a forthcoming collection edited by Cosmo Pieterse entitled *Eleven Short African Plays*. Ngugi's short stories have appeared in *Transition, Penpoint, The New African*, and *Zuka*. He has also contributed a literary essay to *Protest and Conflict in African Literature*.

In the fall of 1970, James Ngugi joined for a year the staff of Northwestern University in Evanston, Illinois.

[1] Ime Ikiddeh in Introduction to James Ngugi, *Weep Not, Child* (London, 1966), p. XII

[2] Martin Tucker in Introduction to James Ngugi, *Weep Not, Child* (New York, 1969), p. 17

[3] Douglas Killam, 'African literature V: novels of disillusion', *Journal of Commonwealth Literature*, Jan. 1969, no. 6, p. 136

[4] Eldred Jones, 'African literature 1966–1967', *African Forum*, vol. 3, no. 1, Summer 1967, pp. 15–16

[5] James Ngugi, 'Satire in Nigeria', in C. Pieterse and D. Munro, eds. *Protest and Conflict in African Literature* (New York and London, 1969), p. 65

[6] Edward Blishen. 'A Report on the Ife Conference on African Writing in English, December 1968', *Cultural Events in Africa*, no. 48, no date, p. 5.

[7] Per Wästberg, ed., *The Writer in Modern Africa* (New York, 1969), p. 25

[8] James Ngugi in an interview in *Cultural Events in Africa*, no. 50, 1969

Abioseh Nicol *(1924–)*

The distinguished Sierra Leonean Ambassador to the United Nations Dr Davidson Nicol has earned a considerable reputation as a short-story writer and poet 'of sensitivity and intellect'.[1] Writing under the pen-name Abioseh Nicol, he has produced two books of short stories: *The Truly Married Woman and Other Stories* (1965) and *Two African Tales: The leopard hunt and The devil at Yolahun bridge* (1965). Of the latter he wrote:

> These stories were written some years ago and have now been modified for my young friends to give them an impression of what happened when we were colonial countries under the rule of Europeans. They owe something to European writers like E.M. Forster, Joyce Cary, Graham Greene and Evelyn Waugh, all of whom I admire and who, themselves, wrote about similar situations. However, being both black and African, I was then on the other side of the fence and perhaps saw things somewhat differently.[2]

Davidson Nicol began writing because

> I wanted to and partly because I found that most of those who wrote about us seldom gave any nobility to their African characters unless they were savages or servants or facing impending destruction. I knew differently. I saw all around me worthy Africans who lived and worked with varying degrees of success, distinction, and happiness. I began to write about them.[3]

In 1952 Nicol was awarded the Margaret Wrong Prize and Medal for Literature in Africa. Since then his stories have been extensively anthologized as has, in more recent years, his poetry (most often 'The Meaning of Africa' and 'African Easter').

Dr Nicol's eminent career as an academic and medical practitioner commenced with his education at the Government Model School and the Prince of Wales School in Freetown, Sierra Leone. In 1943 he went to

Europe, attending the Universities of Cambridge and London, and ultimately receiving degrees in the natural sciences, medicine, and philosophy. After holding research and resident positions at the London Hospital, Dr Nicol returned to Africa. He has since served in the faculty of medicine at Ibadan University, has been an honorary medical officer in Nigeria, a senior pathologist in the Sierra Leone Medical Service, a pathology consultant to the Sierra Leone Government, a member of its Public Service Commission, and director of the National Bank of Sierra Leone. In the capacity of guest lecturer, Davidson Nicol has been to the United States (Yale University, Mayo Clinic, and a U.N.E.S.C.O. conference), Germany, and Ghana. In 1960 he was appointed Principal of Fourah Bay College, and thereafter served as Vice-Chancellor of the entire University of Sierra Leone until 1968, when he returned to the United States in an ambassadorial post.

Dr Nicol has conducted pioneering research into the structure of human insulin and has contributed numerous medical and scientific papers to scholarly journals in addition to his articles on African literature.

Africa: a subjective view, his Aggrey-Fraser-Guggisberg Memorial Lectures presented at the University of Ghana, were published in 1964 in both London and Cambridge, Massachusetts. Here Dr Nicol outlined his personal views:

> I am simply an African, born and bred, searching for wisdom and trying to use what he finds towards the good of his beloved continent, a continent intensely personal, filled with wonderful things, larger than life, only dimly and partially grasped. But now it belongs to us again, and we should see to it that we are always worthy of it.[4]

In 1970 Davidson Nicol edited a collection of writings by Africanus Horton, the early West African nationalist, published simultaneously in England (as *Africanus Horton: the dawn of nationalism in modern Africa*) and in America (as *Black Nationalism in Africa 1867*).

[1]Anne Tibble, *African English Literature* (New York, 1965), p. 114
[2]Abioseh Nicol, *Two African Tales* (London, 1965), Foreword
[3]Abioseh Nicol, *The Truly Married Woman and other stories* (London, 1965), Introduction
[4]Davidson Nicol, *Africa: a subjective view* (London, 1964), p. 80

Lewis Nkosi (1936–   )   SOUTH AFRICA

Lewis Nkosi is primarily an essayist and critic of African letters, and perhaps one of the most distinguished to have emerged in this area. In 1955 he embarked on a career in journalism with the *Ilanga lase Natal* (Natal Sun), a Zulu-English weekly, and the following year joined the staff of South Africa's highly popular *Drum* magazine. When he went to Johannesburg to work for *Drum*, Nkosi records:

> On the whole I was very sober, very young and fiercely ambitious. I was reading an incredible amount; reading always badly. . . .

My sense of honour was propounded out of the romantic novels of Dumas, Kingsley and Marryat and the love I knew best was the love of knights and ladies in the drawing rooms of fifteenth-century Europe. What was happening under my eye was filtered through the moral sieve provided by this foreign literature. It was clear I was using literature as a form of escape; I was using it as a shield against a life of grime and social deprivation.[1]

Speaking for his entire generation. Nkosi feels 'the decade of the fifties was the most shaping influence of our young adulthood . . .'; it was a time in which 'we had no literary heroes, like generations in other parts of the world' and 'we longed desperately for literary heroes we could respect and with whom we could identify.'[2]

While working for *Drum* as chief reporter and later for the *Post* (*Drum's* Sunday newspaper), Nkosi lived in Sophiatown, a ghetto in Johannesburg; a city which Nkosi describes as 'totally without an inner life', where 'people loved quickly . . . lived fitfully; so profligate were they with emotion, so wasteful with their vitality, that it was very often difficult for them to pause and reflect on the passing scene.'[3] And this is partially the reason behind the significant lack of novels as well as plays to come out of South Africa, according to Nkosi.

It is not so much the intense suffering (though this helped a great deal) which makes it impossible for black writers to produce long and complex works of literary genius as it is the very absorbing, violent and immediate nature of experience which impinges on individual life. Unless literature is assumed to be important in itself, for its own sake, unless it is assumed to be its own justification, there was no reason why anyone in our generation should have wanted to write.[4]

Furthermore:

Language must be inhabited, it must be enlarged by usage; South Africans abridge it and stop it from referring too closely to those emotions which they spend almost all their lives trying to obliterate or deny. We cannot be cowards in the lives we live and be brave in the act of creating plays, novels and paintings.[5]

The school year 1960–1961 saw Lewis Nkosi in the United States, a student of journalism at Harvard University. For accepting his Nieman Fellowship to study in the U.S., South Africa issued him with a one-way exit permit and thus barred him from returning. Lewis Nkosi's works are no longer allowed to be published or quoted in his native country. He has since been living in exile.

As a journalist, his articles have appeared in *The New Yorker*, the London *Observer* (for which he toured the South of the U.S.), *The Spectator*, *The Guardian*, *The New Statesman*, *Africa Report*, *Africa Today*, and *Black Orpheus*, among others. His numerous, outspoken, and sometimes controversial articles dealing with African literature have included 'Where does African literature go from here?', 'Fiction by black South Africans', 'African Fiction: Part I – South African protest', and 'African Literature: Part II – English-speaking West Africa'.

Home and Exile, a collection of Nkosi's essays and articles published in London in 1964, was awarded a prize at the Dakar World Festival of Negro Arts. It revealed his background and his thoughts on Johannesburg, apartheid, identity, and New York, as well as eight literary topics. The following year Nkosi's *The Rhythm of Violence*, a play set in Johannesburg, was published in England; reportedly it is the first English-language play to be written by a black South African since 1936.

For the last few years Nkosi has been living in London. He was the literary editor of *The New African* and in 1964 served as moderator and interviewer for the 'African Writers of Today' series, produced by the National Educational Television network in conjunction with London's Transcription Centre.

Lewis Nkosi has expressed views on virtually every aspect of African literature; his opinions have often provoked considerable discussion and controversy. Thus it is perhaps appropriate to conclude with Nkosi's answer to the question, 'What is African literature?':

> ... it seemed to me that, ultimately, what linked various African peoples on the continent was the nature and depth of colonial experience; and this was the final irony. Colonialism had not only delivered them unto themselves, but had delivered them unto each other, had provided them, so to speak, with a common language and an African consciousness; for out of rejection had come an affirmation.[6]

---

[1]Lewis Nkosi, *Home and Exile* (London, 1965), pp. 9, 10
[2]Ibid, pp. 9, 7, 8
[3]Ibid, p. 17
[4]Ibid, p. 17
[5]Ibid, p. 119
[6]Ibid, p. 117

Above: Nzekwu
Left: Nwapa

Flora Nwapa (1931–   )

Florence Nwanzuruaha Nwapa is a doubly distinguished author: she is the only woman to have written a novel in Nigeria, and the first woman in Africa to have had a work of fiction published in London. *Efuru*, her first novel, was released in 1966 by Heinemann Educational Books in their African Writers Series, as was her next novel, *Idu*, published early in 1970. It is the story of a woman in a small town in Nigeria who wants more from life than just children. Extracts from *Idu* appeared in the summer 1968 issue of *African Arts/Arts d'Afrique*.

Flora Nwapa was raised in Oguta in eastern Nigeria, the eldest in a family of six. First educated at Archdeacon Crowther's Memorial Girls' School, and in Lagos at C.M.S. Girls' School, in 1953 she travelled to Britain to attend Edinburgh University for studies culminating in a Diploma in Education. Returning to Nigeria, she has since held several administrative posts within its educational institutions. In Calabar she accepted an appointment as a Woman Education Officer; in Enugu she taught English and geography at Queen's School; at the University of Lagos she was Assistant Registrar. Before the outbreak of the civil war in Nigeria, Flora Nwapa returned to the east of her country.

Onuora Nzekwu (1928–   )

In addition to being the editor of *Nigeria Magazine* since May of 1962, Onuora Nzekwu is the author of three novels and co-author of the children's book *Eze Goes to School*. His first two novels, *Wand of Noble Wood* and *Blade among the Boys*, published in 1961 and 1962 respectively, revolve around the traditional conflict between old and new values. According to John Povey, they expose 'the dilemmas of the young African with all his longings and anger as he seeks a tenable morality amid the conflicting pressures of the pragmatism of his education and the beliefs of his traditions.'[1] His third and latest novel, *Highlife of Lizards*, published in London in 1965, is the story of Agom, a woman childless for many years who 'finally after adversity and various magic spells . . . has a child and becomes a loved wife and an influential and admired woman in her village.'[2]

A Nigerian born in the north-eastern city of Kafanchan, Nzekwu received his education in various northern and eastern Nigerian schools. Enrolled in St Anthony's E.T.C. in 1943, in the following year he began studies at St Charles' Higher Elementary Teacher Training College. Upon graduation he entered the teaching profession and for the next nine years taught in Oturkpo, Onitsha, and Lagos. In 1956 his career took a new direction when he joined the staff of *Nigeria Magazine* as an editorial assistant. During the recent hostilities in Nigeria, Nzekwu was a Biafran partisan.

As a recipient of fellowships from the Rockefeller Foundation and U.N.E.S.C.O., Onuora Nzekwu has twice travelled to Europe and America.

---

[1]John Povey, 'The Novels of Onuora Nzekwu', *Literature East and West*, vol. XII, no. 1, Mar. 1968, p. 74
[2]Ibid., p. 81

Grace Ogot (1930–   )   KENYA

As one of the very few female writers to have emerged from East Africa, and as the only woman to have had her fiction published by the East African Publishing House, Grace Okinyi Ogot occupies a unique position. Born in Kenya's Central Nyanza District, she attended Ng'iya Girls School and Butere High School, after which she trained as a nurse both in Uganda and England. Working at Maseno Hospital as a nursing sister and midwifery tutor, and later in Makerere at University College with the Student Health Service, Grace Ogot's career thereafter took various routes. For fifteen months she was employed as a scriptwriter and broadcaster for the BBC Overseas Service, as a Community Development Officer in Kisumu, and in Nairobi as a Public Relations Officer for the Air India Corporation of East Africa.

Her major contribution to African literature is primarily as a short-story writer. Her stories have been widely anthologized and have appeared in *Black Orpheus, Transition, Présence Africaine*, and *East Africa Journal*. Her first volume of short stories was published in 1968 under the title *Land Without Thunder*. Two years earlier, her one novel, *The Promised Land*, appeared.

Married in 1959 to the historian Bethwell Ogot, Grace Ogot is the mother of three children.

Gabriel Okara *(1921–   )*

Until 1964 Gabriel Okara was known primarily as a Nigerian poet. Before that date his verse had appeared in numerous magazines (in particular in *Black Orpheus*, including its maiden issue), had been translated into several languages, and had been read by the author in Africa, America, and Europe. His poems were widely anthologized. Among the most often quoted were 'The Call of the River Nun', which had won for Okara an award at the 1953 Nigerian Festival of Arts, and 'The Snow Flakes Sail Gently Down', which he wrote from his experience of an American winter. As a prose writer, his short stories included 'The Crooks', again published in *Black Orpheus*.

Then in 1964 André Deutsch issued *The Voice*. This first novel was greeted with mixed reactions. Arthur Ravenscroft, in his introduction to the paperback edition (reissued in both London and New York in the early half of 1970), reviews its initial reception:

> ... some African reviewers found its unconventional use of English unacceptable; they seemed to see it as a novel in a line of development from Amos Tutuola's books. Reviewers abroad were also partly nonplussed by the language, and uncomfortable about its strange symbolism and apparently naive simplicity, which seemed old-fashioned in a world of Western European sophistication. But there were discerning voices, such as M. Macmillan's in *The Journal of Commonwealth Literature* ... who wrote that *The Voice* 'is an interesting and imaginative piece of writing' and that it 'has simplicity of parable and the poignancy of an epitaph'. In 1968 the Canadian novelist Margaret Laurence wrote of it in her book on Nigerian literature, *Long Drums and Cannons*: 'It is certainly one of the most memorable novels to have come out of Nigeria.' I share this view.[1]

The core of this criticism centered largely around Okara's unique and experimental use of the English language: his English translation of some linguistic characteristics of his native Ijaw tongue. Okara himself had already written of his technique in 1963:

> As a writer who believes in the utilisation of African ideas, African philosophy and African folk-lore and imagery to the fullest extent possible, I am of the opinion the only way to use them effectively is to translate them almost literally from the African language native to the writer into whatever European language he is using as his medium of

expression. I have endeavoured in my words to keep as close as possible to the vernacular expressions. For, from a word, a group of words, a sentence and even a name in any African language, one can glean the social norms, attitudes and values of a people.

In order to capture the vivid images of African speech, I had to eschew the habit of expressing my thought first in English. It was difficult at first, but I had to learn. I had to study each Ijaw expression I used and to discover the probable situation in which it was used in order to bring out the nearest meaning in English. I found it a fascinating exercise.[2]

Gabriel Imomotimi Gbaingbain Okara was born in the Ijaw country of the Niger delta. Educated at Government College, Umuahia, he — unlike most Nigerian writers, who often follow an academic path — became a book-binder. He also began writing plays and features for use in broadcasting. Widely regarded as a thoughtful man and poet, self-developed by extensive private reading, Okara has translated a great deal of the folk-lore and poetry of his Ijaw heritage. Throughout most of the past decade, before the outbreak of the Nigerian civil war, he was employed in Enugu as Information Officer for the Eastern Nigerian Government Service.

Gabriel Okara was active on behalf of the Biafran cause during Nigeria's recent civil war and toured the United States with his compatriot and fellow novelist, Chinua Achebe, during part of 1969.

[1] Gabriel Okara, *The Voice* (New York and London, 1970), p. 4
[2] Gabriel Okara, 'African Speech . . . English Words', *Transition*, vol. 3, no. 10, 1963

Christopher Okigbo (1932–1967)   NIGERIA

In 1967 two of Nigeria's outstanding literary figures, poet Christopher Okigbo and novelist Chinua Achebe, launched a publishing company in Enugu. Mr Achebe recounts in an interview in *Transition* that their

idea was that it was necessary at this time to publish books, especially children's books, which would have relevance to our society. This is something we felt very strongly about. We felt we wanted to develop literature for children based on local thought and we set up a firm. Then the war came on and Chris joined the army and I kept on working at the office, but whenever he had some time, he came back and we discussed things.[1]

In May of 1967, Christopher Okigbo had announced that their initial programme would feature new poetry collections by Gabriel Okara and George Awoonor-Williams as well as himself. Later that year it was reported that Christopher Okigbo, a Major in the Biafran army, had been killed in action.

Okigbo began writing poetry in December 1958,

when I knew that I couldn't be anything else than a poet ... I can't say whether the call came from evil spirits or good spirits. But I know that the turning point came in 1958, when I found myself wanting to know myself better, and I had to turn around and look at myself from inside ... I mean myself, just myself, not the background ... But you know that everything has added up to building up the self ... And when I talk of looking inward to myself, I mean turning inward to examine myselves. This of course takes account of ancestors ... Because I do not exist apart from my ancestors.[2]

... I am believed to be a reincarnation of my maternal grandfather, who used to be the priest of the shrine called Ajani, where Idoto, the river goddess, is worshipped. This goddess is the earth mother, and also the mother of the whole family. My grandfather was the priest of this shrine, and when I was born I was believed to be his reincarnation, that is, I should carry on his duties. And although someone else had to perform his functions, this other person was only, as it were, a regent. And in 1958, when I started taking poetry very seriously, it was as though I had felt a sudden call to begin performing my full functions as the priest of Idoto. That is how it happened.[3]

In his lifetime Okigbo saw two volumes of his verse published by Mbari of Ibadan: *Heavensgate* in 1962 and *Limits* in 1964. Speaking of these poems in another *Transition* interview, he said:

My *Heavensgate* ... was influenced by the Impressionist Composers. It is curious how this happens, but this is the truth or part of it. I wrote several parts of *Heavensgate* under the spell of Debussy, César Franck and Ravel. My *Limits* ... was influenced by everything and everybody. But this is not surprising, because the *Limits* were the limits of a dream. It is surprising how many lines of the *Limits* I am not sure are mine and yet do not know whose lines they were originally. But does it matter?[4]

Five years later Okigbo elaborated on his literary influences, saying, 'I think that I've been influenced by various literatures and cultures, right from Classical times to the present day, in English, Latin, Greek and a little French, a little Spanish.'[5] By his own admission, his work was also affected by his childhood in Ojoto, an Ibo village near Onitsha, and Ibo mythology. Literary critics have moreover noted that his sources and models are to be found in Pound, Eliot, the Bible, and Allen Ginsberg's *Howl*; this they attribute to his formal education in the classics.

As testimony to his outstanding achievement, the 1966 Festival of Negro Arts in Dakar awarded Christopher Okigbo its First Prize for Poetry which, however, he declined, saying, 'There is no such thing as Negro art',[6] confirming a statement he had made two years earlier, 'There is no African literature. There is good writing and bad writing — that's all.'[7]

The British poet Peter Thomas, recounting his friendship with Okigbo, recently wrote that Okigbo's father had made certain that his sons received a good education, together with the freedom to plan their own vocational directions. Educated at Government College in Umuahia, Okigbo then studied classics at Ibadan University. After receiving his degree there in 1956, Okigbo acted as Private Secretary to Nigeria's Federal Minister of Research and Information for the following two years, taught for another two years, and then served as Acting Librarian of the University of Nigeria at Nsukka. Although his aspiration was to be a poet, Okigbo continued to gain his livelihood through various means: from Nsukka he moved to the library on the Enugu campus, then became the West Africa representative of Cambridge University Press and West African editor of *Transition* magazine, as well as an editor of Mbari Publications.

Christopher Okigbo is survived by his wife and daughter. A posthumous collection of his complete poetic works, *Labyrinths with Path of Thunder*, will be published simultaneously in New York and London in 1971. In the introduction to this volume, Okigbo wrote in October 1965 that 'Although these poems were written and published separately, they are, in fact, organically related.'[8] In 1971 Evans will publish a full-length study of Okigbo by Sunday Anozie, in their African Writers and Their Work Series.

[1]'Chinua Achebe on Biafra', *Transition*, vol. 7, no. 36, July 1968, p. 36
[2]Marjory Whitelaw, 'Interview with Christopher Okigbo, 1965,' *The Journal of Commonwealth Literature*, July 1970, no. 9, p. 35
[3]Ibid., p. 36
[4]'Transition Conference Questionnaire', *Transition*, vol. 2, no. 5, July—Aug. 1962, p. 12
[5]'Death of Christopher Okigbo', *Transition*, vol. 7, no. 33, p. 18
[6]Ibid., p. 18
[7]Ibid., p. 18
[8]Christopher Okigbo, *Labyrinths with Path of Thunder* (New York and London, 1971), p. XI

Yambo Ouologuem (1940–   )   MALI

Yambo Ouologuem received lavish praise upon the publication of his first novel *Le devoir de violence* in 1968, and was awarded the coveted Prix Renaudot. Following negotiations at the 1968 Frankfurt Book Fair, Harcourt, Brace World in New York and Secker and Warburg in London are preparing English translations of this acclaimed novel, to be titled *Bound to Violence*. It will also appear in Heinemann's African Writers Series.

Ouologuem's novel was greeted as 'perhaps the first African novel worthy of the name' by *Le Monde*.[1] The prominent Nigerian literary critic Abiola Irele described it as 'a meandering succession of sordid happenings, excesses and extravagances, presented as an historical narrative of a fictitious but "typical" African empire . . .' He found the novel's salient idea is 'that the past has only bequeathed to the present generation of Africans a legacy of crime and violence.'[2]

This Malian writer was born of a ruling-class family in the pre-independent Sudan. As a consequence of his family's position, Ouologuem speaks several African languages in addition to his own Dogon; he is also fluent in French, English, and Spanish. He studied in Bamako and Paris, holds degrees in English and philosophy, and is currently preparing his doctoral thesis in sociology.

Ouologuem 'rejects the snobbery which claims that it is not possible to think "African" in French. I am not a victim of French cutlure', he maintains. When he writes in the French language, the language itself is 'simply a tool'.[3]

As a novelist Ouologuem is, in his own words, 'content to denounce — to affirm facts'. Speaking of the 'black man' he says,

> For me there is no 'Negro' problem, there are only problems of class and of human conflict. The French worker with his minimum wage, tied to certain activities, restricted, in some ways ostracised, is a Negro. For me a Jew is simply a badly whitened Negro. I deliberately chose as one of my central characters a Negro who was also of Arab and Jewish background.[4]

And to Ouologuem the future of African literature is bleak, confronted as it is with manifold problems. More precisely, the future 'of African literature of English, French, Portuguese expression', as he prefers to call it, saying 'One should go further and say for instance, Malian literature, Guinean literature.'[5]

> The real problem is that one is in the situation in Africa where one can't write without being tapped on the knuckles by the Government in power; one is creating the national folklore. In each case there are

writers — writers of African origin — but without any kind of personality that is capable of spreading, of conquering the whole continent . . . Besides this there is above all the fact that in Africa, people's mentalities are not yet de-Colonised. People are still very susceptible. It is difficult to instigate a dialogue between ethnic groups, between the tribes themselves.

The problem of African literature is fundamentally linked to that of African unity. It is certain that if these racial and political barriers existing among African people could be pulled down the literature would respond. It is because we haven't yet succeeded in this big step that we have shut ourselves in ghettos of a sort.[6]

His view of the continent is equally dismal; he finds that 'Africa seems to be not so much a mission to be accomplished but a phantasm, governed less by intelligence than by parish pump politicians.'[7]

Yambo Ouologuem has recently written a series of 'letters' expressing his own radical views, which has been published in the volume *Lettres à la France nègre*. He is currently writing a sequel to *Le devoir de violence*. Upon its completion he intends to visit the United States.

[1]*The Guardian*, 28 Nov. 1968, quoted in *Cultural Events in Africa*, no. 47, 1968, p. 6
[2]Abiola Irele, 'A new mood in the African novel', *West Africa*, Sept. 20, 1969, p. 1115
[3]*Cultural Events in Africa*, no. 47, p. 6
[4]Ibid., p. 6
[5]'Yambo Ouologuem (Mali) interviewed by Dr S. Okechukwu Mezu during the African Studies Association, Montreal, October 1969', *Cultural Events in Africa*, no. 61, 1969, p. II
[6]Ibid., pp. I–II
[7]Trans. by Griot, 'Roundabout', *West Africa*, Aug. 16, 1969, p. 961

Sembène Ousmane *(1923–   )*   SENEGAL

From a fisherman, mason, mechanic, and dock-worker to a novelist, short-story writer, and film director of international repute, Sembène Ousmane has travelled a long, varied, and still promising route. Born in the southern region of Senegal in Ziguinchor-Casamance, essentially self-educated, he initially became a fisherman, just like his father. '"I have earned my living since I was 15," Sembène says without bitterness.'[1]

When he moved to Dakar, he worked at manual jobs until the outbreak of World War II. In 1939 he was drafted into the French army and saw action in Italy and in Germany. Returning to Senegal for a brief time, Sembène Ousmane realized that in order to further his literary ambitions he would need to move to France. After working as a docker in Marseilles, he became the trade-union leader of the dockers, but he also began writing.

His first semi-autobiographical novel dating from this period is aptly titled *Le docker noir* (1956), which was followed one year later by *Oh pays, mon beau peuple!* In 1960 *Les bouts de bois de Dieu* appeared in which, once again, Ousmane utilized actual historical events as a basis for his novel: this time, the Niger-Dakar railway strike of 1947. In 1962, *Voltaïque*, a collection of his short stories, was published.

In *L'harmattan*, released in 1964, he wrote:

> Je ne fais pas la théorie du roman africain. Je me souviens pourtant que jadis dans cette Afrique qui passe pour classique, le griot était, non seulement l'élément dynamique de sa tribu, clan, village, mais aussi le témoin patent de chaque événement. C'est lui qui enregistrait, déposait devant tous sous l'arbre du palabre les faits et gestes de chacun. La conception de mon travail découle de cet enseignement: rester au plus près du réel et du peuple.[2]

A new avenue of expression was open to Ousmane when the Moscow Film School invited him to study there. Returning to Dakar, he continued his activities in the field of cinema and completed *Barom Sarret*, a short feature in which he 'looks at the contrasts of Dakar, but with an acutely socially conscious eye.'[3] Ousmane's adaptation of his short story, *La Noire de . . .* (which had appeared in a 1961 issue of *Présence Africaine*) onto film, brought him recognition and several film prizes.

Two short novels, *Véhi Ciosane ou blanche genèse*, and *Le Mandat*, were published in one volume by Présence Africaine in 1965. The latter was reissued in 1969 and a fellow African writer, Mbella Sonne Dipoko, claimed this short novel to be 'a minor masterpiece'.[4] Of Ousmane he wrote: 'He is the leader of the new dynamic realism which is developing in French African writing.'[5] It was this story, when made into a film, that established Sembène Ousmane as an internationally prominent film director. After winning a prize at the Venice Film Festival, in 1969 it was presented as part of the seventh New York Film Festival at Lincoln Center and hailed in the *New York Times* as 'the surprise hit of the festival'.[6] It also brought its director to New York, where he was interviewed by the *Times*.

In this interview Ousmane states, perhaps giving the key to his entire artistic orientation, 'The thing I was trying to do in it was to show Africans some of the deplorable conditions under which they live. When one creates, one doesn't think of the world; one thinks of his own country. It is, after all, the Africans who will ultimately bring about change in Africa — not the Americans or the French or the Russians or the Chinese.' He continued to say that 'he would like to be a Marxist but that is not easy to be done in a society like Africa, where liberty is limited and the economy is controlled by the United States, France, England, Spain, Portugal and Germany.'[7]

[1]Guy Flatley, 'Senegal is Senegal, not Harlem,' *The New York Times*, Nov. 2, 1969, p. 17
[2]Sembène Ousmane, *L'harmattan* (Présence Africaine, 1964), p. 10
[3]*West Africa*, Aug. 9, 1969
[4]*Africa Today*, Aug.–Sept. 1968
[5]Per Wästberg, ed., *The Writer in Modern Africa* (New York, 1969), p. 70
[6]Flatley, p. 17
[7]Ibid., p. 17

Ferdinand Oyono (1929–)   CAMEROON

The similarities between the lives and works of Ferdinand Oyono and Mongo Beti are inescapable. Like his Cameroonian compatriot, Ferdinand Oyono is a Béti, educated in his native land and abroad in France, a satirical novelist who during the late fifties directed his attack primarily toward colonial rule and oppression. And according to at least one critic they are 'both precursors in African literature'; both their works mark 'a watershed in contemporary African literature in French. There is a new element of assurance in their treatment of colonialism as a political force. Although oppressed, the African can turn his back and laugh heartily at his masters. Their biting satire and sarcasm is softened by this frank humour.'[1]

Ferdinand Oyono was born in the small village, N'goulemakong, near Ebolowa, and began his education at the local primary school. His father practised polygamy; his mother, however, was a devout Catholic, and refusing to share her husband, left him and went to work as a seamstress to support her children. The young Oyono worked at the local mission as did his younger sister, and was introduced to a conventional education in the French colonial tradition. It was here, too, that he first became acquainted with what it meant to be the 'boy' of the local missionaries. After attending the local provincial school, his father sent him to France where Oyono first attended the Lycée de Provins, and later studied in the Faculté de Droit, and then the École Nationale d'Administration in Paris. While a student in France — lonely and living under circumstances similar

to those of Camara Laye — Ferdinand Oyono was prompted to write his first two novels: *Une vie de boy* and *Le vieux Nègre et la médaille*, both in 1956. Neither work was especially welcomed by the reviewers. He was enjoying much more success as an actor in the title role in Louis Sapin's *Papa bon Dieu* at the Théâtre d'Alliance Française, where he gained the unanimous approval of the local critics.

Edris Makward points out in his introduction to the American edition, titled *Boy*, that *Une vie de boy* 'denounced openly the excesses of colonial society and above all it showed the awareness of the African and his capacity to see with lucidity the vanity and unfounded claim to "superiority" of the European in Africa.'[2] The French colonial authorities were hardly appreciative of the satire, written in the form of a diary, and therefore Oyono's work was either ignored by literary critics in France or denounced. Today, however, it is receiving its deserved attention. Published in Heinemann's African Writers Series and in Collier's African/American Library, it has been hailed as 'one of the masterpieces of modern African literature'.[3]

Jeanette Kamara has written of Oyono's second novel, *The Old Man and the Medal*, translated and published in London in 1967, that it has 'the quality so rare in modern African writing of bringing together both the comic and sad elements in the situation of pre-independence Africa.'[4]

After the publication of Oyono's first two novels in quick succession, four years went by before his third novel was released. Gerald Moore finds that *Chemin d'Europe* (as yet not translated into English) 'is more ambitious, for it depicts a situation which is in itself diffuse and hard to grasp, the situation of the young man educated beyond his fellows but still not sufficiently so to assure him of a career.'[5] Summarizing Oyono's works, Moore writes:

> Ferdinand Oyono's novels celebrate the disillusionment of the African with the white man's world. His heroes set out in a state of innocent enthusiasm; then comes the moment of truth, opening the door into a new world of bitterness or corrosive resignation. Despite the brilliance of his comic writing, this fatal *consequence* gives a kind of tragic intensity to his plots as a whole, particularly in *Une vie de boy*, his first novel. He is probably the greatest master of construction among African novelists now writing.[6]

Although a fourth novel, *Le pandemonium*, has long been announced, it has not as yet appeared.

Since 1960 Ferdinand Oyono has spent his career in the diplomatic service. He is a Doctor of Law, and after some years in Paris and the French embassy in Rome he was appointed Cameroon's Permanent Representative to the United Nations. Later he served as Ambassador in Brussels and he is currently Ambassador to Liberia.

[1] A. C. Brench, *The Novelists' Inheritance in French Africa* (London, 1967), p. 49, 48
[2] Edris Makward in Introduction to Ferdinand Oyono, *Boy* (New York, 1970). p. VI
[3] Ibid., p. XIV
[4] Jeanette Kamara, book review, in *African Literature Today* no. 3, p. 50
[5] Gerald Moore, 'Ferdinand Oyono and the colonial tragi-comedy', *Présence Africaine*, vol. 18 no. 46, 1963, p. 70
[6] Ibid., p. 61

Guillaume Oyono-Mbia *(1939–   )*   CAMEROON

A relatively new figure on the African literary scene is Guillaume Oyono-Mbia, a young 'prototype bi-lingual' Cameroonian playwright.

The sum of his published credits total thus far two comic plays: *Three Suitors: One Husband* and *Until Further Notice*, published collectively by Methuen of London. The former, originally written in French in 1960 under the title *Trois prétendants . . . un mari*, was first published in 1964 by Editions C.L.E. in Yaoundé, and released again in 1969 in a new and enlarged edition. Initially staged in Yaoundé, 'the story stems from something that happened to one of my cousins,' Oyono-Mbia says, 'who got married in almost exactly the same way as described in *Three suitors*. I just happened to attend the palava where they decided all this. And I was interested in the fact that nobody had consulted her at all. . . . So my first play started as a sort of taking down of everything which was being said during the palava.'[1] In the introduction to the English version, Oyono-Mbia wrote: 'Throughout the comedy, the audience will learn something about the major problems facing Africans today: is it possible to make room for the new while at the same time facing the old?'[2]

Fluent in French, English, and German in addition to his native Bulu Oyono-Mbia 'translated' the French *Trois prétendants* into English. In fact, he 'tried to rewrite it in English rather than translate . . . because we have different mentalities between French-speaking and English-speaking audiences.'[3] Now produced widely throughout the whole of Cameroon (particularly at most school graduation ceremonies), *Three Suitors: One Husband* was performed in England at the University of Keele in 1967 and in France at the Jeune Théâtre Africaine.

Guillaume Oyono-Mbia's comedy *Until Further Notice* was written for radio and in 1967 received first prize in a drama competition organized by the BBC African Service. Early in 1970 it was awarded the newly established El Hadj Ahmadou Ahidjo literary prize, and was issued in a French edition entitled *Jusqu'à nouvel avis* (translated again by the author himself) by Éditions C.L.E.

His latest English-language play, *His Excellency's Train*, is as yet unpublished; he has also written a full-length play in French for radio plus 'some short stories which I refuse to publish because I think they would be more useful as plays.'[4]

The theatre is to this essentially comic playwright 'the only means which can reach illiterate as well as literate people'; he would like to specialize in a kind of participatory theatre where people are 'allowed to take part'.[5]

Guillaume Oyono-Mbia was born in the Cameroon village of Mvoutessi near Sangmélima. He attended the Collège Evangélique de Libamba and in 1964 began studying English and French at the University of Keele, where he graduated in 1969. It was here that he began to write 'by mere accident'. As he says, 'I was preparing for the French *baccalauréat* and this, in fact, led me to write in dramatic dialogue.'[6]

At present, Oyono-Mbia is teaching at Cameroon's Federal University, and is Assistant Head of the Department of English.

[1]'Guillaume Oyono-Mbia, Cameroonian playwright, interviewed by Cosmo Pieterse' in *Cultural Events in Africa*, no. 55, 1969, p. I
[2]Guillaume Oyono-Mbia, *Three Suitors: One Husband. Until Further Notice* (London, 1968) p. 7
[3]*Cultural Events in Africa*, no. 55, p. II
[4]Ibid., p. III
[5]Ibid., p. III
[6]Ibid., p. I

Peter K. Palangyo (1939–   )   TANZANIA

Peter Palangyo is a biologist by training. Out of 150 people at Nkoaranga Primary School in Tanzania he was one of four who went on to Old Moshi Government Secondary School. In 1959 he obtained a government scholarship and began studies in biology and chemistry at St. Olaf College in Minnesota where in 1962 he obtained a B.A. degree. While working toward a graduate degree in human genetics at the University of Minnesota, Palangyo developed a strong interest in literature and decided to return home. He enrolled in Makerere University College and obtained a post-graduate diploma in Education. Since then he has taught in several Tanzanian schools, and was Principal of Lyamungu Secondary School and H.H. Aga Khan Boys' Secondary School, Dar es Salaam. He then went to

the writer's workshop at the University of Iowa. He is now teaching at the
State University of New York, Buffalo.

Dying in the Sun was the first novel by a Tanzanian to be published in
the African Writers Series. As *The Spectator* wrote, 'his tale is about Ntanya,
his hatred for his peasant father, his return home and his progression from
poverty to subsistence and marriage. It also deals with other problems.
His girl-friend and eventual wife neatly describes the rapid piecemeal
changes that come with self-government ... the story is good and
strong...'[1] He is at work on a second novel.

[1] *The Spectator*, 31 January 1969

Okot p'Bitek *(1931–   )*   UGANDA

Ugandan-born Okot p'Bitek attended his native Gulu High School in the
northern part of his country and proceeded to King's College, Budo. He
was a young man of diversified talents: at Budo he composed and produced
an opera, he later toured Britain with Uganda's football team, and his
first literary work, *Lak Tar Miyo Wi Lobo*, a novel written in Lwo, was
published in 1953.

Okot p'Bitek went on to receive a Certificate in Education from Bristol
University, and then an LL.B. from the University College of Wales,
Aberystwyth. His next step was to work for a B.Litt at the Institute of
Social Anthropology in Oxford, where in 1963 he presented his thesis on
Acoli and Lango traditional songs.

Returning to his native Uganda, he joined the staff of the Department
of Sociology at Makerere University College in 1964, and two years later
became a tutor with the Extra-Mural Department.

'It may seem ironical that the first important poem in English to emerge
in Eastern Africa should be a translation from the vernacular original,'[1]
wrote Gerald Moore. He was referring to p'Bitek's *Song of Lawino*, originally written in Luo. Although turned down by several British publishers, it
is now the best-selling title of the East African Publishing House, which
issued this highly praised volume in 1966. The World Publishing Company
of Cleveland issued a separate American edition in 1969.

Founder of the Gulu Festival and Director of Uganda's National Theatre
and National Cultural Centre, p'Bitek subsequently accepted a position
with Nairobi's University College as director of the Western Kenya
section of the Extra-Mural Department. Here in Kenya, at the close of
1968, he initiated and organized the successful Kisumu Arts Festival.
For Okot p'Bitek, the local artists and writers in attendance represented
a small percentage of available talent; hundreds of creative artists remained
obscure in rural areas; to p'Bitek 'these were the real artists'.[2]

A frequent contributor to *Transition* and other journals, Okot p'Bitek's
poems and articles display the same diversity of interests as does his
varied career. They range from poems such as 'Return the Bridewealth'

and 'Harvest', to essays such as his early 'Acholi Folk Tales and Fr. Tempels' *Bantu Philosophy*', to literary criticism, as for example, 'The Self in African Imagery'. Okot p'Bitek published *Song of Ocol*, his second verse collection in 1970; this will be followed by *The Prisoner* and *Song of Malaya* in 1971. Late in 1970 the East African Literature Bureau also released his study *African Religion in Western Scholarship*.

Okot p'Bitek is now a writer in residence at the University of Iowa in the United States.

[1] *Transition*, no. 31, June–July 1967, p. 52
[2] *Cultural Events in Africa*, no. 50, 1969

Lenrie Peters (1932–   )   THE GAMBIA

Poet, novelist, and doctor, Lenrie Peters was born in Bathurst, The Gambia. After receiving his basic education there, in 1949 he moved to Sierra Leone, his parents' native home, where he obtained a Higher School Certificate from Freetown's Prince of Wales School. In 1952 Peters began medical studies at Trinity College, Cambridge; a Pan-Africanist, he became President of the African Student Union. After obtaining his medical degree in 1959, Dr Peters went on to specialize in surgery at a hospital in Guildford, England.

Dr Peters is essentially an urbanized poet writing in English within the European tradition though bringing in African themes and images. Primarily known for his verse first published in *Poems* in 1964 by Mbari, his poetry has since appeared in both African and British journals. In 1967 Heinemann's published *Satellites*, a volume containing 21 poems from the Mbari collection and an additional 34 previously unpublished ones. Lenrie Peters has also written a novel, *The Second Round*, set in Freetown.

A versatile man, Dr Peters' talents also extend to singing and broadcasting. He has participated in BBC programmes, in 'Calling West Africa', and was Chairman of its 'Africa Forum'. He has now returned to The Gambia.

Jean-Joseph Rabéarivelo (1901–1937)   MALAGASY REPUBLIC

Jean-Joseph Rabéarivelo lived and worked in an era when his native country 'Madagascar did not regard itself as part of the African world, a world of which it was only dimly aware.'[1] It was a time in which *négritude* (the philosophy that pervades a number of the works of francophone African writers presented in this volume) was as yet unborn.

Rabéarivelo was born in Antananarivo, Madagascar. He was reared in a poor family by his father, a tailor, and his mother, a woman of noble caste. His formal education ceased when he was only 13 years old, and thereafter he taught himself. He mastered both Spanish and French and used the latter for most of his literary work. Rabéarivelo married young, fathered three children, and meagrely supported himself and his family by working as a proof-reader at Imerina Printing Press.

A passionate devotee of French culture and literature, his primary goal was to get to France. When all his efforts failed, Rabéarivelo (known to be of a romantic and melancholy temperament in addition to being addicted to drugs) committed suicide at the age of 36.

During his short life he wrote seven volumes of poetry, six published in his lifetime, and *Vieilles chansons des pays d'Imerina* published posthumously in 1939. Of his entire opus it is generally agreed that *Presque-songes* and *Traduit de la nuit* — written in French and Hova — are his greatest works, 'the most important', 'the poems of his maturity'. Ulli Beier writes that in these collections alone, particularly the later one, 'he liberated himself completely from French models',[2] and therein lies his contribution to African poetry.

Tracing Jean-Joseph Rabéarivelo's literary development to this pinnacle of achievement Clive Wake writes,

> Rabéarivelo's early poetry is influenced by Baudelaire on the one hand and his own contemporaries in French poetry on the other, poets like Pierre Camo, P.-J. Toulet, Derême, Fontainas, Ormoy, Chabaneix, Vérane, Fagus and others, known nowadays only to the historian of

French poetry. Many of them belonged to a group known as the *Fantaisistes*. Their poetry was full of vague melancholy and a sense of futility much like the poetry of the early French Romantics, although in form they are disciples of Baudelaire and his successors. Rabéarivelo calls them *les poètes les plus délicieux et les plus parfaits de leur génération*. He was fortunate in having as his friend and counsellor in literary matters the poet Pierre Camo who was a civil servant in Madagascar at the time. He encouraged Rabéarivelo to publish and included some of his earliest poems in his review *18° Latitude Sud*. But Camo's most important role was gradually to wean Rabéarivelo from a style which revealed too obviously the influence of his favourite French poets. From Baudelaire and the *Fantaisistes* he acquired however a strong sense of form which is very striking in *Presque-Songes* and *Traduit de la Nuit*. These are the poems of his maturity . . .[3]

Ulli Beier and Gerald Moore have found Jean-Joseph Rabéarivelo to be 'a poet of genius'.[4] Ulli Beier has called him 'one of the greatest French-speaking African poets', 'a poet of cosmic visions'.

The themes of his poems are death, dissolution, catastrophe and sometimes resurrection. . . . The dominant vision of Rabéarivelo is a vision of death. . . . The death he sees is not a specific individual death; it is a cosmic, universal death. . . . Rabéarivelo's poems are clear and precise visions of a strange and personal world. Like Baudelaire, his favourite French poet, Rabéarivelo had a disgust of reality. In his poetry he has destroyed and dismembered reality. And out of the fragments he has built a new mythical world; it is a world of death and frustration, but also transcended by a sad beauty of its own.[5]

During his lifetime his poetry and critical articles on it were published in *La Vie, Le Divan, Les Nouvelles Littéraires*, and *La Dépêche de Toulouse*. Along with Gabriel Razafintsambia he founded and edited (1930–1931) a literary review, *Capricorne*. Unfortunately, his diary remains as yet unpublished.

English translations of Jean-Joseph Rabéarivelo's poems have been made by John Reed and Clive Wake (and included in *A Book of African Verse*) and above all by Ulli Beier and Gerald Moore, whose translations have appeared in *Black Orpheus, Transition, Modern Poetry from Africa*, and in *Jean-Joseph Rabéarivelo: 24 poems* published by Mbari in 1962.

---

[1] Gerald Moore and Ulli Beier, eds., *Modern Poetry from Africa* (Harmondsworth, 1963), p. 17
[2] Ulli Beier, 'Rabéarivelo', *Black Orpheus*, no. 11, p. 10
[3] Clive Wake, ed., *An Anthology of African and Malagasy Poetry in French* (London, 1965), pp. 12–13
[4] Moore and Beier, p. 16
[5] Beier, 'Rabéarivelo,' pp. 10–12

Richard Rive (1931–   )

Unlike most black South African writers, Richard Rive continues to live and write in his native country.

The son of a American seaman and a 'coloured' South African, he was born and raised in District Six in the heart of Cape Town. After attending local schools he received a municipal scholarship, which enabled him to go on to high school where he began writing short stories. In 1949 he graduated with a B.A. degree in English from the University of Cape Town and commenced teaching at Hewat Training College.

Essentially a short-story writer, Rive's early works first appeared in South African journals. They received favourable critical recognition, and have since been translated into over a dozen languages, appearing in *Transition, Contrast, Classic, Présence Africaine*, and several other magazines and anthologies. Bernth Lindfors considers him and Alex La Guma to be 'the most accomplished non-white short story writers in South Africa today'. He finds Rive's style to be 'characterized by strong rhythms, daring images, brisk dialogue and leitmotifs (recurring words, phrases, images) which function as unifying devices within stories.' Lindfors finds his subject-matter 'tsotsis, life in the slums, the consequences of overt protest and the ironies of racial prejudice and color snobbery.'[1]

A volume of Rive's short stories, *African Songs*, was published in East Germany in 1963. In the same year he edited *Quartet*, a collection of stories by four South Africans, one white and two black writers in addition to himself. Again in 1964 he served as editor of *Modern African Prose*, an anthology intended for school use. Rive had come to the conclusion after years of teaching high school English literature in Cape Town that 'important as Shakespeare, Dickens and Sir Walter Scott are, students needed something much more recognizable and immediate in addition (not instead of), in order to synthesize their literary experiences. I would consider it foolhardy to assert that all writers not produced out of the African experience are unacceptable, in favour of local material.'[2]

In 1964 Rive's first full-length novel, *Emergency*, was published in England. Taking its title from the state of emergency declared by the South African government after the Sharpeville massacre, it recounts three days in the life of a 'coloured' school teacher in Cape Town – the days between the massacre and the emergency. Edgar Wright has written that 'Both *Quartet* and *Emergency* voice the protest of the educated, urban, politically conscious South African against the injustice and misery of conditions. The events shape and dominate the literature being produced.'[3] *Emergency* was reissued in 1970 in paperback by Macmillan in New York.

Under the sponsorship of a Farfield Foundation Fellowship, in 1962 Rive toured parts of Africa and Europe studying literary trends in contemporary African-English literature. Altogether he has travelled in some twenty-four African and European countries and has taught in schools in both continents.

Richard Moore Rive is currently teaching English and Latin in a large 'coloured' Cape Town high school, where he also coaches athletics. He is reported to be writing another book, to be published in the near future.

[1]Bernth Lindfors, 'Form and technique in the novels of Richard Rive and Alex La Guma', *Journal of the New African Literature and the Arts*, no. 2, Fall 1966, p. 11
[2]Richard Rive, ed., *Modern African Prose* (London, 1964), p. XI
[3]Edgar Wright, 'New fiction', *Transition*, no. 25, p. 53

David Rubadiri (1930–   )   MALAWI

In 1964 the newly independent republic of Malawi appointed David Rubadiri its first Ambassador to the United States and to the United Nations. This distinction was awarded to a native Nyasaland poet and educator, an activist in Nyasaland's nationalist cause who during the 1959 emergency was arrested and detained by the government. Rubadiri had been schooled in English literature at Makerere University College and King's College at Cambridge University. His career had involved him in active broadcasting in England, teaching in Nyasaland, and directing Soche Hill College in Blanytre.

His literary accomplishments were primarily poetic; his verse was widely anthologized and appeared in the pages of *Transition*. His stature was such that by 1964 he was among those interviewed by the National Educational Television in its African Writers of Today series. '. . . my major interests at this moment are trying to play the little part I can in contributing towards the reconstruction of my country,' he said. With regard to his writing, he felt he was beginning

> to write more like . . . myself as an African who's got roots or beginning to get them, as opposed to the young student who had to live between two worlds, as it were, two values of life. . . . The echoes of the African tradition come to me subconsciously. I hear them, and perhaps this is the only African part or influence that I can confess of; otherwise I think the technical part of it is entirely conditioned by my experience with reading European literature.[1]

Rubadiri returned to Africa in 1965 to take up a teaching post with the Extra-Mural Department at Makerere University College. He continues to write verse, and his drama *Come to Tea* appeared in the July 1965 issue of *New African*. When his first novel, *No Bride Price*, was published in 1967 by the East African Publishing House, 'it was assumed that his earliest work of fiction would unequivocally enhance Eastern African prestige,' wrote David Cook in the *Journal of Commonwealth Literature*.

> David Rubadiri's exceptional power over English words enables him to share his intuitions about people and experiences with his readers succinctly, vividly and memorably. These qualities elevate *No Bride Price* above the growing body of African fiction that aspires to be no more than competent hack-work.[2]

David Rubadiri is at present working for a doctorate at Makerere University College. Together with David Cook he has collected an anthology, *Poems from East Africa*, to be published in the African Writers Series.

[1]David Rubadiri, 'African Writers of Today', program no. 6, broadcast by National Educational Television, 1964
[2]David Cook, 'East and Central Africa', *Journal of Commonwealth Literature*, no. 6, Jan. 1969, p. 9

Sahle Sellassie (1936–)   ETHIOPIA

Sahle Sellassie Berhane Marian was born in the village of Wardena in Ethiopia. He was educated at the Catholic Mission School in Endeber, the seat of the Chaha people's central government, and he attended secondary school in Ethiopia's capital, Addis Ababa. On a fellowship from the French government, Sellassie studied law at Aix-en-Provence for one year. He then came to the United States where he obtained his M.A. in political science in 1963 from the University of California at Los Angeles.

As a graduate student at U.C.L.A., Sahle Sellassie, using Arabic script, wrote the first work ever written in Chaha (an unwritten dialect of Gurage, a Semitic language spoken in Ethiopia), translated by Wolf Leslau, chair-

man of U.C.L.A.'s department of Near Eastern and African languages, as *Shinega's Village: Scenes of Ethiopian Life*. Dr Leslau has praised it as a novel which 'started out to be a work of linguistic scholarship, [and] has ended up as charming literature.'[1] The first Ethiopian novelist to be published in the U.S., Sellassie continued to write under fellowships granted him by the Near Eastern Center and the African Studies Center at U.C.L.A.

Mr Sellassie is also the author of *Wotat Yifredew*, a novel written in Amharic, the national language of Ethiopia. He has published articles and short stories in both English and Amharic in Ethiopian publications and in *Zuka*. Mr Sellassie's most recent novel, *The Afersata*, written in English, appeared in 1969.

[1]'Notes in Transition', *Transition*, vol. 3, no. 13, Mar.–Apr. 1964, p. 46

Francis Selormey (1927–)   GHANA

Francis Kofi Selormey was born in Dzelukofe, near Keta on the Ghanaian coast. His father was the headmaster of the local Christian missionary school and young Selormey received his primary education in Roman Catholic schools. Like his father, he decided to become a teacher and

attended St Augustine's College in Cape Coast. After having studied physical education in both Ghana and Germany, for seven years he was employed by St Francis' Teacher Training College in Hohoe, where he was in charge of physical education. It was at Hohoe, too, that he began writing. From there he moved to Cape Coast to become Senior Regional Sports Organizer with the task of selecting and training young athletes for the Ghana Central Organization of Sport.

In June 1965 'The Witch', a story based on one of his own childhood adventures, was published in *Okyeame*. *The Narrow Path*, subtitled *An African Childhood*, Selormey's autobiographical novel, was published in 1966 in New York and London. The English critic Gerald Moore has written of it, 'The intensity of young Selormey's relationship with his father, his vain search for love where he found only harshness and fear, make his autobiography almost an African equivalent of *Father and Son*.'[1]

Mr Selormey now lives in Accra with his wife and six children, where he is employed by the Ghana Film Corporation as a features and script writer.

[1]Gerald Moore, 'Ghanaian childhoods', *The Journal of Commonwealth Literature*, no. 6, Jan. 1969, p. 51

Léopold Sédar Senghor

(1906–   )   SENEGAL

A 'cultural half-caste' who has embraced poetics, philosophy, and politics, Léopold Sédar Senghor, President of Senegal, has been accorded the tribute of being 'the greatest of the African poets to write in a European language'.[1] Along with Aimé Césaire and Leon Damas, whom he met in Paris in 1928, Senghor's reputation as an apostle of negritude is renowned. He defines it in the following manner:

> *Négritude is the awareness, defense and development of African cultural values. Négritude* is a myth, I agree. And I agree there are false myths, myths which breed division and hatred. *Négritude* as a true myth is the very opposite of these. It is the awareness by a particular social group of

people of its own situation in the world, and the expression of it by means of the concrete image.... However the struggle for *négritude* must not be a negation but *affirmation*. It must be the contribution from us, the peoples of sub-Sahara Africa, to the growth of *Africanity*, and beyond that, to the building of the *Civilization of the Universal*. *Négritude* is part of Africanity, and as such is part of human civilization.... More deeply, in works of art, which are a people's most authentic expression of itself, it is sense of image and rhythm, sense of symbol and beauty. (February 1961)[2]

Quite simply, *négritude* is the *sum total of the values of the civilization of the African world*. It is not racialism, it is culture. (1962)[3]

It is this *spirit* of Negro-African civilization based on the earth and Negro hearts, which is offered to the world — both beings and things — to unify it, to *understand* and to show it. (March 1963)[4]

Senghor was born to Christian parents belonging to the Serer tribe in the small village of Joal, on the Senegalese coast, about 75 miles south of Dakar. His formal education commenced when his father sent him to the nearby Catholic mission at Ngazobil 'to punish me and "straighten me out".'[5] From there he moved to a Seminary and then to the Lycée at Dakar. In 1928 he received a government scholarship and left for France, studying first at the Lycée Louis-le-Grand and then at the Sorbonne, where in 1934 he received his *Licence-ès-lettres*.

Through the personal intervention of the Senegalese deputy Blaise Diagne, Léopold Senghor became a French citizen and the first African to obtain his *agrégation*, a prerequisite for lycée and university teaching in France. In the following years he held French teaching posts at the Lycée Descartes in Tours, and Lycée Marcelin Berthelot at St-Maur des Fosses, near Paris. It was largely during this time that Senghor wrote the poetry that was to appear in his first volume of verse, *Chants d'ombre*, released in 1945.

Clive Wake points out that 'when Seuil published Senghor's first volume of poems ... African poetry as distinct from West Indian poetry made its first appearance in the literary world'.[6] John Reed and Clive Wake find its 'main themes ... are exile, the loneliness and homesickness of an African student in Paris in the 1930's. He recalls his childhood.... This nostalgia for the paradise of childhood with its "innocence of Europe" brings an awareness of a conflict between his African heritage and European culture'.[7] Senghor himself later noted 'that almost all the beings and things which my poems call up for me belong to my canton, a few Serer villages.... I have only to name them to relive the Kingdom of Childhood ...'[8]

When World War II broke out, Senghor joined the French army. He was captured by the Germans and for two years (1940–1942) he remained a prisoner of war. During this time he wrote much of the verse that appeared in *Hosties noires*, published in 1948. Here 'the poet discovers that he is not alone in his exile, but that he is involved in it with those of his compatriots ... fighting a white man's war in Europe, but because of their black skin, treated as inferiors. He discovers his solidarity with the black race but he also realizes that with his education and his poetic gifts he not only can but he has a duty to speak for them'.[9]

The year 1948 also saw the publication of what has been called 'probably the most influential single work of the whole [negritude] movement'[10]: Senghor's *Anthologie de la nouvelle poesie nègre et malgache de langue française*, with a preface by Jean-Paul Sartre (which was later made available separately as *Orphée noir*). 'The poets of the *Anthologie*', according to its editor, 'like those of the oral tradition are above all *auditives*, singers'.[11] Until then, they were for the most part unknown names; today they are part of the canon of French African literature.

Chants pour Naett, published in 1949, celebrates Senghor's 're-discovery' of Africa, symbolized as the woman he loves'.[12] Six years passed before his next volume, *Éthiopiques*, appeared, which includes the now famous poetic transformation of Thomas Mofolo's historical novel *Chaka*. Also in 1956, *Chants d'ombre — Hosties noires* was released in one volume, and in 1961 *Nocturnes*, a sequence of love poems, (which includes the earlier *Chants pour Naett*) was issued.

Poetry to Senghor

> is song even when not actual music. . . . The poem is like a jazz score, where the execution is as important as the text. As I have published each of my collections, this idea has become stronger. And when at the head of a poem I indicate the instruments to be used, this is not mere form of word. . . . I still consider that the poem is only complete when it becomes song, speech and music at the same time.[13]

He finds the distinguishing element in poetry as opposed to prose is 'the monotony of tone . . . it is the seal of négritude, the incantation which gives access to the truth of essential things: to the Forces of the Cosmos'.[14]

After World War II Senghor returned to his teaching post at the Lycée Marcelin Berthelot and in 1944 joined the staff at the École Nationale de la France d'Outre Mer. With his appointment as Senegal's deputy to France's Constituent Assembly in 1945 his political career took root. By 1955 he had become Secretary of State; by 1959 he was head of the Union Progressiste Sénégalaise, a position through which he was able to activate his vision of a United States of Africa. The meagre result, however, was the brief union of Senegal and the Sudan in the Federation of Mali, an alliance which was severed in 1960. Since then Senghor has been President of Senegal and a dominant figure in West Africa. The most recent honour bestowed upon the President has been his membership of the French Academy of Moral and Political Sciences in December 1969, where he took the seat of the late German Chancellor Dr Konrad Adenauer. The previous year he received the 1968 Peace Prize, the distinguished award made annually by the German book trade on the occasion of the international Frankfurt Book Fair.

Senghor's extensive writings reflect his career not only as a poet, but as a major spokesman of the negritude movement, and as a political thinker. One of the most notable of his non-literary works is *Nation et voie africaine du socialisme* published by Présence Africaine in French (1961) and in an English translation by Mercer Cook entitled *Nationhood and the African Road to Socialism* (1962). Abridged American and British editions of this volume appeared later as *On African Socialism*. Other works by Senghor include *Rapport sur la doctrine et le doctrine et le programme du Parti de la Federation Africaine* (1959, also available in English); *Libérte I. Négritude et humanisme* (1964); and, most recently, *Les fondements de l'Africanité ou Négritude et Arabité* (1967) a paper which he submitted to a conference on African unity held in Cairo in 1967. Léopold Senghor's work has been translated into many languages, he has provided prefaces to numerous books, and he has been the subject of several critical studies, some of which are listed in the bibliographic section of this volume.

The British scholars, John Reed and Clive Wake, have been especially active in translating Senghor's prose and poetry into English. They are the joint editors of *Léopold Sédar Senghor: selected poems* (1964), and *Léopold Sédar Senghor: prose and poetry* (1965), and have contributed detailed and lucid introductions to both volumes and an extensive bibliography to the latter. John Reed and Clive Wake were also responsible for the English translation of Senghor's *Nocturnes*, published in the Heinemann African Writers Series in 1970.

[1] John Reed and Clive Wake, eds., *Senghor: prose and poetry* (London, 1965) p. 1
[2] Ibid. p. 97 (from *Discours devant le parlement de Ghana*; unpublished)
[3] Ibid. p. 99 (from *Pierre Teilhard de Chardin et la Politique Africaine*, 1962)
[4] Léopold Senghor, 'Négritude and the concept of universal civilization', *Présence Africaine*, vol. 18, no. 46, p. 11
[5] John Reed and Clive Wake, eds., *Senghor: prose and poetry*, p. 4
[6] Clive Wake, *An Anthology of African and Malagasy Poetry* (London, 1965) p. 1
[7] John Reed and Clive Wake, eds., *Senghor: selected poems* (London, 1964) p. xi
[8] John Reed and Clive Wake, eds., *Senghor: prose and poetry*, p. 92 (from 'Comme les lamantins vont boire à la source', in *Éthiopiques*, 1956)
[9] Clive Wake, *An Anthology of African and Malagasy Poetry* (London, 1965), pp. 15–16.
[10] Gerald Moore, *Seven African Writers* (London, 1962), p. xv
[11] John Reed and Clive Wake, eds., *Senghor: prose and poetry*, p. 93 (from 'Comme les lamantins vont boire à la source', in *Éthiopiques*, 1956)
[12] Clive Wake, *An Anthology of African and Malagasy Poetry* (London, 1965) p. 16
[13] John Reed and Clive Wake, eds., *Senghor: prose and poetry*, pp. 95–96 (from 'Comme les lamantins vont boire à la source', in *Éthiopiques*, 1956)
[14] Ibid. p. 94

Robert Serumaga (1939–)   UGANDA

Robert Serumaga's primary interest is in the theatre. He was the inspiration behind Theatre Limited, a professional acting company based in Uganda, while his business background (an M.A. in economics from Trinity College, Dublin) helped to keep the venture financially sound.

Speaking of the theatre in East Africa, Robert Serumaga finds it necessary to point out that it does not operate

with the same level of formalisation as in Europe. On the other hand, the practice of people getting together to watch the story-teller act out his story, or to hear a musician like the famous Sekinnoomu of Uganda

relate a tale of trenchant social criticism, dramatized in voice, movement and the music of his Ndingidi, has been with us for centuries. And this is the true theatre of East Africa.[1]

Serumaga hopes that Theatre Limited will provide the incentive necessary to give birth to a professional theatre. Though it has been in existence now for two years, he is not unaware of the problems still to be faced. He realizes that 'first and above all, whatever theatrical movement there is must be integrated with and inspired by the society in which it is growing'. Secondly, mass involvement 'will only come about when plays, with their roots firmly embedded in the Africa of today, can be written and produced'.[2]

In the latter part of 1969 at least one such play was produced by Theatre Limited, namely Mr Serumaga's *Elephants*, a play he originally titled *The Fish Net*, and which he says is

> about a man who creates a certain kind of world around himself with the help of friends. He is not aware of having created this world until the holes in its artificiality are blocked up by someone else. I am interested in this idea of a man living in an artificial environment which he has created unknowingly perhaps. We might see all sorts of weaknesses in this life form, but do we stop to contemplate the possibility that if we destroy it, we might destroy the man?[3]

Elephants, with Robert Serumaga in the lead role, was warmly received in Uganda. In April of 1970 Theatre Limited brought the production to Nairobi, where it was welcomed as 'the greatest happening on the East African stage this decade'.[4]

Serumaga has not only acted in his own plays but he has given numerous performances in London and Uganda in plays as diverse as Edward Albee's *Who's Afraid of Virginia Woolf?* and Wole Soyinka's *The Trials of Brother Jero*.

A man of many talents, Robert Serumaga was previously with London's Transcription Centre, where he was producer of a radio programme, *Africa Abroad*. He is also the author of *A Play*, first presented at the National Theatre in Kampala in 1968, and published in the same year by Uganda Publishing House. His poetry has appeared in *Transition*, and in

1969 his first novel *Return to the Shadows* was published by Heinemann in England and the following year by Atheneum in New York.

In mid-1970 Robert Serumaga visited the United States to negotiate the staging of *A Play* in New York, while trying to raise funds for Theatre Limited.

[1]Robert Serumaga, 'Uganda's experimental theatre', *African Arts/Arts d'Afrique* vol. III, no. 3, Spring 1970, p. 52

[2]Ibid., p. 53

[3] Robert Serumaga, *Uganda Argus*, September 19, 1960, quoted in *Cultural Events in Africa*, no. 61, 1969, p. 3

[4]*Daily Nation* (Nairobi, no date) quoted in *Cultural Events in Africa*, no. 63, 1979, p. 2

Wole Soyinka (1934–)   NIGERIA

'Like his Rennaissance progenitors, Soyinka is something of a Universal man: poet, playwright, novelist, critic, lecturer, teacher, actor, translator, politician and publisher. He is all of these',[1] according to the British publisher Rex Collings. And his stature in most of them ranks high.

D. A. N. Jones in the *New York Review of Books* recently wrote, 'I doubt if there is a better dramatic poet in English'.[2] Rex Collings feels that 'above all else Soyinka is a poet'[3] and John Povey finds him 'the most skilful of all African writers ... [his] ... sensitive personal explorations have great poetic merit'.[4] Though *Idandre and other poems* (1967) is his only published collection of verse to date, Soyinka's poems, since their first appearance in an early issue of *Black Orpheus*, have been extensively anthologized, in particular his humorous and satirical 'Telephone Conversation'. In 1969, while imprisoned in Federal Nigeria, Soyinka managed to send two poems to Rex Collings accompanied by a letter in which he wrote, 'I've written a few of these, about the only creative writing that successfully defies philistinic strictures. And nihilistic moods'.[5] A leaflet entitled *Poems*

from Prison was subsequently published by Rex Collings containing them: they were 'Live Burial' and 'Flowers for My Land'.

As a playwright, Wole Soyinka's output has been both prolific and widely praised. With fourteen plays to his credit, half of them published, Soyinka got his first break in the theatre while studying at the Royal Court Theatre in the early fifties. In 1955 this London theatre produced his *The Invention*. Five years later, upon his return to Nigeria, Soyinka formed a national theatre, *The 1960 Masks* (and later the *Orisun Theatre*), for which he wrote a verse play, *A Dance of the Forests*, the winner of a London *Observer* competition. When produced at the Nigerian Independence Celebrations in October 1960, this play created something of a furore. And 'no wonder', comments Robert MacDowell, 'for Soyinka here, as elsewhere is anti-conservative, anti-Négritude, anti-social deadening habits'.[6]

In 1963 Mbari published the first collection of Soyinka's plays in a volume entitled *Three Plays*, containing *The Swamp Dwellers*, *The Trials of Brother Jero*, and *The Strong Breed*. The following year Oxford produced a more substantial collection, *Five Plays*, in which the previous three were included in addition to *A Dance of the Forests* and *The Lion and the Jewel*. Soyinka's plays were not only being published, they were being widely performed as well. In the two theatre capitals of the world, London and New York, Soyinka's plays have been successfully introduced to an international audience. *The Road*, published in 1965, was performed in London the same year in association with the Commonwealth Arts Festival and subsequently won the prize for published drama at the First Festival of Negro Arts at Dakar. The Royal Court Theatre in 1966 followed with a presentation of *The Lion and the Jewel*. In 1967 and 1968 three of Soyinka's plays opened in New York: *The Trials of Brother Jero* and *The Strong Breed* at the off-Broadway Greenwich Mews Theatre, and the following year *Kongi's Harvest* was performed by the Negro Ensemble Company. *Kongi's Harvest* was already the recipient of a prize at the 1966 Dakar Festival of Negro Arts, where it was performed jointly by *The 1960 Masks* and the *Orisun Theatre*. It is currently being made into a motion picture by Omega Films under the direction of Ossie Davis, with Wole Soyinka as Kongi.

Though it is not easy to summarize the voluminous works of Soyinka, it is generally agreed that his technique is that of a satirist. As Robert MacDowell says, he seems 'to be exploring a vast pattern of possibilities, knowing that there are no facile answers. . . . Soyinka is caught up in the infinite possibilities of the mind, and thus his writing touches the lives of all men'. MacDowell notes that Soyinka makes

> use of fascinating devices in his own expressionistic plays: dancing, singing, miming, speeches in verse, flashbacks (sometimes covering eons of time), and characters from the spirit world. He employs techniques familiar at Nigerian festivals, and utilizes any poetic methods which enforce the emotional and intellectual impact of his dramas; in short he has no slavish attachment to the merely naturalistic level of presentation.[7]

In 1966 Wole Soyinka shared with Tom Stoppard the John Whiting drama prize, and while imprisoned in 1969 he was awarded the Jock Campbell *New Statesman* literary prize.

With the publication of his first novel in 1965, Soyinka had embraced every traditional literary genre. *The Interpreters* received for the most part superlative reviews. D. A. N. Jones in the *New York Review of Books* compared it to James Joyce's *Ulysses*:

> Soyinka's novel *The Interpreters*, contains some guidance about the Yoruba gods, but will be best remembered for its Joycean scatology and dashing language: the first sentence — 'Metal on concrete jars my drinklobes' — stands in my head alongside 'stately plump Buck Mulligan'.[8]

John Povey found that Joyce's *Portrait of an Artist* 'is most often brought to mind as one reads Soyinka's novel'.[9]

As a literary critic Wole Soyinka has been an outspoken and controversial figure. He is most often quoted as making the now familiar denunciation of negritude, in which he supposedly said in caustic rebuttal of this philosophy, 'I don't think a tiger has to go around proclaiming his tigritude'. However, in a recording taped by Janheinz Jahn at a conference in Berlin in 1964, Soyinka corrected his many reviewers by saying:

> As Aimé Césaire said, it is quite common for things to be quoted out of context and for portraits to be issued by foreign critics and even by African interviewers which end up by a little bit of distorting the real image. The point is this that, to quote what I said fully, I said 'A tiger does not proclaim his tigritude, he pounces'. In other words: a tiger does not stand in the forest and say: 'I am a tiger'. When you pass where the tiger has walked before, you see the skeleton of the duiker, you know that some tigritude has been emanated there. In other words: the distinction which I was making at this conference [in Kampala, Uganda 1962] was purely a literary one: I was trying to distinguish between propaganda and true poetic creativity. I was saying in other words that what one expected from poetry was an intrinsic poetic quality, not a mere name-dropping.[10]

Soyinka is not only critical of 'negritude', he sees in general that 'publishers hovered like benevolent vultures over the still-born foetus of the African Muse [who] at a given signal . . . tore off bits and pieces and fanned up with powerful wings delusions of significance in commonness and banality'. He finds 'the average published writer in the first few years of the post-colonial era was the most celebrated skin of inconsequence to obscure the true flesh of the African dilemma'. The African writer was never looking inward, 'never truly into the present, never into the obvious symptoms of the niggling, warning, predictable present from which done lay the salvation of ideals'.[11] Soyinka's view of the African artist in the recent past and his hope for the future is a troubled one:

> There can be no further distractions with universal concerns whose balm is spread on abstract wounds, not on the gaping jaws of black inhumanity. A concern with culture strengthens society, but not a

concern with mythology. The artist has always functioned in African society as the record of the mores and experience of his society *and* as the voice of vision in his own time. It is time for him to respond to this essence of himself.[12]

And for Soyinka 'the situation in Africa today is the same as in the rest of the world; it is not one of the tragedies which come of isolated human failures but the very collapse of humanity'.[13] This was Soyinka speaking in 1967 from personal experience. In 1965 he had been detained on a charge that he had substituted his own tape for one supposed to be broadcast by the Prime Minister. Later in 1967, in the midst of Nigeria's civil war, Soyinka, although a Yoruba, was arrested by the Federal Government for alleged pro-Biafran activity and detained in Kaduna Prison. Despite international pleas for his release, Soyinka spent two years in prison. 'Whatever it was I believed in before I was locked up, I came out a fanatic in those things', Soyinka said upon his release in early October 1969. When asked what his role as a writer would now be, he replied:

There are no binding laws of commitment.... Each individual discovers sooner or later his own level and areas of commitment. If I had a choice in the matter I'd rather be a writer with no social commitment. That is by far the most comfortable form of creativity. For many years now I have lived with the knowledge that I could lose my liberty at any time. For reasons which I don't understand and cannot help, I am incapable of any peace of mind under certain social situations. There is nothing I can do about it, I can't change. Before one is a writer, I suppose one is a person.[14]

Born in Abeokuta in Western Nigeria, Soyinka attended Government College and University College in Ibadan. In 1958 he graduated from Leeds University, where he had studied English language and literature. Since he was a producer and director in Nigeria, he toured university theatres in the United States and Australia. In the academic sphere, Soyinka was a research fellow at the University of Ibadan, and Lecturer at the University of Ife, and in the Department of English at Lagos University. He also served as a co-editor of *Black Orpheus* for issues seven to thirteen (June 1960 to November 1964). In 1968 Nelson's released Soyinka's free translation (from the Yoruba) of the late Chief D. O. Fagunwa's novel *Ogboju ode ninu Igbo Irunmale* under the title *The Forest of a Thousand Daemons: a hunter's saga*.

In the fall of 1969 Wole Soyinka returned to the post he had held immediately before his imprisonment as head of the department of drama at the University of Ibadan, where he used a $1,000 grant awarded to him by the Farfield Foundation to help establish a School of Drama. Now, during the summer of 1970, Soyinka is at the Eugene O'Neill Memorial Theatre Centre in Waterford, Connecticut with a troupe of fifteen actors from Nigeria. Here, *Madmen and Specialists*, one of the three plays he wrote during his imprisonment, is being produced, and will be published by Doubleday and Co. early in 1971. Its concern is 'with a problem in my own society', Soyinka says, 'the betrayal of vocation for the attraction of power in one form or another'.[15]

Reportedly Wole Soyinka's next stop is the University of Pennsylvania, where he will take up a teaching appointment, before his return to Nigeria.

Evans will publish in 1971 a full length study on Wole Soyinka by Gerald Moore, in their African Writers and Their Work Series.

[1] Rex Collings, 'A propos', *African Arts/Arts d'Afrique*, vol. II, no. 3, Spring 1969, p. 82

[2] D. A. N. Jones, 'Tribal gods', *New York Review of Books*, July 31, 1969, p. 8

[3] Rex Collings, p. 82

[4] John Povey, 'West African poetry: tradition and change', *Africa Today*, vol. 15, no. 4, Aug./Sept. 1968, p. 7

[5] Wole Soyinka, *Poems from Prison* (London, 1969)

[6] Robert McDowell, 'African drama: West and South', *Africa Today*, vol. 15, no. 4, Aug./Sept. 1968, p. 26

[7] Ibid., p. 25

[8] D. A. N. Jones, p. 8

[9] John Povey, 'Changing themes in the Nigerian novel', *Journal of the New African Literature*, no. 1, Spring 1966, p. 10

[10] Wole Soyinka quoted in Janheinz Jahn, *Neo-African Literature* (London, 1966), pp. 265–266

[11] Wole Soyinka, 'The writer in a modern African state', in Per Wästberg. ed., *The Writer in Modern Africa* (New York, 1969), p. 17

[12] Ibid., p. 21

[13] Ibid., p. 16

[14] Wole Soyinka, 'I met Ojukwu after war began —Soyinka', *Daily Times* (Nigeria), October 13, 1969, p. 7

[15] *The New York Times*, July 20, 1970, p. 22

Efua Theodora Sutherland (1924–   )   GHANA

> I'm on a journey of discovery. I'm discovering my own people. I didn't grow up in rural Ghana — I grew up in Cape Coast with a Christian family. It's a fine family, but there are certain hidden areas of Ghanaian life — important areas of Ghanaian life, that I just wasn't in touch with; in the past four or five years I've made a very concentrated effort to make that untrue. And I feel I know my people now.[1]

Efua Sutherland more than knows her people. She has contributed extensively to their lives through her accomplishments in the literary, dramatic, and teaching professions.

The years 1958–1961 saw the birth of an Experimental Theatre and the Ghana Drama Studio in Accra, both founded by Mrs Sutherland, the latter with the assistance of grants from the Rockefeller Foundation and the Arts Council of Ghana. She conceived the Drama Studio 'as a centre for vigorous experimentation in drama . . . as eventually being a formative process in developing writers.' As she says:

> The Drama Studio has really come as another expression of my desire to have more and more people interested in writing — primarily for children. But later on it turned out that not everyone is interested in writing for children, although there are a great many interested in writing. To give another reason why people would want to write I

started to build the Drama Studio and develop the experimental theatre programme.[2]

In 1962 two of Mrs Sutherland's plays, *Foriwa* and *Edufa*, were performed at the Drama Studio for the first time. Later published in *Okyeame* (a Ghanaian literary magazine she helped establish) in 1964 and 1966 respectively, they have both since been issued in book form in Ghana. Productions at the studio have also included Efua Sutherland's one-act play *You Swore an Oath* and *Odasani*, a Ghanaian interpretation of *Everyman*. A versatile playwright, her publications also include *The Marriage of Anansewa*, a fantasy *The Pineapple Child*, and *Nyamekye*. Combining her lifelong interest in children with her literary abilities, she has written several children's plays as well: *Tweedledum and Tweedledee, Two Rhythm Plays: Vulture! Vulture! and Tahinta* (published by Ghana's State Publishing Corporation in 1968) and *Ananse and the Dwarf Brigade*.

Efua Sutherland feels that the language problem in Ghana will ultimately force English to become the national language. She is therefore 'pushing with the objective of a bilingual society in . . . mind.'[3]

> Some of my writing for children is in both English and Akan; I am anxious that children are started off bilingually in the schools. This can't happen unless there is literature in support of it. So this is all part of my experimental programme — to find out what can be translated in both languages towards this end.[4]

In 1961 Efua Sutherland's first book, a pictorial essay for children titled *The Roadmakers*, was published. A joint endeavour in the same genre, *Playtime in Africa*, was issued the following year, with photographs contributed by the American Willis E. Bell (who later also supplied photographs for the publication of *Two Rhythm Plays*) and text by Mrs Sutherland. Published in New York by Atheneum, this highly popular volume is now in its sixth printing.

In 1963 Efua Sutherland was granted a research appointment in African literature and drama at the University of Ghana's Institute of African Studies. She is currently connected with the School of Drama in Legon and directing the Kusum Agoromba, a theatre group based on the Ghana Drama Studio, performing at Accra schools, churches, and training colleges, and planning to travel throughout the country.

Efua Sutherland received her formal education at Ghana's Saint Monica's School and Teacher Training College, Homerton College in Cambridge for teacher training, and as a linguistics student at the University of London's School of Oriental and African Studies. Returning to her native country in the early 1950s, she married the American William Sutherland, had three children, taught in Ghana, and assisted her husband in the establishment of a school in the Transvolta.

[1] *Cultural Events in Africa*, no. 42, 1968, p. III
[2] Ibid., p. I
[3] Ibid., p. II
[4] Ibid., p. III

Amos Tutuola (1920–)

I am the native of Abeokuta. . . . Abeokuta is 64 miles to Lagos. When I was about 7 years old, one of my father's cousins whose name is Dalley, a nurse in the African hospital, took me from my father to his friend Mr F. O. Monu, an Ibe man, to live with him as a servant and to send me to school instead of paying me money.

I started my first education at the Salvation Army School, Abeokuta, in the year 1934, and Mr Monu was paying my school fees regularly. . . .

But as I had a quicker brain than the other boys in our class . . . I was given the special promotion. . . .

Having spent two years with my master, he was transferred to Lagos in 1936, and I followed him through his kindness. . . .

A few weeks after we arrived in Lagos, I was admitted into a school called Lagos High School. . . .

I attended this school for a year, and my weekly report card columns were always marked 1st position. . . . the Principal of this school promoted me from Std. II to Std. IV and he also allowed me to attend the school free of charge for one year.

But having passed from Std. IV to V the following year, I was unable to remain with my master any longer, because the severe punishments given me at home by this woman were too much for me. . . . When I reached home, I refused to go back to Lagos. . . .

. . . Again, I started to attend the school at Abeokuta. . . .

At the end of that year, I passed from Std. V to VI, and after I spent nine months on Std. VI my father, who was paying the school fees, etc., died unexpectedly (1939). Now, there was none of my family who volunteered to assist me to further my studies.[1]

Amos Tutuola, the first African writer to achieve international fame, signed this part of his autobiography on 17 April 1952, and in 1953 it was appended to the Grove Press edition of *The Palm-wine Drinkard*.

Twelve years later he elaborated on his life:

Having failed to further my education, I went to my father's farm. I planted plenty of corn on which I put all my hope that when they yielded, I would sell them and pay my school fees, etc. out of the money realised. But to my disappointment, there were no sufficient rains that year which could make the crops to yield well. Then having failed to help myself to further my education, I went back to Lagos in the early part of 1940.

I stayed with my brother when I came back to Lagos in 1940. In the same year, I started to learn smithery. At the end of 1942, I joined the R.A.F. as a blacksmith and discharged as a grade two blacksmith. . . . I got employment in the Department of Labour, Lagos, in 1946, as a messenger. I was still in this hardship and poverty, when one night, it came to my mind to write my first book — the Palm-wine Drinkard and I wrote it within a few days successfully because I was a story-teller when I was in the school. So since then I have become a writer.[2]

Amos Tutuola submitted *The Palm-wine Drinkard* to the United Society for Christian Literature, who passed it on to the London publisher, Faber and Faber. It was written in a somewhat unconventional, if not extraordinary English: Faber's smoothed out its roughest edges and the book was published almost entirely in its original form in 1952.

Two months later, Dylan Thomas, writing in the London *Observer*, gave it a highly laudatory review, calling it a 'brief, thronged, grisly and bewitching story. . . . Nothing is too prodigious or too trivial to put down in this tall, devilish story.'[3] English and American critics alike hailed it a remarkable success. An American edition followed in 1953 and by the time Janheinz Jahn published his bibliography in 1965, he was able to note six translated editions. Tutuola's most severe critics were his fellow Nigerians, who criticized him for his lack of education, his imperfect English, his adaptations from Yoruba oral literature, and for presenting a disparaging image of Nigeria.

Bernth Lindfors writes that Tutuola has recently

acknowledged that there are many stories like his written in Yoruba and has written in a letter that he read *Pilgrim's Progress* and *The Arabian Nights* in 1948, just two years before *The Palm-wine Drinkard* was written. He has also told Eric Larabee that he enjoyed reading Joyce Cary's *Mister Johnson* and Edith Hamilton's *Mythology* which presumably is the book responsible for enlarging his folkloric vocabulary.[4]

Since *The Palm-wine Drinkard*, Tutuola has written *My Life in the Bush of Ghosts* (1954), *Simbi and the Satyr of the Dark Jungle* (1955), *The Brave African Huntress* (1958), and *Feather Woman of the Jungle* (1962). His latest literary efforts have utilized the short-story form.

In 1964 Tutuola wrote:

I joined the Nigerian Broadcasting Service . . . as a storekeeper and have since then been promoted to the senior grade. I married in 1947 and have already got three children. . . . In 1957, I asked for a transfer to Ibadan, Western Nigeria, in order to be in close with Prof. Collis of the University of Ibadan, and I was transferred to Ibadan in December of the same year. In 1958, Prof. Collis who has interest in my books, taught

me how to write the Palm-wine Drinkard in form of a play. . . . I am one
of the founders of the 'MBARI CLUB', the writers and publishers organ-
isation, in Ibadan.⁵

Amos Tutuola remains a controversial figure. Bernth Lindfors aptly
writes of him: 'No one denies that Tutuola is an extraordinary writer. The
issue seems to be whether as a writer he is extraordinarily good, extraordinarily bad or extraordinarily lucky.'⁶

A full-length study of Amos Tutuola has recently been made by Harold
Collins in a book entitled *Tutuola*, in Twayne's World Authors series.

¹ Amos Tutuola, *The Palm-wine Drinkard* (New York, 1953), pp. 126—128
² Amos Tutuola, 'A Short Biography' (A letter written to Faber and Faber, London), 14 July
1964
³ Dylan Thomas, *The Observer* (London), 6 July 1952, p. 7
⁴ Bernth Lindfors, 'Amos Tutuola and his critics', *Abbia*, Mai-Août 1969, pp. 115—116
⁵ Amos Tutuola, 'A Short Biography'
⁶ Lindfors, p. 113

Gérald Félix Tchicaya U Tam'si

(1931–   )   CONGO BRAZZAVILLE

This Congolese poet in voluntary exile has resided in Paris since 1946,
when he accompanied his father, who was then his country's First Deputy,
to the French National Assembly, to France. Tchicaya U Tam'si thereafter
studied at the Orleans Lycée and later at the Lycée Janson de Sailly in
Paris. And although he views his native country from abroad, Gerald
Moore points out that 'the poetic landscape of U Tam'si, the materials of
his imagination, his whole sensibility, the very music of his life, have all
been shaped by Africa.'¹

In 1963 Moore called U Tam'si 'a poet of some importance and the most
prolific black poet of French expression to appear since Césaire';² in 1967

he saw him 'emerging as the outstanding poet of French expression among those who have been publishing since the war.'[3] Through both his critical articles and translations of his poetry, Gerald Moore has probably done more than anyone else to introduce U Tam'si to the English-speaking world, in particular to Anglophone Africa. Moore's first English translations of his poetry appeared in early issues of both *Black Orpheus* (no. 13) and *Transition* (no. 9).

U Tam'si's published works consist of six books of verse and one of African legends: *Le mauvais sang* (1955), *Feu de brousse* (1957), *À triche-coeur* (1960), *Epitome* (with an introduction by Léopold Sédar Senghor) (1962), *Le ventre* (1964), *L'arc musical* (1969), and *Légendes Africaines* (1969). In 1964 Mbari published *Brush fire*, containing English translations from *Feu de brousse*, and Heinemann now have published some English translations of U Tam'si's verse in a volume entitled *Selected Poems*.

Gerald Moore finds that U Tam'si's poetry has been influenced by many things: 'the inspiration of Césaire and beyond him the technique and example of the Surrealistes; the sculpture, music, dancing and poetry of the Congo; and not least his own poetic genius.'[4]

> Each of his books is unified by the constant re-working and exploration of a fairly fixed vocabulary of images which he continually places in new relations to each other.
>
> The physical intensity with which U Tam'si explores the landscape of the world and his own being cannot be fully matched by any other poet now working in Africa, but his general relationship to the elements of landscape and his insistence on the physical and temporal unity of all experience, with energy as the uniting principle, can be found equally in the work of many other African writers.[5]

U Tam'si himself records that his poetry 'is a spoken poetry, not a written poetry, even though it is on paper. A spoken poetry does not obey the same laws as a written poetry which follows a grammatical logic. My logic is my own, it is a logic of reverberation in a way.' He admits of two different strains in his poetry:

> There is a permanent feature in my writing which is a kind of black humour, an inner grin, a sort of chuckle. I laugh at myself when I can and this comes out in my writing.
>
> Certainly there is in my writing this universe, this loneliness, sadness of man — man everywhere, whether he be black, white, yellow etc.[6]

As a freelance writer and journalist, U Tam'si has contributed to both English and French reviews, and in 1960 he became editor of the journal *Congo*. He has written, produced, and directed many radio broadcasts, concentrating in particular on the adaptation of African stories and legends for this medium. He has also served as an officer of U.N.E.S.C.O.

At the 1967 African-Scandinavian Writers' Conference held in Stockholm, U Tam'si expressed his view of the writer in a modern African state:

> Je pense que l'écrivain que je pourrais être, que je suis peut-être, militerait plutôt pour trouver l'intimité la plus stricte auprès de 200

lecteurs et leur communiquer ce que je pense être le message, plutôt que d'aller le dire sur une place publique. Ceci dit en général. Donc, pour ma part, je ne vois pas d'autre devoir pour un écrivain que d'écrire et d'être un homme, tout simplement. Son rôle, encore une fois, c'est d'être un homme.[7]

[1] Gerald Moore, 'Surrealism and negritude in the poetry of Tchikaya U Tam'si', *Black Orpheus*, no. 13, November 1963, p. 12

[2] Ibid., p. 5

[3] Gerald Moore, 'The Negro poet and his landscape', *Black Orpheus*, no. 22, August 1967, p. 35

[4] Moore, 'Surrealism and negritude', p. 12

[5] Moore, 'The Negro poet', pp. 36, 38

[6] 'Tchikaya U Tam'si interviewed by Edris Makward during the African Studies Association Conference held at Montreal, October 1969', *Cultural Events in Africa*, no. 60, 1969 pp. III, II, IV

[7] Tchicaya U Tam'si, 'The writer in a modern African state', in Per Wästberg, ed., *The Writer in Modern Africa* (New York, 1969), p. 30

ESSENTIAL ADDRESSES

PUBLISHERS
USA

Africana Publishing Corporation
101 Fifth Avenue
New York, N.Y. 10003

African Studies Association
218 Shiffman Humanities Center,
Brandeis University
Waltham, Mass. 02154

Alfred A. Knopf, Inc.
501 Madison Avenue
New York, N.Y. 10022

Astor-Honor, Inc.
26 East 42nd St.
New York, N.Y. 10017

Atheneum Publishers
122 East 42nd St.
New York, N.Y. 10017

Cambridge University Press
32 East 57th St.
New York, N.Y. 10022

Dodd, Mead and Co.
79 Madison Avenue
New York, N.Y. 10016

Doubleday and Company, Inc.
277 Park Avenue
New York, N.Y. 10017

E. P. Dutton & Co., Inc.
201 Park Avenue South
New York, N.Y. 10016

Fawcett World Library
67 West 44th St.
New York, N.Y. 10036

Farrar, Strauss and
Giroux, Inc.
19 Union Sq. West
New York, N.Y. 10003

Grove Press, Inc.
80 University Place
New York, N.Y. 10003

Harcourt, Brace & World, Inc.
757 Third Avenue
New York, N.Y. 10017

Harper & Row, Publishers
49 East 33rd St.
New York, N.Y. 10016

Hill and Wang, Inc.
141 Fifth Avenue
New York, N.Y. 10010

Houghton Mifflin Co.
2 Park St.
Boston, Mass. 02107

Humanities Press Inc.
303 Park Avenue South
New York, N.Y. 10010

Indiana University Press
Tenth and Morton Sts.
Bloomington, Ind. 47401

International Publishers Co., Inc.
381 Park Avenue South
New York, N.Y. 10016

Jefferson Bookshop Inc.
100 East 16th St.
New York, N.Y. 10003

John Day Company
200 Madison Avenue
New York, N.Y. 10016

Johnson Reprint Corporation
111 Fifth Avenue
New York, N.Y. 10003

Kraus Reprint Corp.,
16 East 46th Street,
New York, N.Y. 10017; and
FL-9491 Nendeln, Liechtenstein

Little Brown and Co.
34 Beacon St.
Boston, Mass. 02106

McGraw-Hill Co. Inc.
330 West 42nd St.
New York, N.Y. 10036

Macmillan Co.
866 Third Avenue
New York, N.Y. 10022

Negro Universities Press
(& Greenwood Press)
51 Riverside Avenue
Westport, Conn. 06880

New American Library, Inc.
1301 Avenue of the Americas
New York, N.Y. 10019

Northwestern University Press
1735 Benson Avenue
Evanston, Ill. 60201

October House Inc.
55 West 13th St.
New York, N.Y. 10010

Odyssey Press, Inc.
55 Fifth Avenue
New York, N.Y. 10003

Oxford University Press
200 Madison Avenue
New York, N.Y. 10016

Penguin Books, Inc.
7110 Ambassador Road
Baltimore, Md. 21207

Pergamon Press, Inc.
Maxwell House
Fairview Park
Elmsford, N.Y. 10523

Praeger Publishers, Inc.
111 Fourth Avenue
New York, N.Y. 10003

Random House, Inc.
457 Madison Avenue
New York, N.Y. 10022

The Third Press
444 Central Park West
New York, N.Y. 10025

University of California Press
2223 Fulton St.
Berkeley, Calif. 94720

University of Wisconsin Press
P.O. Box 1379
Madison, Wisconsin 53701

Vanguard Press, Inc.
424 Madison Avenue
New York, N. 10017

Walker and Company
720 Fifth Avenue
New York, N.Y. 10019

United Kingdom

George Allen and Unwin Ltd
40 Museum St.
London W.C.1

A. J. Arnold and Son Ltd
Butterley St.
Hunslet La.
Leeds 10

Associated Book Publishers
(Andover), Ltd
Northway, Andover
Hants

Cambridge University Press
Bentley Ho.
P.O. Box 92
200 Euston Road
London N.W.1

Frank Cass and Co. Ltd
67 Great Russell St.
London W.C.1

Collier-Macmillan Ltd
10 South Audley St.
London W.1

Rex Collings Ltd
6 Paddington St.
London W.1

William Collins, Sons and Co. Ltd
14 St James's Pl.
London S.W.1

André Deutsch Ltd
105 Great Russell St.
London W.C.1

Evans Brothers Ltd
Montague Ho.
Russell Sq.
London W.C.1

Faber and Faber Ltd
24 Russell Sq.
London W.C.1

Ginn and Co. Ltd
18 Bedford Row
London W.C.1

Victor Gollancz Ltd
14 Henrietta St.
Covent Garden
London W.C.2

Gregg International Publishers Ltd
1 Westmead, Farnborough
Hants

George G. Harrap and Co. Ltd
182 High Holborn
London W.C.1

Heinemann Educational Books Ltd
48 Charles St.
London W.1

Hodder and Stoughton Ltd
St Paul's Ho., Warwick La.
London E.C.4

Hutchinson Publishing Group Ltd
178–202 Great Portland St.
London W.1

Longman Group Ltd.
Longman House, Burnt Mill
Harlow
Essex

Lutterworth Press
4 Bouverie St.
London E.C.4

Macmillan and Co. Ltd
Little Essex St.
London W.C.2

Methuen and Co. Ltd
11 New Fetter La.
London E.C.4

Frederick Muller Ltd
Ludgate Ho.
110 Fleet St.
London E.C.4

Thomas Nelson and Sons Ltd
36 Park St.
London W.1

New English Library Ltd
Bernard's Inn, Holborn
London E.C.1

Peter Owen Ltd
12 Kendrick Mews
Kendrick Pl.
London S.W.7

Oxford University Press
Ely Ho., 37 Dover St.
London W.1

Pall Mall Press Ltd
5 Cromwell Pl.
London S.W.7

Pan Books Ltd
33 Tothill St.
London S.W.1

Panaf Books
89 Fleet St.
London E.C.4

Panther Books Ltd
3 Upper James St.
Golden Sq.
London W.1

Penguin Books Ltd
Harmondsworth
Middx.

Pergamon Press Ltd
Headington Hill Hall
Oxford

Routledge and Kegan Paul Ltd
68–74 Carter La.
London E.C.4

Arthur H. Stockwell Ltd
Elms Court, Torrs Park
Ilfracombe
Devon

University of London Press Ltd
St Paul's House
Warwick La.
London E.C.4

Writers Forum
262 Randolph Avenue
London W.9

France

Édit. Caractère
40 rue de Collisée
Paris 8

Libr. Flammarion et Cie.
26 rue Racine
Paris 6

Édit. Gallimard
5 rue Sébastien-Bottin
Paris 7

Édit. Jean Grassin
50 rue Rodier
Paris 9

Libr. Hachette
79 Bd. Saint-Germain
Paris 6

Édit. René Juillard
8 rue Garancière
Paris 6

Édit. Robert Laffont
6 Place Saint-Sulpice
Paris 6

Édit. Albin Michel
22 rue Huyghens
Paris 14

Édit. Nalis
65 rue de Courcelles
Paris 8

Libr. Fernand Nathan et Cie.
9 rue Méchain
Paris 14

Nouvelles Édit. Debresse
17 rue Duguay-Trouin
Paris 6

Nouvelles Édit. Latines
1 rue Palatine
Paris 6

Édit. Pierre-Jean Oswald
16 rue des Capucines
14 — Honfleur — Paris

Libr. Plon
8 rue Garancière
Paris 6

Présence Africaine
25 bis rue des Ecoles
Paris 5

Édit. Séghers
118 rue de Vaugirard
Paris 6

Édit. du Seuil
27 rue Jacob
Paris 6

Other Europe

Edit. Gérard & Cie
65 rue de Limbourg
Verviers
Belgium

Institut de Sociologie Solvay
Université Libre de Bruxelles
44 avenue Jeanne
Brussels 5
Belgium

Moritz Diesterweg
6000 Frankfurt (M) 1
Hochstrasse 31
Germany

Sevens Seas Books
Berlin
(order from Deutsche Buch
Export und Import GmbH
Leninstrasse 16
Postfach 160
601 Leipzig
German Democratic Republic)

N. V. Brill
Oude Riyn 33a
Leiden
The Netherlands

Mouton Publishers
5 Harderstraat
P.O. Box 1132
The Hague
The Netherlands

Africa[1]

African Universities Press
P.O. Box 1287
Lagos
Nigeria

U.S. distributor:
Africana Publishing Corp., New York
U.K. distributor:
Ginn and Co., London

Ánowuo Educational Publ.
2R McCarthy Hill
Accra
Ghana

A. A. Balkema
P.O. Box 3117
93 Kerom St.
Cape Town
South Africa

Éditions C.L.E.
B.P. 4048
Yaoundé
Cameroun

U.S. distributor:
Africana Publishing Corp., New York

East African Literature Bureau
P.O. Box 30022
Nairobi
Kenya

U.K. distributor: University Press of
Africa
1 West Street Tavistock Devon

East African Publishing House
Uniafric House
Koinange Street
P.O. Box 30571
Nairobi
Kenya

U.S. distributor:
Northwestern Univ. Press, Evanston, Ill.
U.K. distributor:
Heinemann Educ. Books, London

Ghana Publishing Corp.
P.O. Box 4348
Accra

Ibadan University Press
Ibadan University
Ibadan
Nigeria

U.S. distributor:
Africana Publishing Corp., New York

Inst. of African Studies
Univ. of Ibadan
Ibadan
Nigeria
(distributed by University
Bookshop Nigeria Ltd, Ibadan)

Mambo Press
Gwelo
Rhodesia

Mbari Club
P.O. Box 1463
Ibadan
Nigeria

U.S. distributor: (partial list only)
Northwestern Univ. Press, Evanston, Ill.

[1]for a comprehensive directory of African publishers, see *Africana Library Journal*, vol. 1, no. 2, Summer, 1970, pp. 11—16, and supplement in vol. 1, no. 4, Winter, 1970, pp. 33—34.

National Educational
Comp. of Zambia Ltd
P.O. Box 2664
Lusaka
Zambia

Uganda Publishing House Ltd
P.O. Box 2923
Kampala
Uganda

Witwatersrand Univ. Press
University Park
Johannesburg
South Africa

BOOKSELLERS AND DEALERS

[who specialize and/or hold *substantial* stocks of African literature[1]]

United Kingdom

B. H. Blackwell Ltd
48—51 Broad St.
Oxford

Dillon's University Bookshop Ltd
1 Malet St.
London W.C.1

W. Heffer and Sons
3—4 Petty Cury
Cambridge

Kegan Paul, Trench, Trubner and Co.
43 Great Russell St.
London, W.C.1

France

Librairie Présence Africaine
24 rue des Ecoles
Paris 5

Librairie du Camée
M. et M. Trochon,
3 rue de Valence
Paris 5

United States

Africana Center
International University Booksellers, Inc.
101 Fifth Avenue
New York, N.Y. 10003
(Wholesale only)

The Cellar Bookshop
Box 6
College Park Station
Detroit, Mich. 48221

Drum and Spear Bookstore
2701 14th Street, N.W.
Washington, D.C. 20009

University Place Bookshop
740 Broadway, 13th floor
New York, N.Y. 10003
(formerly at 69 University Place)

Africa

Centre de Littérature Evangélique
C.L.E.
B.P. 4048
Yaoundé
Cameroun

Librairie Congolaise
B.P. 2100
Kinshasa
Rep. of the Congo

G. P. Giannopoulos
B.O. Box 120
Addis Ababa
Ethiopia

Menno Bookstore
P.O. Box 1236
Addis Ababa
Ethiopia

R.J. Moxon
The Atlas Bookshop
P.O. Box M160
Accra
Ghana

University Bookshop,
University of Ghana
P.O. Box 1
Legon
Ghana

Librairie Africaine
B.P. 328
Abidjan
Ivory Coast

University College Bookshop
University College
Nairobi
Kenya

S. J. Moore Bookshop
P.O. Box 31062
Nairobi
Kenya

The Times Bookshop
P.O. Box 445
Blantyre
Malawi

[1]A comprehensive list of *general* Africana dealers is provided in the *Special Bibliographic Series*, vol. 6, 1969 of the African Bibliographic Center. (Distributed by Negro Universities Press, Westport, Conn.)

La Librairie de Madagascar
B.P. 402
Tananarive
Malagasy Republic

University Bookshop Nigeria Ltd
University of Ibadan
Ibadan
Nigeria

Nigerian Book Suppliers Ltd
8 Lake St.
P.O. Box 3870
Lagos
Nigeria

University of Ife Bookshop Ltd.
University of Ife
Ile-Ife
Nigeria
(*branch at Ibadan*)

Librairie Clairafrique
B.P. 2005
Dakar
Senegal

Fourah Bay College Bookshop Ltd
University of Sierra Leone
Freetown
Sierra Leone

C. Struik
P.O. Box 1144
Cape Town
South Africa

Sudan Bookshop
P.O. Box 156
Khartoum
Sudan

University Bookshop
University College
Dar-es-Salaam
Tanzania

Dar es Salaam Bookshop
P.O. Box 9030
Dar se Salaam
Tanzania

Makerere University Bookshop
University College
Makerere
Kampala
Uganda

University of Zambia Bookshop
The University of Zambia
Lusaka
Zambia

INDEX

This index lists all authors, editors and critics included in the bibliography. Furthermore, it cites writers whose work, thus far, has only appeared in anthologies. However, these anthologies are indexed only for those writers who fall within the scope of this bibliography. Therefore, a black writer from Portuguese Africa or a white South African author, for example, who have been anthologized, are *not* covered.

Nationalities of *African* authors (where known) are identified by country symbols as follows:

BO	–BOTSWANA	MAU	–MAURITIUS
BU	–BURUNDI	MR	–MALAGASY REPUBLIC
C	–CAMEROON	N	–NIGERIA
CAR	–CENTRAL AFRICAN REPUBLIC	NI	–NIGER
CH	–CHAD	R	–RWANDA
COB	–CONGO BRAZZAVILLE	RH	–RHODESIA
COK	–CONGO KINSHASA	S	–SENEGAL
D	–DAHOMEY	SA	–SOUTH AFRICA
E	–ETHIOPIA	SL	–SIERRA LEONE
G	–GHANA	SO	–SOMALILAND
GA	⌐GABON	SU	–SUDAN
GAM	–GAMBIA	SW	–SWAZILAND
GU	–GUINEA	SWA	–SOUTH WEST AFRICA
IC	–IVORY COAST	T	–TANZANIA
K	–KENYA	TO	–TOGO
L	–LESOTHO	U	–UGANDA
LI	–LIBERIA	UV	–UPPER VOLTA
M	–MALI	Z	–ZAMBIA
MA	–MALAWI		

Entry numbers appear in roman type face. **Page** numbers (pp. **96** through **199**), are in **bold**, and periodical and magazine titles are in *italics* followed by the **page** reference. The abbreviation BIOG. followed by a page number in **bold** indicates that a biography of the author is included.

The letter 'A' is prefixed to the entry number(s) of an anthology(ies) in which the author's work appears. In addition, writers who have thus far only been published in anthologies are indexed similarly. However, we were unable to obtain and index a small number of anthologies, including those not yet published at the time of going to press. These are: 100, 107, 117, 122, 123, 142 and 330. Folkloristic literature and verse collections from secondary schools have *not* been indexed.

Example: Aluko, T. M. (N) 228, 229, 230, 231,
                          A70, A82
                      BIOG. **121**

This indicates that works by Timothy Aluko, a Nigerian writer, are listed as entries 228 through 231; his writing has been anthologized in Berry's *Africa Speaks* (entry 70), and in Edwards's *Modern African Narrative* (entry 82); and a biography of him appears on page **121**. (Additional page references might refer to periodical articles by an author).

Abbia **102**
Abbs, A. (G) 144
Abdoul, R. 97
Aboderin, S. F. (N) A111
Abraham, W. E. (G) 639
Abrahams, L. 392
Abrahams, P. (SA) 400, 401, 402, 403, 404, 405, 406, 407, 408, 409
A77, A78, A79, A81, A82, A83v.I, A86, A87, A88, A89, A92, A101, A110, A111, A112v.I, A112v.II
BIOG. **115**
Abrash, B. 1
Abruquah, J. W. (G) 145, 146
Achebe, C. (N) 219, 220, 221, 222, 223, 682, 795
A69, A70, A76, A79, A82, A83v.I, A89, A94, A99, A101, A109, A110, A112v.I, A118, A119, A121v.II, A124, A195
96, 101
BIOG. **117**
Achiriga, J. J. (N) 11
Actes du Colloque sur la littérature africaine d'expression française 24
Adali-Mortty, G. (G) 139
A87
Ademola, F. (N) 195
Adeyemo, G. A. (N) A197
Adiko, A. (IC) A118
Africa Report **108**
Africa Today **108**
African Affairs **108**
African Arts/Arts d'Afrique **102**
Africa Centre, The 14
African Forum **108**
African Literature Today **102**
African Notes **108**
African Studies **108**
African Studies Bulletin (African Studies Review) **108**
Africana Library Journal **108**
Afrifa, A. A. (G) 640
Afro-Asian Theatre Bulletin **108**
Afro-Asian Writings **109**
Agboro, J. A. (N) A115
Aggrey, J. (G) A111, A112v.II
Agunwa, C. (N) 224
Ahuma, S. A. (G) A83
Aidoo, A. A. (G) 147, 148, 149
A65, A66, A69, A76, A94, A99, A102
BIOG. **120**

Aig-Imoukhuede, F. A. (N) A87, A98, A118, A197
Aiyegbusu, T. (U) A328
Ajao, A. (N) A83
Ajose, A. (N) 683, 684
Akar, J. (SL) A128
Akiga, B. (N) 225
A75, A81, A83v.I
Akinsemoyin, K. (N) 685, 686, 687
A128
Ako, O. D. (G) 149
Akogbo, B. (N)
Akpabot, A. (N) 226, 688, 689
A102
Akpan, N. U. (N) 227, 690
Akpoko, A. (U) 329
Akpoyoware, M. (N) A197
Albert, M. O. (N) A75
Alene, C. (C) A442
Alima, E. (C) A442
Allary, J. 4
Aluko, T. M. (N) 228, 229, 230, 231
A70, A82
BIOG. **121**
Amadi, E. (N) 232, 233
BIOG. **122**
Amali, S. O. O. (N) 234, 235, 236
A65
American Society of African Culture 25
Amosu, M. 2
Ananou, D. (TO) A75, A112v.II
Andrzejewski, B. W. 326
Anghoff, C. 65
Anizoba, R. (N) 691
Annan, K. (G) A94
Anozie, S. O. (N) 779
Apoko, A. (N) A73
Apronti, J. (G) A98, A115
Arhurst, F. S. (G) A88
Armah, A. K. (G) 151, 152, 796
A139
BIOG. **123**
Armah, K. (G) 641
Armattoe, R. E. G. (G) 153
A108, A111, A127, A128
Asalache, K. (K) 342
A98, A114, A115
Asare, B. (G) 154
Asheri, J. (N) 692
Ateli, M. (N) A115
Atiyah, E. (SU) A83

Reference: Meaning
roman — entry number
bold face — page number
italics — periodicals and magazines
BIOG. — biography of author
Prefix A — author's work appears in one or several anthologies
(S) — nationality of African authors (see key, page **207**)

Attah, E. (N) A102
Awolowo, O. (N) 642, 643, 644
Awoonor, K. (G) 139, 780, 797, 810
A106
  BIOG. **124**
(*see also* Awoonor-Williams, G.)
Awoonor-Williams, G. (G) 155, 156
A65, A98, A99, A108, A114, A118, A119, A127
(*see also*, Awoonor, K.)
Ayissi, L. M. (C) 446, 447
A442
Azikiwe, N. (N) 645, 646

Ba, A. H. (M) 529
A66, A92
Ba Shiru **109**
Babalola, S. A. (N) 196
A80, A108
Badian, S. (M) 530, 531
A91, A112v.I A112v.II
Balewa, Sir. A. A. T. (N) 237, 647
Balogun, S. I. (N) 26, 543
Banham, M. 197
98
Banks-Henries, A. D. (LI) 189
Baratte, T. 3
Barclay, E. (LI) A87
Bart-Williams, G. (SL) A66, A114, A115, A116
Basner, M. 384
Bassir, O. (N) 123
Battestini, M. 444, 445, 485, 494, 505, 528,
  546, 547, 548
Bazarrabusa, T. (U) A74
Bebey, F. (C) 448, 449, 798
A120
  BIOG. **126**
Bediako, A. K. (G) 157, 158
(*see also* Asare, B.)
Bedwei, A. (G) A94
Beier, U. 27, 66, 67, 68, 69, 98, 198, 199,
  204, 205, 693
99, 100, 101
Belinga, E. M. S. 28
A92
Bemba, S. (COB) A99
Bengono, J. (C) 450
Bereng, D. C. (L) A394
Bereng, M. (L) A111
Berry, J. P. 70
Beti, M. (C) 451, 452, 453, 454, 799
A31, A70, A72, A75, A77, A79, A83v.II,
  A85, A89, A90, A91, A92, A103, A112v.I,
  A112v.II
  BIOG. **128**
(*see also* Boto, E.)
Bgoya, W. (T) A335
Bhalo, A. N. (K) 343
Bhêly-Quenum, O. (D) 486, 487
A77, A92, A112v.II
Bingo **109**
Biyidi, A. (*see* Beti, M.)

Black Academy Review **109**
Black Orpheus **103**
Blay, J. B. (G) 694, 800
A86, A88
Blyden, E. (LI) A83v.II
Boeti, D. (SA) 410
A392
Bognini, J. M. (IC) 507
A77, A98, A120
Bol. V. P. 4
Bolamba, A. R. (COK) 608
A74, A77, A91, A98, A99
Boni, N. (UV) A72, A75, A85, A112v.II
Books Abroad **109**
Boruett, W. K. (K) 344
Boto, E. (C) 456
A77, A103
(*see also* Beti, M.)
Boundzeki-Dongala, E. (COK) A98
Bown, L. 29
Brand, D. (SA) A102, A395
Brench, A. C. 30, 31
98
Brew, K. (G) 159
A73, A74, A87, A98, A99, A108, A114, A115,
  A116, A118, A119, A127, A139
Brown, C. E. (N) A111
Brownlee, P. 71
Brutus, D. (SA) 411, 412
A92, A98, A99, A102, A119, A392, A395
  BIOG. **130**
Buahin, P. K. (G) A94
*Bulletin of the Association for African Literature
  in English* **103**
Buraga, J. (U) 364
Busara **104**
Busia, K. A. (G) 648, 649
A70, A81
Bwana, M. (K) A112v.II

Camara, S. (GU) 495
Cameroun Littéraire Le **109**
Caputo, N. (SA) A77
Carlin, M. (U) 814, 815
Carroll, D. 781
Cartey, W. 32, 695
Casely-Hayford, G. M. (G) A127
Casely-Hayford, J. E. (G) 160
A70, A75, A88, A94, A111, A118, A121v.II,
  A124, A127
Cassirer, T. **101**
Caverhill, N. 72
Cazziol, R. J. 788
Chache, T. (T) A70, A76, A118, A328
Chadwick, H. M. 33
Chadwick, N. K. 33
Chagula, L. (SA) A70
Chaplin, J. (U) A65
Charimo **109**
Chemba, Y. S. (U) A335
Chibule, A. (K?) 696

210

Chisiza, D. K. (SA) A101
Choonara, I. (SA) A395
Christofer, O. (N) A92
Cissoko, S. (S) 550
Citashe, I. W. W. (SA) A86, A88
Clark, J. P. (N) 200, 238, 239, 240, 241, 242, 243, 244
A78, A87, A92, A96, A98, A108, A114, A115, A118, A119, A127, A195
98, 99
BIOG. **132**
Clark, L. E. 73
Clarke, P. (SA) A87, A116
Classic, The **109**
Clinton, J. V. (N) 697
Cadjoe, T. A. (G) A111
Cole, A. (SL) 698
Cole, R. W. (SL) 312
A83v.I, A101
Colin, R. 33, 34
Collins, H. 201, 202
Conch, The **104**
Congrès des Ecrivains et Artistes Noirs, Deuxième 37
Congrès International des Ecrivains et Artistes Noirs 53
Conton, W. (SL) 313
A70, A76, A83v.I, A94, A109, A110, A112v.II, A119, A124, A729
BIOG. **134**
Contrast **109**
Cook, D. 327, 328, 789
Cook, M. 36
Copans, J. 544
Cope, T. 391, 394
Coupez, A. 631
Crowder, M. 29, 747
96
Cudjoe, S. D. (TO) A108
Cultural Events in Africa **104**
Current Bibliography on African Affairs, A **109**

Dadié, B. (IC) 508, 509, 510, 511, 512, 513, 514, 515, 516, 517, 518, 519, 801
A72, A77, A81, A85, A86, A90, A91, A92, A97, A013, A108, A112v.I, A112v.II, A118, A120, A121v.II, A127
BIOG. **135**
Dahal, C. (K?) 699
Danquah, J. B. (G) 161, 162
A87

Darlite **104**
Dathorne, O. R. 74, 75
99
Davies, J. S. (SL) A128
Decker, T. (SL) 700
A74
de Graft, J. C. (G) 163, 164
A65, A139
de Graft-Hanson (G) 165
Dei-Anang, M. F. (G) 166, 167, 168, 169, 170, 171
A74, A86, A87, A88, A92, A115, A127
Dembele, S. (M) A112v.II
Dempster, R. T. (LI) 190, 191, 192
A87
Denny, N. 76
Deressa, S. (E) A65
Dervain, E. (C) 457, 458
A92
Dholomo, H. (SA) 413, 414
A74
Dholomo, R. R. (SA) 415
A75
Dia, M. (S) 650
A86
Diakhaté, L. (S) 551, 552, 553
Diallo, B. (S) 554
Diboti, E. M. 77
Dick, J. B. 78, 79
Dickson, T. (N) 701
Diop, B. 555, 556, 557, 558, 559, 560
A31, A66, A72, A81, A85, A86, A88, A90, A92, A95, A98, A99, A103, A108, A111, A112v.I, A112v.II, A113, A119, A120, A121v.II, A127, A128
BIOG. **137**
Diop, D. (S) 561
A77, A78, A81, A85, A86, A87, A92, A97, A98, A99, A108, A111, A113, A118, A119, A120, A127, A128
BIOG. **139**
Diop, O. S. (*see* Socé, D.)
Diouara, B. B. (M) A92
Dipoko, M. S. (C) 131, 132
A70, A98, A99, A106, A118, A127, A172
97
BIOG. **140**
Djoleto, A. (G) 172
A70
Dobrin, M. (K) 718
Dogbeh, R. (D) 77, 488, 489, 490, 491

Dombi **104**
Dongmo, J. (C) A92, A442
Doob, L. 80, 702
Dosunmu, S. (N?) A106
Dove-Danquah, M. (G) A88, A118, A121v.II
Drachler, J. 81
Dressler, C. P. 777
Drum **109**
Dudley, D. R. 38
Duodo, C. (G) 173
A95, A139
Dzovo, E. V. K. (G) 703

Easmon, R. S. (SL) 314, 315, 316
A65, A94, A99, A109
BIOG. **142**
East Africa Journal **109**
East, N. B. 5
96
Echeruo, M. J. C. (N) 245
A98, A102, A114, A115, A119, A127
Echezona, W. W. C. (N) A101
Edwards, P. 82, 83, 124
Egbuna, O. B. (N) 246, 247, 816
Egudu, R. N. (N) A65, A98, A102, A114, A115
Ekwensi, C. (N) 248, 249, 250, 251, 252, 253,
   254, 255, 704, 705, 706, 707, 708, 709,
   710, 711, 712, 713
A66, A70, A76, A82, A83v.II, A88, A94,
   A99, A110, A111, A112v.I, A112v.II, A115,
   A119, A121v.II, A195, A197
BIOG. **142**
Ekwere, J. D. (N) A195, A197
El-Miskery, S. A. (T) A115
Eliet, E. 37
English Studies in Africa **109**
Epangya-Yonde, E. (C) 483
A85, A92
Epelle, S. (N) A108
Equiano, O. (N) 256
A83v.I, A119, A121v.II, A124
Eric, S. (N?) A75
Esan, Y. (N) A128, A197
Essama, D. (C) A442
Ethiopia Observer **109**
Euba, F. (N) A105
Evans-Pritchard, E. E. 322
Evembé, F. (C) 460
Ewandé, D. (C) 459
Expression **110**
Eyakuze, V. (SA) A328

Fadl, E. S. H. (SU) 324
Fafunwa, B. (N) A88
Fagunwa, D. O. (N) 257
A66, A69, A112v.II, A121v.II
Faleti, A. (N) A87
Fall, M. (S) 562, 563
A92
Faye, N. G. M. (S) 564

Feuser, W. 75
Fiawoo, F. K. (G) A87
Finnegan, R. 311, 782
'First word' **97**
Fodeba, K. (GU) 496, 497
A86, A92
Forrest, R. 84
Fouda, B. J. 441
Fox, D. C. 329
Freeman, R. A. (N) A65
Fuja, A. (N) 203
Furay, M. **100**

Gabre-Medhin, T. (E) 337
Garg, K. C. (T) A115
Gashe, M. (K) A87
Gatanyu, R. J. M. (K) 345
Gatheru, R. J. M. (K) 346
Gatuiria, J. (K) A74, A128, A328
Gbadamosi, B. (N) 204, 205
A65,
   A69, A75, A111
George, C. (SL) 317
A128
Gicaru, M. (K) A82, A83v.I, A112v.II
Gichuru, S. (K) 714
Gicogo, G. K. (K) A328
Gleason, J. 125, **99**
Gologo, M. (M) A112v.II
Goodwin, K. L. 783
Gordimer, N. 392
Graham-White, A. **96**
Green, R. 330, **100**
Gresshoff, N. M. 393
Guibert, A. 545
Guma, S. M. 380
Gwala, T. H. (SA) A398
Gwengwe, J. W. (N) 715

Haji, M. M. (T?) A328
Hama, B. (NI) A91
Hamann, W. 85
Harries, L. 331, 332
Harvard University Library 6
Hassan, M. (N) A124
Hazoumé, P. (D) 492
A75, A112v.II
Head, B. (SA) 416, 802
Henderson, S. E. 36
Hendrickse, B. **97**
Henshaw, J. E. (N) 258, 259, 260, 261
A96
Higo, A. (N) A98, A108, A197
Hiheta, R. K. (G) 174
Hinawy, M. A. (K) A111
Hoh, I. K. (N) 716
Hokororo, A. M. (K?) 328
Horatio-Jones, E. B. (N) A75
Howard University Library 7, 8
Hughes, L. 86, 87, 88
Hunter, C. (K?) 717

Huntingford, G. W. B. 336
Hutchinson, A. (SA) 417, 418
A70, A81, A92, A94, A96, A105, A110,
 A112v.II, A119
BIOG. **144**

Ibadan **110**
Ibongia, J. (K) 718
Ife-Writing **110**
Ijeoma, J. (N) A102
Ijimere, O. (N) A198
Ike, V. C. (N) 263, 264
A83v.II, A89
Ikelle-Matiba, J. (C) 461
A85, A92, A112v.II
Ikiddeh, I. (N) 89, A105
Ilunga-Kabongo, A. (COK) A102
Irele, A. (N) 90
A197
100
Iroaganachi, J. O. (N) A121v.II
Irungu, D. (K?) 719
Isaak, T. N. (C) 462
Ismaili, R. R. (D) A102
Issa, I. (NI) A91

Jabavu, N. (SA) 419, 420
A101, A112v.II, A119
Jablow, A. A83v.I
Jahn, J. 9, 38, 39, 55, 777
97
Japuonjo, R. (K) 720
Jeune Afrique **110**
Jewel of Africa, The **104**
Joachim, P. (D) 493
A97, A99
Johnson, L. (SL) A65, A102
Johnston, H. A. S. 206
Jolobe, J. R. (SA) A74, A108
Jones, E. (SL) 109
A65, A94
97
Jones-Quartey, K. A. B. (G) A87
98
Jordan, A. C. (SA) A80, A87
Journal of Commonwealth Literature **105**
*Journal of the Language Association of Eastern
 Africa* **110**
*Journal of the New African Literature and the
 Arts, The* **105**

*Journal of the Nigerian English Studies
 Association* **110**
July, R. W. 40
100
Justin, A. 90, 91

Kachingwe, A. (MA) 385
Kagamé, A. (R) 632, 633, 634
A74
Kaggwa, M. (U) A328
Kagwe, S. (K) A328
Kahiga, S. (K) 347
A70
Kala, J. (K) 721
Kamanzi, T. 631
Kamera, W. D. (T) A335
Kane, C. H. (S) 565, 566
A31, A69, A72, A75, A77, A85, A90, A91,
 A92, A103, A112v.II
Kane, M. (S?) **99, 101**
Kanié, A. (IC) A92
Kariara, J. (K) A70, A74, A75, A110, A114,
 A328
Karibo, M. (N) A74, A108, A128, A197
Karienye, M. (U) A328
Kariuki, J. M. (K) 651
A82, A92, A98, A99
Karo, B. (N) A83v.I, A101
Kassam, A. (K) A335
Kassam, S. (K) A65, A75
Kassam, Y. O. (T) A115, A74
Kaunda, K. (Z) 652, 653
A70
Kawegere, F. (T) 722
Kay, K. (G) 723
A105
Kayira, L. (MA) 386, 387, 388, 803
A101
BIOG. **145**
Kayo, P. (C) A98
Kayper-Mensah, A. (G) A74, A139
Kazembe, M. (Z) A83v.I
Kenyatta, J. (K) 654, 655, 656
A70, A79, A80, A81, A83v.II, A86, A92,
 A101, A111
Kéré, A. K. (UV) A118
Kesteloot, L. 41, 92
Kgositsile, K. (SA) 811
A98, A102, A395
Khaketla, B. M. (SA) A394

Reference: Meaning
roman — entry number
bold face — page number
italics — periodicals and magazines
BIOG. — biography of author
Prefix A — author's work appears in one or several anthologies
(S) — nationality of African authors (see key, page **207**)

Khunga, C. (U?) A328
Kibera, L. (K) 347
A70
Kilekwa, P. (Z) A83v.II
Killam, G. D. 207
Kimbugwe, H. S. (*see* Seruma, E.)
Kimenye, B. (U) 365, 366, 724
A70, A76, A95
King, B. 784
King, D. (SL) 318
A115
Kinteh, R. (GAM) 135
Kironde, E. (U) 367
Klimá, V. 785
Knappert, J. 333, 334, 791
Koelle, S. W. 93
Koffi, R. A. (G) A103, A112v.II
Kokunda, V. (U) A328
Komey, E. A. (G) 94
A87, A94, A98, A119, A139
Konadu, A. (G) 175, 176, 177, 178, 179, 180
BIOG. **147**
Koné, M. (IC) 520, 521, 522
Kotei, S. I. A. (G) 140
Kourouma, A. (IC) 523
Kouyaté, S. B. (M) A92
Krige, U. 394
Krog, E. W. 390
Kuguru, P. (K) 725
Kumalo, P. (SA) A88
Kunene, D. P. (SA) 381, 792
A102
Kunene, M. (SA) 421
A98, A99, A115, A395
Kyei, K. G. (G) A87
Kyendo, K. (K) 726

Ladipo, D. (N) 265, 266, 267
A198
L'Afrique Actuelle **110**
L'Afrique Littéraire et Artistique **105**
Lagneau, L. 442
La Guma, A. (SA) 422, 423, 424, 425
A66, A69, A75, A76, A79, A94, A95, A99,
A112v.II, A119, A392, A396, A398
BIOG. **148**
Laluah, A. (G) A86, A87, A88, A128
Lang, D. M. 38
Lanham, P. 383
Lantum, D. (C?) 727
Larson, C. 95
97, 99
Latino, J. (GU) A74
Laurence, M. 208
Laye, C. (GU) 499, 500, 501, 502, 503, 504
A31, A66, A72, A73, A77, A79, A81, A83v.I,
A85, A86, A89, A90, A91, A92, A99, A101,
A103, A110, A111, A112v.I, A119,
A121v.II, A124, A729
BIOG. **150**
Lee M. 327

Lemma, M. (E) 817
Leshoai, B. L. (L) 728
Lesoro, E. A. S. (SA) A394
Lewis, I. M. 326
Liberty, Z. (LI) A102
Lienhardt, P. A. 361
Lijembe, J. A. (K) 329
Lindfors, B. 209, 210, 211
96, 97
Literary Review, The **110**
Literature East and West **110**
Litto, F. M. 96
Loba, A. (IC) 524
A31, A72, A75, A77, A85, A91, A99, A103,
A112v.I
lo Liyong, T. (U) 42, 368, 369, 812
A65, A335
100, 101
BIOG. **152**
Lomax, A. 97
Lukumbi, E. T. (COK) 609
Lumumba, P. (COK) 657
A87
Luthuli, A. (SA) 658
A79, A81

Maddy, P. (SL) 818
A105, A106
Mahood, M. M. **98**
Maimane, A. (SA) A105
Maimo, S. (C) 133, 134
Makerere Journal **110**
Makiwane, T. (SA) A88
Makumi, J. (K) 730
Makunyi, D. (K) 734, 735
Makward, E. 43, **100**
Malangatana, V. (SA) A87
Maley, A. 736
Malinwa, D. N. (T) A75
Malonga, J. (COB) A31, A75, A77, A91,
A92, A112v.I
Mandela, N. (SA) 659
Mangoaela, Z. S. (L) A74, A394
Manley, D. 729
Manyase, L. T. (SA) A394
Maragwanda, J. W. (Z) A112v.II
Markwei, M. (G) A65, A88
Martie, M. (G) A108
Massiye, A. S. (U) 370
Matindi, A. (K?) 731, 732
Matip, B. (C) 463
A72, A92, A112v.I, A112v.II
Matshikiza, T. (SA) 426
A88, A99, A392
Matthews, J. (SA) A70, A76, A94, A95,
A110, A396
Maunick, E. (MAU) A92
Mawazo **110**
Mayo, S. P. C. (Z) A65
Mayssal, H. (C) 464
Mazrui, A. (K) 804

Mbiti, J. (K) 340, 348, 349
A98, A112v.II, A335
Mbotela, J. J. (K) A83v.I
Mbowa, R. (U) A115
Mboya, T. (K) 660, 819
A88
Medhen, T. G. (E) A118
Melone, T. 44, 443
99
Memmi, A. 10
Menga, G. (COB) 598
Mensah, A. K. (G) A108
Mercier, R. 444, 445, 485, 494, 505, 528, 546, 547, 548
Mezu, S. O. (N) 549, 805
A102
Mila **110**
Milner-Brown, A. L. (G) A87
Mkapa, B. (T) A114, A328
Modisane, B. (SA) 427
A66, A74, A79, A82, A86, A87, A88, A92, A98, A111, A398
Modisane, W. (*see* Modisane, B.)
Modupe, P. (GU) 188
A70, A119, A124, A729
Mofolo, T. (L) 382
A79, A81, A83v.II, A111, A112v.II A119, A121v.II
Mohamadou, E. (C) 464
Mohamedali, H. (K) A335
Mohome, P. M. (L) **100**
Mokhomo, M. A. (SA) A394
Moore, B. T. (L) 193, 194
Moore, G. 45, 46, 47, 98, 786
97, 99
Moore, J. A. 126
Mopeli-Paulus, A. S. (L) 383, 384
Moran **110**
Morel, M. (SA) A86, A88
Morris, C. (Z) 652
Morris, H. 363
Moser, G. M. **97**
Motsisi, C. (SA) A75, A76, A94, A392
Mphahlele, E. (SA) 94, 99, 428, 429, 430, 431, 432, 661, 806
A66, A70, A75, A76, A81, A82, A83v.I, A87, A88, A89, A92, A94, A95, A99, A102, A110, A112v.I, A119, A121v.II, A392, A398
97, 100
BIOG. **154**

Mqhayi, S. E. K. (SA) A81, A394
Muffet, D. J. M. 733
Mulaisho, D. (Z) 807
Mulikita, F. M. (Z) 439, 440
Munonye, J. (N) 267, 268, 808
Munro, D. 52
Murphy, A. 736
Murray, A. A. (SA) 433
Mushiete, P. 100
Musukwa, J. W. A. (T) A112v.II
Mutabaruka, J. (R) A92, A99
Mutiga, J. (K) A114, A119, A328, A335
Mvomo, R. M. (C) 465

Naaman, A. Y. 11
Nagenda, J. (U) A76, A114, A115, A328
Nagenda, M. (U) 737
Naigiziki, J. S. (R) 635, 636, 637
A111
Nair, S. (U) A65
Nakasa, N. (SA) A392
Nassar, O. A. (R) A335
National Book League 12, 13, 14
National Educational Television 48
Nazareth, P. (U?) A328
Ndao, C. A. (S) 567
Ndebeka, M. (COB) 599
Ndlovu, J. (RH) A102
Ndoro, J. (K) 738
Ndu, P. N. (N) A98, A115
Ndungu, F. (K?) 740
Neogy, R. (U) A114
Neuendorffer, M. J. 754
New African, The **105**
New Coin **110**
New Writing from Zambia **105**
Nexus **106**
Ngandé, C. (C) A92, A442
Ngani, A. Z. (SA) A394
Ngibuini, P. K. (R?) 739
Ng'Ombo, C. (K) 350
Ng'Osos, D. (K) 741
Ngo Mai, J. (C) 466
Ngugi, J. (K) 351, 352, 353, 354
A70, A75, A76, A82, A83v.II, A89, A94, A95, A106, A109, A110, A118, A119, A121v.II, A328
BIOG. **157**
Ngulukulu, N. G. (K) A328
Niane, D. T. (M) 532, 533
A72, A92, A112v.II

Niang, L. (S) 568
Nicol, A. (SL) 319, 320
A74, A79, A81, A82, A83v.II, A86, A87, A88,
    A94, A95, A99, A108, A110, A111, A114,
    A115, A118, A119, A124, A127, A128
BIOG. **159**
(*see also* Nicol, D.)
Nicol, D. 662
97, 99
(*see also* Nicol, A.)
Nigeria Magazine **110**
Njau, R. (U) A106
Njoku, M. C. (K) A65
Njoroge, J. K. (K) 742, 743, 744
Njururi, N. (K) 431
Nketia, J. H. A. (G) A80, A88
Nkosi, L. (SA) 434, 435
A96, A99, A392, A398
97
BIOG. **160**
Nkrumah, K. (G) 663, 664, 665, 666, 667,
    668, 669, 670, 671, 672
A86, A88, A92, A111
Nockolds, E. (*see* Abbs, A.)
Nokan, C. (IC) 525, 526, 527
A72, A98
Nolen, B. 101
Noronha, B. (K) A115
Northwestern University Libraries 15
Nortje, K. A. (SA) A98, A395
Nouktar, D. M. (M?) A103
Nouvelle somme de poésie du monde noir 49
Ntantala, P. (SA) A86, A88
Ntara, S. Y. (MA) A75
Ntuyahaga, M. (BU) A121v.II
Nwankwo, N. (N) 269, 745, 746
A74, A89, A94, A119, A195
Nwanodi, O. G. (N) 270
Nwapa, F. (N) 271, 272
BIOG. **163**
Nweke, C. (N) A87
Nwoga, D. (N) 127
101
Nyabongo, A. K. (U) A80
Nyembezi, C. L. S. (SA) 394
Nyerere, J. K. (T) 673, 674
A70, A101
Nyunai, J. P. (C) 467, 468, 469
A92, A442
Nzekwu, O. (N) 273, 274, 275, 747
A99, A110, A112v.II, A119, A195
BIOG. **163**
Nzioki, J. M. (N?) 329
Nzouankeu, J. M. (C) 470
A92

Obumselu, B. (N) **98**
Obeng, R. E. (G) 181
A75
Obiechina, E. (N) **98, 100**
Obika, F. (N) A111

Obudo, N. (K) A65, A114
Ocansey, J. E. (G) A83v.II
Ochieng, P. (R) A335
Oculi, O. (U) 371, 372
Odinga, O. (K) 675
Odita, E. O. (N) A102
Odu **110**
Ofori, H. (G) A96
Ogieriaikhi, E. (N) 276
Ogot, G. (K) 355, 356
A76, A94, A99
BIOG. **164**
Ogot, P. (K) 748, 749
Ojike, M. (N) 277, 278, 279
A101
Ojuka, A. (N?) A335
Okafor-Omali, D. (N) A79
Okai, J. (G) 182
A115
Okala, L. (K) 335
Okara, G. (N) 280
A66, A74, A76, A86, A87, A88, A92, A94,
    A97, A98, A108, A114, A115, A116, A118,
    A119, A127, A128, A195
BIOG. **165**
Okeke, U. (N) 793
A115
Okigbo C. (N) 281, 282, 283
A78, A87, A97, A98, A108, A114, A115, A118,
    A119, A127, A128, A195
BIOG. **166**
Okogie, M. O. (N) 284
Okoro, A. (N) 750, 751
Okpaku, J. O. (N) 102
A65, A102
100
Okpewho, I. (N) 285
Okwu, E. C. (N) A115
Okyeame **106**
Olagoke, D. O. (N) 752, 753
Oleghe, P. (N) A108, A128, A197
Olela, H. (K) 754
Olisa, O. (N) A75
Ologoudou, E. (D) A98, A118
Omali, D. O. (N) A 729
Ombede, P. L. (*see* Philombe, R.)
Omolo, L. O. (K) 755
Onadipe, K. (N) 736, 756, 757, 758, 759,
    820
Onyejeli, B. (N) A114
Opara, R. (N) A75, A195
Ophir **110**
Opoku, A. A. (G) A87
Oppong-Affi, A. M. (G) 760
Osadebay, D. C. (N) A80, A87, A114, A127,
    A128
O'Sullivan, Rev. J. 141
Ouana, I. M. (M) A112v.II
Ouedrago, G. (UV) A102
Ouologuem, Y. (M) 534, 535, 536
A98, A118

216

BIOG. **168**
Ousmane, S. (S) 569, 570, 571, 572, 573,
574, 575, 809
A31, A72, A75, A85, A90, A91, A92, A95,
A103, A112v.I, A112v.II, A118
BIOG. **170**
Owiti, H. (K) A102
Owomoyela, O. (N) A102
Owosu, M. (G) 761
Owoyele, D. (N) A94, A195
Oyono, F. (C) 471, 472, 473, 474, 475
A75, A77, A85, A86, A90, A91, A92, A99,
A112v.I
BIOG. **172**
Oyono-Mbia, G. (C) 476, 477, 478
A92
BIOG. **174**
Ozila **106**

Packman, B. 103
Palangyo, P. (T) 360
BIOG. **175**
Panafrica **110**
Páricsy, P. 16, 51
96
Parkes, F. K. (G) 183
A74, A86, A87, A88, A108, A114, A115,
A118, A127, A128, A139
p'Bitek, O. (U) 373, 374, 813
A73
BIOG. **176**
Pederek, S. (G) A88, A128
Penpoint **111**
Perham, M. 104
Peters, L. (GAM) 136, 137, 138
A74, A89, A97, A98, A99, A108, A114, A115,
A118, A119, A127, A128
BIOG. **177**
Philombe, R. (C) 479, 480, 481
A92, A442
Pieterse, C. (SA) 52, 105, 106, 395
A105
Plaatje, S. O. (SA) 436
A75, A119
Pliya, J. (D) A99
Porter, D. 17, 18
Povey, J. 65
98, 99
Présence Africaine **106**
Press, J. 54
Purple Renoster, The **111**

Quaison-Sackey, A. (G) 676
Quenum, M. (D) A91, A112v.II
Quenum, O. (*see* Bhêly-Quenum, O.)
Quillateau, C. 506

Rabéarivelo, J. J. (MR) 611, 612, 613, 614,
615, 616, 617, 618, 619
A74, A78, A92, A88, A108, A113, A118
BIOG. **178**
Rabémananjara, J. (MR) 620, 621, 622, 623,
624, 625, 626, 627
A74, A92, A108, A113
Radford, W. L. 107
Raditladi, L. D. (BO) A111
Ramitloa, M. D. (SA) A398
Ramsaran, J. 19, 55
Ranaivo, F. (MR) 628, 629, 630
A80, A92, A108, A113, A118, A119
Rattray, R. S. (G) A80
Ravenscroft, A. 212
99
Redford, W. 762, 763
Reed, J. 108
99, 100
Reindorf, C. C. (G) 121v.II
Research in African Literatures **106**
Reynault, C. 86
Ricard, A. 213
Ridout, R. 109
Rive, R. (SA) 110, 396, 437, 438
A76, A86, A87, A88, A94, A99, A110, A111,
A112v.II, A118, A396, A398
BIOG. **180**
Robert, S. (T) A119, A121v.II
Roberts, J. (K) A65
Robinson, C. H. 214
Rose, B. W. 71
Rotimi, O. (N) 286
Rowe, E. (SL) 321
Rubadiri, D. (MA) 389, 789
A70, A74, A87, A98, A108, A111, A114,
A115, A116, A118, A328, A335
BIOG. **181**
Ruganda, J. M. (U) A65, A115, A335
Ruhumbika, G. (T) 362
Ruoro, P. (K) A65, A102
Rutherford, P. 111
Rwakyaka, P. (U) A65, A115

Sadji, A. (S) 576, 577, 578
A31, A72, A75, A77, A85, A91, A92, A112v.I
A112v.II

Reference: Meaning
roman — entry number
bold face — page number
italics — periodicals and magazines
BIOG. — biography of author
Prefix A — author's work appears in one or several anthologies
(S) — nationality of African authors (see key, page **207**)

St. John-Parsons, D. 128
Sainville, L. 112
Salih, T. (SU) 324, 325
Sancho, I. A82
Sarbah, J. M. (G) A75
Sartre, J. P. 56
Schapera, I. 379
Schomburg Collection of Negro Literature
  and History 20
Seboni, M. (BO) A111
Segooa, W. (BO) A394
Segun, M. (N) 764
  A115, A195, A729
Seid, J. B. (CH) 596, 597
  A72, A92, A112v.II
Sellassie, S. (E) 338, 339
  BIOG. 182
Selormey, F. (G) 184
  A70, A124
  BIOG. 183
Sembène, O. (see Ousmane, S.)
Senghor, L. S. (S) 113, 579, 580, 581, 582,
  583, 584, 585, 586, 587, 588, 589, 590,
  677, 678
  A73, A74, A75, A77, A78, A79, A81, A85,
  A86, A87, A88, A91, A92, A97, A98, A99,
  A101, A108, A111, A113, A118, A119,
  A120, A127, A128
  100
  BIOG. 184
Sentongo, N. (SA) A95
Sentso, D. (SA) A111
Sergeant, H. 114, 115, 116
Seruma, E. (U) 375
Serumaga, R. (U) 376, 377
  BIOG. 187
Sey, K. (G) A139
Shapiro, N. R. 117
Shears, G. 21
Shelton, A. J. 118
  98
Shepherd, R. H. W. 397
Shore, H. I. 398
  98
Shore-Bos, M. 398
Shuaibu, M. (N) A124
Sibthorpe, A. B. C. (SL) A75
Simon, B. (SA) 410
  A392
Sinah, M. W. (SL) A111
Sinda, M. (COB) A86, A108, A120
Sissoko, F. D. (M) 537, 538, 539, 540, 541,
  542
Sitati, P. (K) A65
Sithole, N. (RH) 679
Skinner, N. 215, 216
Socé, O. (S) 591, 592, 593, 594, 595
  A69, A75, A77, A86, A92, A99, A103,
  A112v.I, A112v.II
Société Africaine de Culture 57
Society of African Culture 58

Sofala, S. A. (N) 287
Solarin, T. (N) 288
Sondhi, K. (K) A99, A106
Songa, P. W. (U) A335
South Africa: Information and Analysis 111
South African Outlook 111
Soyinka, W. (N) 289, 290, 291, 292, 293, 294,
  295, 296, 297, 298, 299, 794
  A74, A75, A78, A79, A86, A87, A88, A92,
  A97, A98, A99, A108, A114, A115, A119,
  A127, A195
  98, 101
  BIOG. 189
Ssemuwanga, J. B. K. (U) A65, A74, A115
Stuart, D. 98
Studies in Black Literature 111
Sutherland, E. T. (G) 185, 186, 187, 765
  A76, A86, A88, A92, A96, A110, A118, A119,
  A139
  BIOG. 193
Sutu-Mthimkhulu, S. D. R. (L) A74, A394
Swanzy, H. (G) 142
Syad, W. (SO) 638
Syracuse University. Maxwell Graduate
  School of Citizenship and Public Affairs.
  Program of Eastern African Studies 217

Taiwo, O. (N) 129, 766, 767
Takir, I. (MAU) A112v.II
Tatti-Loutard, J. B. (COB) 484
  A98
Tchicaya U Tam'si, G. F. (see U Tam'si,
  T. G. F.)
Tejani, A. (U) A115
ten Raa, E. 395
Tetteh-Lartey, A. C. V. (G) 768
Themba, C. (SA) A86, A88, A94, A99, A392
Theroux, P. 100
Thomas, I. B. (N) A75
Thomas, L. V. 100
Tibble, A. 119
Touré, S. (GU) 680, 681
  A75, A86
Towo-Atangana, F. (C) 482
  A92
Towo-Atangana, G. (C) 482
  A92
Transition 107
Traoré, B. 59
Tsaro-Wiwa, K. (N?) A75
Tshakatumba, W. (COB) A118
Tshibamba, P. L. (COK) A91
Tucker, M. 60
Tutuola, A. (N) 300, 301, 302, 303, 304, 305,
  306
  A69, A75, A81, A83v.I, A86, A88, A92,
  A94, A95, A99, A110, A111, A112v.II,
  A119, A121v.II, A124, A195
  BIOG. 195

Udeagu, O. (N) A88

Ufahamu **111**
Ukoli, N. M. (N?) 769
Ukwu, U. I. (N) A108, A128
Ulasi, A. L. (N) 307
Umeasiegbu, R. N. (N) 308
Umukoro, G. (N) Ai97
University of London. School of Oriental
    and African Studies 22
U Tam'si, T. G. F. (COB) 600, 601, 602, 603,
    604, 605, 606, 607
A74, A87, A92, A98, A99, A118, A120
BIOG. **197**
Uwemedimo, R. (N?) 770
Uzodinma, E. C. (N) 309, 310

Valette, P. 610
Vaughan, J. K. (N) A86, A88
Vilakazi, B. W. (SA) A74, A87, A111, A394
von Grunebaum, G. E. 61
von Meijer, G. 23

Wachira, G. (K) 357
Waciumba, C. (K) 358, 771, 772
Wade, M. 787
Waiguru, J. (U) A114, A328
Waiyaki, E. (K) A335
Wake, C. 108, 120
101
Wali, O. (N) **99**
Walker, A. R. (G) A91
Walsh, W. 218

Wangeci, A. (K) A335
Wangusa, T. (U) A75, A115
Warren, J. 171
Wästberg, P. 62
Watts, M. E. 143
Wauthier, C. 63, 64
Wegesa, B. S. (U) 378
WEST AFRICA **111**
When I awoke 773
Whiteley, W. H. 121
Wilkov, A. 399
Williams, R. (SA) A398
Wimbush, D. (N) 774, 775
Winful, E. A. (G) A115, A139
Wonodi, O. (N) A65, A98, A114, A115,
    A127
Wright, E. **101**

Yako, S. J. P. (SA) A394
Yassin, M. (SL) 776
Yondo, E. E. (C) A86, A442
Young, P. **101**
Young, T. C. 122

Zankli, B. (N) A65
Zell, H. M. 130
Zerbo, J. J. (UV) A85
Zirimu, E. N. A328
Zobel, J. (S) A77, A92, A99
Zuka **107**

Reference: Meaning
roman — entry number
bold face — page number
italics — periodicals and magazines
BIOG. — biography of author
Prefix A — author's work appears in one or several anthologies
(S) — nationality of African authors (see key, page **207**)